FROM A SKETCH by J.C.WARD. ESQ.

LITH.OF SARONY & MAJOR.

SAN FRANCISCO IN NOVEMBER, 1848.

NEW YORK GEO. P. PUTNAM.

ELDORADO

ADVENTURES IN THE PATH OF EMPIRE

A VOYAGE TO CALIFORNIA, VIA PANAMA; LIFE IN SAN FRANCISCO
AND MONTEREY; PICTURES OF THE GOLD REGION, AND
EXPERIENCES OF MEXICAN TRAVEL.

BY

BAYARD TAYLOR

WITH ILLUSTRATIONS BY THE AUTHOR.

Skyhorse Publishing

Eldorado: Volume 1 was first published 1850 by George P. Putnam, New York.
Eldorado: Volume 2 was first published 1850 by George P. Putnam, New York.
First Skyhorse Publishing edition 2015.

Skyhorse Publishing books may be purchased in bulk at special discounts for sales promotion, corporate gifts, fund-raising, or educational purposes. Special editions can also be created to specifications. For details, contact the Special Sales Department, Skyhorse Publishing, 307 West 36th Street, 11th Floor, New York, NY 10018 or info@skyhorsepublishing.com.

Skyhorse® and Skyhorse Publishing® are registered trademarks of Skyhorse Publishing, Inc.®, a Delaware corporation.

Visit our website at www.skyhorsepublishing.com.

10 9 8 7 6 5 4 3 2 1

Library of Congress Cataloging-in-Publication Data is available on file.

Cover design by Rain Saukas

Print ISBN: 978-1-62914-714-7
Ebook ISBN: 978-1-62914-930-1

Printed in the United States of America

TO

EDWARD F. BEALE, LIEUT., U. S. N.

THIS WORK IS DEDICATED

WITH

THE AUTHOR'S ESTEEM AND AFFECTION.

VOLUME I

LIST OF ILLUSTRATIONS.

PREFACE.

THIS work requires but few words in the way of introduction. Though the author's purpose in visiting California was not to write a book, the circumstances of his journey seemed to impose it upon him as a duty, and all his observations were made with this end in view. The condition of California, during the latter half of the year 1849, was as transitory as it was marvellous; the records which were then made can never be made again. Seeing so much that was worthy of being described—so many curious and shifting phases of society—such examples of growth and progress, most wonderful in their first stage—in a word, the entire construction of a new and sovereign State, and the establishment of a great commercial metropolis on the Pacific coast—the author suffered no opportunity to pass, which might qualify him to preserve their fleeting images. As he was troubled by no dreams of gold, and took no part in exciting schemes of trade, he has hoped to give an impartial coloring to the picture. His impressions of California are those of one who went to see and write, and who sought to do both faithfully. Whatever may be the faults of his work, he trusts this endeavor will be recognized.

A portion, only, of the pages which follow, were included in the original letters which appeared in the columns of the New-York Tribuné. Many personal incidents, and pictures of society as it then existed in California, noted down at the time, have been added, and a new form given to the materials obtained. The account of the author's journey across Mexico, is now published for the first time. The Report of Hon. T. Butler King, on California Affairs, has been added as an Appendix, since many of the author's own statements receive from it additional confirmation, and since those wishing to learn something of California, will desire to possess it in a permanent form.

If, when a new order of things has been established and what has occurred is looked upon as a phenomenon of the Past, some of these pages should be preserved as a record and remembrance thereof, the object of this work will be fully accomplished.

CONTENTS OF VOL. I.

1*

CONTENTS.

ELDORADO.

CHAPTER I.

FROM NEW YORK TO CHAGRES.

On the 28th of June, 1849, I sailed from New York, in the U. S. Mail steamship Falcon, bound for Chagres. About eight months had elapsed since the tidings of an Eldorado in the West reached the Atlantic shore. The first eager rush of adventurers was over, yet there was no cessation to the marvellous reports, and thousands were only waiting a few further repetitions, to join the hordes of emigration. The departure of a steamer was still something of an incident. The piers and shipping were crowded with spectators, and as the Falcon moved from her moorings, many a cheer and shout of farewell followed her. The glow and excitement of adventure seemed to animate even those who remained behind, and as for our passengers, there was scarcely one who did not feel himself more or less a hero. The deck rang with songs, laughter and gaily-spoken anticipations of roving life and untold treasure, till we began to feel the heavy swell rolling inward from Sandy Hook.

Rough weather set in with the night, and for a day or two we were all in the same state of torpid misery. Sea-sickness—next to Death, the greatest leveler—could not, however, smooth down the striking contrasts of character exhibited among the pas-

1

sengers. Nothing less than a marvel like that of California could have brought into juxtaposition so many opposite types of human nature. We had an officer of the Navy, blunt, warm-hearted and jovial; a captain in the merchant service, intelligent and sturdily-tempered; Down-Easters, with sharp-set faces—men of the genuine stamp, who would be sure to fall on their feet wherever they might be thrown; quiet and sedate Spaniards; hilarious Germans; and some others whose precise character was more difficult to determine. Nothing was talked of but the land to which we were bound, nothing read but Frémont's Expedition, Emory's Report, or some work of Rocky Mountain travel.

After doubling Cape Hatteras, on the second day out, our monotonous life was varied by the discovery of a distant wreck. Captain Hartstein instantly turned the Falcon's head towards her, and after an hour's run we came up with her. The sea for some distance around was strewed with barrels, fragments of bulwarks, stanchions and broken spars. She was a schooner of a hundred tons, lying on her beam ends and water-logged. Her mainmast was gone, the foremast broken at the yard and the bowsprit snapped off and lying across her bows. The mass of spars and rigging drifted by her side, surging drearily on the heavy sea. Not a soul was aboard, and we made many conjectures as to their fate.

We lay to off Charleston the fourth night, waiting for the mails, which came on board in the morning with a few forlorn-looking passengers, sick and weary with twenty-four hours' tossing on the swells. In the afternoon we saw Tybee Lighthouse, through the veil of a misty shower. The sun set among the jagged piles of a broken thunder-cloud, and ribbon-like streaks of lightning darted all round the horizon. Our voyage now began to have a real interest. With the next sunrise, we saw the Lighthouse of St. Augustine and ran down the shores of Florida, inside the Gulf Stream, and close to the edges of the banks of coral. The passengers clustered on the bow, sitting with their feet hanging over the guards, and talking of Ponce de Leon, De Soto, and the early Spanish adventurers. It was unanimously voted that the present days were as wonderful as those, and each individual emigrant entitled to equal credit for daring and enterprise. I found it delightful to sit all day leaning over the rails, watching the play of flying-fish, the floating of purple nautili on the water, or looking off to the level line of the shore. Behind a beach of white sand, half a mile in breadth and bordered by dense thickets, rise the interminable forests of live oak, mangrove and cypress. The monotony of this long extent of coast is only broken by an occasional lagoon, where the deep green of the woods comes down upon the lighter green of the coral shoals, or by the huts of wreckers and their trim, duck-like crafts, lying in the offings. The temperature was delicious, with a light, cloudy sky, and a breeze as soft and balmy as that of our northern May. The afternoons commenced with a heavy thunder-shower, after which the wind came fresh from the land, bringing us a rank vegetable odor from the cypress swamps.

On the morning of July 5th, I took a station on the wheel-house, to look out for Cuba. We had left Florida in the night, and the waves of the Gulf were around us. The sun, wheeling near the zenith, burned fiercely on the water. I glowed at my post, but not with his beam. I had reached the flaming boundary of the Tropics, and felt that the veil was lifting from an unknown world. The far rim of the horizon seemed as if it would never break into an uneven line. At last, towards noon, Capt. Hartstein handed me the ship's glass. I swept the southern distance, and discerned a single blue, conical peak rising from the water—the well-known Pan of Matanzas. As we drew nearer, the Iron Mountains—a rugged chain in the interior—rose, then the green hills along the coast, and finally the white beach and bluffs, the coral reefs and breakers. The shores were buried in vegetation. The fields of young sugar-cane ran along the slopes; palms waved from the hill-tops, and the country houses of planters lay deep in the valleys, nestling in orange groves. I drank in the land-wind—a combination of all tropical perfumes in one full breath of cool air—with an enjoyment verging on intoxication, while, point beyond point, we followed the enchanting coast.

We ran under the battlements of the Moro at six o'clock, and turning abruptly round the bluff of dark rock on which it is built, the magnificent harbor opened inland before us. To the right lay the city, with its terraced houses of all light and brilliant colors, its spacious public buildings, spires, and the quaint, half-oriental pile of its cathedral, in whose chancel repose the ashes of Christopher Columbus. The immense fortress of the Moro crowned the height on our left, the feathery heads of palm-trees peering above its massive, cream-colored walls. A part of the garrison were going through their evening exercises on the beach. Numberless boats skimmed about on the water, and a flat ferry-steamer, painted green and yellow, was on its way to the suburb of Regoles. Around the land-locked harbor, two miles in width, rose green hills, dotted with the country palaces of the nobility. Over all this charming view glowed the bright hues of a southern sunset.

On account of the cholera at New York, we were ordered up to the Quarantine ground and anchored beside the hulk of an old frigate, filled with yellow-fever patients. The Health Officers received the mail and ship's papers at the end of a long pole, and dipped them in a bucket of vinegar. The boats which brought us water and vegetables were attended by Cuban soldiers, in white uniform, who guarded against all contact with us. Half-naked slaves, with the broad, coarse features of the natives of Congo, worked at the pump, but even they suffered the rope-end or plank which had touched our vessel, to drop in the water before they handled it. After sunset, the yellow-fever dead were buried and the bell of a cemetery on shore tolled mournfully at intervals. The steamer Isabel, and other American ships, were anchored beside us, and a lively conversation between the crews broke the stillness of the tropical moonlight resting on the water. Now and then they struck into songs, one taking up a new strain as the other ceased—in the style of the Venetian gondoliers, but with a different effect. "Tasso's echoes" are another thing from "the floating scow of old Virginny." The lights of the city gleamed at a distance, and over them the flaming beacon of the Moro. Tall palms were dimly seen on the nearer hills, and the damp night-air came heavy with the scent of cane-fields, orange groves and flowers.

A voyage across the Gulf is the perfection of sea-traveling. After a detention of eighteen hours at Havana, we ran under the frowning walls of the Moro, out on its sheet of brilliant blue water, specked with white-caps that leaped to a fresh north-easter. The waves are brighter, the sky softer and purer, the sunsets more mellow than on the Atlantic, and the heat, though ranging from 88° to 95° in the shade, is tempered by a steady and delicious breeze.

Before catching sight of land, our approach to the Mississippi was betrayed by the water. Changing to a deep, then a muddy green, which, even fifteen or twenty miles from shore, rolls its

stratum of fresh water over the bed of denser brine, it needed no
soundings to tell of land ahead.   The light on the South Pass
was on our starboard at dusk.   The arm of the river we entered
seemed so wide in the uncertain light, that, considering it as one
of five, my imagination expanded in contemplating the size of the
single flood, bearing in its turbid waves the snows of mountains
that look on Oregon, the ice of lakes in Northern Minesota and
the crystal springs that for a thousand miles gush from the western slope of the Alleghanies.   When morning came, my excited
fancies seemed completely at fault.   I could scarcely recognize
the Father of Waters in the tortuous current of brown soap-suds,
a mile in width, flowing between forests of willow and cypress on
one side and swamps that stretched to the horizon on the other.
Everything exhibited the rank growth and speedy decay of tropi
cal vegetation   The river was filled with floating logs, which
were drifted all along the shore.   The trees, especially the
cypress, were shrouded in gray moss, that hung in long streamers
from the branches, and at intervals the fallen thatch of some deserted cabin was pushed from its place by shrubbery and wild
vines.

Near the city, the shores present a rich and cultivated aspect.
The land is perfectly flat, but the forest recedes, and broad fields
of sugar cane and maize in ear come down to the narrow levee
which protects them from the flood.   The houses of the planters,
low, balconied and cool, are buried among orange trees, acacias,
and the pink blossoms of the crape myrtle.   The slave-huts adjoining, in parallel rows, have sometimes small gardens attached,
but are rarely shaded by trees.

I found New Orleans remarkably dull and healthy.   The city
was enjoying an interregnum between the departure of the cholera

and the arrival of the yellow fever. The crevasse, by which half the city had lately been submerged, was closed, but the effects of the inundation were still perceptible in frequent pools of standing water, and its scenes daily renewed by incessant showers. The rain came down, "not from one lone cloud," but as if a thousand cisterns had been stove in at once. In half an hour after a shower commenced, the streets were navigable, the hack-horses splashing their slow way through the flood, carrying home a few drenched unfortunates.

The Falcon was detained four days, which severely tested the temper of my impatient shipmates. I employed the occasional gleams of clear weather in rambling over the old French and Spanish quarters, riding on the Lafayette Railroad or driving out the Shell Road to the cemetery, where the dead are buried above ground. The French part of the city is unique and interesting. All the innovation is confined to the American Municipalities, which resemble the business parts of our Northern cities. The curious one-storied dwellings, with jalousies and tiled roofs, of the last century, have not been disturbed in the region below Canal street. The low houses, where the oleander and crape myrtle still look over the walls, were once inhabited by the luxurious French planters, but now display such signs as " Magazin des Modes," " Au bon marché," or " Perrot, Coiffeur." Some of the more pretending mansions show the *porte cochère* and heavy barred windows of the hotels of Paris, and the common taverns, with their smoky aspect and the blue blouses that fill them, are exact counterparts of some I have seen in the Rue St. Antoine. The body of the Cathedral, standing at the head of the Place d' Armes, was torn down, and workmen were employed in building a prison in its stead ; but the front, with its venerable tower and refreshing appearance of antiquity, will remain, hiding behind its changeless face far different passions and darker spectacles than in the Past.

The hour of departure at length arrived. The levee opposite our anchorage, in Lafayette City, was thronged with a noisy multitude, congregated to witness the embarcation of a hundred and fifty additional passengers. Our deck became populous with tall, gaunt Mississipians and Arkansans, Missouri squatters who had pulled up their stakes yet another time, and an ominous number of professed gamblers. All were going to seek their fortunes in California, but very few had any definite idea of the country or the voyage to be made before reaching it. There were among them some new varieties of the American—long, loosely-jointed men, with large hands and feet and limbs which would still be awkward, whatever the fashion of their clothes. Their faces were lengthened, deeply sallow, overhung by straggling locks of straight black hair, and wore an expression of settled melancholy. The corners of their mouths curved downwards, the upper lip drawn slightly over the under one, giving to the lower part of the face that cast of destructiveness peculiar to the Indian. These men chewed tobacco at a ruinous rate, and spent their time either in dozing at full length on the deck or going into the fore-cabin for 'drinks.' Each one of them carried arms enough for a small company and breathed defiance to all foreigners.

We had a voyage of seven days, devoid of incident, to the Isthmus. During the fourth night we passed between Cuba and Yucatan. Then, after crossing the mouth of the Gulf of Honduras, where we met the south-eastern trades, and running the gauntlet of a cluster of coral keys, for the navigation of which no chart can be positively depended upon, we came into the deep

water of the Caribbean Sea.   The waves ran high under a dull
rain and raw wind, more like Newfoundland weather than the
tropics.   On the morning of the eighth day, we approached land.
All hands gathered on deck, peering into the mist for the first
glimpse of the Isthmus.   Suddenly a heavy rain-cloud lifted, and
we saw, about five miles distant, the headland of Porto Bello—a
bold, rocky promontory, fringed with vegetation and washed at
its foot by a line of snowy breakers.   The range of the Andes of
Darien towered high behind the coast, the further summits lost in
the rain.   Turning to the south-west, we followed the magnificent
sweep of hills toward Chagres, passing Navy Bay, the Atlantic
terminus of the Panama Railroad.   The entrance is narrow, between two bold bluffs, opening into a fine land-locked harbor,
surrounded by hills.

  Chagres lies about eight miles to the west of this bay, but the
mouth of the river is so narrow that the place is not seen till you
run close upon it.   The eastern shore is high and steep, cloven
with ravines which roll their floods of tropical vegetation down to
the sea.   The old castle of San Lorenzo crowns the point, occupying a position somewhat similar to the Moro Castle at Havana,
and equally impregnable.   Its brown battlements and embrasures
have many a dark and stirring recollection.   Morgan and his
buccaneers scaled its walls, took and leveled it, after a fight in
which all but thirty-three out of three hundred and fourteen de-
fenders were slain, some of them leaping madly from the precipice
into the sea.   Strong as it is by nature, and would be in the hands
of an enterprising people, it now looks harmless enough with a few
old cannon lying lazily on its ramparts.   The other side of the
river is flat and marshy, and from our place of anchorage we could
only see the tops of some huts among the trees.
            1*

We came to anchor about half past four. The deck was already covered with luggage and everybody was anxious to leave first. Our captain, clerk, and a bearer of dispatches, were pulled ashore in the steamer's boat, and in the meantime the passengers formed themselves into small companies for the journey up the river. An immense canoe, or " dug-out," manned by half-naked natives shortly came out, and the most of the companies managed to get agents on board to secure canoes for them. The clerk, on his return, was assailed by such a storm of questions—the passengers leaning half-way over the bulwarks in their eagerness for news— that for a few minutes he could not make himself heard. When the clamor subsided, he told us that the Pacific steamer would sail from Panama on the 1st of August, and that the only canoes to be had that night were already taken by Captain Hartstein, who was then making his way up the Rio Chagres, in rain and thick darkness. The trunks and blankets were therefore taken below again and we resigned ourselves to another night on board, with a bare chance of sleep in the disordered state-rooms and among the piles of luggage. A heavy cloud on the sea broke out momently into broad scarlet flashes of lightning, surpassing any celestial pyrotechnics I ever witnessed. The dark walls of San Lorenzo, the brilliant clusters of palms on the shore and the green, rolling hills of the interior, leaped at intervals out of the gloom, as vividly seen as under the noon-day sun.

CHAPTER II.

CROSSING THE ISTHMUS.

I LEFT the Falcon at day-break in the ship's boat. We rounded the high bluff on which the castle stands and found beyond it a shallow little bay, on the eastern side of which, on low ground, stand the cane huts of Chagres. Piling up our luggage on the shore, each one set about searching for the canoes which had been engaged the night previous, but, without a single exception, the natives were not to be found, or when found, had broken their bargains. Everybody ran hither and thither in great excitement, anxious to be off before everybody else, and hurrying the naked boatmen, all to no purpose. The canoes were beached on the mud, and their owners engaged in re-thatching their covers with split leaves of the palm. The doors of the huts were filled with men and women, each in a single cotton garment, composedly smoking their cigars, while numbers of children, in Nature's own clothing, tumbled about in the sun. Having started without breakfast, I went to the " Crescent City" Hotel, a hut with a floor to it, but could get nothing. Some of my friends had fared better at one of the native huts, and I sat down to the remains of their meal, which was spread on a hen-coop beside the door. The pigs of the vicinity and several lean dogs surrounded me to offer their services, but maintained a respectful silence, which is more than could be said of pigs at home. Some pieces of pork fat, with fresh bread and a draught of sweet spring water from a cocoa shell, made me a delicious repast.

A returning Californian had just reached the place, with a box containing $22,000 in gold-dust, and a four-pound lump in one hand. The impatience and excitement of the passengers, already at a high pitch, was greatly increased by his appearance. Life and death were small matters compared with immediate departure from Chagres. Men ran up and down the beach, shouting, gesti- ulating, and getting feverishly impatient at the deliberate habits of the natives; as if their arrival in California would thereby be at all hastened. The boatmen, knowing very well that two more steamers were due the next day, remained provokingly cool and unconcerned. They had not seen six months of emigration with- out learning something of the American habit of going at full speed. The word of starting in use on the Chagres River, is " go- ahead !" Captain C—— and Mr. M——, of Baltimore, and myself, were obliged to pay $15 each, for a canoe to Cruces. We chose a broad, trimly-cut craft, which the boatmen were covering with fresh thatch. We stayed with them until all was ready, and they had pushed it through the mud and shoal water to the bank before Ramos's house. Our luggage was stowed away, we took our seats and raised our umbrellas, but the men had gone off for provisions and were not to be found. All the other canoes were equally in limbo. The sun blazed down on the swampy shores, and visions of yellow fever came into the minds of the more timid travelers. The native boys brought to us bottles of fresh water, biscuits and fruit, presenting them with the words: " bit !" " pi- cayune !" " Your bread is not good," I said to one of the shirtless traders. "Si, *Señor !*" was his decided answer, while he tossed back his childish head with a look of offended dignity which charmed me. While sitting patiently in our craft, I was much diverted by seeing one of our passengers issue from a hut with a native on each arm, and march them resolutely down to the river. Our own men appeared towards noon, with a bag of rice and dried pork, and an armful of sugar-cane. A few strokes of their broad paddles took us from the excitement and noise of the landing-place to the seclusion and beauty of the river scenery.

Our chief boatman, named Ambrosio Mendez, was of the mixed Indian and Spanish race. The second, Juan Crispin Bega, belonged to the lowest class, almost entirely of negro blood. He was a strong, jovial fellow, and took such good care of some of our small articles as to relieve us from all further trouble about them. This propensity is common to all of his caste on the Isthmus. In addition to these, a third man was given to us, with the assurance that he would work his passage; but just as we were leaving, we learned that he was a runaway soldier, who had been taken up for theft and was released on paying some sub-alcalde three bottles of liquor, promising to quit the place at once. We were scarcely out of sight of the town before he demanded five dollars a day for his labor. We refused, and he stopped working. Upon our threatening to set him ashore in the jungle, he took up the paddle, but used it so awkwardly and perversely that our other men lost all patience. We were obliged, however, to wait until we could reach Gatun, ten miles distant, before settling matters. Juan struck up "Oh Susanna !" which he sang to a most ludicrous imitation of the words, and I lay back under the palm leaves, looking out of the stern of the canoe on the forests of the Chagres River.

There is nothing in the world comparable to these forests.   No
description that I have ever read conveys an idea of the splendid
overplus of vegetable life within the tropics.   The river, broad,
and with a swift current of the sweetest water I ever drank, winds
between walls of foliage that rise from its very surface.   All the
gorgeous growths of an eternal Summer are so mingled in one
impenetrable mass, that the eye is bewildered.   From the rank
jungle of canes and gigantic lilies, and the thickets of strange
shrubs that line the water, rise the trunks of the mango, the ceiba,
the cocoa, the sycamore and the superb palm.   Plaintains take
root in the banks, hiding the soil with their leaves, shaken and
split into immense plumes by the wind and rain.   The zapote,
with a fruit the size of a man's head, the gourd tree, and other
vegetable wonders, attract the eye on all sides.   Blossoms of
crimson, purple and yellow, of a form and magnitude unknown in
the North, are mingled with the leaves, and flocks of paroquets
and brilliant butterflies circle through the air like blossoms blown
away.   Sometimes a spike of scarlet flowers is thrust forth like
the tongue of a serpent from the heart of some convolution of un-
folding leaves, and often the creepers and parasites drop trails and
streamers of fragrance from boughs that shoot half-way across the
river.   Every turn of the stream only disclosed another and more
magnificent vista of leaf, bough and blossom.   All outline of the
landscape is lost under this deluge of vegetation.   No trace of the
soil is to be seen ; lowland and highland are the same ; a mountain is but a higher swell of the mass of verdure.   As on the
ocean, you have a sense rather than a perception of beauty.   The
sharp, clear lines of our scenery at home are here wanting.   What
shape the land would be if cleared, you cannot tell.   You gaze
upon the scene before you with a never-sated delight, till your

brain aches with the sensation, and you close your eyes, over-whelmed with the thought that all these wonders have been from the beginning—that year after year takes away no leaf or blossom that is not replaced, but the sublime mystery of growth and decay is renewed forever.

In the afternoon we reached Gatun, a small village of bamboo huts, thatched with palm-leaves, on the right bank of the river. The canoes which preceded us had already stopped, and the boatmen, who have a mutual understanding, had decided to remain all night. We ejected our worthless passenger on landing, notwithstanding his passive resistance, and engaged a new boatman in his place, at $8. I shall never forget the forlorn look of the man as he sat on the bank beside his bag of rice, as the rain began to fall. Ambrosio took us to one of the huts and engaged hammocks for the night. Two wooden drums, beaten by boys, in another part of the village, gave signs of a coming fandango, and, as it was Sunday night, all the natives were out in their best dresses. They are a very cleanly people, bathing daily, and changing their dresses as often as they are soiled. The children have their heads shaved from the crown to the neck, and as they go about naked, with abdomens unnaturally distended, from an exclusive vegetable diet, are odd figures enough. They have bright black eyes, and are quick and intelligent in their speech and motions.

The inside of our hut was but a single room, in which all the household operations were carried on. A notched pole, serving as a ladder, led to a sleeping loft, under the pyramidal roof of thatch. Here a number of the emigrants who arrived late were stowed away on a rattling floor of cane, covered with hides. After a supper of pork and coffee, I made my day's notes by the light of a miserable starveling candle, stuck in an empty bottle, but had not written far before my paper was covered with fleas. The owner of the hut swung my hammock meanwhile, and I turned in, to secure it for the night. To lie there was one thing, to sleep another. A dozen natives crowded round the table, drinking their aguardiente and disputing vehemently ; the cooking fire was on one side of me, and every one that passed to and fro was sure to give me a thump, while my weight swung the hammock so low, that all the dogs on the premises were constantly rubbing their backs under me. I was just sinking into a doze, when my head was so violently agitated that I started up in some alarm. It was but a quarrel about payment between the Señora and a boatman, one standing on either side. From their angry gestures, my own head and not the reckoning, seemed the subject of contention.

Our men were to have started at midnight, but it was two hours later before we could rouse and muster them together. We went silently and rapidly up the river till sunrise, when we reached a cluster of huts called Dos Hermanos (Two Brothers.) Here we overtook two canoes, which, in their anxiety to get ahead, had been all night on the river. There had been only a slight shower since we started ; but the clouds began to gather heavily, and by the time we had gained the ranche of Palo Matida a sudden cold wind came over the forests, and the air was at once darkened. We sprang ashore and barely reached the hut, a few paces off, when the rain broke over us, as if the sky had caved in. A dozen lines of white electric heat ran down from the zenith, followed by crashes of thunder, which I could feel throbbing in the earth under my feet. The rain drove into one side of the cabin and out the other, but we wrapped ourselves in India-rubber cloth and kept out the wet and chilling air. During the whole day the river rose rapidly and we were obliged to hug the bank closely, running under the boughs of trees and drawing ourselves up the rapids by those that hung low.

I crept out of the snug nest where we were all stowed as closely as three unfledged sparrows, and took my seat between Juan and Ambrosio, protected from the rain by an India-rubber poncho. The clothing of our men was likewise waterproof, but without seam or fold. It gave no hindrance to the free play of their muscles, as they deftly and rapidly plied the broad paddles Juan kept time to the Ethiopian melodies he had picked up from the emigrants, looking round from time to time with a grin of satisfaction at his skill. I preferred, however, hearing the native songs, which the boatmen sing with a melancholy drawl on the final syllable of every line, giving the music a peculiar but not unpleasant effect, when heard at a little distance. There was one, in particular, which he sang with some expression, the refrain running thus:

" Ten piedad, piedad de mis penas,
Ten piedad, piedad de mi amor !"
(Have pity on my sufferings—have pity on my love !)

Singing begets thirst, and perhaps Juan sang the more that he might have a more frequent claim on the brandy. The bottle was then produced and each swallowed a mouthful, after which he dipped his cocoa shell in the river and took a long draught. This is a universal custom among the boatmen, and the traveler is obliged to supply them. As a class, they are faithful, hardworking and grateful for kindness. They have faults, the worst of which are tardiness, and a propensity to filch small articles; but good treatment wins upon them in almost every case. Juan said to me in the beginning " *soy tu amigo yo*," (*Americanicè :* I am thy friend, *well* I am,) but when he asked me, in turn, for every article of clothing I wore, I began to think his friendship not the most disinterested.   Ambrosio told me that they would serve no one well who treated them badly.   " If the Americans are good, we are good ; if they abuse us, we are bad.   We are black, but *muchos caballeros*," (very much of gentlemen,) said he.   Many blustering fellows, with their belts stuck full of pistols and bowie-knives, which they draw on all occasions, but take good care not to use, have brought reproach on the country by their silly conduct.   It is no bravery to put a revolver to the head of an unarmed and ignorant native, and the boatmen have sense enough to be no longer terrified by it.

We stopped the second night at Peña Blanca, (the White Rock,) where I slept in the loft of a hut, on the floor, in the midst of the family and six other travelers.   We started at sunrise, hoping to reach Gorgona the same night, but ran upon a sunken log and were detained some time.   Ambrosio finally released us by jumping into the river and swimming ashore with a rope in his teeth.   The stream was very high, running at least five miles an hour, and we could only stem it with great labor.   We passed the ranches of Agua Salud, Varro Colorado and Palan-quilla, and shortly after were overtaken by a storm on the river. We could hear the rush and roar of the rain, as it came towards us like the trampling of myriad feet on the leaves.   Shooting under a broad sycamore we made fast to the boughs, covered ourselves with India-rubber, and lay under our cool, rustling thatch of palm, until the storm had passed over.

The character of the scenery changed somewhat as we advanced.   The air was purer, and the banks more bold and steep.

The country showed more signs of cultivation, and in many places the forest had been lopped away to make room for fields of maize, plantain and rice. But the vegetation was still that of the tropics and many were the long and lonely reaches of the river, where we glided between piled masses of bloom and greenery. I remember one spot, where, from the crest of a steep hill to the edge of the water, descended a flood, a torrent of vegetation. Trees were rolled upon trees, woven into a sheet by parasitic vines, that leaped into the air like spray, from the topmost boughs. When a wind slightly agitated the sea of leaves, and the vines were flung like a green foam on the surface of the river, it was almost impossible not to feel that the flood was about rushing down to overwhelm us.

We stopped four hours short of Gorgona, at the hacienda of San Pablo, the residence of Padre Dutaris, curé of all the interior. Ambrosio took us to his house by a path across a rolling, open savanna, dotted by palms and acacias of immense size. Herds of cattle and horses were grazing on the short, thick-leaved grass, and appeared to be in excellent condition. The padre owns a large tract of land, with a thousand head of stock, and his ranche commands a beautiful view up and down the river. Ambrosio was acquainted with his wife, and by recommending us as *buenos caballeros*, procured us a splendid supper of fowls, eggs, rice boiled in cocoa milk, and chocolate, with baked plantains for bread. Those who came after us had difficulty in getting anything. The padre had been frequently cheated by Americans and was therefore cautious. He was absent at the time, but his son Felipe, a boy of twelve years old, assisted in doing the honors with wonderful grace and self-possession. His tawny skin was as soft as velvet, and his black eyes sparkled like jewels. He is almost the only living model of the Apollino that I ever saw. He sat in the hammock with me, leaning over my shoulder as I noted down the day's doings, and when I had done, wrote his name in my book, in an elegant hand. I slept soundly in the midst of an uproar, and only awoke at four o'clock next morning, to hurry our men in leaving for Gorgona.

The current was very strong and in some places it was almost impossible to make headway. Our boatmen worked hard, and by dint of strong poling managed to jump through most difficult places. Their naked, sinewy forms, bathed in sweat, shone like polished bronze. Ambrosio was soon exhausted, and lay down; but Miguel, our *corps de reserve*, put his agile spirit into the work and flung himself upon the pole with such vigor that all the muscles of his body quivered as the boat shot ahead and relaxed them. About half-way to Gorgona we rounded the foot of Monte Carabali, a bold peak clothed with forests and crowned with a single splendid palm. This hill is the only one in the province from which both oceans may be seen at once.

As we neared Gorgona, our men began repeating the ominous words : " *Cruces—mucha colera.*" We had, in fact, already heard of the prevalence of cholera there, but doubted, none the less, their wish to shorten the journey. On climbing the bank to the village, I called immediately at the store of Mr. Miller, the only American resident, who informed me that several passengers by the Falcon had already left for Panama, the route being reported passable. In the door of the alcalde's house, near at hand, I met Mr. Powers, who had left New York a short time previous to my departure, and was about starting for Panama on foot, mules being very scarce. While we were deliberating whether to go on to Cruces, Ambrosio beckoned me into an adjoining hut.

The owner, a very venerable and dignified native, received me swinging in his hammock. He had six horses which he would furnish us the next morning, at $10 the head for riding animals, and $6 for each 100 lbs. of freight. The bargain was instantly concluded.

Now came the settlement with our boatmen. In addition to the fare, half of which was paid in Chagres, we had promised them a *gratificacion*, provided they made the voyage in three days. The contract was not exactly fulfilled, but we thought it best to part friends and so gave them each a dollar. Their antics of delight were most laughable. They grinned, laughed, danced, caught us by the hands, vowed eternal friendship and would have embraced us outright, had we given them the least encouragement. Half an hour afterwards I met Juan, in a clean shirt and white pantaloons. There was a heat in his eye and a ruddiness under his black skin, which readily explained a little incoherence in his speech. "*Mi amigo!*" he cried, "*mi buen amigo!* give me a bottle of beer!" I refused. "But," said he, "we are friends; surely you will give your dear friend a bottle of beer." "I don't like my dear friends to drink too much;" I answered. Finding I would not humor him, as a last resort, he placed both hands on his breast, and with an imploring look, sang:

> " Ten piedad, piedad de mis penas,
> Ten piedad, piedad de mi amor !"

I burst into a laugh at this comical appeal, and he retreated, satisfied that he had at least done a smart thing.

During the afternoon a number of canoes arrived, and as it grew dark the sound of the wooden drums proclaimed a fandango.

The aristocracy of Gorgona met in the Alcalde's house ; the *plebs* on a level sward before one of the huts. The dances were the same, but there was some attempt at style by the former class. The ladies were dressed in white and pink, with flowers in their hair, and waltzed with a slow grace to the music of violins and guitars. The Alcalde's daughters were rather pretty, and at once became favorites of the Americans, some of whom joined in the fandango, and went through its voluptuous mazes at the first trial, to the great delight of the natives. The Señora Catalina, a rich widow, of pure Andalusian blood, danced charmingly. Her little head was leaned coquettishly on one side, while with one hand she held aloft the fringed end of a crimson scarf, which rested lightly on the opposite shoulder. The dance over, she took a guitar and sang, the subject of her song being "*los amigos Americanos.*" There was less sentiment, but more jollity, at the dances on the grass. The only accompaniment to the wooden drums was the " *ña, ña, ña,*" of the women, a nasal monotone, which few ears have nerve to endure. Those who danced longest and with the most voluptuous spirit, had the hats of all the others piled upon them, in token of applause. These half-barbaric orgies were fully seen in the pure and splendid light poured upon the landscape from a vertical moon.

Next morning at daybreak our horses—tough little mustangs, which I could almost step over—were at the door. We started off with a guide, trusting our baggage to the honesty of our host, who promised to send it the same day. A servant of the Alcalde escorted us out of the village, cut us each a good stick, pocketed a real and then left us to plunge into the forests. The path at the outset was bad enough, but as the wood grew deeper and darker and the tough clay soil held the rains which had fallen, it became finally a narrow gully, filled with mud nearly to our horses' bellies. Descending the steep sides of the hills, they would step or slide down almost precipitous passes, bringing up all straight at the bottom, and climbing the opposite sides like cats. So strong is their mutual confidence that they invariably step in each other's tracks, and a great part of the road is thus worn into holes three feet deep and filled with water and soft mud, which spirts upward as they go, coating the rider from head to foot.

The mountain range in the interior is broken and irregular. The road passes over the lower ridges and projecting spurs of the main chain, covered nearly the whole distance to Panama by dense forests. Above us spread a roof of transparent green, through which few rays of the sunlight fell. The only sounds in that leafy wilderness were the chattering of monkeys as they cracked the palm-nuts, and the scream of parrots, flying from tree to tree. In the deepest ravines spent mules frequently lay dead, and high above them, on the large boughs, the bald vultures waited silently for us to pass. We overtook many trains of luggage, packed on the backs of bulls and horses, tied head-to-tail in long files. At intervals, on the road, we saw a solitary ranche, with a cleared space about it, but all the natives could furnish us was a cup of thick, black coffee.

After ascending for a considerable distance, in the first half of our journey, we came to a level table-land, covered with palms, with a higher ridge beyond it. Our horses climbed it with some labor, went down the other side through clefts and gullies which seemed impassable, and brought us to a stream of milky blue water, which, on ascertaining its course with a compass, I found to be a tributary of the Rio Grande, flowing into the Pacific at Panama. We now hoped the worst part of our route was over, but this was a terrible deception. Scrambling up ravines of slippery clay, we went for miles through swamps and thickets, urging forward our jaded beasts by shouting and beating. Going down a precipitous bank, washed soft by the rains, my horse slipped and made a descent of ten feet, landing on one bank and I on another. He rose quietly, disengaged his head from the mud and stood, flank-deep, waiting till I stepped across his back and went forward, my legs lifted to his neck. This same adventure happened several times to each of us on the passage across.

As we were leaving Gorgona, our party was joined by a long Mississippian, whose face struck me at the first glance as being peculiarly cadaverous. He attached himself to us without the least ceremony, leaving his own party behind. We had not ridden far before he told us he had felt symptoms of cholera during the night, and was growing worse. We insisted on his returning to Gorgona at once, but he refused, saying he was "bound to go through." At the first ranche on the road we found another traveler, lying on the ground in a state of entire prostration. He was attended by a friend, who seemed on the point of taking the epidemic, from his very fears. The sight of this case no doubt operated on the Mississippian, for he soon became so racked with pain as to keep his seat with great difficulty. We were alarmed; it was impossible to stop in the swampy forest, and equally impossible to leave him, now that all his dependence was on us. The only thing resembling medicine in our possession, was a bottle of claret. It was an unusual remedy for cholera, but he insisted on drinking it.

After urging forward our weary beasts till late in the afternoon, we were told that Panama was four hours further. We pitied the poor horses, but ourselves more, and determined to push ahead. After a repetition of all our worst experience, we finally struck the remains of the paved road constructed by the buccaneers when they held Panama. I now looked eagerly forward for the Pacific, but every ridge showed another in advance, and it grew dark with a rain coming up. Our horses avoided the hard pavement and took by-paths through thickets higher than our heads. The cholera-stricken emigrant, nothing helped by the claret he drank, implored us, amid his groans, to hasten forward. Leaning over the horse's neck, he writhed on his saddle in an agony of pain, and seemed on the point of falling at every step. We were far in advance of our Indian guide and lost the way more than once in the darkness. At last he overtook us, washed his feet in a mudhole, and put on a pair of pantaloons. This was a welcome sign to us, and in fact, we soon after smelt the salt air of the Pacific, and could distinguish huts on either side of the road. These gave place to stone houses and massive ruined edifices, overgrown with vegetation. We passed a plaza and magnificent church, rode down an open space fronting the bay, under a heavy gate-way, across another plaza and through two or three narrow streets, hailed by Americans all the way with: "Are you the Falcon's passengers?" "From Gorgona?" "From Cruces?" till our guide brought us up at the Hotel Americano.

Thus terminated my five days' journey across the Isthmus—decidedly more novel, grotesque and adventurous than any trip of similar length in the world. It was rough enough, but had nothing that I could exactly call hardship, so much was the fatigue balanced by the enjoyment of unsurpassed scenery and a continual sensation of novelty. In spite of the many dolorous accounts which have been sent from the Isthmus, there is nothing, at the worst season, to deter any one from the journey.

CHAPTER III.

I saw less of Panama than I could have wished. A few hasty
rambles through its ruined convents and colleges and grass-grown
plazas—a stroll on its massive battlements, lumbered with idle
cannon, of the splendid bronze of Barcelona—were all that I could
accomplish in the short stay of a day and a half. Its situation at
the base of a broad, green mountain, with the sea washing three
sides of the narrow promontory on which it is built, is highly picturesque, yet some other parts of the bay seem better fitted for
the purposes of commerce. Vessels of heavy draught cannot
anchor within a mile and a half of the city, and there is but one
point where embarkation, even in the shallow " dug-outs" of the
natives, is practicable. The bottom of the bay is a bed of rock,
which, at low tide, lies bare far out beyond the ramparts. The
south-eastern shore of the bay belongs to the South-American
Continent, and the range of lofty mountains behind it is constantly
wreathed with light clouds, or shrouded from view by the storms
which it attracts. To the west the green islands of Taboga, and
others, rise behind one another, interrupting the blue curve of the
watery horizon. The city was already half American. The native boys whistled Yankee Doodle through the streets, and Se-

ñoritas of the pure Castilian blood sang the Ethiopian melodies of Virginia to their guitars. Nearly half the faces seen were American, and the signs on shops of all kinds appeared in our language. On the morning after I arrived, I heard a sudden rumbling in the streets, and observing a general rush to the windows, followed the crowd in time to see the first cart made in Panama—the work of a Yankee mechanic, detained for want of money to get further.

We found the hotels doing a thriving business, though the fare and attendance were alike indifferent. We went to bed, immediately after reaching the Hotel Americano, that our clothes might be washed before morning, as our luggage had not arrived. Nearly all the passengers were in a similar predicament. Some ladies, who had ridden over from Cruces in male attire, a short time previous, were obliged to sport their jackets and pantaloons several days before receiving their dresses. Our trust in the venerable native at Gorgona was not disappointed; the next morning his mule was at the door, laden with our trunks and valises. Some of the passengers, however, were obliged to remain in Panama another month, since, notwithstanding the formal contract of the Alcalde of Gorgona, their luggage did not arrive before the sailing of the steamer.

The next day nearly all of our passengers came in. There had been a heavy rain during the night, and the Gorgona road, already next to impassable, became actually perilous. A lady from Maine, who made the journey alone, was obliged to ford a torrent of water above her waist, with a native on each side, to prevent her from being carried away. A French lady who crossed was washed from her mule, and only got over by the united exertions of seven men.

The roads from Cruces and Gorgona enter on the eastern side of the city, as well as the line of the railroad survey. The latter, after leaving Limon Bay, runs on the north side of the Chagres River till it reaches Gorgona, continuing thence to Panama in the same general course as the mule route. It will probably be extended down the Bay to some point opposite the island of Taboga, which is marked out by Nature as the future anchorage ground and dépôt of all the lines touching at Panama. The engineers of the survey accomplished a great work in fixing the route within so short a space of time. The obstacles to be overcome can scarcely be conceived by one who has never seen tropical vegetation or felt tropical rains. The greatest difficulty in constructing the road is the want of stone, though this is in some degree supplied by abundance of lignum-vitæ and other durable wood. The torrents of rain during the summer season will require the side-hill cuttings to be made of unusual strength. The estimated cost of the road appears small, especially when the value of labor is taken into consideration. The natives are not to be depended on, and there is some risk in taking men from the United States half way to California.

Panama is one of the most picturesque cities on the American Continent. Its ruins—if those could be called ruins which were never completed edifices—and the seaward view from its ramparts, on a bright morning, would ravish the eye of an artist. Although small in limit, old and terribly dilapidated, its situation and surroundings are of unsurpassable beauty. There is one angle of the walls where you can look out of a cracked watch-tower on the sparkling swells of the Pacific, ridden by flocks of snow-white pelicans and the rolling canoes of the natives—where your vision, following the entire curve of the Gulf, takes in on either side nearly a hundred miles of shore. The ruins of the Jesuit Church of San Felipe, through which I was piloted by my friend, Lieutenant Beale, reminded me of the Baths of Caracalla. The majestic arches spanning the nave are laden with a wilderness of shrubbery and wild vines which fall like a fringe to the very floor. The building is roofless, but daylight can scarcely steal in through the embowering leaves. Several bells, of a sweet, silvery ring, are propped up by beams, in a dark corner, but from the look of the place, ages seem to have passed since they called the crafty brotherhood to the *oracion*. A splendid College, left incomplete many years ago, fronts on one of the plazas. Its Corinthian pillars and pilasters of red sandstone are broken and crumbling, and from the crevices at their base spring luxuriant bananas, shooting their large leaves through the windows and folding them around the columns of the gateway.

There were about seven hundred emigrants waiting for passage, when I reached Panama. All the tickets the steamer could possibly receive had been issued and so great was the anxiety to get on, that double price, $600, was frequently paid for a ticket to San Francisco. A few days before we came, there was a most violent excitement on the subject, and as the only way to terminate the dispute, it was finally agreed to dispose by lot of all the tickets for sale. The emigrants were all numbered, and those with tickets for sailing vessels or other steamers excluded. The remainder then drew, there being fifty-two tickets to near three hundred passengers. This quieted the excitement for the time, though there was still a continual under-current of speculation and intrigue which was curious to observe. The disappointed candidates, for the most part, took passage in sailing vessels, with a prospect of seventy days' voyage before them. A few months previous, when three thousand persons were waiting on the Isth-mus, several small companies started in the log canoes of the natives, thinking to reach San Francisco in them ! After a voy-age of forty days, during which they went no further than the Island of Quibo, at the mouth of the Gulf, nearly all of them re-turned ; the rest have not since been heard of.

The passengers were engaged in embarking all the afternoon of the second day after my arrival. The steamer came up to within a mile and a half of the town, and numbers of canoes plied be-tween her and the sea-gateway. Native porters crowded about the hotels, clamoring for luggage, which they carried down to the shore under so fervent a heat that I was obliged to hoist my umbrella. One of the boatmen lifted me over the swells for the sake of a *medio*, and I was soon gliding out along the edge of the breakers, startling the pelicans that flew in long lines over the water. I was well satisfied to leave Panama at the time ; the cholera, which had already carried off one-fourth of the native population, was making havoc among the Americans, and several of the Falcon's passengers lay at the point of death.

CHAPTER IV.

THE PACIFIC COAST OF MEXICO.

THE following morning, at eleven o'clock, the last canoe-load of mails came on board. Ten minutes afterwards our parting gun was fired, and its echoes had not died away when the paddles were in motion and the boat heading for Taboga. We ran past several steep volcanic islands, matted in foliage, and in an hour came-to before Taboga, which is to Panama what Capri is to Naples, only that it is far more beautiful. In the deep and secure roadstead one may throw a stone from the ship's deck into the gardens of orange and tamarind fringing the beach. The village lies beside a cocoa grove in a sheltered corner, at the foot of hills which rise in terraces of luxuriant vegetation to the height of a thousand feet. The mass of palm, cocoa, banana and orange trees is unbroken from the summit to the water's edge. The ravine behind the village contains an unfailing spring of sweet water, from which all vessels touching at Panama are supplied. The climate is delightful and perfectly healthy.

The steamer Oregon was lying high and dry on the beach, undergoing repairs, having injured her keel by running on a rock during the voyage down. The remarkable adaptation of Taboga for a dry dock was shown by the fact that while at high tide the

Oregon floated, at low tide one might walk around her on dry ground; by building two walls and a gate in front, the dry dock would be complete. This is the only place between Cape Horn and San Francisco where such a thing is possible. These un- rivaled advantages, as well as the healthiness of Taboga and its splendid scenery, point it out as the stopping-place for steamers and passengers, if not the commercial dépôt of this part of the Pacific.

A voyage from Panama to San Francisco in the year 1849, can hardly be compared to sea-life in any other part of the world or at any previous period. Our vessel was crowded fore and aft: exercise was rendered quite impossible and sleep was each night a new experiment, for the success of which we were truly grateful. We were roused at daylight by the movements on deck, if not earlier, by the breaking of a hammock-rope and the thump and yell of the unlucky sleeper. Coffee was served in the cabin; but, as many of the passengers imagined that, because they had paid a high price for their tickets, they were conscientiously obligated to drink three cups, the late-comers got a very scanty allowance. The breakfast hour was nine, and the table was obliged to be fully set twice. At the first tingle of the bell, all hands started as if a shot had exploded among them; conversation was broken off in the middle of a word; the deck was instantly cleared, and the passengers, tumbling pell-mell down the cabin-stairs, found every seat taken by others who had probably been sitting in them for half an hour. The bell, however, had an equally convulsive effect upon these. There was a confused grabbing motion for a few seconds, and lo! the plates were cleared. A chicken parted in twain as if by magic, each half leaping into an opposite plate; a dish of sweet potatoes vanished before a single hand; beefsteak flew in all directions ; and while about half the passengers had all their breakfast piled at once upon their plates, the other half were regaled by a " plentiful lack." The second table was but a repetition of these scenes, which dinner—our only additional meal—renewed in the afternoon. To prevent being driven, in self-defence, into the degrading habit, eight of us secured one end of the second table, shut off by the mizen-mast from the long arms that might otherwise have grabbed our share. Among our company of two hundred and fifty, there were, of course, many gentlemen of marked refinement and intelligence from various parts of the Union—enough, probably, to leaven the large lump of selfishness and blackguardism into which we were thrown. I believe the controlling portion of the California emigration is intelligent, orderly and peaceable ; yet I never witnessed so many disgusting exhibitions of the lowest passions of humanity, as during the voyage. At sea or among the mountains, men completely lose the little arts of dissimulation they practise in society. They show in their true light, and very often, alas ! in a light little calculated to encourage the enthusiastic believer in the speedy perfection of our race.

The day after leaving Panama we were in sight of the promontory of Veraguas and the island of Quibo, off Central America. It is a grand coast, with mountain ranges piercing the clouds. Then, for several days, we gave the continent a wide berth, our course making a chord to the arc of the Gulf of Tehuantepec. The sea was perfectly tranquil, and we were not molested by the inexorable demon that lodges in the stomachs of landsmen. Why has never a word been said or sung about sunset on the Pacific ? Nowhere on this earth can one be overvaulted with such a glory of colors. The sky, with a ground-hue of rose towards the west and purple towards the east, is mottled

2*

and flecked over all its surface with light clouds, running through
every shade of crimson, amber, violet and russet-gold. There is
no dead duskiness opposite the sunken sun ; the whole vast shell
of the firmament glows with an equal radiance, reduplicating its
hues on the glassy sea, so that we seem floating in a hollow sphere
of prismatic crystal. The cloud-strata, at different heights in
the air, take different coloring ; through bars of burning carmine
one may look on the soft, rose-purple folds of an inner curtain,
and, far within and beyond that, on the clear amber-green of the
immaculate sky. As the light diminishes, these radiant vapors
sink and gather into flaming pyramids, between whose pinnacles
the serene depth of air is of that fathomless violet-green which
we see in the skies of Titian.

The heat, during this part of the voyage, was intolerable.
The thermometer ranged from 82° to 84° at night, and 86° to
90° by day—a lower temperature than we frequently feel in the
North, but attended by an enervating languor such as I never
before experienced. Under its influence one's energies flag,
active habits of mind are thrown aside, the imagination grows
faint and hazy, the very feelings and sensibilities are melted and
weakened. Once, I panted for the heat and glare and splendid
luxuriance of tropical lands, till I almost made the god of the
Persians my own. I thought some southern star must have been
in the ascendant at my birth, some glowing instinct of the South
been infused into my nature. Two months before, the thought of
riding on that summer sea, with the sun over the mast-head,
would have given a delicious glow to my fancy. But all my vision
of life in the tropics vanished before the apathy engendered by
this heat. The snowy, bleak and sublime North beckoned me
like a mirage over the receding seas. Gods ! how a single sough

of keen north-west wind down some mountain gorge would have beaten a march of exulting energy to my spirit! how my veins would have tingled to the sound, and my nerves stiffened in the healthy embraces of that ruder air!

After a week of this kind of existence we passed the sun's latitude, and made the mountains of Mexico. The next night we came-to at the entrance of the harbor of Acapulco, while the ship's boat went to the city, some two miles distant. In about two hours it returned, bringing us word that thirty or forty Americans were waiting passage, most of whom were persons who had left Panama in the Humboldt in March, and who had already been three months in port. Captain Bailey determined to take them on board, and the Panama felt her way in through the dark, narrow entrance.

It was midnight. The beautiful mountain-locked basin on which Acapulco is built was dimly visible under the clouded moon, but I could discern on one side the white walls of the Fort on a rocky point, with the trees of the Alameda behind it, and still further the lights of the town glittering along the hill. As we approached the Fort we were hailed, but as a response was not immediately made the light was suddenly extinguished. Some one called out "*fuero! fuero!*" (outside!) and our boat, which had been sent out a second time, returned, stating that a file of soldiers drawn up on the beach had opposed any landing. It was followed by another, with four oars, containing a messenger from the Governor, who announced to us, in good English, that we were not allowed to come so near the town, but must lie off in the channel; the cholera, they had learned, was at Panama, and quarantine regulations had been established at Acapulco. This order was repeated, and the Panama then moved to the other side of the harbor. The boat, however, came out again, bringing a declaration from the Governor that if we did not instantly fall back to a certain channel between two islands, we should be fired upon. Rather than get into a quarrel with the alarmed authorities or be subjected to delay, we got under way again, and by sunrise were forty miles nearer San Blas.

We had on board a choice gang of blacklegs, among whom were several characters of notoriety in the United States, going out to extend the area of their infernal profession. About a dozen came on from New Orleans by the Falcon and as many from New York by the Crescent City. They established a branch at Panama, immediately on their arrival, and two or three remained to take charge of it. They did not commence very fortunately; their first capital of $500 having been won in one night by a lucky padre. Most of them, with the devil's luck, drew prizes in the ticket lottery, while worthy men were left behind. After leaving Acapulco, they commenced playing *monte* on the quarter-deck, and would no doubt have entrapped some unwary passengers, had not the Captain put a stop to their operations. These characters have done much, by their conduct on the Isthmus and elsewhere, to earn for us the title of "Northern barbarians," and especially, by wantonly offending the religious sentiment of the natives. I was told of four who entered one of the churches with their hats pulled fast over their brows, and, marching deliberately up the aisle, severally lighted their cigars at the four tapers of the altar. The class was known to all on board and generally shunned.

There is another class of individuals whom I would recommend travelers to avoid. I saw several specimens on the Isthmus. They are miserable, melancholy men, ready to yield up their last breath at any moment. They left home prematurely, and now humbly acknowledge their error. They were not made for traveling, but they did not know it before. If you would dig a hole and lay them in it, leaving only their heads above ground, they would be perfectly contented. Let them alone; do not even express your sympathy. Then their self-pity will change to indignation at your cold-heartedness, and they will take care of themselves for very spite.

Our track, now, was along and near the coast—a succession of lofty mountain ranges, rising faint and blue through belts of cloud. Through a glass, they appeared rugged and abrupt, scarred with deep ravines and divided by narrow gorges, yet exhibiting, nearly to their summits, a rich clothing of forests. The shore is iron-bound and lined with breakers, yet there are many small bays and coves which afford shelter to fishing and coasting vessels and support a scanty population. The higher peaks of the inland chain are occasionally seen when the atmosphere is clear. One morning the Volcano of Colima, distant ninety miles " as the bird flies," came into sight, shooting its forked summits far above the nearer ranges. It is in the province of Jalisco, near Lake Chapala, and is 16,000 feet in height—a greater than Mount Blanc! I was delighted with Cuba and the Isthmus, but forgot them at once when I viewed the grand outline of this coast, the only approach to which is seen in the Maritime Alps, on leaving Genoa.

On the third morning from Acapulco, we saw the lofty group of mountains bounding the roadstead of San Blas on the East. The islands called Las Tres Marias were visible, ten miles distant, on our left. They are too small and scattering to break the heavy seas and " southers" which come in to the very end of the

bight on which San Blas is built. Vessels of light draught may
run across a narrow bar between breakers and find safe anchorage in a little inlet on the northern side, but those which are
obliged to lie in the open road are exposed to considerable danger.
A high white rock, of singular form, about a quarter of a mile
from the shore, serves as a landmark for vessels. The village,
which is a little larger than Chagres, and like it a collection of
cane huts with a few stone houses, lies on one side of the inlet
before mentioned, on flat swampy ground, and surrounded by rank
forests and jungles. A mile behind it, on a high, precipitous
rock, is the Presidio of San Blas, now almost deserted, all business being transacted at the village on shore.

We came-to, a mile from the place, and were soon after visited
by the Alcalde, who, after exchanging the ordinary courtesies informed us there were plenty of provisions on shore, and departed,
saying nothing of quarantine. A flock of cayucas, paddled by
the natives, followed him and swarmed around us, ready to take
passengers at three rials apiece. Three or four of us took one of
these craft, and were paddled ashore, running on the edge of the
breakers which roared and dashed along the mouth of the inlet.
We landed on a beach, ancle-deep in sand and covered with mustangs, mules and donkeys, with a sprinkling of natives. Our
passengers were busy all over the village, lugging strings of
bananas and plantains, buying cool water-jars of porous earth,
gathering limes and oranges from the trees, or regaling themselves
at the fondas with fresh spring-water, (not always unmixed,)
tortillas and fried pork. Several gentlemen who had come overland from Vera Cruz, awaited our arrival, and as the place was
very unhealthy they were not long in embarking.

In company with some friends, I set out for the old Presidio on the cliff. The road led through swampy forests till we reached the foot of the ascent. A native passed us, on a sharp-trotting mule : " *Donde va, hombre ?*" " *Tépic,*" was his answer. Up we went, scrambling over loose stones, between banana thickets and flowering shrubs, till we gained a rocky spur near the summit. Here the view to the north, toward Mazatlan, was very fine. Across the marshy plain many leagues in breadth, bordering the sea, we traced the Rio Grande of the West by the groves of syca-more on its banks ; beyond it another lateral chain of the Sierra Madre rose to the clouds. Turning again, we entered a deserted court-yard, fronted by the fort, which had a covered gallery on the inside. The walls were broken down, the deep wells in the rock choked up and the stone pillars and gateways overrun with rank vines. From the parapet, the whole roadstead of San Blas lay at our feet, and our steamer, two miles off, seemed to be within hail.

This plaza opened on another and larger one, completely covered with tall weeds, among which the native pigs rooted and meditated by turns. A fine old church, at the farther end, was going to ruin, and the useless bells still hung in its towers. Some of the houses were inhabited, and we procured from the natives fresh water and delicious bananas. The aspect of the whole place, picturesque in its desolation, impressed me more than anything on the journey, except the church of San Felipe, at Panama. The guns of the Presidio were spiked by Commander Dupont, during the war ; there has been no garrison there for many years.

We descended again, made our purchases of fruit, and reached the beach just as the steamer's gun signalized us to return. The cayuca in which we embarked was a round log, about ten feet long, rolling over the swells with a ticklish facility. We lay flat in

the bottom, not daring to stir hand or foot for fear of losing
the exact balance which kept us upright, and finally reached the
gangway, where we received a sound cursing from one of the
ship's crew for trusting ourselves in such a craft. A dozen
others, pulling for life, came behind us, followed by a launch
bringing two live bullocks for our provender. A quarrel broke
out between one of our new passengers and a native, in which
blows were exchanged. The question was then raised " whether
a nigger was as good as a white man," and like the old feuds of
the *Bianchi* and the *Neri* in Tuscany, the contest raged fiercely
for the rest of the day.

The morning mist rose from the summits of the Sierra Madre
of Durango. As we neared Mazatlan, a light smoke was discerned
far on our left ; and we had not been long in the harbor before the
California came rounding in, her passengers cheering us as she
passed and dropped anchor between us and the town. She looked
somewhat weather-beaten, but was a pleasant sight to our eyes.
Conversation was kept up between the two ships so long as they
were in hearing, the Panama's passengers inquiring anxiously
about the abundance of gold, and the Californians assuring them
that it was as plenty as ever.

Few ports present a more picturesque appearance from the sea
than Mazatlan. The harbor, or roadstead, open on the west to
the unbroken swells of the Pacific, is protected on the north and
south by what were once mountain promontories, now split into
parallel chains of islands, separated by narrow channels of sea.
Their sides are scarred with crags, terminating toward the sea in
precipices of dark red rock, with deep caverns at the base, into
which the surf continually dashes. On approaching the road,
these islands open one beyond the other, like a succession of shift-

ing views, the last revealing the white walls of Mazatlan, rising gradually from the water, with a beautiful back-ground of dim blue mountains. The sky was of a dazzling purity, and the whole scene had that same clearness of outline and enchanting harmony of color which give the landscapes of Italy their greatest charm. As we ran westward on the Tropic of Cancer across the mouth of the Gulf, nothing could exceed the purity of the atmosphere.

CHAPTER V.

"There is California!" was the cry next morning at sunrise.
"Where?" "Off the starboard bow." I rose on my bunk in
one of the deck state-rooms, and looking out of the window, watched
the purple mountains of the Peninsula, as they rose in the fresh,
inspiring air. We were opposite its southern extremity, and I
scanned the brown and sterile coast with a glass, searching for
anything like vegetation. The whole country appeared to be a
mass of nearly naked rock, nourishing only a few cacti and some
stunted shrubs. At the extreme end of the Peninsula the valley
of San José opens inland between two ranges of lofty granite
mountains. Its beautiful green level, several miles in width,
stretched back as far as the eye could reach. The town lies near
the sea ; it is noted for the siege sustained by Lieut. Haywood and
a small body of American troops during the war. Lying deep
amid the most frightfully barren and rugged mountains I ever saw,
the valley of San José which is watered by a small river, might
be made a paradise. The scenery around it corresponded strikingly with descriptions of Syria and Palestine. The bare, yellow
crags glowed in the sun with dazzling intensity, and a chain of
splintered peaks in the distance wore the softest shade of violet.

In spite of the forbidding appearance of the coast, a more peculiar and interesting picture than it gave can hardly be found on the Pacific. Cape San Lucas, which we passed toward evening, is a bold bluff of native granite, broken into isolated rocks at its points, which present the appearance of three distinct and perfectly-formed pyramids. The white, glistening rock is pierced at its base by hollow caverns and arches, some of which are fifteen or twenty feet high, giving glimpses of the ocean beyond. The structure of this cape is very similar to that of The Needles on the Isle of Wight.

On the 12th of August we passed the island of Santa Marguerita, lying across the mouth of a bay, the upper extremity of which is called Point San Lazaro. Here, the outline of the coast, as laid down on the charts in use, is very incorrect. The longitude is not only placed too far eastward by twenty to thirty miles, but an isolated mountain, rising from the sea, eight miles northwest of Point San Lazaro, is entirely wanting. This mountain—a summit of barren rock, five miles in length and about a thousand feet in hight, is connected with the coast by a narrow belt of sand, forming a fine bay, twelve miles deep, curving southward till it strikes Point San Lazaro. The northern point of the headland is bordered by breakers, beyond which extends a shoal. Here the current sets strongly in shore, and here it was that a whale-ship was lost a few months since, her crew escaping to wander for days on an arid desert, without water or vegetation. The Panama, on her downward trip, ran on the shoal and was obliged to lay-to all night; in the morning, instead of the open sea promised by the chart, the crags of the unknown headland rose directly in front of her. The coast, as far as I could see with a good glass, presented an unbroken level of glaring white sand, which must extend in-

land for fifty or sixty miles, since, under the clearest of skies, no
sign of rock or distant peak was visible. The appearance of the
whole Peninsula, in passing—the alternations of bleak mountain,
blooming plain and wide salt desert—the rumors of vast mineral
wealth in its unknown interior and the general want of intelligence
in relation to it—conspired to excite in me a strong wish to traverse it from end to end.

The same evening we doubled Cape San Lucas, we met the
ship Grey Eagle, of Philadelphia, one of the first of the California
squadron. She was on her way from San Francisco to Mazatlan,
with two hundred passengers on board, chiefly Mexicans. Three
cheers were given and returned, as the vessels passed each other.
The temperature changed, as we left the tropics behind and met
the north-western trades; the cool winds drove many passengers
from the deck, and the rest of us had some chance for exercise.
All were in the best spirits, at the prospect of soon reaching our
destination, and the slightest thread of incident, whereto a chance
for amusement might be hung, was eagerly caught up. There
was on board a man of rather grave demeanor, who, from the
circumstance of having his felt hat cocked up like a general's,
wearing it square across his brows and standing for long whiles
with his arms folded, in a meditative attitude, had been generally
nicknamed "Napoleon." There was no feature of his face like
the great Corsican's, but from the tenacity with which he took his
stand on the mizen-yard and folded his arms every evening, the
passengers supposed he really imagined a strong resemblance.
One of those days, in a spirit of mischief, they bought a felt hat,
gave it the same cocked shape, and bribed one of the negro cooks
to wear it and take off Napoleon. Accordingly, as the latter began ascending the shrouds to his favorite post, the cook went up

the opposite side. Napoleon sat down on the yard, braced himself against the mast and folded his arms ; the cook, slyly watching his motions, imitated them with a gravity which was irresistible. All the passengers were by this time gathered on the quarter-deck, shouting with laughter : it was singular how much merriment so boyish a trick could occasion. Napoleon bore it for a time with perfect stolidity, gazing on the sunset with unchanged solemnity of visage. At last, getting tired of the affair, he looked down on the crowd and said : " you have sent me a very fit representative of yourselves." The laugh was stopped suddenly, and from that time forth Napoleon was not disturbed in his musings.

The only other point of interest which we saw on the Peninsular coast, was Benito Island, off the Bay of Sebastian Viscaino, so named, after the valiant discoverer of California. Two mornings after, I saw the sun rise behind the mountains back of San Diego. Point Loma, at the extremity of the bay, came in sight on the left, and in less than an hour we were at anchor before the hide-houses at the landing place. The southern shore of the bay is low and sandy ; from the bluff hights on the opposite side a narrow strip of shingly beach makes out into the sea, like a natural breakwater, leaving an entrance not more than three hundred yards broad. The harbor is the finest on the Pacific, with the exception of Acapulco, and capable of easy and complete defense. The old hide-houses are built at the foot of the hills just inside the bay, and a fine road along the shore leads to the town of San Diego, which is situated on a plain, three miles distant and barely visible from the anchorage. Above the houses, on a little eminence, several tents were planted, and a short distance further were several recent graves, surrounded by paling. A number of people were clustered on the beach, and boats laden with passengers and freight, instantly put off to us. In a few minutes after our gun was fired, we could see horsemen coming down from San Diego at full gallop, one of whom carried behind him a lady in graceful riding costume. In the first boat were Colonel Weller, U. S. Boundary Commissioner, and Major Hill, of the Army. Then followed a number of men, lank and brown " as is the ribbed sea-sand"—men with long hair and beards, and faces from which the rigid expression of suffering was scarcely relaxed. They were the first of the overland emigrants by the Gila route, who had reached San Diego a few days before. Their clothes were in tatters, their boots, in many cases, replaced by moccasins, and, except their rifles and some small packages rolled in deerskin, they had nothing left of the abundant stores with which they left home.

We hove anchor in half an hour, and again rounded Point Loma, our number increased by more than fifty passengers. The Point, which comes down to the sea at an angle of 60° has been lately purchased by an American, for what purpose I cannot imagine, unless it is with the hope of speculating on Government when it shall be wanted for a light-house. In the afternoon we passed the island of Santa Catalina, which is about twelve miles in length, rising to a height of 3,000 feet above the sea, and inhabited by herds of wild goats. Santa Cruz and Santa Rosa, which lie opposite Santa Barbara and separated from it by the channel of the same name, were left behind us in the night, and the next day we were off Cape Conception, the Cape Horn of California. True to its character, we had a cold, dense fog, and violent head-winds; the coast was shrouded from sight.

The emigrants we took on board at San Diego were objects of

general interest. The stories of their adventures by the way sounded more marvellous than anything I had heard or read since my boyish acquaintance with Robinson Crusoe, Captain Cook and John Ledyard. Taking them as the average experience of the thirty thousand emigrants who last year crossed the Plains, this California Crusade will more than equal the great military expeditions of the Middle Ages in magnitude, peril and adventure. The amount of suffering which must have been endured in the savage mountain passes and herbless deserts of the interior, cannot be told in words. Some had come by way of Santa Fé and along the savage hills of the Gila; some, starting from Red River, had crossed the Great Stake Desert and taken the road from Paso del Norte to Tueson in Sonora; some had passed through Mexico and after spending one hundred and four days at sea, run into San Diego and given up their vessel; some had landed, weary with a seven months' psssage around Cape Horn, and some, finally, had reached the place on foot, after walking the whole length of the Californian Peninsula.

The emigrants by the Gila route gave a terrible account of the crossing of the Great Desert, lying west of the Colorado. They described this region as scorching and sterile—a country of burning salt plains and shifting hills of sand, whose only signs of human visitation are the bones of animals and men scattered along the trails that cross it. The corpses of several emigrants, out of companies who passed before them, lay half-buried in sand, and the hot air was made stifling by the effluvia that rose from the dry carcases of hundreds of mules. There, if a man faltered, he was gone; no one could stop to lend him a hand without a likelihood of sharing his fate. It seemed like a wonderful Providence to these emigrants, when they came suddenly upon a large and swift stream of fresh water in the midst of the Desert, where, a year previous, there had been nothing but sterile sand. This phenomenon was at first ascribed to the melting of snow on the mountains, but later emigrants traced the river to its source in a lake about half a mile in length, which had bubbled up spontaneously from the fiery bosom of the Desert.

One of the emigrants by the Sonora route told me a story of a sick man who rode behind his party day after day, unable to keep pace with it, yet always arriving in camp a few hours later. This lasted so long that finally little attention was paid to him and his absence one night excited no apprehension. Three days passed and he did not arrive. On the fourth, a negro, traveling alone and on foot, came into camp and told them that many miles behind a man lying beside the road had begged a little water from him and asked him to hurry on and bring assistance. The next morning a company of Mexicans came up and brought word that the man was dying. The humane negro retraced his steps forty miles, and arrived just as the sufferer breathed his last. He lifted him in his arms; in the vain effort to speak, the man expired. The mule, tied to a cactus by his side, was already dead of hunger.

I was most profoundly interested in the narrative of a Philadelphian, who, after crossing Mexico from Tampico to San Blas, embarked for San Francisco, and was put ashore by his own request, at Cape San Lucas. He had three or four companions, the party supposing they might make the journey to San Diego in thirty or forty days, by following the coast. It was soon found, however, that the only supply of water was among the mountains of the interior, and they were obliged to proceed on foot to the valley of San José and follow the trail to La Paz, on the Californian Gulf. Thence they wandered in a nearly opposite direction to Todos Santos Bay, on the Pacific, where they exchanged some of their arms for horses. The route led in a zigzag direction across the mountain chain, from one watering-place to another, with frequent *jornadas* (journeys without water,) of thirty, forty and even sixty miles in length. Its rigors were increased by the frightful desolation of the country, and the deep gullies or *arroyos* with which it is seamed. In the beds of these they would often lose the trail, occasioning them many hours' search to recover it. The fruit of the cactus and the leaves of succulent plants formed their principal sustenance. After a month of this travel they reached San Ignacio, half-way to San Diego, where their horses failed them ; the remainder of the journey was performed on foot. The length of the Peninsula is about eight hundred miles, but the distance traveled by these hardy adventurers amounted to more than fifteen hundred.

Among the passengers who came on board at San Diego, was Gen. Villamil, of the Republic of Ecuador, who was aid to Bolivar during the war of South-American independence. After the secession of Ecuador from Columbia, he obtained from Gen. Flores a grant of one of the Galapagos Islands—a group well known to whalers, lying on the equator, six hundred miles west of Guayaquil. On this island, which he named Floriana, he has lived for the past sixteen years. His colony contains a hundred and fifty souls, who raise on the light, new soil, abundant crops of grain and vegetables. The island is fifteen miles in length, by twelve in breadth, lying in lat. 1° 30' S. and its highest part is about 5,000 feet above the level of the sea. The soil is but from twelve to eighteen inches deep, yet such is the profusion of vegetable growth, that, as Gen. Villamil informed me, its depth has in many places increased six inches

since he first landed there.   The supply of water is obtained in a
very singular manner.   A large porous rock, on the side of one of
the mountains, seems to serve as an outlet or filter for some subterranean vein, since on its base, which is constantly humid, the
drops collect and fall in sufficient abundance to supply a large
basin in the rock below.   Pipes from this deposit convey the water
to the valley.   Its quality is cool, sweet and limpid, and the
rocky sponge from which it drips never fails in its supply.

We were within sight of the Coast Range of California all day,
after passing Cape Conception.   Their sides are spotted with
timber, which in the narrow valleys sloping down to the sea appeared to be of large growth.   From their unvarying yellow hue,
we took them to be mountains of sand, but they were in reality
covered with natural harvests of wild oats, as I afterwards learned,
on traveling into the interior.   A keen, bracing wind at night
kept down the fog, and although the thermometer fell to.52°,
causing a general shiver on board, I walked the deck a long time,
noting the extraordinary brilliancy of the stars in the pure air.
The mood of our passengers changed very visibly as we approached
the close of the voyage ; their exhilarant anticipations left them,
and were succeeded by a reaction of feeling that almost amounted
to despondency.   The return to laborious life after a short ex-
emption from its cares, as in the case of travel, is always attended
with some such feeling, but among the California emigrants it was
intensified by the uncertainty of their venture in a region where all
the ordinary rules of trade and enterprise would be at fault.

When I went on deck in the clear dawn, while yet

> "The maiden splendors of the morning-star
> Shook in the steadfast blue,"

we were rounding Point Pinos into the harbor of Monterey. As we drew near, the white, scattered dwellings of the town, situated on a gentle slope, behind which extended on all sides the celebrated Pine Forest, became visible in the grey light. A handsome fort, on an eminence near the sea, returned our salute. Four vessels, shattered, weather-beaten and apparently deserted, lay at anchor not far from shore. The town is larger than I expected to find it, and from the water has the air of a large New-England village, barring the *adobe* houses. Major Lee and Lieut. Beale, who went ashore in the steamer's boat, found Gen. Riley, the Civil Governor, very ill with a fever. As we were preparing to leave, the sun rose over the mountains, covering the air with gold brighter than ever was scratched up on the Sacramento. The picturesque houses of Monterey, the pine woods behind and the hills above them, glowed like an illuminated painting, till a fog-curtain which met us at the mouth of the harbor dropped down upon the water and hid them all from sight.

At last the voyage is drawing to a close. Fifty-one days have elapsed since leaving New York, in which time we have, in a manner, coasted both sides of the North-American Continent, from the parallel of 40° N. to its termination, within a few degrees of the Equator, over seas once ploughed by the keels of Columbus and Balboa, of Grijalva and Sebastian Viscaino. All is excitement on board ; the Captain has just taken his noon observation. We are running along the shore, within six or eight miles' distance ; the hills are bare and sandy, but loom up finely through the deep blue haze. A brig bound to San Francisco, but fallen off to the leeward of the harbor, is making a new tack on our left, to come up again. The coast trends somewhat more to the westward, and a notch or gap is at last visible in its lofty outline.

An hour later ; we are in front of the entrance to San Francisco Bay. The mountains on the northern side are 3,000 feet in hight, and come boldly down to the sea. As the view opens through the splendid strait, three or four miles in width, the island rock of Alcatraz appears, gleaming white in the distance. An inward-bound ship follows close on our wake, urged on by wind and tide. There is a small fort perched among the trees on our right, where the strait is narrowest, and a glance at the formation of the hills shows that this pass might be made impregnable as Gibraltar. The town is still concealed behind the promontory around which the Bay turns to the southward, but between Alcatraz and the island of Yerba Buena, now coming into sight, I can see vessels at anchor. High through the vapor in front, and thirty miles distant, rises the peak of Monte Diablo, which overlooks everything between the Sierra Nevada and the Ocean. On our left opens the bight of Sousolito, where the U. S. propeller Massachusetts and several other vessels are at anchor.

At last we are through the Golden Gate—fit name for such a magnificent portal to the commerce of the Pacific ! Yerba Buena Island is in front ; southward and westward opens the renowned harbor, crowded with the shipping of the world, mast behind mast and vessel behind vessel, the flags of all nations fluttering in the breeze ! Around the curving shore of the Bay and upon the sides of three hills which rise steeply from the water, the middle one receding so as to form a bold amphitheatre, the town is planted and seems scarcely yet to have taken root, for tents, canvas, plank, mud and adobe houses are mingled together with the least apparent attempt at order and durability. But I am not yet on shore. The gun of the Panama has just announced our arrival to the people on land. We glide on with the tide, past the U. S. ship Ohio and opposite the main landing, outside of the forest of masts. A dozen boats are creeping out to us over the water; the signal is given—the anchor drops—our voyage is over.

CHAPTER VI.

FIRST IMPRESSIONS OF SAN FRANCISCO.

I LEFT the Panama, in company with Lieut. Beale, in the boat of the U. S. ship Ohio, which brought Lieutenant Ells on board. We first boarded the noble ship, which, even in San Francisco harbor, showed the same admirable order as on our own coast. She had returned from Honolulu a few days previous, after an absence of three months from California. The morning of our arrival, eighteen of her men had contrived to escape, carrying with them one of the boats, under fire from all the Government vessels in the harbor. The officers were eager for news from home, having been two months without a mail, and I was glad that my habit of carrying newspapers in my pockets enabled me to furnish them with a substantial gratification. The Ohio's boat put us ashore at the northern point of the anchorage, at the foot of a steep bank, from which a high pier had been built into the bay. A large vessel lay at the end, discharging her cargo. We scrambled up through piles of luggage, and among the crowd collected to witness our arrival, picked out two Mexicans to carry our trunks to a hotel. The barren side of the hill before us was covered with tents and canvas houses, and nearly in front a large two-story building displayed the sign : " Fremont Family Hotel."

As yet, we were only in the suburbs of the town. Crossing the shoulder of the hill, the view extended around the curve of the bay, and hundreds of tents and houses appeared, scattered all over the heights, and along the shore for more than a mile. A furious wind was blowing down through a gap in the hills, filling the streets with clouds of dust. On every side stood buildings of all kinds, begun or half-finished, and the greater part of them mere canvas sheds, open in front, and covered with all kinds of signs, in all languages. Great quantities of goods were piled up in the open air, for want of a place to store them. The streets were full of people, hurrying to and fro, and of as diverse and bizarre a character as the houses : Yankees of every possible variety, native Californians in *sarapes* and sombreros, Chilians, Sonorians, Kanakas from Hawaii, Chinese with long tails, Malays armed with their everlasting creeses, and others in whose embrowned and bearded visages it was impossible to recognize any especial nationality. We came at last into the plaza, now dignified by the name of Portsmouth Square. It lies on the slant side of the hill, and from a high pole in front of a long one-story adobe building used as the Custom House, the American flag was flying. On the lower side stood the Parker House—an ordinary frame house of about sixty feet front—and towards its entrance we directed our course.

Our luggage was deposited on one of the rear porticos, and we discharged the porters, after paying them two dollars each—a sum so immense in comparison to the service rendered that there was no longer any doubt of our having actually landed in California. There were no lodgings to be had at the Parker House—not even a place to unroll our blankets ; but one of the proprietors accompanied us across the plaza to the City Hotel, where we obtained a room with two beds at $25 per week, meals being in addition $20 per week. I asked the landlord whether he could send a porter for our trunks. "There is none belonging to the house," said he; "every man is his own porter here." I returned to the Parker House, shouldered a heavy trunk, took a valise in my hand and carried them to my quarters, in the teeth of the wind. Our room was in a sort of garret over the only story of the hotel; two cots, evidently of California manufacture, and covered only with a pair of blankets, two chairs, a rough table and a small looking-glass, constituted the furniture. There was not space enough between the bed and the bare rafters overhead, to sit upright, and I gave myself a severe blow in rising the next morning without the proper heed. Through a small roof-window of dim glass, I could see the opposite shore of the bay, then partly hidden by the evening fogs. The wind whistled around the eaves and rattled the tiles with a cold, gusty sound, that would have imparted a dreary character to the place, had I been in a mood to listen.

Many of the passengers began speculation at the moment of landing. The most ingenious and successful operation was made by a gentleman of New York, who took out fifteen hundred copies of The Tribune and other papers, which he disposed of in two hours, at one dollar a-piece! Hearing of this I bethought me of about a dozen papers which I had used to fill up crevices in packing my valise. There was a newspaper merchant at the corner of the City Hotel, and to him I proposed the sale of them, asking him to name a price. "I shall want to make a good profit on the retail price," said he, "and can't give more than ten dollars for the lot." I was satisfied with the wholesale price, which was a gain of just four thousand per cent!

I set out for a walk before dark and climbed a hill back of

the town, passing a number of tents pitched in the hollows. The scattered houses spread out below me and the crowded shipping in the harbor, backed by a lofty line of mountains, made an imposing picture. The restless, feverish tide of life in that little spot, and the thought that what I then saw and was yet to see will hereafter fill one of the most marvellous pages of all history, rendered it singularly impressive. The feeling was not decreased on talking that evening with some of the old residents, (that is, of six months' standing,) and hearing their several experiences. Every new-comer in San Francisco is overtaken with a sense of complete bewilderment. The mind, however it may be prepared for an astonishing condition of affairs, cannot immediately push aside its old instincts of value and ideas of business, letting all past experiences go for naught and casting all its faculties for action, intercourse with its fellows or advancement in any path of ambition, into shapes which it never before imagined. As in the turn of the dissolving views, there is a period when it wears neither the old nor the new phase, but the vanishing images of the one and the growing perceptions of the other are blended in painful and misty confusion. One knows not whether he is awake or in some wonderful dream. Never have I had so much difficulty in establishing, satisfactorily to my own senses, the reality of what I saw and heard.

I was forced to believe many things, which in my communications to The Tribune I was almost afraid to write, with any hope of their obtaining credence. It may be interesting to give here a few instances of the enormous and unnatural value put upon property at the time of my arrival. The Parker House rented for $110,000 yearly, at least $60,000 of which was paid by gamblers, who held nearly all the second story. Adjoining it on

3*

the right was a canvas-tent fifteen by twenty-five feet, called "Eldorado," and occupied likewise by gamblers, which brought $40,000.
On the opposite corner of the plaza, a building called the "Miner's
Bank," used by Wright & Co., brokers, about half the size of a
fire-engine house in New York, was held at a rent of $75,000.
A mercantile house paid $40,000 rent for a one-story building of
twenty feet front; the United States Hotel, $36,000; the Post-
Office, $7,000, and so on to the end of the chapter. A friend of
mine, who wished to find a place for a law-office, was shown a
cellar in the earth, about twelve feet square and six deep, which
he could have at $250 a month. One of the common soldiers at
the battle of San Pasquale was reputed to be among the mil-
lionaires of the place, with an income of $50,000 *monthly*. A
citizen of San Francisco died insolvent to the amount of $41,000
the previous Autumn. His administrators were delayed in
settling his affairs, and his real estate advanced so rapidly in value
meantime, that after his debts were paid his heirs had a yearly
income of $40,000. These facts were indubitably attested;
every one believed them, yet hearing them talked of daily, as
matters of course, one at first could not help feeling as if he had
been eating of "the insane root."

The prices paid for labor were in proportion to everything else.
The carman of Mellus, Howard & Co. had a salary of $6,000 a
year, and many others made from $15 to $20 daily. Servants
were paid from $100 to $200 a month, but the wages of the
rougher kinds of labor had fallen to about $8. Yet, notwith-
standing the number of gold-seekers who were returning enfeebled
and disheartened from the mines, it was difficult to obtain as many
workmen as the forced growth of the city demanded. A gentleman who arrived in April told me he then found but thirty or

forty houses ; the population was then so scant that not more than twenty-five persons would be seen in the streets at any one time. Now, there were probably five hundred houses, tents and sheds, with a population, fixed and floating, of six thousand. People who had been absent six weeks came back and could scarcely recognize the place. Streets were regularly laid out, and already there were three piers, at which small vessels could discharge. It was calculated that the town increased daily by from fifteen to thirty houses; its skirts were rapidly approaching the summits of the three hills on which it is located.

A curious result of the extraordinary abundance of gold and the facility with which fortunes were acquired, struck me at the first glance. All business was transacted on so extensive a scale that the ordinary habits of solicitation and compliance on the one hand and stubborn cheapening on the other, seemed to be entirely forgotten. You enter a shop to buy something; the owner eyes you with perfect indifference, waiting for you to state your want ; if you object to the price, you are at liberty to leave, for you need not expect to get it cheaper; he evidently cares little whether you buy it or not. One who has been some time in the country will lay down the money, without wasting words. The only exception I found to this rule was that of a sharp-faced Down-Easter just opening his stock, who was much distressed when his clerk charged me seventy-five cents for a coil of rope, instead of one dollar. This disregard for all the petty arts of money-making was really a refreshing feature of society. Another equally agreeable trait was the punctuality with which debts were paid, and the general confidence which men were obliged to place, perforce, in each other's honesty. Perhaps this latter fact was owing, in part, to the impossibility of protecting wealth, and consequent dependence on an honorable regard for the rights of others.

About the hour of twilight the wind fell ; the sound of a gong called us to tea, which was served in the largest room of the hotel. The fare was abundant and of much better quality than we expected—better, in fact, than I was able to find there two months later. The fresh milk, butter and excellent beef of the country were real luxuries after our sea-fare. Thus braced against the fog and raw temperature, we sallied out for a night-view of San Francisco, then even more peculiar than its daylight look. Business was over about the usual hour, and then the harvest-time of the gamblers commenced. Every " hell" in the place, and I did not pretend to number them, was crowded, and immense sums were staked at the monte and faro tables. A boy of fifteen, in one place, won about $500, which he coolly pocketed and carried off. One of the gang we brought in the Panama won $1,500 in the course of the evening, and another lost $2,400. A fortunate miner made himself conspicuous by betting large piles of ounces on a single throw. His last stake of 100 oz. was lost, and I saw him the following morning dashing through the streets, trying to break his own neck or that of the magnificent *garañon* he bestrode.

Walking through the town the next day, I was quite amazed to find a dozen persons busily employed in the street before the United States Hotel, digging up the earth with knives and crumbling it in their hands. They were actual gold-hunters, who obtained in this way about $5 a day. After blowing the fine dirt carefully in their hands, a few specks of gold were left, which they placed in a piece of white paper. A number of children were engaged in the same business, picking out the fine grains by applying to them the head of a pin, moistened in their mouths. I was told of a small boy having taken home $14 as the result of one day's labor. On climbing the hill to the Post Office I observed in places, where the wind had swept away the sand, several glittering dots of the real metal, but, like the Irishman who kicked the dollar out of his way, concluded to wait till I should reach the heap. The presence of gold in the streets was probably occasioned by the leakings from the miners' bags and the sweepings of stores; though it may also be, to a slight extent, native in the earth, particles having been found in the clay thrown up from a deep well.

The arrival of a steamer with a mail ran the usual excitement and activity of the town up to its highest possible notch. The little Post Office, half-way up the hill, was almost hidden from sight by the crowds that clustered around it. Mr. Moore, the new Postmaster, who was my fellow-traveler from New York, barred every door and window from the moment of his entrance, and with his sons and a few clerks, worked steadily for two days and two nights, till the distribution of twenty thousand letters was completed. Among the many persons I met, the day after landing, was Mr. T. Butler King, who had just returned from an expedition to the placers, in company with General Smith. Mr. Edwin Bryant, of Kentucky, and Mr. Durivage, of New Orleans, had arrived a few days previous, the former by way of the Great Salt Lake, and the latter by the northern provinces of Mexico and the Gila. I found the artist Osgood in a studio about eight feet square, with a head of Captain Sutter on his easel. He had given up gold-digging, after three months of successful labor among the mountains.

I could make no thorough acquaintance with San Francisco

during this first visit. Lieutenant Beale, who held important
Government dispatches for Colonel Frémont, made arrangements
to leave for San José on the second morning, and offered me a
seat on the back of one of his mules. Our fellow-passenger,
Colonel Lyons, of Louisiana, joined us, completing the mystic
number which travelers should be careful not to exceed. We
made hasty tours through all the shops on Clay, Kearney, Washington and Montgomery streets, on the hunt of the proper equipments. Articles of clothing were cheaper than they had been or
were afterwards ; tolerable blankets could be had for $6 a pair ;
coarse flannel shirts, $3 ; Chilian spurs, with rowels two inches
long, $5, and Mexican sarapes, of coarse texture but gay color,
$10. We could find no saddle-bags in the town, and were neces-
sitated to pack one of the mules. Among our camping materials
were a large hatchet and plenty of rope for making lariats ; in
addition to which each of us carried a wicker flask slung over one
shoulder. We laid aside our civilized attire, stuck long sheath-
knives into our belts, put pistols into our pockets and holsters, and
buckled on the immense spurs which jingled as they struck the
ground at every step. Our " animals" were already in waiting ;
an *alazan*, the Californian term for a sorrel horse, a beautiful
brown mule, two of a cream color and a dwarfish little fellow
whose long forelock and shaggy mane gave him altogether an
elfish character of cunning and mischief.

CHAPTER VII.

TO THE SAN JOAQUIN, ON MULEBACK.

It was noon before we got everything fairly in order and moved slowly away from the City Hotel, where a number of our fellow-passengers—the only idlers in the place, because just arrived—were collected to see us start. Shouldering our packs until we should be able to purchase an *aparéjo*, or pack-saddle, from some Mexican on the road, and dragging after us two reluctant mules by their lariats of horse-hair, we climbed the first " rise," dividing the town from the Happy Valley. Here we found a party of Sonorians encamped on the sand, with their mules turned loose and the harness scattered about them. After a little bargaining, we obtained one of their pack-saddles for eight dollars. Lieut. Beale jumped down, caught the little mule—which to his great surprise he recognized as an old acquaintance among the Rocky Mountains during the previous winter—and commenced packing. In my zeal to learn all the mysteries of mountain-life, I attempted to alight and assist him ; but alas ! the large rowel of my spur caught in the folds of a blanket strapped to the saddle, the girth slipped and I was ingloriously thrown on my back. The Sonorians laughed heartily, but came forward and re-adjusted the saddle with a willingness that reconciled me to their mirth.

All was finally arranged and we urged our mules along in the sand, over hills covered with thickets of evergreen oak. The guns of the Ohio, fired for the obsequies of ex-president Polk, echoed among the mountains of the bay, and companies of horsemen, coming in from the interior, appeared somewhat startled at the sound. Three miles from San Francisco is the old Mission of Dolores, situated in a sheltered valley, which is watered by a perpetual stream, fed from the tall peaks towards the sea. As we descended a long sand-hill before reaching the valley, Picayune, our pack-mule, suddenly came to a stop. Lieut. Beale, who had a most thorough knowledge of mule-craft, dismounted and untied the lash-rope ; the pack had slightly shifted, and Picayune, who was as knowing as he was perverse, would not move a step till it was properly adjusted. We now kept the two loose mules in advance and moved forward in better order. The mountains beyond the Mission are bleak and barren and the dire north-west wind, sweeping in from the sea through their gorges, chilled us to the bones as we rode over them.

After ascending for some distance by a broad road, in which, at short intervals, lay the carcasses of mules and horses, attended by flocks of buzzards, we passed through a notch in the main chain, whence there was a grand look-out to the sea on one side, to the bay on the other. We were glad, however, to descend from these raw and gusty heights, along the sides of the mountains of San Bruno, to the fertile and sheltered plains of Santa Clara. Large herds of cattle are pastured in this neighborhood, the grass in the damp flats and wild oats on the mountains, affording them sufficient food during the dry season. At Sanchez' Ranche, which we reached just before sunset, there was neither grass nor barley and we turned our mules supperless into the corral. The Señora

Sanchez, after some persuasion, stirred up the fire in the mud kitchen and prepared for us a *guisado* of beef and onions, with some rank black tea. As soon as it was dark, we carried our equipments into the house, and by a judicious arrangement of our saddles, blankets and clothes, made a grand bed for three, where we should have slept, had fleas been lobsters. But as they were fleas, of the largest and savagest kind, we nearly perished before morning. Rather than start for the day with starved animals, we purchased half a *fanega*—a little more than a bushel— of wheat, for $5. Mr. Beale's horse was the only one who did justice to this costly feed, and we packed the rest on the back of little Picayune, who gave an extra groan when it was added to his load.

Our road now led over broad plains, through occasional belts of timber. The grass was almost entirely burnt up, and dry, gravelly arroyos, in and out of which we went with a plunge and a scramble, marked the courses of the winter streams. The air was as warm and balmy as May, and fragrant with the aroma of a species of gnaphalium, which made it delicious to inhale. Not a cloud was to be seen in the sky, and the high, sparsely-wooded mountains on either hand, showed softened and indistinct through a blue haze. The character of the scenery was entirely new to me. The splendid valley, untenanted except by a few solitary rancheros living many miles apart, seemed to be some deserted location of ancient civilization and culture. The wooded slopes of the mountains are lawns, planted by Nature with a taste to which Art could add no charm. The trees have nothing of the wild growth of our forests ; they are compact, picturesque, and grouped in every variety of graceful outline. The hills were covered to the summit with fields of wild oats, coloring them as far as the eye could reach, with tawny gold, against which the dark, glossy green of the oak and cypress showed with peculiar effect. As we advanced further, these natural harvests extended over the plain, mixed with vast beds of wild mustard, eight feet in height, under which a thick crop of grass had sprung up, furnishing sustenance to the thousands of cattle, roaming everywhere unherded. The only cultivation I saw was a small field of maize, green and with good ears.

I never felt a more thorough, exhilarating sense of freedom than when first fairly afloat on these vast and beautiful plains. With the mule as my shallop, urged steadily onward past the tranquil isles and long promontories of timber ; drinking, with a delight that almost made it a flavor on the palate, the soft, elastic, fragrant air ; cut off, for the time, from every irksome requirement of civilization, and cast loose, like a stray, unshackled spirit, on the bosom of a new earth, I seemed to take a fresh and more perfect lease of existence. The mind was in exquisite harmony with the outer world, and the same sensuous thrill of Life vibrated through each. The mountains showed themselves through the magical screen of the haze ; far on our left the bay made a faint, glimmering line, like a rod of light, cutting off the hardly-seen hills beyond it, from the world ; and on all sides, from among the glossy clumps of bay and evergreen oak, the chirrup and cheery whistle of birds rang upon the air.

After a ride of twenty-five miles without grass, water or sign of habitation, we stopped to rest at a ranche, in the garden of which I found a fine patch of grape vines, laden with flourishing bunches. We watered our mules with a basket of Indian manufacture, so closely plaited that scarcely a drop found its way through. At the ranche we met an emigrant returning from the mines, and were strongly advised to turn back. He had evidently mistaken his capacity when he came to California. "You think you are very wise," said he, "and you'll believe nothing; but it won't be long before you'll find out the truth of my words. You'll have to sleep on the ground every night and take care of your own animals; and you may think yourselves lucky if you get your regular meals." We fully agreed with him in every respect, but he took it all for unbelieving irony. At Whisman's ranche, two miles further, we stopped to dinner. The sight of a wooden house gladdened our eyes, and still more so that of the home-made bread, fresh butter and milk which Mrs. Whisman set before us. The family had lived there nearly two years and were well contented with the country. The men go occasionally to the mines and dig, but are prudent enough not to neglect their farming operations. The grass on the vega before the house was still thick and green, and a well fifteen feet deep supplied them with good water. The vegetables in their garden, though planted late, were growing finely; the soil is a rich, dark loam, now as cracked and dry as a cinder, but which, under the Winter and Spring rains, is hidden by a deluge of vegetable bloom.

As evening drew on the white spire of Santa Clara Mission showed in the distance, and an hour's sharp riding brought us in front of its old white-washed walls. The buildings, once very spacious in extent, are falling into ruin, and a single monk in the corridor, habited in a very dirty cowl and cassock, was the only saintly inhabitant we saw. The Mission estate, containing twenty-five thousand head of cattle and many square leagues of land, was placed by Gen. Kearney in charge of Padre del Real, President of the Missions of the North. The Padre, however, exceeded his powers by making leases of the Mission lands to emigrants and others,

and devoting the proceeds to the benefit of the Church Personal.
At the time we passed, several frame houses had sprung up
around the Mission, on grounds thus leased. Beyond the buildings, we entered a magnificent road, three miles in length, and
shaded by an avenue of evergreen oaks, leading to Pueblo San
José, which we reached at dusk.

Pueblo San José, situated about five miles from the southern
extremity of the Bay of San Francisco, and in the mouth of the
beautiful valley of San José, is one of the most flourishing inland
towns in California. On my first visit, it was mainly a collection
of adobe houses, with tents and a few clapboard dwellings, of the
season's growth, scattered over a square half-mile. As we were
entering, I noticed a little white box, with pillars and triangular
façade in front, and remarked to my friend that it had certainly
been taken bodily from Lynn and set down there. Truly enough,
it was a shoe store! Several stores and hotels had been opened
within a few weeks, and the price of lots was only lower than those
of San Francisco. We rode into an open plaza, a quarter of a
mile in length, about which the town was built, and were directed
to the Miner's Home, a decent-looking hotel, near its northern
end. Our mules were turned into a stable at hand; tea, with the
substantial addition of beefsteak, was served to us, and lighting
the calumet, we lounged on the bench at the door, enjoying that
repose which is only tasted after wearisome travel. Lieut. Beale
went off to seek Col. Frémont, who was staying at the house of
Mr. Grove Cook; Col. Lyons and myself lay down on the floor
among half a dozen other travelers and fleas which could not be
counted.

In the morning we went with Lieut. Beale to call upon Col.
Frémont, whom we found on the portico of Mr. Cook's house,

wearing a sombrero and Californian jacket, and showing no trace of the terrible hardships he had lately undergone. It may be interesting to the thousands who have followed him, as readers may, on his remarkable journeys and explorations for the past eight years, to know that he is a man of about thirty-five years of age ; of medium height, and lightly, but most compactly knit—in fact, I have seen in no other man the qualities of lightness, activity, strength and physical endurance in so perfect an equilibrium. His face is rather thin and embrowned by exposure ; his nose a bold aquiline and his eyes deep-set and keen as a hawk's. The rough camp-life of many years has lessened in no degree his native refinement of character and polish of manners. A stranger would never suppose him to be the Columbus of our central wildernesses, though when so informed, would believe it without surprise.

After the disastrous fate of his party on the head waters of the Rio del Norte, Col. Frémont took the southern route through Sonora, striking the Gila River at the Pimos Village. It was exceedingly rough and fatiguing, but he was fortunate enough to find in the bottoms along the river, where no vegetation had been heard of or expected, large patches of wild wheat. The only supposition by which this could be accounted for, was that it fell from the store-wagons attached to Major Graham's command, which passed over the route the previous autumn. Otherwise, the bursting forth of a river in the midst of the Great Desert, which I have already mentioned, and the appearance of wheat among the sterile sands of the Gila, would seem like a marvellous coincidence, not wholly unsuited to the time. Col. Frémont had just returned from the Mariposa River, where his party of men was successfully engaged in gold-digging. In addition, he had commenced a more secure business, in the establishment of a steam saw-mill at Pueblo San José. The forests of redwood close at hand make fine timber, and he had a year's work engaged before the mill was in operation. Lumber was then bringing $500 per thousand feet, and not long before brought $1,500.

At the house of Mr. Cook we also saw Andrew Sublette, the celebrated mountaineer, who accompanied Lieut. Beale on hi overland journey, the winter before. He was lame from scurvy brought on by privations endured on that occasion and his subsequent labors in the placers. Sublette, who from his bravery and daring has obtained among the Indians the name of Kee-ta-tah-ve-sak, or One-who-walks-in-fire, is a man of about thirty-seven, of fair complexion, long brown hair and beard, and a countenance expressing the extreme of manly frankness and integrity. Lieut. Beale, who has the highest admiration of his qualities, related to me many instances of his heroic character. Preuss and Kreuzfeldt, Frémont's old campaigners, who so narrowly escaped perishing among the snows of the central chain, were at the Miner's Home, at the time of our stay.

About noon we saddled our mules, laid in a stock of provisions and started for Stockton. At the outset, it was almost impossible to keep the animals in order; Picayune, in spite of his load, dashed out into the mustard fields, and Ambrose, our brown mule, led us off in all sorts of zigzag chases. The man to whom we had paid $2 a head for their night's lodging and fare, had absolutely starved them, and the poor beasts resisted our efforts to make them travel. In coursing after them through the tall weeds, we got off the trail, and it was some time before we made much progress towards the Mission of San José. The valley, fifteen miles in breadth, is well watered and may be made to produce the finest

wheat crops in the world. It is perfectly level and dotted all over
its surface with clumps of magnificent oaks, cypresses and sycamores. A few miles west of the Pueblo there is a large forest of
red wood, or California cypress, and the quicksilver mines of Santa
Clara are in the same vicinity. Sheltered from the cold winds of
the sea, the climate is like that of Italy. The air is a fluid balm.

Before traveling many miles we overtook a Sonorian riding on
his *burro* or jackass, with a wooden bowl hanging to the saddle
and a crowbar and lance slung crosswise before him. We offered
him the use of our extra mule if he would join us, to which he
gave a willing consent. Burro was accordingly driven loose laden
with the gold-hunting tools, and our Bedouin, whom we christened
Tompkins, trotted beside us well pleased. At the Mission of San
José we dispatched him to buy meat, and for half a dollar he
brought us at least six yards, salted and slightly dried for transportation. The Mission—a spacious stone building, with court-
yard and long corridors—is built upon the lower slope of the
mountains dividing San Francisco Bay from the San Joaquin
valley, and a garden extends behind it along the banks of a little
stream.

The sight of a luxuriant orchard peeping over the top of its
mud walls, was too tempting to be resisted, so, leaving Lieutenant
Beale to jog ahead with Tompkins and the loose animals, Colonel
Lyons and myself rode up the hill, scrambled over and found
ourselves in a wilderness of ripening fruit. Hundreds of pear
and apple trees stood almost breaking with their harvest, which
lay rotting by cart-loads on the ground. Plums, grapes, figs and
other fruits, not yet ripened, filled the garden. I shall never
forget how grateful the pears of San José were to our parched
throats, nor what an alarming quantity we ate before we found it

possible to stop. I have been told that the garden is irrigated
during the dry season, and that where this method is practicable,
fruit trees of all kinds can be made to yield to a remarkable
extent.

Immediately on leaving the Mission we struck into a narrow
cañon among the mountains, and following its windings reached
the "divide," or ridge which separates the streams, in an hour.
From the summit the view extended inland over deep valleys and
hazy mountain ranges as far as the vision could reach. Lines of
beautiful timber followed the course of the arroyos down the sides,
streaking the yellow hue of the wild oats, which grew as thickly
as an ordinary crop at home. Descending to a watered valley, we
heard some one shouting from a slope on our left, where a herd of
cattle was grazing. It was Lieut. Beale, who had chosen our
camping-ground in a little glen below, under a cluster of oaks.
We unpacked, watered our mules, led them up a steep ascent,
and picketed them in a thick bed of oats. I had taken the lash-
rope, of plaited raw-hide, for the purpose of tethering Ambrose,
but Tompkins, who saw me, cried : " *Cuidado ! hay bastante
coyotes aqui*," (Take care ! there are plenty of coyotes here)—
which animals invariably gnaw in twain all kinds of ropes except
hemp and horse-hair. The picketing done, we set about cooking
our supper ; Tompkins was very active in making the fire, and
when all was ready, produced a good dish of stewed beef and
tortillas, to which we added some ham, purchased in San José
at eighty cents the pound. We slept under the branching
curtains of our glen chamber, wakened only once or twice by the
howling of the coyotes and the sprinkling of rain in our faces.
By sunrise we had breakfast and started again.

The first twenty miles of our journey passed through one of

the most beautiful regions in the world. The broad oval valleys, shaded by magnificent oaks and enclosed by the lofty mountains of the Coast Range, open beyond each other like a suite of palace chambers, each charming more than the last. The land is admirably adapted for agricultural or grazing purposes, and in a few years will become one of the most flourishing districts in California.

We passed from these into hot, scorched plains, separated by low ranges of hills, on one of which is situated Livermore's Ranche, whose owner, Mr. Livermore, is the oldest American resident in the country, having emigrated thither in 1820. He is married to a native woman, and seems to have entirely outgrown his former habits of life. We obtained from him dinner for ourselves and mules at $2 25 each ; and finding there was neither grass nor water for twenty-five miles, made an early start for our long afternoon's ride. The road entered another cañon, through which we toiled for miles before reaching the last " divide." On the summit we met several emigrant companies with wagons, coming from Sutter's Mill. The children, as brown and wild-looking as Indians, trudged on in the dust, before the oxen, and several girls of twelve years old, rode behind on horses, keeping together the loose animals of the party. Their invariable greeting was : " How far to water ?"

From the top of the divide we hailed with a shout the great plain of San Joaquin, visible through the openings among the hills, like a dark-blue ocean, to which the leagues of wild oats made a vast beach of yellow sand. At least a hundred miles of its surface were visible, and the hazy air, made more dense by the smoke of the burning tulé marshes, alone prevented us from seeing the snowy outline of the Sierra Nevada. After descending

VOL. I.   4

and traveling a dozen miles on the hot, arid level, we reached a
slough making out from the San Joaquin. The sun had long been
down, but a bright quarter-moon was in the sky, by whose light
we selected a fine old tree for our place of repose. A tent,
belonging to some other travelers, was pitched at a little distance.

Feeling the ground with our hands to find the spots where the
grass was freshest, we led our mules into a little tongue of
meadow-land, half-embraced by the slough, and tied them to the
low branches, giving them the full benefit of their tether. Tompkins complained of illness, and rolling himself in his sarape, lay
down on the plain, under the open sky. We were too hungry to
dispose of the day so quickly; a yard of jerked beef was cut off, and
while Lieut. Beale prepared it for cooking, Col. Lyons and myself wandered about in the shadow of the trees, picking up everything that cracked under our feet. The clear red blaze of the
fire made our oak-tree an enchanted palace. Its great arms, that
arched high above us and bent down till they nearly reached the
ground, formed a hollow dome around the columnar trunk, which
was fretted and embossed with a thousand ornaments of foliage.
The light streamed up, momentarily, reddening the deeps within
deeps of the bronze-like leaves; then sinking low again, the shadows returned and the stars winked brightly between the wreathed
mullions of our fantastic windows.

The meal finished, we went towards the tent in our search for
water. Several sleepers, rolled in their blankets, were stretched
under the trees, and two of them, to our surprise, were enjoying
the luxury of musquito bars. On the bank of the slough, we
found a shallow well, covered with dead boughs; Lieut. Beale,
stretching his hand down towards the water, took hold of a snake,
which was even more startled than he. Our quest was repaid by

a hearty draught, notwithstanding its earthy flavor, and we betook ourselves to sleep. The mosquitos were terribly annoying; after many vain attempts to escape them, I was forced to roll a blanket around my head, by which means I could sleep till I began to smother, and then repeat the operation. Waking about midnight, confused and flushed with this business, I saw the moon, looming fiery and large on the horizon. "Surely," thought I, with a half-awake wandering of fancy, " the moon has been bitten by mosquitos, and that is the reason why her face is so swollen and inflamed."

Five miles next morning took us to the San Joaquin, which was about thirty yards in width. Three Yankees had " squatted" at the crossing, and established a ferry; the charge for carrying over a man and horse was $2, and as this route was much traveled, their receipts ranged from $500 to $1,000 daily. In addition to this, they had a tavern and grazing camp, which were very profitable. They built the ferry-boat, which was a heavy flat, hauled across with a rope, with their own hands, as well as a launch of sixty tons, doing a fine business between Stockton and San Francisco. Tompkins, who perhaps imagined that some witchcraft of ours had occasioned his illness, here left us, and we saw his swarthy face no more. Disengaging our loose mules from a corral full of horses, into which they had dashed, from a sudden freak of affection, we launched into another plain, crossed in all directions by tulé swamps, and made towards a dim shore of timber twelve miles distant.

CHAPTER VIII.

CAMP-LIFE, AND A RIDE TO THE DIGGINGS.

As we came off the scorching calm of the plain into the shadow of the trees, we discerned two tents ahead, on a gentle knoll. This was the camp of Major Graham, who commanded the expedition sent from Monterey, Mexico, overland into California, in the summer of 1848. He was employing a little time, before returning home, in speculating on his own account and had established himself near Stockton with a large herd of horses and cattle, on which he was making good profits. Lieut. Beale was an old acquaintance of the Major's, and as friends of the former we were made equally welcome. We found him sitting on a camp-stool, outside the tent, wearing a hunting-jacket and broad-brimmed white hat. With a prompt hospitality that would take no denial, he ordered our mules driven out to his *caballada*, had our packs piled up in the shade of one of his oaks, and gave directions for dinner. For four days thereafter we saw the stars through his tree-tops, between our dreams, and shared the abundant fare of his camp-table, varying the delightful repose of such life by an occasional gallop into Stockton. Mr. Callahan, an old settler, who had pitched his tent near Major Graham's, went out every morning to hunt elk among the tulé, and we were daily supplied with steaks

BAYARD TAYLOR.

LITH. OF SARONY & MAJOR.

LOWER BAR, MOKELUMNE RIVER.

NEW YORK GEO. P. PUTNAM.

and cutlets from his spoils. In the early morning the elk might be seen in bands of forty or fifty, grazing on the edge of the marshes, where they were sometimes lassoed by the native vaqueros, and taken into Stockton. We saw the coyotes occasionally prowling along the margin of the slough, but they took good care to sneak off before a chance could be had to shoot them. The plain was perforated in all directions by the holes of a large burrowing squirrel, of a gray color, and flocks of magpies and tufted partridges made their covert in the weeds and wild oats.

Our first visit to Stockton was made in company, on some of Major Graham's choicest horses. A mettled roan *canalo* fell to my share, and the gallop of five miles without check was most inspiring. A view of Stockton was something to be remembered. There, in the heart of California, where the last winter stood a solitary ranche in the midst of tulé marshes, I found a canvas town of a thousand inhabitants, and a port with twenty-five vessels at anchor! The mingled noises of labor around—the click of of hammers and the grating of saws—the shouts of mule drivers —the jingling of spurs—the jar and jostle of wares in the tents— almost cheated me into the belief that it was some old commercial mart, familiar with such sounds for years past. Four months, only, had sufficed to make the place what it was; and in that time a wholesale firm established there (one out of a dozen) had done business to the amount of $100,000. The same party had just purchased a lot eighty by one hundred feet, on the principal street, for $6,000, and the cost of erecting a common one-story clapboard house on it was $15,000.

I can liken my days at Major Graham's camp to no previous phase of my existence. They were the realization of a desire sometimes felt, sometimes expressed in poetry, but rarely enjoyed in complete fulfilment. In the repose of Nature, unbroken day or night; the subtle haze pervading the air, softening all sights and subduing all sounds; the still, breathless heat of the day and the starry hush of the night—the oak-tree was for me a perfect Castle of Indolence. Lying at full length on the ground, in listless ease, whichever way I looked my eye met the same enchanting groupage of the oaks, the same glorious outlines and massed shadows of foliage; while frequent openings, through the farthest clumps, gave boundless glimpses of the plain beyond. Scarcely a leaf stirred in the slumberous air; and giving way to the delicate languor that stole in upon my brain, I seemed to lie apart from my own mind and to watch the lazy waves of thought that sank on its shores without a jar. All effort—even the memory of effort—came like a sense of pain. It was an abandonment to rest, like that of the " Lotos-Eaters," and the feeling of these lines, not the words, was with me constantly:

> " Why should we toil alone,
> We only toil, who are the first of things,
> And make perpetual moan,
> Still from one sorrow to another thrown;
> Nor ever fold our wings
> And cease from wanderings,
> Nor steep our brows in slumber's holy balm:
> Nor harken what the inner spirit sings,
> ' There is no joy but calm!' "

There is one peculiarity about the Californian oaks, which I do not remember to have seen noticed. In the dry heat of the long summer seasons, their fibre becomes brittle, and frequently at noon-day, when not a breath of air is stirring, one of their stout arms parts from the trunk without the slightest warning sound, and drops bodily to the earth. More than one instance is related, in which persons have been killed by their fall. For this reason the native Californians generally camp outside of the range of the limbs.

After discussing our further plans, it was decided to visit the Mokelumne Diggings, which were the most accessible from Stockton. Accordingly, on Monday morning, our mules were driven in from the plain and saddled for the journey. The sun was shining hotly as we rode over the plain to Stockton, and the tent-streets of the miraculous town glowed like the avenues of a brick-kiln. The thermometer stood at 98°, and the parched, sandy soil burnt through our very boot-soles. We therefore determined to wait till evening before starting for another stage to the Moke-lumne. While waiting in the tent of Mr. Belt, the alcalde of the place, I made acquaintance with two noted mountaineers—Mr. William Knight, the first man who followed in the track of Lewis and Clark, on the Columbia River, and White Elliott, a young Missourian, who for ten years had been rambling through New Mexico and the Rocky Mountains. The latter had been one of Lieut. Beale's men on the Gila, and the many perils they then shared gave their present meeting a peculiar interest. Elliott, who, young as he was, had undergone everything that could harden and toughen a man out of all sensibility, colored like a young girl; his eyes were wet and he scarcely found voice to speak. I had many opportunities of seeing him afterwards and appreciating his thorough nobleness and sincerity of character.

Mr. Raney, who had just established a line of conveyance to the Mokelumne, kindly offered to accompany us as far as his ranche on the Calaveras River, twenty-four miles distant. We started at four o'clock, when a pleasant breeze had sprung up,

and rode on over the level plain, through beautiful groves of oak.
The trail was crossed by deep, dry arroyos, which, in the rainy
season, make the country almost impassable ; now, however, the
very beds of the tulé marshes were beginning to dry up. The air
was thicker than ever with the smoke of burning tulé, and as we
journeyed along in the hazy moonlight, the lower slopes of the
mountains were not visible till we reached Mr. Raney's ranche,
which lies at their base. We gave our tired mules a good feed of
barley, and, after an excellent supper which he had prepared, betook ourselves to rest. The tent was made of saplings, roofed
with canvas, but had cost $1,000 ; the plain all around was
covered deep with dust, which the passing trains of mules kept
constantly in the air. Nevertheless, for the first time in several
days, we slept in a bed—the bed of Calaveras River, and in the
deepest hollow of its gold-besprinkled sands. The stream, which
in the spring is thirty feet deep, was perfectly dry, and the timber
on its banks made a roof far above, which shut out the wind and
sand, but let in the starlight. Heaping the loose gravel for pil-
lows, we enjoyed a delightful sleep, interrupted only once by the
howling of a large gray wolf, prowling in the thickets over us.

While waiting for breakfast, I saw a curious exemplification of
the careless habits of the miners, in regard to money. One of
the mule-drivers wanted to buy a pistol which belonged to another, and as the article was in reality worth next to nothing,
offered him three dollars for it. "I will sell nothing for such a
beggarly sum," said the owner: "you are welcome to take the
pistol." The other took it, but laid the three dollars on a log, saying : "you must take it, for I shall never touch it again." "Well,"
was the reply, "then I'll do what I please with it ;" and he flung
the dollars into the road and walked away. An Irishman who

stood by, raked in the dust for some time, but only recovered about half the money.

Leaving the ranche soon after sunrise, we entered the hills The country was dotted with picturesque clumps of oak, and, as the ground became higher and more broken, with pines of splendid growth. Around their feet were scattered piles of immense cones, which had been broken up for the sake of the spicy kernels they contain. Trails of deer could be seen on all the hills, leading down to chance green spots in the hollows, which a month since furnished water. Now, however, the ground was parched as in a furnace ; the vegetation snapped like glass under the hoofs of our mules, and the cracks and seams in the arid soil seemed to give out an intense heat from some subterranean fire. In the glens and *cañadas*, where the little air stirring was cut off, the mercury rose to 110° ; perspiration was dried as soon as formed, and I began to think I should soon be done to a turn.

After traveling about fourteen miles, we were joined by three miners, and our mules, taking a sudden liking for their horses, jogged on at a more brisk rate. The instincts of the mulish heart form an interesting study to the traveler in the mountains. I would, were the comparison not too ungallant, liken it to a woman's, for it is quite as uncertain in its sympathies, bestowing its affections where least expected, and when bestowed, quite as constant, so long as the object is not taken away. Sometimes a horse, sometimes an ass, captivates the fancy of a whole drove of mules ; but often an animal nowise akin. Lieut. Beale told me that his whole train of mules once took a stampede on the plains of the Cimarone, and ran half a mile, when they halted in apparent satisfaction. The cause of their freak was found to be a buffalo calf, which had strayed from the herd. They were frisking around it

4*

in the greatest delight, rubbing their noses against it, throwing up
their heels and making themselves ridiculous by abortive attempts
to neigh and bray, while the poor calf, unconscious of its attractive
qualities, stood trembling in their midst. It is customary to
have a horse in the *atajos*, or mule-trains, of the traders in
Northern Mexico, as a sort of magnet to keep together the separate
atoms of the train, for, whatever the temptation, they will never
stray far from him.

We turned from the main road, which led to the Upper Bar,
and took a faint trail leading over the hills to the Lower Bar.
The winding *cañon* up which we passed must be a paradise in
Spring ; even at the close of August the dry bed of the stream
was shaded by trees of every picturesque form that a painter
could desire. Crossing several steep spurs, we reached the top of
the divide overlooking the Mokelumne Valley, and here one of
the most charming mountain landscapes in the world opened to
our view. Under our very feet, as it seemed, flowed the river,
and a little corner of level bottom, wedged between the bases of
the hills, was dotted with the tents of the gold-hunters, whom we
could see burrowing along the water. The mountains, range
behind range, spotted with timber, made a grand, indistinct
background in the smoky air,—a large, fortress-like butte, toward
the Cosumne River, the most prominent of all. Had the atmosphere been clearer, the snowy crown of the Nevada, beyond all,
would have made the picture equal to any in Tyrol.

Coming down the almost perpendicular side of the hill, my
saddle began to slip over the mule's straight shoulders, and, dis-
mounting, I waded the rest of the way knee-deep in dust. Near
the bottom we came upon the Sonorian Town, as it was called,
from the number of Mexican miners encamped there. The place,

which was a regularly laid-out town of sapling houses, without walls and roofed with loose oak boughs, had sprung up in the wilderness in three weeks : there were probably three hundred persons living in or near it. Under the open canopies of oak we heard, as we passed along, the jingle of coin at the monte tables, and saw crowds gathered to watch the progress of the game. One of the first men Lieutenant Beale saw was Baptiste Perrot, a mountaineer who had been in his overland party. He kept a hotel, which was an open space under a branch roof ; the appliances were two tables of rough plank, (one for meals and one for monte,) with logs resting on forked limbs as seats, and a bar of similar materials, behind which was ranged a goodly stock of liquors and preserved provisions. We tethered our mules to a stump in the rear of the hotel, hastened supper, and made ourselves entirely at home.

CHAPTER IX.

OUR first move was for the river bottom, where a number of Americans, Sonorians, Kanakas and French were at work in the hot sun. The bar, as it was called, was nothing more nor less than a level space at the junction of the river with a dry arroyo or " gulch," which winds for about eight miles among the hills. It was hard and rocky, with no loose sand except such as had lodged between the large masses of stone, which must of course be thrown aside to get at the gold. The whole space, containing about four acres, appeared to have been turned over with great labor, and all the holes slanting down between the broken strata of slate, to have been explored to the bottom. No spot could appear more unpromising to the inexperienced gold-hunter. Yet the Sonorians, washing out the loose dust and dirt which they scraped up among the rocks, obtained from $10 to two ounces daily. The first party we saw had just succeeded in cutting a new channel for the shrunken waters of the Mokelumne, and were commencing operations on about twenty yards of the river-bed, which they had laid bare. They were ten in number, and their only implements were shovels, a rude cradle for the top layer of earth, and flat wooden bowls for washing out the sands. Baptiste took one of the bowls which was full of sand, and in five minutes showed us a dozen grains of bright gold. The company had made in the forenoon about three pounds; we watched them at their work till the evening, when three pounds more were produced, making an average of seven ounces for each man. The gold was of the purest quality and most beautiful color. When I first saw the men, carrying heavy stones in the sun, standing nearly waist-deep in water, and grubbing with their hands in the gravel and clay, there seemed to me little virtue in resisting the temptation to gold digging; but when the shining particles were poured out lavishly from a tin basin, I confess there was a sudden itching in my fingers to seize the heaviest crowbar and the biggest shovel.

A company of thirty, somewhat further down the river, had made a much larger dam, after a month's labor, and a hundred yards of the bed were clear. They commenced washing in the afternoon and obtained a very encouraging result. The next morning, however, they quarreled, as most companies do, and finally applied to Mr. James and Dr. Gillette, two of the principal operators, to settle the difficulty by having the whole bed washed out at their own expense and taking half the gold. As all the heavy work was done, the contractors expected to make a considerable sum by the operation. Many of the Americans employed Sonorians and Indians to work for them, giving them half the gold and finding them in provisions. Notwithstanding the enormous prices of every article of food, these people could be kept for about a dollar daily—consequently those who hire them profited handsomely.

After we had taken the sharp edge off our curiosity, we returned to our quarters. Dr. Gillette, Mr. James, Captain Tracy and several other of the miners entertained us with a hospitality as gratifying as it was unexpected. In the evening we sat down to a supper prepared by Baptiste and his partner, Mr. Fisher, which completed my astonishment at the resources of that wonderful land. There, in the rough depth of the hills, where three weeks before there was scarcely a tent, and where we expected to live on jerked beef and bread, we saw on the table green corn, green peas and beans, fresh oysters, roast turkey, fine Goshen butter and excellent coffee. I will not pretend to say what they cost, but I began to think that the fable of Aladdin was nothing very remarkable, after all. The genie will come, and had come to many whom I saw in California ; but the rubbing of the lamp —aye, there's the rub. There is nothing in the world so hard on the hands.

I slept soundly that night on the dining-table, and went down early to the river, where I found the party of ten bailing out the water which had leaked into the river-bed during the night. They were standing in the sun, and had two hours' hard work before they could begin to wash. Again the prospect looked uninviting, but when I went there again towards noon, one of them was scraping up the sand from the bed with his knife, and throwing it into a basin, the bottom of which glittered with gold. Every knifeful brought out a quantity of grains and scales, some of which were as large as the finger-nail. At last a two-ounce lump fell plump into the pan, and the diggers, now in the best possible humor, went on with their work with great alacrity. Their forenoon's digging amounted to nearly six pounds. It is only by such operations as these, through associated labor, that great profits are to be made in those districts which have been visited by the first eager horde of gold hunters. The deposits most easily reached are soon exhausted by the crowd, and the labor required to carry on further work successfully deters single individuals from attempting it. Those who, retaining their health, return home disappointed, say they have been humbugged about the gold, when in fact, they have humbugged themselves about the *work*. If any one expects to dig treasures out of the earth, in California, without severe labor, he is wofully mistaken. Of all classes of men, those who pave streets and quarry limestone are best adapted for gold diggers.

Wherever there is gold, there are gamblers. Our little village boasted of at least a dozen monte tables, all of which were frequented at night by the Americans and Mexicans. The Sonorians left a large portion of their gold at the gaming tables, though it was calculated they had taken $5,000,000 out of the country during the summer. The excitement against them prevailed also on the Mokelumne, and they were once driven away; they afterwards quietly returned, and in most cases worked in companies, for the benefit and under the protection of some American. They labor steadily and faithfully, and are considered honest, if well watched. The first colony of gold-hunters attempted to drive out all foreigners, without distinction, as well as native Californians. Don Andres Pico, who was located on the same river, had some difficulty with them until they could be made to understand that his right as a citizen was equal to theirs.

Dr. Gillette, to whom we were indebted for many kind attentions, related to me the manner of his finding the rich gulch which attracted so many to the Mokelumne Diggings. The word *gulch*, which is in general use throughout the diggings, may not be familiar to many ears, though its sound somehow expresses its. meaning, without further definition. It denotes a mountain ravine, differing from ravines elsewhere as the mountains of California

differ from all others—more steep, abrupt and inaccessible. The
sound of *gulch* is like that of a sudden plunge into a deep hole,
which is just the character of the thing itself. It bears the same
relation to a ravine that a " cañon" does to a pass or gorge.
About two months previous to our arrival, Dr. Gillette came
down from the Upper Bar with a companion, to " prospect" for
gold among the ravines in the neighborhood. There were no
persons there at the time, except some Indians belonging to the
tribe of José Jesus. One day at noon, while resting in the shade
of a tree, Dr. G. took a pick and began carelessly turning up the
ground. Almost on the surface, he struck and threw out a lump
of gold of about two pounds weight. Inspired by this unexpected
result, they both went to work, laboring all that day and the next,
and even using part of the night to quarry out the heavy pieces
of rock. At the end of the second day they went to the village
on the Upper Bar and weighed their profits, which amounted to
fourteen pounds ! They started again the third morning under
pretence of hunting, but were suspected and followed by the other
diggers, who came upon them just as they commenced work.
The news rapidly spread, and there was soon a large number of
men on the spot, some of whom obtained several pounds per
day, at the start. The gulch had been well dug up for the large
lumps, but there was still great wealth in the earth and sand, and
several operators only waited for the wet season to work it in a
systematic manner.

The next day Col. Lyons, Dr. Gillette and myself set out on a
visit to the scene of these rich discoveries. Climbing up the
rocky bottom of the gulch, as by a staircase, for four miles, we
found nearly every part of it dug up and turned over by the
picks of the miners. Deep holes, sunk between the solid strata

or into the precipitous sides of the mountains, showed where veins of the metal had been struck and followed as long as they yielded lumps large enough to pay for the labor. The loose earth, which they had excavated, was full of fine gold, and only needed washing out. A number of Sonorians were engaged in dry washing this refuse sand—a work which requires no little skill, and would soon kill any other men than these lank and skinny Arabs of the West. Their mode of work is as follows :—Gathering the loose dry sand in bowls, they raise it to their heads and slowly pour it upon a blanket spread at their feet. Repeating this several times, and throwing out the worthless pieces of rock, they reduce the dust to about half its bulk ; then, balancing the bowl on one hand, by a quick, dexterous motion of the other they cause it to revolve, at the same time throwing its contents into the air and catching them as they fall. In this manner everything is finally winnowed away except the heavier grains of sand mixed with gold, which is carefully separated by the breath. It is a laborious occupation, and one which, fortunately, the American diggers have not attempted. This breathing the fine dust from day to day, under a more than torrid sun, would soon impair the strongest lungs.

We found many persons at work in the higher part of the gulch, searching for veins and pockets of gold, in the holes which had already produced their first harvest. Some of these gleaners, following the lodes abandoned by others as exhausted, into the sides of the mountain, were well repaid for their perseverance. Others, again, had been working for days without finding anything. Those who understood the business obtained from one to four ounces daily. Their only tools were the crowbar, pick and knife, and many of them, following the veins under strata of rock which lay deep below the surface, were obliged to work while lying flat on their backs, in cramped and narrow holes, sometimes kept moist by springs. They were shielded, however, from the burning heats, and preserved their health better than those who worked on the bars of the river.

There are thousands of similar gulches among the mountains, nearly all of which undoubtedly contain gold. Those who are familiar with geology, or by carefully noting the character of the soil and strata where gold is already found, have learned its indications, rarely fail in the selection of new spots for digging. It is the crowd of those who, deceived in their extravagant hopes, disheartened by the severe labor necessary to be undergone, and bereft of that active and observing spirit which could not fail to win success at last, that cry out with such bitterness against the golden stories which first attracted them to the country. I met with hundreds of such persons, many of whom have returned home disgusted forever with California. They compared the diggings to a lottery, in which people grew rich only by accident or luck. There is no such thing as accident in Nature, and in proportion as men understand her, the more sure a clue they have to her buried treasures. There is more gold in California than ever was said or imagined : ages will not exhaust the supply. From what I first saw on the Mokelumne, I was convinced that the fabled Cibao of Columbus, splendid as it seemed to his eager imagination, is more than realized there.

I went up in the ravines one morning, for about two miles, looking for game. It was too late in the day for deer, and I saw but one antelope, which fled like the wind over the top of the mountain. I started a fine hare, similar in appearance to the European, but of larger size. A man riding down the trail, from the Double Spring, told us he had counted seven deer early in the morning, beside numbers of antelopes and partridges. The grizzly bear and large mountain wolf are frequently seen in the more thickly timbered ravines. The principal growth of the mountains is oak and the California pine, which rises like a spire to the height of two hundred feet. The *piñons*, or cones, are much larger and of finer flavor, than those of the Italian stone-pine. As far as I could see from the ridges which I climbed, the mountains were as well timbered as the soil and climate will allow. A little more rain would support as fine forests as the world can produce. The earth was baked to a cinder, and from 11 A. M. to 4 P. M. the mercury ranged between 98° and 110°.

There was no end to the stories told by the diggers, of their own and others' experiences in gold-hunting. I could readily have made up a small volume from those I heard during the four days I spent on the Mokelumne. In the dry diggings especially, where the metal frequently lies deep, many instances are told of men who have dug two or three days and given up in despair, while others, coming after them and working in the same holes, have taken out thousands of dollars in a short time. I saw a man who came to the river three weeks before my visit, without money, to dig in the dry gulch. Being very lazy, he chose a spot under a shady tree, and dug leisurely for two days without making a cent. He then gave up the place, when a little German jumped into his tracks and after a day's hard work weighed out $800. The unlucky digger then borrowed five ounces and started a boarding-house. The town increased so fast that the night I arrived he sold out his share (one-third) of the concern for $1,200. Men were not troubled by the ordinary ups and downs of business, when it was so easy for one of any enterprise to recover his foothold. If a person lost his all, he was perfectly indifferent; two weeks of hard work gave him enough to start on, and two months, with the usual luck, quite reinstated him.

The largest piece found in the rich gulch weighed eleven pounds. Mr. James, who had been on the river since April, showed me a lump weighing sixty-two ounces—pure, unadulterated gold. We had a visit one day from Don Andres Pico, commander of the California forces during the war. He had a company of men digging at the Middle Bar, about a mile above. He is an urbane, intelligent man, of medium stature, and of a natural gentility of character which made him quite popular among the emigrants.

From all I saw and heard, while at the Mokelumne Diggings, I judged there was as much order and security as could be attained without a civil organization. The inhabitants had elected one of their own number Alcalde, before whom all culprits were tried by a jury selected for the purpose. Several thefts had occurred, and the offending parties been severely punished after a fair trial. Some had been whipped and cropped, or maimed in some other way, and one or two of them hung. Two or three who had stolen largely had been shot down by the injured party, the general feeling among the miners justifying such a course when no other seemed available. We met near Livermore's Ranche, on the way to Stockton, a man whose head had been shaved and his ears cut off, after receiving one hundred lashes, for stealing ninety-eight pounds of gold. It may conflict with popular ideas of morality, but, nevertheless, this extreme course appeared to have produced good results. In fact, in a country without not only bolts and bars, but any effective system of law and government, this Spartan severity of discipline seemed the only security against the most frightful disorder. The result was that, except some petty

acts of larceny, thefts were rare. Horses and mules were sometimes taken, but the risk was so great that such plunder could not
be carried on to any extent. The camp or tent was held invio-
late, and like the patriarchal times of old, its cover protected all
it enclosed. Among all well-disposed persons there was a tacit
disposition to make the canvas or pavilion of rough oak-boughs as
sacred as once were the portals of a church.

Our stay was delayed a day by the illness of Lieut. Beale, who
had been poisoned a few days previous by contact with the *rhus
toxicodendron*, which is very common in California. His impatience to reach San Francisco was so great that on Saturday afternoon we got ready to return to Stockton. Our bill at the hotel
was $11 a day for man and mule—$4 for the man and $7 for the
mule. This did not include lodgings, which each traveler was expected to furnish for himself. Some slight medical attendance,
furnished to Lieut. Beale, was valued at $48. The high price
of mule-keep was owing to the fact of barley being $1 per quart
and grass $1 per handful. Dr. Gillette took a lame horse which
had just come down from a month's travel among the snowy
ridges, where his rider had been shot with an Indian arrow, and
set out to accompany us as far as Stockton. One of our mules,
which was borrowed for the occasion at Raney's Ranche, had
been reclaimed by its owner, and I was thus reduced to the necessity of footing it. In this order, we left the town just before
sunset, and took a mule-path leading up the steep ascent.

CHAPTER X.

INSTEAD of retracing our steps through the fiery depth of the cañon, we turned off eastward through a gap in the hills and took a road leading to the Double Spring. The doctor insisted on my mounting behind him on the limping horse, and we had an odd ride of it, among the dusky glens and hollows. At the Double Spring, where a large tent was pitched, three of us were furnished with supper, at a cost of $11—not an exorbitant price, if our appetites were considered. It was decided to push on the same night to another ranche, seven miles distant, and I started in advance, on foot. The road passed between low hills, covered with patches of chapparal, the usual haunt of grizzly bears. I looked sharply at every bush, in the dim moonlight ; my apprehensions were a little raised by the thought of a miner whom I had seen one evening come down to the Mokelumne, pale as a sheet, after having been chased some distance by a huge she-bear, and by the story told me at the Double Spring, of the bones of two men, picked clean, having been found on the road I was traveling. I was not sorry, therefore, to hear the halting tramp of the doctor's horse behind me ; the others came up after awhile, and we reached the tent. The landlord lay asleep in one corner ; we tied our animals to a tree, made one bed in common against the side of the tent, and were soon locked in sound repose.

Lieut. Beale, who was still unwell and anxious to hurry on, woke us at the peep of day, and after giving a spare feed to our mules, we took the road again. As the doctor and I, mounted on the lame horse, were shuffling along in advance, we espied a venerable old animal before us, walking in the same direction. The doctor slipped off the bridle, ran forward and caught him without any difficulty. There was no sign of any camp to be seen, and we came to the conclusion that the horse was an estray, and we might therefore lawfully make use of him. He was the most grotesque specimen of horseflesh I ever saw—lame like our own—and with his forehead broken in above the eyes, which did not prevent his having a nose of most extraordinary length and prominence. The doctor bridled him and mounted, leaving me his own horse and saddle, so that we were about equally provided. By dint of shouting and kicking we kept the beasts in a sort of shambling gallop till we reached Raney's Ranche, where the doctor took the precaution of removing the bridle and letting the horse stand loose ; the custom of the miners being, to shoot a man who puts his gear on your horse and rides him without leave.

As it happened, the precaution was not ill-timed ; for, while we lay inside the tent on a couple of benches, we heard an exclamation from some one outside. " There you are !" said the voice ; " what do you mean, you old rascal ? how came you here ? you know you never left me before, you know you did n't !"— Then, turning to the tent-keeper, who was standing by the cooking-fire, he enquired : " how did that horse get here ?" " Why," answered the former, with a slight variation of the truth, " he was driven in this morning by some men who found him in the road, about three miles from here.   The men have gone on to Stockton, but left him, thinking he might have an owner somewhere, though he don't look like it."   " Three miles!" ejaculated the voice : " it was six miles from here, where I camped, and the horse never left me before ; you know you did n't, you rascal !"   Then, coming into the tent, he repeated the whole story to us, who marvelled exceedingly that the horse should have left.   " He does n't look to be much," added the man, " but I've had him two years among the mountains, and never saw sich another wonderful knowin' animal."

Sergeant Falls, who owned a ranche in the neighborhood, came along shortly after with a *caballada* which he was driving into Stockton.   The day was hot, but a fine breeze blew over the hazy plain and rustled the groves of oak as we went past them on a sweeping gallop, which was scarcely broken during the whole ride of twenty-five miles.   No exercise in the world is so exciting and inspiring as the traveling gait or " lope" of the Californian horse. I can compare it to nothing but the rocking motion of a boat over a light sea.   There is no jar or jolt in the saddle ; the rider sits lightly and securely, while the horse, obeying the slightest touch of the rein, carries him forward for hours without slackening his bounding speed.   Up and down the steep sides of an arroyo—over the shoulder of a mountain, or through the flinty bed of some dry lake or river—it is all the same.   One's blood leaps merrily along his veins, and the whole frame feels an elastic warmth which exquisitely fits it to receive all sensuous impressions.   Ah ! if horse-flesh were effortless as the wind, indestructible as adamant, what motion of sea or air—what unwearied agility of fin or steady sweep of wing—could compare with it ?   In the power of thus speeding onward at will, as far as the wish might extend, one would forget his desire to soar.

I saw at the Pueblo San José a splendid pied horse belonging to Col. Frémont—the gift of Don Pio Pico—on which he had frequently ridden to San Francisco, a distance of fifty-five miles, within seven hours. When pushed to their utmost capacity, these horses frequently perform astonishing feats. The saddles in common use differ little from the Mexican ; the stirrups are set back, obliging the rider to stand rather than sit, and the seat corresponds more nearly to the shape of the body than the English saddle. The horses are broken by a halter of strong rope, which accustoms them to be governed by a mere touch of the rein. On first attempting to check the gallop of one which I rode, I thoughtlessly drew the rein as strongly as for a hard-mouthed American horse. The consequence was, he came with one bound to a dead stop and I flew bolt upwards out of the saddle ; but for its high wooden horn, I should have gone over his head.

At Raney's Ranche, our notice was attracted to the sad spectacle of a man, lying on the river bank, wasted by disease, and evidently near his end. He was a member of a company from Massachusetts, which had passed that way three weeks before, not only refusing to take him further, but absolutely carrying with them his share of the stores they had brought from home. This, at least, was the story told me on the spot, but I hope it was untrue. The man had lain there from day to day, without medical aid, and dependant on such attention as the inmates of the tent were able to afford him. The Dr. left some medicines with him, but it was evident to all of us that a few days more would terminate his sufferings.

All the roads from Stockton to the mines were filled with *atajos* of mules, laden with freight. They were mostly owned by Americans, many of them by former trappers and mountaineers, but the packers and drivers were Mexicans, and the *aparéjos* and *alforjas* of the mules were of the same fashion as those which, for three hundred years past, have been seen on the hills of Grenada and the Andalusian plains. With good mule-trains and experienced packers, the business yielded as much as the richest diggings. The placers and gulches of Mokelumne as well as Murphy's Diggings and those on Carson's Creek, are within fifty-five miles of Stockton; the richest diggings on the Stanislaus about sixty, and on the Tuolumne seventy. The price paid for carrying to all the nearer diggings averaged 30 cents per lb. during the summer. A mule-load varies from one to two hundred lbs., but the experienced carrier could generally reckon beforehand the expenses and profits of his trip. The intense heat of the season and the dust of the plains tended also to wear out a team, and the carriers were often obliged to rest and recruit themselves. One of them, who did a good business between Stockton and the Lower Bar of the Mokelumne, told me that his profits were about $3,000 monthly.

I found Stockton more bustling and prosperous than ever. The limits of its canvas streets had greatly enlarged during my week of absence, and the crowd on the levee would not disgrace a much larger place at home. Launches were arriving and departing daily for and from San Francisco, and the number of mule-trains, wagons, etc., on their way to the various mines with freight and supplies kept up a life of activity truly amazing. Stockton was first laid out by Mr. Weaver, who emigrated to the country seven years before, and obtained a grant of eleven square leagues from the Government, on condition that he would obtain settlers for the whole of it within a specified time. In planning the town of Stockton, he displayed a great deal of shrewd business tact, the sale of lots having brought him upwards of $500,000. A great disadvantage of the location is the sloughs by which it is surrounded; which, in the wet season, render the roads next to impassable. There seems, however, to be no other central point so well adapted for supplying the rich district between the Mokelumne and Tuolumne, and Stockton will evidently continue to grow with a sure and gradual growth.

I witnessed, while in the town, a summary exhibition of justice. The night before my arrival, three negroes, while on a drunken revel, entered the tent of a Chilian, and attempted to violate a female who was within. Defeated in their base designs by her husband, who was fortunately within call, they fired their pistols at the tent and left. Complaint was made before the Alcalde, two of the negroes seized and identified, witnesses examined, a jury summoned, and verdict given, without delay. The principal offender was sentenced to receive fifty lashes and the other twenty —both to leave the place within forty-eight hours under pain of death. The sentence was immediately carried into execution; the negroes were stripped, tied to a tree standing in the middle of the principal street, and in presence of the Alcalde and Sheriff received their punishment. There was little of that order and respect shown which should accompany even the administration of impromptu law; the bystanders jeered, laughed, and accompanied every blow with coarse and unfeeling remarks. Some of the more intelligent professed themselves opposed to the mode of punishment, but in the absence of prisons or effective guards could suggest no alternative, except the sterner one of capital punishment.

The history of law and society in California, from the period of the golden discoveries, would furnish many instructive lessons to the philosopher and the statesman. The first consequence of the unprecedented rush of emigration from all parts of the world into a country almost unknown, and but half reclaimed from its original barbarism was to render all law virtually null, and bring the established authorities to depend entirely on the humor of the population for the observance of their orders. The countries which were nearest the golden coast—Mexico, Peru, Chili, China and the Sandwich Islands—sent forth their thousands of ignorant adventurers, who speedily outnumbered the American population. Another fact, which none the less threatened serious consequences, was the readiness with which the worthless and depraved class of our own country came to the Pacific Coast. From the beginning, a state of things little short of anarchy might have been reasonably awaited.

Instead of this, a disposition to maintain order and secure the rights of all, was shown throughout the mining districts. In the absence of all law or available protection, the people met and adopted rules for their mutual security—rules adapted to their situation, where they had neither guards nor prisons, and where the slightest license given to crime or trespass of any kind must inevitably have led to terrible disorders. Small thefts were punished by banishment from the placers, while for those of large amount or for more serious crimes, there was the single alternative of hanging. These regulations, with slight change, had been continued up to the time of my visit to the country. In proportion as the emigration from our own States increased, and the digging community assumed a more orderly and intelligent aspect, their severity had been relaxed, though punishment was still strictly administered for all offences. There had been, as nearly as I could learn, not more than twelve or fifteen executions in all, about half of which were inflicted for the crime of murder. This awful responsibility had not been assumed lightly, but after a fair trial and a full and clear conviction, to which was added, I believe in every instance, the confession of the criminal.

In all the large digging districts, which had been worked for some time, there were established regulations, which were faithfully observed. Alcaldes were elected, who decided on all disputes of right or complaints of trespass, and who had power to summon juries for criminal trials. When a new placer or gulch was discovered, the first thing done was to elect officers and extend the area of order. The result was, that in a district five hundred miles long, and inhabited by 100,000 people, who had neither government, regular laws, rules, military or civil protection, nor even locks or bolts, and a great part of whom possessed wealth enough to tempt the vicious and depraved, there was as much security to life and property as in any part of the Union, and as small a proportion of crime. The capacity of a people for self-government was never so triumphantly illustrated. Never, perhaps, was there a community formed of more unpropitious elements ; yet from all this seeming chaos grew a harmony beyond what the most sanguine apostle of Progress could have expected.

The rights of the diggers were no less definitely marked and strictly observed. Among the hundreds I saw on the Mokelumne and among the gulches, I did not see a single dispute nor hear a word of complaint. A company of men might mark out a race of any length and turn the current of the river to get at the bed, possessing the exclusive right to that part of it, so long as their undertaking lasted. A man might dig a hole in the dry ravines, and so long as he left a shovel, pick or crowbar to show that he still intended working it, he was safe from trespass. His tools might remain there for months without being disturbed. I have seen many such places, miles away from any camp or tent, which the digger had left in perfect confidence that he should find all right on his return. There were of course exceptions to these rules—the diggings would be a Utopia if it were not so—but they were not frequent. The Alcaldes sometimes made awkward decisions, from inexperience, but they were none the less implicitly obeyed. I heard of one instance in which a case of trespass was settled to the satisfaction of both parties and the Sheriff ordered to pay the costs of Court—about $40. The astonished functionary remonstrated, but the power of the Alcalde was supreme, and he was obliged to suffer.

The treatment of the Sonorians by the American diggers was one of the exciting subjects of the summer. These people came into the country in armed bands, to the number of ten thousand in all, and took possession of the best points on the Tuolumne, Stanislaus and Mokelumne Rivers. At the Sonorian camp on the Stanislaus there were, during the summer, several thousands of them, and the amount of ground they dug up and turned over is almost incredible. For a long time they were suffered to work peaceably, but the opposition finally became so strong that they were ordered to leave. They made no resistance, but quietly backed out and took refuge in other diggings. In one or two places, I was told, the Americans, finding there was no chance of having a fight, coolly invited them back again ! At the time of my visit, however, they were leaving the country in large numbers, and there were probably not more than five thousand in all scattered along the various rivers. Several parties of them, in revenge for the treatment they experienced, committed outrages on their way home, stripping small parties of the emigrants by the Gila route of all they possessed. It is not likely that the country will be troubled with them in future.

Abundance of gold does not always beget, as moralists tell us, a grasping and avaricious spirit. The principles of hospitality were as faithfully observed in the rude tents of the diggers as they could be by the thrifty farmers of the North and West. The cosmopolitan cast of society in California, resulting from the commingling of so many races and the primitive mode of life, gave a character of good-fellowship to all its members; and in no part of the world have I ever seen help more freely given to the needy, or more ready coöperation in any humane proposition. Personally, I can safely say that I never met with such unvarying kindness from comparative strangers.

CHAPTER XI.

A NIGHT-ADVENTURE IN THE MOUNTAINS.

On reaching Stockton, Lieut. Beale and Col. Lyons decided to return to San Francisco in a launch, which was to leave the same evening. This was thought best, as mule-travel, in the condition of the former, would have greatly aggravated his illness. The mules were left in my charge, and as the management of five was an impossibility for one man, it was arranged that I should wait three days, when Mr. R. A. Parker and Mr. Atherton, of San Francisco, were to leave. These gentlemen offered to make a single *mulada* of all our animals, which would relieve me from my embarrassment. I slept that night in Mr. Lane's store, and the next morning rode out to Graham's Camp, where the Major received me with the same genial hospitality. For three days longer I shared the wildwood fare of his camp-table and slept under the canopy of his oaks. Long may those matchless trees be spared to the soil—a shore of cool and refreshing verdure to all who traverse the hot plains of San Joaquin!

Messrs. Parker and Atherton, with three other gentlemen and two servants, made their appearance about sunset. My mules had already been caught and lariated, and joining our loose animals, we had a *mulada* of eight, with eight riders to keep them in order. The plain was dark when we started, and the trail stretched like a dusky streak far in advance. The mules gave us infinite trouble at first, darting off on all sides; but, by dint of hard chasing, we got them into regular file, keeping them in a furious trot before us. The volumes of dust that rose from their feet, completely enveloped us; it was only by counting the tails that occasionally whisked through the cloud, that we could tell whether they were in order. One of my spurs gave way in the race, but there was no stopping to pick it up, nor did we halt until, at the end of twelve miles, the white tent of the ferry came in sight.

We crossed and rode onward to my old camping-place on the slough. A canvas tavern had been erected on a little knoll, since my visit, and after picketing our animals in the meadow, we proceeded to rouse the landlord. The only person we could find was an old man, lying under a tree near at hand; he refused to stir, saying there was nothing to eat in the tent, and he would not get up and cook at that time of night. My fellow-travelers, accustomed to the free-and-easy habits of California, entered the tent without ceremony and began a general search for comestibles. The only things that turned up were a half-dozen bottles of ale in a dusty box and a globular jar of East-India preserves, on which odd materials we supped with a hearty relish. The appetite engendered by open-air life in California would have made palatable a much more incongruous meal. We then lay down on the sloping sides of the knoll, rolled in a treble thickness of blankets, for the nights were beginning to grow cool. I was awakened once or twice by a mysterious twitching of my bed-clothes and a scratching noise, the cause of which was explained when I arose in the morning. I had been sleeping over half a

5*

dozen squirrel-holes, to the great discomfort of the imprisoned tenants.

The old denizen of the place, in better humor after we had paid for our unceremonious supper, set about baking tortillas and stewing beef, to which we added two cans of preserved turtle soup, which we found in the tent. Our mules had scattered far and wide during the night, and several hours elapsed before they could be herded and got into traveling order. The face of the broad plain we had to cross glimmered in the heat, and the Coast Range beyond it was like the phantom of a mountain-chain. We journeyed on, hour after hour, in the sweltering blaze, crossed the divide and reached Livermore's Ranche late in the afternoon. My saddle-mule was a fine gray animal belonging to Andrew Sublette, which Lieut. Beale had taken on our way to Stockton, leaving his own *alazan* at the ranche. Mr. Livermore was absent, but one of his vaqueros was prevailed upon, by a bribe of five dollars, to take the mule out to the corral, six miles distant, and bring me the horse in its stead. I sat down in the door of the ranche to await his arrival, leaving the company to go forward with all our animals to a camping-ground, twelve miles further.

It was quite dark when the vaquero rode up with the *alazan*, and I lost no time in saddling him and leaving the ranche. The trail, no longer confined among the hills, struck out on a circular plain, ten miles in diameter, which I was obliged to cross. The moon was not risen; the soil showed but one dusky, unvaried hue; and my only chance of keeping the trail was in the sound of my horse's feet. A streak of gravelly sand soon put me at fault, and after doubling backwards and forwards a few times, I found myself adrift without compass or helm. In the uncertain gloom, my horse blundered into stony hollows, or, lost in the mazes of the oaks, startled the buzzards and mountain vultures from their roost. The boughs rustled, and the air was stirred by the muffled beat of their wings : I could see them, like unearthly, boding shapes, as they swooped between me and the stars. At last, making a hazard at the direction in which the trail ran, I set my course by the stars and pushed steadily forward in a straight line.

Two hours of this dreary travel passed away : the moon rose, lighting up the loneliness of the wide plain and the dim, silvery sweep of mountains around it. I found myself on the verge of a steep bank, which I took to be an arroyo we had crossed on the outward journey. Getting down with some difficulty, I rode for more than a mile over the flinty bed of a lake, long since dried up by the summer heats. At its opposite side I plunged into a ghostly wood, echoing with the dismal howl of the wolves, and finally reached the foot of the mountains. The deep-sunken glen, at whose entrance I stood, had no familiar feature ; the tall clumps of chapparal in its bottom, seemed fit haunts for grizzly bear ; and after following it for a short distance, I turned about and urged my horse directly up the steep sides of the mountain.

It was now midnight, as near as I could judge by the moon, and I determined to go no further. I had neither fire-arms, matches nor blankets—all my equipments having gone on with the pack-mule—and it was necessary to choose a place where I could be secure from the bears, the only animal to be feared. The very summit of the mountain seemed to be the safest spot ; there was a single tree upon it, but the sides, for some distance below, were bare, and if a " grizzly" should come up one side, I could dash down the other. Clambering to the top, I tied my horse to the tree, took the saddle for a pillow, and coiling into the smallest possible compass, tried to cover myself with a square yard of saddle-blanket. It was too cold to sleep, and I lay there for hours, with aching bones and chattering teeth, looking down on the vast, mysterious depths of the landscape below me. I shall never forget the shadowy level of the plain, whose belts and spots of timber were like clouds in the wan light—the black mountain-gulfs on either hand, which the incessant yell of a thousand wolves made seem like caverns of the damned—the far, faint shapes of the distant ranges, which the moonshine covered, as with silver gossamer, and the spangled arch overhead, doubly lustrous in the thin air. Once or twice I fell into a doze, to dream of slipping off precipices and into icy chasms, and was roused by the snort of my horse, as he stood with raised ears, stretching the lariat to its full length.

When the morning star, which was never so welcome, brought the daylight in its wake, I saddled and rode down to the plain. Taking a course due north, I started off on a gallop and in less than an hour recovered the trail. I had no difficulty in finding the beautiful meadow where the party was to have camped, but there was no trace of them to be seen ; the mules, as it happened, were picketed behind some timber, and the men, not yet arisen, were buried out of sight in the rank grass. I rode up to some *milpas*, (brush-huts,) inhabited by Indians, and for two reals obtained a boiled ear of corn and a melon, which somewhat relieved my chill, hungry condition. Riding ahead slowly, that my horse might now and then crop a mouthful of oats, I was finally overtaken by Mr. Atherton, who was in advance of the company. We again took our places behind the mules, and hurried on to the Mission of San José.

Mr. Parker had been seized with fever and chills during the night, and decided to rest a day at the Pueblo San José. Messrs.

Atherton and Patterson, with myself, after breakfasting and making a hasty visit to the rich pear-trees and grape-vines of the garden, took a shorter road, leading around the head of the bay to Whisman's Ranche. We trotted the twenty-five miles in about four hours, rested an hour, and then set out again, hoping to reach San Francisco that night. It was too much, however, for our mules ; after passing the point of Santa Clara mountain they began to scatter, and as it was quite dark, we halted in a grove near the Ruined Mission. We lay down on the ground, supperless and somewhat weary with a ride of about seventy miles. I slept a refreshing sleep under a fragrant bay-tree, and was up with the first streak of dawn to look after my mules. Once started, we spurred our animals into a rapid trot, which was not slackened till we had passed the twenty miles that intervened between us and the Mission Dolores.

When I had climbed the last sand-hill, riding in towards San Francisco, and the town and harbor and crowded shipping again opened to the view, I could scarcely realize the change that had taken place during my absence of three weeks. The town had not only greatly extended its limits, but seemed actually to have doubled its number of dwellings since I left. High up on the hills, where I had seen only sand and chapparal, stood clusters of houses ; streets which had been merely laid out, were hemmed in with buildings and thronged with people ; new warehouses had sprung up on the water side, and new piers were creeping out toward the shipping ; the forest of masts had greatly thickened ; and the noise, motion and bustle of business and labor on all sides were incessant. Verily, the place was in itself a marvel. To say that it was daily enlarged by from twenty to thirty houses may not sound very remarkable after all the stories that have been told ; yet this, for a country which imported both lumber and houses, and where labor was then $10 a day, is an extraordinary growth. The rapidity with which a ready-made house is put up and inhabited, strikes the stranger in San Francisco as little short of magic. He walks over an open lot in his before-breakfast stroll—the next morning, a house complete, with a family inside, blocks up his way. He goes down to the bay and looks out on the shipping—two or three days afterward a row of storehouses, staring him in the face, intercepts the view.

I found Lieut. Beale and Col. Lyons, who gave me an amusing account of their voyage on the San Joaquin. The " skipper" of the launch in which they embarked knew nothing of navigation, and Lieut. Beale, in spite of his illness, was obliged to take command. The other passengers were a company of Mexican miners. After tacking for two days among the tulé swamps, the launch ran aground ; the skipper, in pushing it off, left an oar in the sand and took the boat to recover it. Just then a fine breeze sprang up and the launch shot ahead, leaving the skipper to follow. That night, having reached a point within two miles of the site of an impossible town, called New-York-of-the-Pacific, the passengers left in a body. The next day they walked to the little village of Martinez, opposite Benicia, a distance of twenty-five miles, crossing the foot of Monte Diablo. Here they took another launch, and after tossing twelve hours on the bay, succeeded in reaching San Francisco.

At the United States Hotel I again met with Colonel Frémont, and learned the particulars of the magnificent discovery which had just been made upon his ranche on the Mariposa River. It was nothing less than a vein of gold in the solid rock—the first which had been found in California. I saw some specimens which were in Col. Frémont's possession. The stone was a reddish quartz, filled with rich veins of gold, and far surpassing the specimens brought from North Carolina and Georgia. Some stones picked up on the top of the quartz strata, without particular selection, yielded two ounces of gold to every twenty-five pounds. Col. Frémont informed me that the vein had been traced for more than a mile. The thickness on the surface is two feet, gradually widening as it descends and showing larger particles of gold. The dip downward is only about 20°, so that the mine can be worked with little expense. The ranche upon which it is situated was purchased by Col. Frémont in 1846 from Alvarado, former Governor of the Territory. It was then considered nearly worthless, and Col. F. only took it at the moment of leaving the country, because disappointed in obtaining another property. This discovery made a great sensation thoughout the country, at the time, yet it was but the first of many such. The Sierra Nevada is pierced in every part with these priceless veins, which will produce gold for centuries after every spot of earth from base to summit shall have been turned over and washed out.

Many of my fellow-passengers by the Panama were realizing their dreams of speedy fortune ; some had already made $20,000 by speculating in town lots. A friend of mine who had shipped lumber from New York to the amount of $1000 sold it for $14,000. At least seventy-five houses had been imported from Canton, and put up by Chinese carpenters. Washing was $8 a dozen, and as a consequence, large quantities of soiled linen were sent to the antipodes to be purified. A vessel just in from Canton brought two hundred and fifty dozen, which had been sent out a few months before ; another from the Sandwich Islands brought one hundred dozen, and the practice was becoming general.

CHAPTER XII.

A BETTER idea of San Francisco, in the beginning of September, 1849, cannot be given than by the description of a single day. Supposing the visitor to have been long enough in the place to sleep on a hard plank and in spite of the attacks of innumerable fleas, he will be awakened at daylight by the noises of building, with which the hills are all alive. The air is temperate, and the invariable morning fog is just beginning to gather. By sunrise, which gleams hazily over the Coast Mountains across the Bay, the whole populace is up and at work. The wooden buildings unlock their doors, the canvas houses and tents throw back their front curtains; the lighters on the water are warped out from ship to ship; carts and porters are busy along the beach; and only the gaming-tables, thronged all night by the votaries of chance, are idle and deserted. The temperature is so fresh as to inspire an active habit of body, and even without the stimulus of trade and speculation there would be few sluggards at this season.

As early as half-past six the bells begin to sound to breakfast, and for an hour thenceforth, their incessant clang and the braying of immense gongs drown all the hammers that are busy on a hundred roofs. The hotels, restaurants and refectories of all kinds are already as numerous as gaming-tables, and equally various in kind. The tables d'hôte of the first class, (which charge $2 and upwards the meal,) are abundantly supplied. There are others, with more simple and solid fare, frequented by the large class who have their fortunes yet to make. At the United States and California restaurants, on the plaza, you may get an excellent beefsteak, scantily garnished with potatoes, and a cup of good coffee or chocolate, for $1. Fresh beef, bread, potatoes, and all provisions which will bear importation, are plenty; but milk, fruit and vegetables are classed as luxuries, and fresh butter is rarely heard of. On Montgomery street, and the vacant space fronting the water, venders of coffee, cakes and sweetmeats have erected their stands, in order to tempt the appetite of sailors just arrived in port, or miners coming down from the mountains.

By nine o'clock the town is in the full flow of business. The streets running down to the water, and Montgomery street which fronts the Bay, are crowded with people, all in hurried motion. The variety of characters and costumes is remarkable. Our own countrymen seem to lose their local peculiarities in such a crowd, and it is by chance epithets rather than by manner, that the New-Yorker is distinguished from the Kentuckian, the Carolinian from the Down-Easter, the Virginian from the Texan. The German and Frenchman are more easily recognized. Peruvians and Chilians go by in their brown ponchos, and the sober Chinese, cool and impassive in the midst of excitement, look out of the oblique corners of their long eyes at the bustle, but are never tempted to venture from their own line of business. The eastern side of the plaza, in front of the Parker House and a canvas hell called the Eldorado, are the general rendezvous of business and amusement

—combining 'change, park, club-room and promenade all in one. There, everybody not constantly employed in one spot, may be seen at some time of the day. The character of the groups scattered along the plaza is oftentimes very interesting. In one place are three or four speculators bargaining for lots, buying and selling " fifty varas square " in towns, some of which are canvas and some only paper ; in another, a company of miners, brown as leather, and rugged in features as in dress ; in a third, perhaps, three or four naval officers speculating on the next cruise, or a knot of genteel gamblers, talking over the last night's operations.

The day advances. The mist which after sunrise hung low and heavy for an hour or two, has risen above the hills, and there will be two hours of pleasant sunshine before the wind sets in from the sea. The crowd in the streets is now wholly alive. Men dart hither and thither, as if possessed with a never-resting spirit. You speak to an acquaintance—a merchant, perhaps. He utters a few hurried words of greeting, while his eyes send keen glances on all sides of you ; suddenly he catches sight of somebody in the crowd ; he is off, and in the next five minutes has bought up half a cargo, sold a town lot at treble the sum he gave, and taken a share in some new and imposing speculation. It is impossible to witness this excess and dissipation of business, without feeling something of its influence. The very air is pregnant with the magnetism of bold, spirited, unwearied action, and he who but ventures into the outer circle of the whirlpool, is spinning, ere he has time for thought, in its dizzy vortex.

But see ! the groups in the plaza suddenly scatter ; the city surveyor jerks his pole out of the ground and leaps on a pile of boards ; the venders of cakes and sweetmeats follow his example, and the place is cleared, just as a wild bull which has been racing down Kearney street makes his appearance. Two vaqueros, shouting and swinging their lariats, follow at a hot gallop; the dust flies as they dash across the plaza. One of them, in mid-career, hurls his lariat in the air. Mark how deftly the coil unwinds in its flying curve, and with what precision the noose falls over the bull's horns! The horse wheels as if on a pivot, and shoots off in an opposite line. He knows the length of the lariat to a hair, and the instant it is drawn taught, plants his feet firmly for the shock and throws his body forward. The bull is " brought up " with such force as to throw him off his legs. He lies stunned a moment, and then, rising heavily, makes another charge. But by this time the second vaquero has thrown a lariat around one of his hind legs, and thus checked on both sides, he is dragged off to slaughter.

The plaza is refilled as quickly as it was emptied, and the course of business is resumed. About twelve o'clock, a wind begins to blow from the north-west, sweeping with most violence through a gap between the hills, opening towards the Golden Gate. The bells and gongs begin to sound for dinner, and these two causes tend to lessen the crowd in the streets for an hour or two. Two o'clock is the usual dinner-time for business men, but some of the old and successful merchants have adopted the fashionable hour of five. Where shall we dine to-day? the restaurants display their signs invitingly on all sides; we have choice of the United States, Tortoni's, the Alhambra, and many other equally classic resorts, but Delmonico's, like its distinguished original in New York, has the highest prices and the greatest variety of dishes. We go down Kearney street to a two-story wooden house on the corner of Jackson. The lower story is a market; the walls are garnished with quarters of beef and mutton; a huge pile of Sandwich Island squashes fills one corner, and several cabbage-heads, valued at $2 each, show themselves in the window. We enter a little door at the end of the building, ascend a dark, narrow flight of steps and find ourselves in a long, low room, with ceiling and walls of white muslin and a floor covered with oil-cloth.

There are about twenty tables disposed in two rows, all of them so well filled that we have some difficulty in finding places. Taking up the written bill of fare, we find such items as the following :

SOUPS.
Mock Turtle $0 75
St. Julien 1 00

FISH.
Boiled Salmon Trout, Anchovy
    sauce 1 75

BOILED.
Leg Mutton, caper sauce . . 1 00
Corned Beef, Cabbage, . . . 1 00
Ham and Tongues 0 75

ENTREES.
Fillet of Beef, mushroom
    sauce $1 75
Veal Cutlets, breaded . . . 1 00
Mutton Chop 1 00
Lobster Salad 2 00
Sirloin of Venison 1 50
Baked Maccaroni 0 75
Beef Tongue, sauce piquante 1 00

So that, with but a moderate appetite, the dinner will cost us $5, if we are at all epicurean in our tastes. There are cries of " steward !" from all parts of the room—the word " waiter" is not considered sufficiently respectful, seeing that the waiter may have been a lawyer or merchant's clerk a few months before. The dishes look very small as they are placed on the table, but they are skilfully cooked and very palatable to men that have ridden in from the diggings. The appetite one acquires in California is something remarkable. For two months after my arrival, my sensations were like those of a famished wolf.

In the matter of dining, the tastes of all nations can be gratified here. There are French restaurants on the plaza and on Dupont street ; an extensive German establishment on Pacific street ; the *Fonda Peruana ;* the Italian Confectionary ; and three Chinese houses, denoted by their long three-cornered flags of yellow silk. The latter are much frequented by Americans, on account of their excellent cookery, and the fact that meals are $1 each, without regard to quantity. Kong-Sung's house is near the water; Whang-Tong's in Sacramento Street, and Tong-Ling's in Jackson street. There the grave Celestials serve up their chow-chow and curry, besides many genuine English dishes; their tea and coffee cannot be surpassed.

The afternoon is less noisy and active than the forenoon. Merchants keep within-doors, and the gambling-rooms are crowded with persons who step in to escape the wind and dust. The sky takes a cold gray cast, and the hills over the bay are barely visible in the dense, dusty air. Now and then a watcher, who has been stationed on the hill above Fort Montgomery, comes down and reports an inward-bound vessel, which occasions a little excitement among the boatmen and the merchants who are awaiting consignments. Towards sunset, the plaza is nearly deserted; the wind is merciless in its force, and a heavy overcoat is not found unpleasantly warm. As it grows dark, there is a lull, though occasional gusts blow down the hill and carry the dust of the city out among the shipping.

The appearance of San Francisco at night, from the water, is unlike anything I ever beheld. The houses are mostly of canvas, which is made transparent by the lamps within, and transforms them, in the darkness, to dwellings of solid light. Seated on the slopes of its three hills, the tents pitched among the chapparal to the very summits, it gleams like an amphitheatre of fire. Here and there shine out brilliant points, from the decoy-lamps of the gaming-houses; and through the indistinct murmur of the streets comes by fits the sound of music from their hot and crowded precincts. The picture has in it something unreal and fantastic; it impresses one like the cities of the magic lantern, which a motion of the hand can build or annihilate.

The only objects left for us to visit are the gaming-tables, whose day has just fairly dawned. We need not wander far in search of one. Denison's Exchange, the Parker House and Eldorado stand side by side; across the way are the Verandah and Aguila de Oro; higher up the plaza the St. Charles and Bella Union; while dozens of second-rate establishments are scattered through the less frequented streets. The greatest crowd is about the Eldorado; we find it difficult to effect an entrance. There are about eight tables in the room, all of which are thronged; copper-hued Kanakas, Mexicans rolled in their sarapes and Peruvians thrust through their ponchos, stand shoulder to shoulder with the brown and bearded American miners. The stakes are generally small, though when the bettor gets into " a streak of luck," as it is called, they are allowed to double until all is lost or the bank breaks. Along the end of the room is a spacious bar, supplied with all kinds of bad liquors, and in a sort of gallery, suspended under the ceiling, a female violinist tasks her talent and strength of muscle to minister to the excitement of play.

The Verandah, opposite, is smaller, but boasts an equal attraction in a musician who has a set of Pandean pipes fastened at his chin, a drum on his back, which he beats with sticks at his elbows, and cymbals in his hands. The piles of coin on the monte tables clink merrily to his playing, and the throng of spectators, jammed together in a sweltering mass, walk up to the bar between the tunes and drink out of sympathy with his dry and breathless throat. At the Aguila de Oro there is a full band of Ethiopian serenaders, and at the other hells, violins, guitars or wheezy accordeons, as the case may be. The atmosphere of these places is rank with tobacco-smoke, and filled with a feverish, stifling heat, which communicates an unhealthy glow to the faces of the players. We shall not be deterred from entering by the heat and smoke, or the motley characters into whose company we shall be thrown. There are rare chances here for seeing human nature in one of its most dark and exciting phases. Note the variety of expression in the faces gathered around this table ! They are playing monte, the favorite game in California, since the chances are considered more equal and the opportunity of false play very slight. The dealer throws out his cards with a cool, nonchalant air ; indeed, the gradual increase of the hollow square of dollars at his left hand is not calculated to disturb his equanimity. The two Mexicans in front, muffled in their dirty sarapes, put down their half-dollars and dollars and see them lost, without changing a muscle. Gambling is a born habit with them, and they would lose thousands with the same indifference. Very different is the demeanor of the Americans who are playing ; their good or ill luck is betrayed at once by involuntary exclamations and changes of countenance, unless the stake should be very large and absorbing, when their anxiety, though silent, may be read with no less certainty. They have no power to resist the fascination of the game. Now counting their winnings by thousands, now dependent on the kindness of a friend for a few dollars to commence anew, they pass hour after hour in those hot, unwholesome dens. There is no appearance of arms, but let one of the players, impatient with his losses and maddened by the poisonous fluids he has drank, threaten one of the profession, and there will be no scarcity of knives and revolvers.

There are other places, where gaming is carried on privately

and to a more ruinous extent—rooms in the rear of the Parker
House, in the City Hotel and other places, frequented only by the
initiated.   Here the stakes are almost unlimited, the players being
men of wealth and apparent respectability.   Frequently, in the
absorbing interest of some desperate game the night goes by un-
heeded and morning breaks upon haggard faces and reckless hearts.
Here are lost, in a few turns of a card or rolls of a ball, the product
of fortunate ventures by sea or months of racking labor on land.
How many men, maddened by continual losses, might exclaim in
their blind vehemence of passion, on leaving these hells :

> "Out, out, thou strumpet, Fortune !   All you gods,
>   In general synod, take away her power ;
>   Break all the spokes and fellies from her wheel,
>   And bowl the round nave down the hill of heaven,
>   As low as to the fiends !"

BAYARD TAYLOR.

MONTEREY.

NEW YORK, GEO. P. PUTNAM.

LITH OF SARONY & MAJOR.

CHAPTER XIII.

INCIDENTS OF A WALK TO MONTEREY.

I STAYED but four or five days in San Francisco on my return. The Convention, elected to form a constitution for California, was then in session at Monterey, and, partly as an experiment, partly for economy's sake, I determined to make the journey of one hundred and thirty miles on foot. Pedestrianism in California, however, as I learned by this little experience, is something more of a task than in most countries, one being obliged to carry his hotel with him. The least possible bedding is a Mexican sarape, which makes a burdensome addition to a knapsack, and a loaf of bread and flask of water are inconvenient, when the mercury stands at 90° Besides, the necessity of pushing forward many miles to reach "grass and water" at night, is not very pleasant to the foot-sore and weary traveler. A mule, with all his satanic propensities, is sometimes a very convenient animal.

Dressed in a complete suit of corduroy, with a shirt of purple flannel and boots calculated to wear an indefinite length of time, I left San Francisco one afternoon, waded through the three miles of deep sand to the Mission, crossed the hills and reached Sanchez' Ranche a little after dark. I found the old man, who is said to dislike the Americans most cordially, very friendly. He set before me a supper of beef stewed in red-peppers and then gave me a bed—an actual bed—and, wonder of wonders! without fleas. Not far from Sanchez there is a large adobe house, the ruins of a former Mission, in the neighborhood of which I noticed a grove of bay-trees. They were of a different species from the Italian bay, and the leaves gave out a most pungent odor. Some of the trees were of extraordinary size, the trunk being three feet in diameter. They grew along the banks of a dry arroyo, and had every appearance of being indigenous. I found the *jornada* of twenty-five miles to Secondini's Ranche, extremely fatiguing in the hot sun. I entered the ranche panting, threw my knapsack on the floor and inquired of a handsome young Californian, dressed in blue calzoneros : " Can you give me anything to eat ?" " *Nada—nad-i-t-a !*" he answered, sharpening out the sound with an expression which meant, as plain as words could say it : " nothing ; not even the little end of nothing !"

I was too hungry to be satisfied with this reply, and commenced an inventory of all the articles on hand. I found plenty of French brandy, *mescal* and various manufactured wines, which I rejected ; but my search was at last rewarded by a piece of bread, half a Dutch cheese and a bottle of ale, nearly all of which soon disappeared. Towards night, some of the vaqueros brought in a cow with a lariat around her horns, threw her on the ground and plunged a knife into her breast. A roaring fire was already kindled behind the house, and the breath had not been many seconds out of the cow's body, before pieces of meat, slashed from her flank, were broiling on the coals. When about half cooked, they were snatched out, dripping with the rich, raw juices of the animal, and eaten as a great delicacy. One of the vaqueros handed me a large slice, which I found rather tough, but so remarkably sweet and nutritious that I ate it, feeling myself at the time little better than a wolf.

I left Secondini's at daybreak and traveled twelve miles to the Mission of Santa Clara, where, not being able to obtain breakfast, I walked into the garden and made a meal of pears and the juicy fruit of the cactus. Thence to Pueblo San José, where I left the road I had already traveled, and took the broad highway running southward, up the valley of San José. The mountains were barely visible on either side, through the haze, and the road, perfectly level, now passed over wide reaches of grazing land, now crossed park-like tracts, studded with oaks and sycamores—a charming interchange of scenery. I crossed the dry bed of Coyote Creek several times, and reached Capt. Fisher's Ranche as it was growing dusk, and a passing traveler warned me to look out for bears.

Capt. Fisher, who is married to a Californian lady and has lived many years in the country, has one of the finest ranches in the valley, containing four square leagues of land, or about eighteen thousand acres. There are upon it eighteen streams or springs, two small orchards, and a vineyard and garden. He purchased it at auction about three years since for $3,000, which was then considered a high price, but since the discovery of gold he has been offered $80,000 for it. I was glad to find, from the account he gave me of his own experience as a farmer, that my first impressions of the character of California as an agricultural country, were fully justified. The barren, burnt appearance of the plains during the summer season misled many persons as to the value of the country in this respect. From all quarters were heard complaints of the torrid heat and arid soil under which large rivers dry up and vegetation almost entirely disappears. The possibility of raising good crops of any kind was vehemently denied, and the bold assertion made that the greater part of California is worthless, except for grazing purposes. Capt. Fisher informed me, however, that there is no such wheat country in the world. Even with the imperfect plowing of the natives, which does little more than scratch up the surface of the ground, it produces a hundred-fold. Not only this, but, without further cultivation, a large crop springs up on the soil the second and sometimes even the third year. Capt. Fisher knew of a ranchero who sowed twenty fanegas of wheat, from which he harvested one thousand and twenty fanegas. The second year he gathered from the same ground eight hundred fanegas, and the third year six hundred. The unvarying dryness of the climate after the rains have ceased preserves grain of all kinds from rot, and perhaps from the same circumstance, the Hessian fly is unknown. The mountain-sides, to a considerable extent, are capable of yielding fine crops of wheat, barley and rye, and the very summits and ravines on which the wild oats grow so abundantly will of course give a richer return when they have been traversed by the plow.

Corn grows upon the plains, but thrives best in the neighborhood of streams. It requires no irrigation, and is not planted until after the last rain has fallen. The object of this, however, is to avoid the growth of weeds, which, were it planted earlier, would soon choke it, in the absence of a proper system of farming. The use of the common cultivator would remove this difficulty, and by planting in March instead of May, an abundant crop would be certain. I saw several hundred acres which Capt. Fisher had on his ranche. The ears were large and well filled, and the stalks, though no rain had fallen for four months, were as green and fresh as in our fields at home. Ground which has been plowed and planted, though it shows a dry crust on the top, retains its moisture to within six inches of the surface; while close beside it, and on the same level, the uncultured earth is seamed with heat, and vegetation burned up. The valley of San José is sixty miles in length, and contains at least five hundred square miles of level plain, nearly the whole of which is capable of cultivation. In regard to climate and situation, it is one of the most favored parts of California, though the valleys of Sonoma, Napa, Bodega, and nearly the whole of the Sacramento country, are said to be equally fertile.

Vegetables thrive luxuriantly, and many species, such as melons, pumpkins, squashes, beans, potatoes, etc., require no further care than the planting. Cabbages, onions, and all others which are transplanted in the spring, are obliged to be irrigated. Grape vines in some situations require to be occasionally watered; when planted on moist slopes, they produce without it. A Frenchman named Vigne made one hundred barrels of wine in one year, from a vineyard of about six acres, which he cultivates at the Mission San José. Capt. Fisher had a thousand vines in his garden, which were leaning on the earth from the weight of their fruit. Many of the clusters weighed four and five pounds, and in bloom, richness and flavor rivaled the choicest growth of Tuscany or the Rhine. The vine will hereafter be an important product of California, and even Burgundy and Tokay may be superseded on the tables of the luxurious by the vintage of San José and Los Angeles.

Before reaching Fisher's Ranche, I noticed on my left a bold spur striking out from the mountain-range. It terminated in a bluff, and both the rock and soil were of the dark-red color of Egyptian porphyry, denoting the presence of cinnabar, the ore of quicksilver. The veins of this metal contained in the mountain are thought to be equal to those of the mines of Santa Clara, which are on the opposite side of the valley, about eight miles from Pueblo San José.

The following morning I resumed my walk up the valley. The soft, cloudless sky—the balmy atmosphere—the mountain ranges on either hand, stretching far before me until they vanished in purple haze—the sea-like sweep of the plain, with its islands and shores of dark-green oak, and the picturesque variety of animal life on all sides, combined to form a landscape which I may have seen equalled but never surpassed. Often, far in advance beyond the belts of timber, a long blue headland would curve out from the mountains and seem to close up the beautiful plain ; but after the road had crossed its point, another and grander plain expanded for leagues before the eye. Nestled in a warm nook on the sunny side of one of these mountain capes, I found the ranche of Mr. Murphy, commanding a splendid prospect. Beyond the house and across a little valley, rose the conical peak of El Toro, an isolated mountain which served as a landmark from San José nearly to Monterey.

I was met at the door by Mr. Ruckel of San Francisco, who, with Mr. Everett of New York, had been rusticating a few days in the neighborhood. They introduced me to Mr. Murphy and his daughter, Ellen, both residents of the country for the last six years. Mr. Murphy, who is a native of Ireland, emigrated from Missouri, with his family, in 1843. He owns nine leagues of land (forty thousand acres) in the valley, and his cottage is a well-known and welcome resting-place to all the Americans in the country. During the war he remained on the ranche in company with his daughter, notwithstanding Castro's troops were scouring the country, and all other families had moved to the Pueblo for protection. His three sons were at the same time volunteers under Frémont's command.

After dinner Mr. Murphy kindly offered to accompany me to the top of El Toro. Two horses were driven in from the caballada and saddled, and on these we started, at the usual sweeping speed. Reaching the foot of the mountain, the lithe and spirited animals climbed its abrupt side like goats, following the windings of cattle-paths up the rocky ridges and through patches of stunted oak and chapparal, till finally, bathed in sweat and panting with the toil, they stood on the summit. We looked on a vast and wonderful landscape. The mountain rose like an island in the sea of air, so far removed from all it overlooked, that everything was wrapped in a subtle violet haze, through which the features of the scene seemed grander and more distant than the reality. West of us, range behind range, ran the Coast Mountains, parted by deep, wild valleys, in which we could trace the course of streams, shaded by the pine and the giant redwood. On the other side, the valley of San José, ten miles in width, lay directly at our feet, extending to the North and South, beyond point and headland, till either extremity was lost in the distance. The unvarying yellow hue of mountain and plain, except where they were traversed by broad belts of dark green timber, gave a remarkable effect to the view. It was not the color of barrenness and desolation and had no character of sadness or even monotony. Rather, glimmering through the mist, the mountains seemed to have arrayed themselves in cloth of gold, as if giving testimony of the royal metal with which their veins abound.

After enjoying this scene for some time, we commenced the descent. The peak slanted downward at an angle of 45°, which

rendered it toilsome work for our horses. I was about half-way
down the summit-cone, when my saddle, slipping over the horse's
shoulders, suddenly dropped to his ears. I was shot forward and
alighted on my feet two or three yards below, fortunately retaining
the end of the lariat in my hand. For a few minutes we performed
a very spirited *pas de deux* on the side of the mountain, but Mr.
Murphy coming to my assistance, the horse was finally quieted and
re-saddled. The afternoon was by this time far advanced, and I
accepted Mr. Murphy's invitation to remain for the night. His
pleasant family circle was increased in the evening by the arrival
of Rev. Mr. Dowiat, a Catholic Missionary from Oregoñ, who
gave us an account of the Indian massacre the previous winter.
He was on the spot the day of its occurrence and assisted in in-
terring the bodies of Dr. Whitman and his fellow-victims.

I traveled slowly the next day, for the hot sand and unaccus-
tomed exercise were beginning to make some impression on my
feet. Early in the afternoon I reached some *milpas* standing in
the middle of a cornfield. A handsome young ranchero came
dashing up on a full gallop, stopping his horse with a single bound
as he neared me. I asked him the name of the ranche, and
whether he could give me a dinner. "It is Castro's Ranche," he
replied ; " and I am a Castro. If you want water-melons, or dinner
either, don't go to the other milpas, for they have nothing: venga !"
and off he started, dashing through the corn and over the melon
patches, as if they were worthless sand. I entered the milpa,
which resembled an enormous wicker crate. In default of chairs
I sat upon the ground, and very soon a dish of tortillas, one of
boiled corn and another of jerked beef, were set before me. There
was no need of knives and forks ; I watched the heir of the Castros,
placed a tortilla on one knee and plied my fingers with an assiduity

equal to his own, so that between us there was little left of the repast. He then picked out two melons from a large pile, rolled them to me, and started away again, doubtless to chase down more customers.

The road crossed the dry bed of a river, passed some meadows of fresh green grass and entered the hills on the western side of the valley. After passing the divide, I met an old Indian, traveling on foot, of whom I asked the distance to San Juan. His reply in broken Spanish was given with a comical brevity : " San Juan— two leagues—you sleep—I sleep rancho—you walk—I walk ; *anda, vamos !*" and pointing to the sun to signify that it was growing late, he trudged off with double speed. By sunset I emerged from the mountains, waded the Rio Pajaro, and entered on the valley of San Juan, which stretched for leagues before me, as broad and beautiful as that I had left. The road, leading directly across it, seemed endless ; I strained my eyes in vain looking for the Mission. At last a dark spot appeared some distance ahead of me. " Pray heaven," thought I, " that you be either a house, and stand still, or a man, and come forward." It was an Indian vaquero, who pointed out a dark line, which I could barely discern through the dusk. Soon afterwards the sound of a bell, chiming vespers, broke on the silence, but I was still more weary before I reached the walls where it swung.

At the inn adjoining the Mission I found Rev. Mr. Hunt, Col. Stewart, Capt. Simmons and Mr. Harrison, of San Francisco. We had beds, but did not sleep much ; few travelers, in fact, sleep at any of the Missions, on account of the dense population. In the morning I made a sketch of the ruined building, filled my pockets with pears in the orchard, and started up a cañada to cross the mountains to the plain of Salinas River. It was a mule-path,

6*

impracticable for wagons, and leading directly up the face of the dividing ridge. Clumps of the madrono—a native evergeen, with large, glossy leaves, and trunk and branches of bright purple—filled the ravines, and dense thickets of a shrub with a snow-white berry lined the way. From the summit there was a fine mountain-view, sloping off on either hand into the plains of San Juan and Salinas.

Along this road, since leaving San José, I met constantly with companies of emigrants from the Gila, on their way to the diggings. Many were on foot, having had their animals taken from them by the Yuma Indians at the crossing of the Colorado. They were wild, sun-burned, dilapidated men, but with strong and hardy frames, that were little affected by the toils of the journey. Some were mounted on mules which had carried them from Texas and Arkansas; and two of the Knickerbocker Company, having joined their teams to a wagon, had begun business by filling it with vegetables at the Mission, to sell again in the gold district. In a little glen I found a party of them camped for a day or two to wash their clothes in a pool which had drained from the meadows above. The companies made great inroads on my progress by questioning me about the gold region. None of them seemed to have any very definite plan in their heads. It was curious to note their eagerness to hear " golden reports" of the country, every one of them betraying, by his questioning, the amount of the fortune he secretly expected to make. " Where would you advise me to go ?" was the first question. I evaded the responsibility of a direct answer, and gave them the general report of the yield on all the rivers. " How much can I dig in a day ?" This question was so absurd, as I could know nothing of the physical strength, endurance or geological knowledge of the emigrant, that I invariably refused to

make a random answer, telling them it depended entirely on themselves. But there was no escaping in this manner. " Well, how
much do you *think* I can dig in a day ?" was sure to follow, and I
was obliged to satisfy them by replying : " Perhaps a dollar's
worth, perhaps five pounds, perhaps nothing !"

They spoke of meeting great numbers of Sonorians on their way
home—some of whom had attempted to steal their mules and
provisions. Others, again, who had reached the country quite
destitute, were kindly treated by them. The Yuma and Maricopas
Indians were the greatest pests on the route. They had met with
no difficulty in passing through the Apache country, and, with the
exception of some little thieving, the Pimos tribes had proved
friendly. The two former tribes, however, had united their forces,
which amounted to two thousand warriors, and taken a hostile position among the hills near the Colorado crossing. There had
been several skirmishes between them and small bodies of emigrants, in which men were killed on both sides. A New York
Company lost five of its members in this manner. Nearly all the
persons I met had been seven months on the way. They reported
that there were about ten thousand persons on the Gila, not more
than half of whom had yet arrived in California. Very few of
the original companies held together, most of them being too large
for convenience.

Descending a long cañada in the mountains, I came out at the
great Salinas Plain. At an Indian ranche on the last slope,
several cart-loads of melons were heaped beside the door, and I
ate two or three in company with a traveler who rode up, and
who proved to be a spy employed by Gen. Scott in the Mexican
campaign. He was a small man, with a peculiar, keen gray eye,
and a physiognomy thoroughly adapted for concealing all that was

passing in his mind. His hair was long and brown, and his
beard unshorn ; he was, in fact, a genuine though somewhat
diminutive type of Harvey Birch, differing from him likewise in a
courteous freedom of manner which he had learned by long familiarity with Spanish habits. While we sat, slicing the melons
and draining their sugary juice, he told me a story of his capture
by the Mexicans, after the battles in the Valley. He was carried
to Queretaro, tried and sentenced to be shot, but succeeded in
bribing the sergeant of the guard, through whose means he succeeded in escaping the night before the day of execution. The
sergeant's wife, who brought his meals to the prison in a basket,
left with him the basket, a *rebosa* and petticoat, in which he arrayed
himself, after having shaved off his long beard, and passed out un-
noticed by the guard. A good horse was in waiting, and he never
slacked rein until he reached San Juan del Rio, eleven leagues
from Queretaro.

To strike out on the plain was like setting sail on an unknown
sea. My companion soon sank below the horizon, while I, whose
timbers were somewhat strained, labored after him. I had some
misgivings about the road, but followed it some four or five miles,
when, on trying the course with a compass, I determined to leave
it and take the open plain. I made for a faint speck far to the
right, which, after an hour's hard walking showed itself to be a
deserted ranche, beside an *ojo de agua*, or marshy spring. Fortunately, I struck on another road, and perseveringly followed it
till dusk, when I reached the ranche of Thomas Blanco, on the
bank of the Salinas River. Harvey Birch was standing in the
door, having arrived an hour before me. Tortillas and frijoles
were smoking on the table—a welcome sight to a hungry man !
Mr. Blanco, who treated us with g nuine kindness, then gave us

good beds, and I went to sleep with the boom of the surf on the shore of the distant bay ringing in my ears.

Mr. Blanco, who is married to a Californian woman, has been living here several years. His accounts of the soil and climate fully agreed with what I had heard from other residents. There is a fine garden on the ranche, but during his absence at the placers in the summer, all the vegetables were carried away by a band of Sonorians, who loaded his pack-mules with them and drove them off. They would even have forcibly taken his wife and her sister with them, had not some of her relatives fortunately arrived in time to prevent it.

I was so lame and sore the next morning, that I was fain to be helped over the remaining fifteen miles to Monterey, by the kind offer of Mr. Shew of Baltimore, who gave me a seat in his wagon. The road passed over sand-hills, covered only with chapparal, and good for nothing except as a shooting-ground for partridges and hares. The view of the town as you approach, opening through a gap between two low, piny hills, is very fine. Though so far inferior to San Francisco in size, the houses were all substantially built, and did not look as if they would fly off in a gale of wind. They were scattered somewhat loosely over a gentle slope, behind which ran a waving outline of pine-covered mountains. On the right hand appeared the blue waters of the bay, with six or seven vessels anchored near the shore. The American flag floated gaily in the sunshine above the fort on the bluff and the Government offices in the town, and prominent among the buildings on the high ground stood the Town Hall—a truly neat and spacious edifice of yellow stone, in which the Constitutional Convention was then sitting.

In spite of the additional life which this body gave to the place, my first impression was that of a deserted town. Few people were stirring in the streets ; business seemed dull and stagnant ; and after hunting half an hour for a hotel, I learned that there was none. In this dilemma I luckily met my former fellow-traveler, Major Smith, who asked me to spread my blanket in his room, in the *cuartel*, or Government barracks. I willingly complied, glad to find a place of rest after a foot-journey which I declared should be my last in California.

CHAPTER XIV.

MAJOR SMITH, who was Paymaster for the stations of Monterey and San Diego, had arrived only a few days previous, from the latter place. He was installed in a spacious room in the upper story of the *cuartel*, which by an impromptu partition of muslin, was divided into an office and bedroom. Two or three empty freight-boxes, furnished as a great favor by the Quarter Master, served as desk, table and wash-stand. There were just three chairs for the Major, his brother and myself, so that when we had a visit, one of us took his seat on a box. The only bedding I brought from San Francisco was a sarape, which was insufficient, but with some persuasion we obtained a soldier's pallet and an armful of straw, out of which we made a comfortable bed. We were readily initiated into the household mysteries of sweeping, dusting, etc., and after a few days' practice felt competent to take charge of a much larger establishment.

I took my meals at the *Fonda de la Union*, on the opposite side of the street. It was an old, smoky place not uncomfortably clean, with a billiard-room and two small rooms adjoining, where the owner, a sallow Mexican, with his Indian cook and *muchacho*, entertained his customers. The place was frequented by a number of the members and clerks of the Convention, by all rambling Americans or Californians who happened to be in Monterey, and occasionally a seaman or two from the ships in the harbor. The charges were usually $1 per meal; for which we were furnished with an *olla* of boiled beef, cucumbers and corn, an *asado* of beef and red-pepper, a *guisado* of beef and potatoes, and two or three cups of execrable coffee. At the time of my arrival this was the only restaurant in the place, and reaped such a harvest of *pesos*, that others were not long in starting up.

There was one subject, which at the outset occasioned us many sleepless nights. In vain did we attempt to forego the contemplation of it; as often as we lay down on our pallets, the thought would come uncalled, and very soon we were writhing under its attacks as restlessly as Richard on his ghost-haunted couch. It was no imaginary disturbance; it assailed us on all sides, and without cessation. It was an annoyance by no means peculiar to California; it haunts the temples of the Incas and the halls of the Montezumas; I have felt it come upon me in the Pantheon of Rome, and many a traveler has bewailed its visitation while sleeping in the shadow of the Pyramid. Nothing is more positively real to the feelings, nothing more elusive and intangible to the search. You look upon the point of its attack, and you see it not; you put your finger on it, and it is not there!

We tried all the means in our power to procure a good night's rest. We swept out the room, shook out the blankets and tucked ourselves in so skillfully that we thought no flea could effect an entrance—but in vain. At last, after four nights of waking torment, I determined to give up the attempt; I had become so nervous by repeated failures that the thought of it alone would have prevented sleep. At bed-time, therefore, I took my blankets, and went up into the pine woods behind the town. I chose a warm corner between some bushes and a fallen log; the air was misty and chill and the moon clouded over, but I lay sheltered and comfortable on my pillow of dry sticks. Occasionally a partridge would stir in the bushes by my head or a squirrel rustle among the dead leaves, while far back in the gloomy shadows of the forest the coyotes kept up an endless howl. I slept but indifferently, for two or three fleas had escaped the blanket-shaking, and did biting enough for fifty.

After many trials, I finally nonplussed them in spite of all their cunning. There is a thick green shrub in the forest, whose powerful balsamic odor is too much for them. After sweeping the floor and sprinkling it with water, I put down my bed, previously well shaken, and surrounded it with a chevaux-de-frise of this shrub, wide enough to prevent their overleaping it. Thus moated and palisaded from the foe, I took my rest unbroken, to his utter discomfiture.

Every day that I spent in Monterey, I found additional cause to recede from my first impression of the dullness of the place. Quiet it certainly is, to one coming from San Francisco; but it is only dull in the sense that Nice and Pisa are dull cities. The bustle of trade is wanting, but to one not bent on gold-hunting, a delicious climate, beautiful scenery, and pleasant society are a full compensation. Those who stay there for any length of time, love the place before they leave it—which would scarcely be said of San Francisco.

The situation of Monterey is admirable. The houses are built on a broad, gentle slope of land, about two miles from Point Pinos, the southern extremity of the bay. They are scattered over an extent of three quarters of a mile, leaving ample room for the growth of the town for many years to come. The outline of the hills in the rear is somewhat similar to those of Staten Island, but they increase in height as they run to the south-east, till at the distance of four miles they are merged in the high mountains of the Coast Range. The northern shore of the bay is twenty miles distant, curving so far to the west, that the Pacific is not visible from any part of the town. Eastward, a high, rocky ridge, called the Toro Mountains, makes a prominent object in the view, and when the air is clear the Sierra de Gavilàn, beyond the Salinas plains, is distinctly visible.

During my visit the climate was mild and balmy beyond that of the same season in Italy. The temperature was that of mid-May at home, the sky for the greater part of the time without a cloud, and the winds as pleasant as if tempered exactly to the warmth of the blood. A thermometer hanging in my room only varied between 52° and 54°, which was about 10° lower than the air without. The siroccos of San Francisco are unknown in Monterey; the mornings are frequently foggy, but it always clears about ten o'clock, and remains so till near sunset. The sky at noonday is a pure, soft blue.

The harbor of Monterey is equal to any in California. The bight in which vessels anchor is entirely protected from the north-westers by Sea-Gull Point, and from the south-eastern winds by mountains in the rear. In the absence of light-houses, the dense fog renders navigation dangerous on this coast, and in spite of an entrance twenty-five miles in breath, vessels frequently run below Point Pinos, and are obliged to anchor on unsafe ground in Car-mel Bay. A road leads from the town over the hills to the ex-Mission of Carmel, situated at the head of the bay, about four miles distant. Just beyond it is Point Lobos, a promontory on the coast, famous for the number of seals and sea-lions which congregate there at low tide. A light-house on Point Pinos and another on Point Lobos would be a sufficient protection to navigation for the present, and I understand that the agents of the Government have recommended their erection.

The trade of Monterey is rapidly on the increase. During my stay of five weeks, several houses were built, half a dozen stores opened and four hotels established, one of which was kept by a Chinaman. There were at least ten arrivals and departures of vessels, exclusive of the steamers, within that time, and I was credibly informed that the Collector of the Port had, during the previous five months, received about $150,000 in duties. Provisions of all kinds are cheaper than at San Francisco, but merchandize brings higher prices. At the Washington House, kept by a former private in Col. Stevenson's regiment, I obtained excellent board at $12 per week. The building, which belongs to an Italian named Alberto Tusconi, rented for $1,200 monthly. Rents of all kinds were high, $200 a month having been paid for rooms during the session of the Convention. Here, as in San Francisco, there are many striking instances of sudden prosperity. Mr. Tusconi, whom I have just mentioned, came out five years before, as a worker in tin. He was without money, but obtained the loan of some sheets of tin, which he manufactured into cups and sold. From this beginning he had amassed a fortune of $50,000, and was rapidly adding to his gains.

There was a good deal of speculation in lots, and many of the sales, though far short of the extravagant standard of San Francisco, were still sufficiently high. A lot seventy-five feet by twenty-five, with a small frame store upon it, was sold for $5,000. A one-story house, with a lot about fifty by seventy-five feet, in

the outskirts of the town, was held at $6,000. This was about
the average rate of property, and told well for a town which a
year previous was deserted, and which, only six months before,
contained no accommodations of any kind for the traveler.

There is another circumstance which will greatly increase the
commercial importance of Monterey. The discoveries of gold
mines and placers on the Mariposa, and the knowledge that gold
exists in large quantities on the Lake Fork, King's River and the
Pitiuna—streams which empty into the Tularé Lakes on their
eastern side—will hereafter attract a large portion of the mining
population into that region. Hitherto, the hostility of the Indians
in the southern part of the Sierra Nevada, and the richness of
more convenient localities, have hindered the gold diggers from
going beyond the Mariposa. The distance of these rivers from
San Francisco, and the great expense of transporting supplies to
the new mining district, will naturally direct a portion of the im-
porting trade to some more convenient seaport. Monterey, with
the best anchorage on the coast, is one hundred and twenty-five
miles nearer the Tularé Lakes. By bridging a few arroyos, an
excellent wagon road can be made through a pass in the Coast
Range, into the valley of San Joaquin, opening a direct communication with the southern placers.

The removal of the Seat of Government to the Pueblo San
José, will not greatly affect the consequence of the place. The
advantages it has lost, are, at most, a slight increase of population, and the custom of the Legislature during its session. This
will be made up in a different way ; a large proportion of the
mining population, now in the mountains, will come down to the
coast to winter and recruit themselves after the hardships of the
Fall digging. Of these, Monterey will attract the greater portion,

as well from the salubrity of its climate as the comparative cheapness of living. The same advantages will cause it to be preferred, hereafter, as the residence of those who have retired from their golden labors. The pine-crowned slopes back of the town contain many sites of unsurpassed beauty for private residences.

With the exception of Los Angeles, Monterey contains the most pleasant society to be found in California. There is a circle of families, American and native, residing there, whose genial and refined social character makes one forget his previous ideas of California life. In spite of the lack of cultivation, except such instruction as the priests were competent to give, the native population possesses a natural refinement of manner which would grace the most polished society. They acknowledge their want of education; they tell you they grow as the trees, with the form and character that Nature gives them; but even uncultured Nature in California wears all the ripeness and maturity of older lands. I have passed many agreeable hours in the houses of the native families. The most favorite resort of Americans is that of Doña Augusta Ximeno, the sister of Don Pablo de la Guerra. This lady, whose active charity in aiding the sick and distressed has won her the enduring gratitude of many and the esteem of all, has made her house the home of every American officer who visits Monterey. With a rare liberality, she has given up a great part of it to their use, when it was impossible for them to procure quarters, and they have always been welcome guests at her table. She is a woman whose nobility of character, native vigor and activity of intellect, and above all, whose instinctive refinement and winning grace of manner, would have given her a complete supremacy in society, had her lot been cast in Europe or the United States. During the session of the Convention, her house was the favorite resort of all the leading members, both American and Californian. She was thoroughly versed in Spanish literature, as well as the works of Scott and Cooper, through translations, and I have frequently been surprised at the justness and elegance of her remarks on various authors. She possessed, moreover, all those bold and daring qualities which are so fascinating in a woman, when softened and made graceful by true feminine delicacy. She was a splendid horsewoman, and had even considerable skill in throwing the lariat.

The houses of Señor Soveranez and Señor Abrego were also much visited by Americans The former gentleman served as a Captain in Mexico during the war, but since then has subsided into a good American citizen. Señor Abrego, who is of Mexican origin, was the most industrious Californian I saw in the country. Within a few years he had amassed a large fortune, which was in no danger of decreasing. I attended an evening party at his house, which was as lively and agreeable as any occasion of the kind well could be. There was a tolerable piano in his little parlor, on which a lady from Sydney, Australia, played " Non piu mesta" with a good deal of taste. Two American gentlemen gave us a few choice flute duetts, and the entertainment closed by a quadrille and polka, in which a little son of Señor Abrego figured, to the general admiration.

The old and tranquil look of Monterey, before the discovery of the placers, must have seemed remarkable to visitors from the Atlantic side of the Continent. The serene beauty of the climate and soft, vaporous atmosphere, have nothing in common with one's ideas of a new, scarce-colonized coast ; the animals, even, are those of the old, civilized countries of Europe. Flocks of ravens croak from the tiled roofs, and cluster on the long adobe walls ; magpies chatter in the clumps of gnarled oak on the hills, and as you pass through the forest, hares start up from their coverts under the bearded pines. The quantity of blackbirds about the place is astonishing ; in the mornings they wheel in squadrons about every house-top, and fill the air with their twitter.

But for the interest occasioned by the Convention, and the social impulse given to Monterey by the presence of its members, the town would hardly have furnished an incident marked enough to be remembered. Occasionally there was an arrival at the anchorage—generally from San Francisco, San Diego or Australia— which furnished talk for a day or two. Then some resident would give a fandango, which the whole town attended, or the Alcalde would decree a general *horn-burning*. This was nothing less than the collecting of all the horns and heads of slaughtered animals, scattered about the streets, into large piles, which burned through half the night, filling the air with a most unpleasant odor. When the atmosphere happened to be a little misty, the red light of these fires was thrown far up along the hills.

I learned some very interesting facts during my stay, relative to the products of California. Wisconsin has always boasted of raising the largest crops of talking humanity, but she will have to yield the palm to the new Pacific State, where the increase of population is entirely without precedent. A native was pointed out to me one day as the father of thirty-six children, twenty of whom were the product of his first marriage, and sixteen of his last. Mr. Hartnell, the Government translator, has a family of twenty-one children. Señor Abrego, who had been married twelve years, already counted as many heirs. Several other couples in the place had from twelve to eighteen ; and the former number, I was told, is the usual size of a family in California. Whether or not this remarkable fecundity is attributable to the climate, I am unable to tell.

The Californians, as a race, are vastly superior to the Mexicans. They have larger frames, stronger muscle, and a fresh, ruddy complexion, entirely different from the sallow skins of the tierra caliente or the swarthy features of those Bedouins of the West, the Sonorians. The families of pure Castilian blood resemble in features and build, the descendants of the Valencians in Chili and Mexico, whose original physical superiority over the natives of the other provinces of Spain, has not been obliterated by two hundred years of transplanting. Señor Soveranez informed me that the Californian soldiers, on account of this physical distinction, were nicknamed " Americanos" by the Mexicans. They have no national feeling in common with the latter, and will never forgive the cowardly deportment of the Sonorians toward them, during the recent war. Their superior valor, as soldiers, was amply experienced by our own troops, at the battle of San Pasquale.

I do not believe, however, that the majority of the native population rejoices at the national change which has come over the country. On the contrary, there is much jealousy and bitter feeling among the uneducated classes. The vast tides of emigration from the Atlantic States thrice outnumbered them in a single year, and consequently placed them forever in a hopeless minority. They witnessed the immediate extinction of their own political importance, and the introduction of a new language, new customs, and new laws. It is not strange that many of them should be opposed to us at heart, even while growing wealthy and prosperous under the marvellous change which has been wrought by the enterprise of our citizens. Nevertheless, we have many warm friends, and the United States many faithful subjects, among them. The intelligent and influential faction which aided us during the war, is still faithful, and many who were previously discontented, are now loudest in their rejoicing. Our authorities have acted toward them with constant and impartial kindness. By pursuing a similar course, the future government of the State will soon obliterate the differences of race and condition, and all will then be equally Californian and American citizens.

CHAPTER XV.

In some respects, the political history of California for the year 1849, is without a parallel in the annals of any nation. The events are too recent for us to see them in the clear, defined outlines they will exhibit to posterity; we can only describe them as they occurred, throwing the strongest light on those points which now appear most prominent.

The discovery of the Gold Region of California occurred in little more than a month after the Treaty of Guadalupe Hidalgo, by which the country was ceded to the United States. Congress having adjourned without making provision for any kind of civil organization, the Military Government established during the war continued in force, in conjunction with the local laws in force under the Mexican rule—a most incongruous state of things, which gave rise to innumerable embarrassments. Meanwhile, the results of the gold discovery produced a complete revolution in society, upturning all branches of trade, industry or office, and for a time completely annulling the Government. Mexico and the South American republics sent their thousands of adventurers into the country like a flood, far outnumbering the native population. During the winter of 1848-9, the state of affairs was most critical;

the American and foreign miners were embittered against each other ; the authorities were without power to enforce their orders, and there seemed no check to restrain the free exercise of all lawless passions. There *was* a check, however—the steady integrity and inborn capacity for creating and upholding Law, of a portion of the old American settlers and emigrants newly arrived. A single spark of Order will in time irradiate and warm into shape a world of disorderly influences.

In the neglect of Congress to provide for the establishment of a Territorial Government, it was at first suggested that the People should provisionally organize such a Government among themselves. Various proposals were made, but before any decisive action was had on the subject, another and more appropriate form was given to the movement, chiefly through the labor and influence of a few individuals, who were countenanced by the existing authorities. This was, to call a Convention for the purpose of drafting a State Constitution, that California might at once be admitted into the Union, without passing through the usual Territorial stage—leaping with one bound, as it were, from a state of semi-civilization to be the Thirty-First Sovereign Republic of the American Confederacy. The vast influx of emigration had already increased the population beyond the required number, and the unparalleled speed with which Labor and Commerce were advancing warranted such a course, no less than the important natural resources of the country itself. The result of this movement was a proclamation from Gov. Riley, recommending that an election of Delegates to form such a Convention be held on the first of August, 1849.

Gen. Riley, the Civil Governor appointed by the United States, Gen. Smith, and Mr. T. Butler King, during a tour through the mining districts in the early part of summer, took every occasion to interest the people in the subject, and stimulate them to hold preparatory meetings. The possibility of calling together and keeping together a body of men, many of whom must necessarily be deeply involved in business and speculation, was at first strongly doubted. In fact, in some of the districts named in the proclamation, scarcely any move was made till a few days before the day of election. It was only necessary, however, to kindle the flame ; the intelligence and liberal public spirit existing throughout the country, kept it alive, and the election passed over with complete success. In one or two instances it was not held on the day appointed, but the Convention nevertheless admitted the delegates elected in such cases.

Party politics had but a small part to play in the choice of candidates. In the San Francisco and Sacramento districts there might have been some influences of this kind afloat, and other districts undoubtedly sent members to advocate some particular local interest. But, taken as a body, the delegates did honor to California, and would not suffer by comparison with any first State Convention ever held in our Republic. I may add, also, that a perfect harmony of feeling existed between the citizens of both races. The proportion of native Californian members to the American was about equal to that of the population. Some of the former received nearly the entire American vote—Gen. Vallejo at Sonoma, Antonio Pico at San José, and Miguel de Pedrorena at San Diego, for instance.

The elections were all over, at the time of my arrival in California, and the 1st of September had been appointed as the day on which the Convention should meet. It was my intention to have been present at that time, but I did not succeed in reaching Monterey until the 19th of the month. The Convention was not regularly organized until the 4th, when Dr. Robert Semple, of the Sonoma District, was chosen President and conducted to his seat by Capt. Sutter and Gen. Vallejo. Capt. William G. Marcy, of the New-York Volunteer Regiment, was elected Secretary, after which the various post of Clerks, Assistant Secretaries, Translators, Doorkeeper, Sergeant-at-Arms, etc., were filled. The day after their complete organization, the officers and members of the Convention were sworn to support the Constitution of the United States. The members from the Southern Districts were instructed to vote in favor of a Territorial form of Government, but expressed their willingness to abide the decision of the Convention. An invitation was extended to the Clergy of Monterey to open the meeting with prayer, and that office was thenceforth performed on alternate days by Padre Ramirez and Rev. S. H. Willey.

The building in which the Convention met was probably the only one in California suited to the purpose. It is a handsome, two-story edifice of yellow sandstone, situated on a gentle slope, above the town. It is named "Colton Hall," on account of its having been built by Don Walter Colton, former Alcalde of Monterey, from the proceeds of a sale of city lots. The stone of which it is built is found in abundance near Monterey; it is of a fine, mellow color, easily cut, and will last for centuries in that mild climate. The upper story, in which the Convention sat, formed a single hall about sixty feet in length by twenty-five in breadth. A railing, running across the middle, divided the members from the spectators. The former were seated at four long tables, the President occupying a rostrum at the further end, over which were suspended two American flags and an extraordinary picture of Washington, evidently the work of a native artist. The appearance of the whole body was exceedingly dignified and intellectual, and parliamentary decorum was strictly observed. A door in the centre of the hall opened on a square balcony, supported by four pillars, where some of the members, weary with debate, came frequently to enjoy the mild September afternoon, whose hues lay so softly on the blue waters of the bay.

The Declaration of Rights, which was the first subject before the Convention, occasioned little discussion. Its sections being general in their character and of a liberal republican cast, were nearly all adopted by a nearly unanimous vote. The clause prohibiting Slavery was met by no word of dissent; it was the universal sentiment of the Convention. It is unnecessary to recapitulate here the various provisions of the Constitution; it will be enough to say that they combined, with few exceptions, the most enlightened features of the Constitutions of older States. The election of Judges by the people—the rights of married women to property—the establishment of a liberal system of education—and other reforms of late introduced into the State Governments east of the Rocky Mountains, were all transplanted to the new soil of the Pacific Coast.

The adoption of a system of pay for the officers and members of the Convention, occasioned some discussion. The Californian members and a few of the Americans patriotically demanded that the Convention should work for nothing, the glory being sufficient. The majority overruled this, and finally decided that the members should receive $16 per day, the President $25, the Secretary and Interpreter $28, the Clerks $23 and $18, the Chaplain $16, the Sergeant-at-Arms $22 and the Doorkeeper $12. The expenses of the Convention were paid out of the " Civil Fund," an accumulation of the duties received at the ports. The funds were principally silver, and at the close of their labors it was amusing to see the members carrying their pay about town tied up in handkerchiefs or slung in bags over their shoulders. The little Irish boy, who acted as page, was nearly pressed down by the weight of his wages.

One of the first exciting questions was a clause which had been crammed through the Convention on its first reading, prohibiting the entrance of free people of color into the state. Its originator was an Oregon man, more accustomed to and better fitted for squatter life than the dignity of legislation. The members, by the time it was brought up for second reading, had thought more seriously upon the question, and the clause was rejected by a large majority: several attempts to introduce it in a modified form also signally failed.

It was a matter of regret that the question of suffrage could not have been settled in an equitable and satisfactory manner. The article first adopted by the Convention, excluding Indians and Negroes, with their descendants, from the privilege of voting, was, indeed, modified by a proviso offered by Mr. de la Guerra, which gave the Legislature the power of admitting Indians or the descendants of Indians, by a two-thirds concurrent vote, to the right of suffrage. This was agreed to by many merely for the purpose of settling the question for the present; but the native members will not be content to let it rest. Many of the most wealthy and respectable families in California have Indian blood in their veins, and even a member of the Convention, Dominguez, would be excluded from voting under this very clause.

The Articles of the Constitution relating to the Executive, Judicial and Legislative Departments occupied several days, but the debates were dry and uninteresting. A great deal of talk was expended to no purpose, several of the members having the same

morbid ambition in this respect, as may be found in our legislative assemblies on this side of the mountains. A member from
Sacramento severely tried the patience of the Convention by his
long harangues; another was clamorous, not for his own rights but
those of his constituents, although the latter were suspected of
being citizens of Oregon. The Chair occasionally made a bung-
ling decision, whereupon two of the members, who had previously
served in State Assemblies, would aver that in the whole course
of their legislative experience they had never heard of such a
thing. Now and then a scene occurred, which was amusing
enough. A section being before the Convention, declaring that
every citizen arrested for a criminal offence should be tried by a
jury of his peers, a member, unfamiliar with such technical terms,
moved to strike out the word " peers." " I don't like that word
' peers,' " said he ; " it a'int republican ; I'd like to know what
we want with *peers* in this country—we're not a monarchy, and
we've got no House of Parliament. I vote for no such law."

The boundary question, however, which came up towards the
close of the Convention, assumed a character of real interest and
importance. The great point of dispute on this question was the
eastern limit of the State, the Pacific being the natural boundary
on the West, the meridian of 42° on the North, and the Mexican line, run in conformity with the treaty of Queretaro, on
the South. Mr. Hastings, a member from Sacramento, moved
that the eastern boundary, beginning at the parallel of 42°, should
follow the meridian of 118° W. long. to 38° N. thence running
direct to the intersection of the Colorado with 114° W. following
that river to the Mexican line. This was proposed late on Monday night, and hurried through by a bare majority. Messrs.
Gwin and Halleck, of the Boundary Committee, with all the Cali-

fornian members, and some others, opposed this proposition, claiming that the original Spanish boundary, extending to the line of New Mexico, should be adopted. With some difficulty a reconsideration of the vote was obtained, and the House adjourned without settling the question.

The discussion commenced in earnest the next morning. The members were all present, and as the parties were nearly balanced the contest was very animated and excited. It assumed, in fact, more of a party character than any which had previously come up. The grounds taken by the party desiring the whole territory were that the Convention had no right to assume another boundary than that originally belonging to California; that the measure would extend the advantages and protecting power of law over a vast inland territory, which would otherwise remain destitute of such protection for many years to come; that, finally, it would settle the question of Slavery for a much greater extent of territory, and in a quiet and peaceful manner. The opposite party—that which advocates the Sierra Nevada as the boundary line—contended that the Constitution had no right to include the Mormon settlers in the Great Salt Lake country in a State, whose Constitution they had no share in forming, and that nearly the whole of the country east of the Sierra Nevada was little better than a desert.

After a hot discussion, which lasted the whole day, the vote was reversed, and the report of the Boundary Committee (including all the Territory as far as New Mexico) adopted. The opposition party, defeated after they were sure of success, showed their chagrin rather noisily. At the announcement of the vote, a dozen members jumped up, speaking and shouting in the most confused and disorderly manner. Some rushed out of the room;

7*

others moved an adjournment ; others again protested they would
sign no Constitution, embodying such a provision.   In the midst
of this tumult the House adjourned.   The defeated party were
active throughout, and procured a second reconsideration.   Major
Hill, delegate from San Diego, then proposed the following boundary : a line starting from the Mexican Boundary and following
the course of the Colorado to lat. 35° N., thence due north to the
Oregon Boundary.   Such a line, according to the opinion of both
Capt. Sutter and Gen. Vallejo, was the limit set by the Mexican
Government to the civil jurisdiction of California.   It divides the
Great Central Basin about two-thirds of the distance between the
Sierra Nevada and the Great Salt Lake.   This proposition was
adopted, but fell through on second reading, when the boundary
which had first passed was reädopted by a large vote.   When it
came to be designated on the map, most of the members were
better satisfied than they had anticipated.   They had a State with
eight hundred miles of sea-coast and an average of two hundred
and fifty miles in breadth, including both sides of the Sierra Nevada and some of the best rivers of the Great Basin.   As to the
question of Slavery, it will never occasion much trouble.   The
whole Central Region, extending to the Sierra Madre of New
Mexico, will never sustain a slave population.   The greater part
of it resembles in climate and general features the mountain
steppes of Tartary, and is better adapted for grazing than agriculture.   It will never be settled so long as an acre of the rich loam
of Oregon or the warm wheat-plains of California is left untenanted.

One of the subjects that came up about this time was the de-
sign of a Great Seal for the State.   There were plenty of ideas in
the heads of the members, but few draughtsmen, and of the eight

or ten designs presented, some were ludicrous enough. The choice finally fell upon one drawn by Major Garnett, which was, in reality, the best offered. The principal figure is Minerva, with her spear and Gorgon shield, typical of the manner in which California was born, full-grown, into the Confederacy. At her feet crouches a grizzly bear, certainly no very appropriate supporter for the Gorgon shield. The wheat-sheaf and vine before him illustrate the principal agricultural products of the country, and are in good keeping—for Ceres sat beside Minerva in the councils of the gods. Near at hand is a miner with his implements, in the distance the Bay of San Francisco, and still further the Sierra Nevada, over which appears the single word : " EUREKA !"

The discussion on the subject was most amusing. None of the designs seemed at first to tally with the taste of the Convention, as each district was anxious to be particularly represented. The Sacramento members wanted the gold mines ; the San Francisco members wanted the harbor and shipping ; the Sonoma members thought no seal could be lawful without some reminder of their noted " bear flag ;" while the Los Angeles and San Diego members were clamorous for the rights of their vines, olives and wild horses —so that, no doubt, the seal they chose was the most satisfactory to all. The sum of $1,000 was voted to Mr. Lyon, one of the Secretaries, for the purpose of having it engraved. The Convention also voted the sum of $10,000 to Mr. J. Ross Browne, its reporter, on his contracting to furnish one thousand printed copies of the entire proceedings in English and three hundred in Spanish. This sum also included the remuneration for his labors as a stenographer.

After discussing various plans for meeting the expenses of the

State, at the outset, an ordinance was adopted, (subject to the action of Congress,) the substance of which was as follows :

1. One section out of every quarter township of the public lands shall be granted to the State for the use of the schools. 2. Seventy-two sections of unappropriated land within the State shall be granted to the State for the establishment and support of a University. 3. Four sections, selected under direction of the Legislature, shall be granted for the use of the State in establishing a Seat of Government and erecting buildings. 4. Five hundred thousand acres of public lands, in addition to the same amount granted to new States, shall be granted for the purpose of defraying the expenses of the State Government. And five per cent of the proceeds of the sale of public lands, after deducting expenses, shall be given for the encouragement of learning. 5. All salt springs, with the land adjoining, shall be granted to the use of the State.

It may probably be thought, on reading these various provisions for the filling of the State Treasury, that the appetite for gold must surely grow by what it feeds on. California, nevertheless, had some reason for making so many exacting demands. The expenses of the Government, at the start, will necessarily be enormous ; and the price of labor so far exceeds the value of real estate, that the ordinary tax on property would scarcely be a drop in the bucket. The cost of erecting buildings and supporting the various branches of government will greatly surpass that to which any state has ever been subjected. In paying the expenses of the Convention from the Civil Fund, Gov. Riley in many instances took upon himself weighty responsibilities ; but the circumstances under which he acted were entirely without precedent. His course was marked throughout by great prudence and good sense.

Towards the close of the Convention, those of the members who aspired to still further honor, commenced caucusing and the canvassing of influence for the coming election. Several announced themselves as candidates for various offices, and in spite of vehement disclaimers to the contrary the lines of old parties were secretly drawn. Nevertheless, it is impossible at present to pronounce correctly on the political character of the State; it will take some time for the native Californians to be drilled into the new harness, and I suspect they will frequently hold the balance of power.

One of the most intelligent and influential of the Californians is Gen. Mariano Guadalupe Vallejo, whom I had the pleasure of meeting several times during my stay in Monterey. As Military Commandant, during the Governorship of Alvarado, he exercised almost supreme sway over the country. He is a man of forty-five years of age, tall and of a commanding presence; his head is large, forehead high and ample, and eyes dark, with a grave, dignified expression. He is better acquainted with our institutions and laws than any other native Californian.

Among the other notable members were Covarrubias, formerly Secretary of Government, and José Antonio Carrillo, the right-hand man of Pio Pico. The latter is upward of fifty-five years of age—a small man with frizzled hair and beard, gray eyes, and a face strongly expressive of shrewdness and mistrust. I saw him, one day, dining at a restaurant with Gen. Castro—the redoubtable leader of the Californian troops, in Upper and Lower California. Castro is a man of medium height, but stoutly and strongly made. He has a very handsome face; his eyes are large and dark, and his mouth is shaded by moustaches with the gloss and color of a raven's wing, meeting on each side with his whis-

kers.   He wore the sombrero, jacket and calzoneros of the country.   His temperament, as I thought, seemed gloomy and satur-
nine, and I was gravely informed by a Californian who sat opposite me, that he meditated the reconquest of the country !

Capt. Sutter's appearance and manners quite agreed with my
preconceived ideas of him.   He is still the hale, blue-eyed, jovial
German—short and stout of stature, with broad forehead, head
bald to the crown, and altogether a ruddy, good-humored expression of countenance.   He is a man of good intellect, excellent
common sense and amiable qualities of heart.   A little more
activity and enterprise might have made him the first man in
California, in point of wealth and influence.

CHAPTER XVI.

THE day and night immediately preceding the dissolution of the Convention far exceeded in interest all the former period of its existence. I know not how I can better describe the closing scenes than by the account which I penned on the spot, at the time :

The Convention yesterday (October 12) gave token of bringing its labors to a close ; the morning session was short and devoted only to the passing of various miscellaneous provisions, after which an adjournment was made until this morning, on account of the Ball given by the Convention to the citizens of Monterey. The members, by a contribution of $25 each, raised the sum of $1,100 to provide for the entertainment, which was got up in return for that given by the citizens about four weeks since.

The Hall was cleared of the forum and tables and decorated with young pines from the forest. At each end were the American colors, tastefully disposed across the boughs. Three chandeliers, neither of bronze nor cut-glass, but neat and brilliant withal, poured their light on the festivities. At eight o'clock—the fashionable ball-hour in Monterey—the guests began to assemble, and in an hour afterward the Hall was crowded with nearly all the

Californian and American residents. There were sixty or seventy
ladies present, and an equal number of gentlemen, in addition to
the members of the Convention. The dark-eyed daughters of
Monterey, Los Angeles and Santa Barbara mingled in pleasing
contrast with the fairer bloom of the trans-Nevadian belles. The
variety of feature and complexion was fully equalled by the variety
of dress. In the whirl of the waltz, a plain, dark, nun-like robe
would be followed by one of pink satin and gauze ; next, perhaps,
a bodice of scarlet velvet with gold buttons, and then a rich
figured brocade, such as one sees on the stately dames of Titian.

The dresses of the gentlemen showed considerable variety, but
were much less picturesque. A complete ball-dress was a happiness attained only by the fortunate few. White kids could not be
had in Monterey for love or money, and as much as $50 was paid
by one gentleman for a pair of patent-leather boots. Scarcely a
single dress that was seen belonged entirely to its wearer, and I
thought, if the clothes had power to leap severally back to their
respective owners, some persons would have been in a state of
utter destitution. For my part, I was indebted for pantaloons and
vest to obliging friends. The only specimen of the former article
which I could get, belonged to an officer whose weight was considerably more than two hundred, but I managed to accommodate
them to my proportions by a liberal use of pins, notwithstanding
the difference of size. Thus equipped, with a buff military vest,
and worsted gaiters with very square toes, I took my way to the
Hall in company with Major Smith and his brother.

The appearance of the company, nevertheless, was genteel and
respectable, and perhaps the genial, unrestrained social spirit that
possessed all present would have been less had there been more
uniformity of costume. Gen. Riley was there in full uniform,

with the yellow sash he won at Contreras ; Majors Canby, Hill and
Smith, Captains Burton and Kane, and the other officers stationed
in Monterey, accompanying him. In one group might be seen
Capt. Sutter's soldierly moustache and clear blue eye ; in another,
the erect figure and quiet, dignified bearing of Gen. Vallejo. Don
Pablo de la Guerra, with his handsome, aristocratic features, was
the floor manager, and gallantly discharged his office. Conspicuous
among the native members were Don Miguel de Pedrorena and
Jacinto Rodriguez, both polished gentlemen and deservedly popular. Dominguez, the Indian member, took no part in the dance,
but evidently enjoyed the scene as much as any one present. The
most interesting figure to me was that of Padre Ramirez, who, in
his clerical cassock, looked on until a late hour. If the strongest
advocate of priestly gravity and decorum had been present, he
could not have found in his heart to grudge the good old padre the
pleasure that beamed upon his honest countenance.

The band consisted of two violins and two guitars, whose music
made up in spirit what it lacked in skill. They played, as it
seemed to me, but three pieces alternately, for waltz, contra-dance
and quadrille. The latter dance was evidently an unfamiliar one,
for once or twice the music ceased in the middle of a figure. Each
tune ended with a funny little squeak, something like the whistle
of the octave flute in *Robert le Diable*. The players, however,
worked incessantly, and deserved good wages for their performance.
The etiquette of the dance was marked by that grave, stately
courtesy, which has been handed down from the old Spanish times.
The gentlemen invariably gave the ladies their hands to lead them
to their places on the floor ; in the pauses of the dance both parties
stood motionless side by side, and at its conclusion the lady was
bravely led back to her seat.

At twelve o'clock supper was announced. The Court-Room in the lower story had been fitted up for this purpose, and, as it was not large enough to admit all the guests, the ladies were first conducted thither and waited upon by a select committee. The refreshments consisted of turkey, roast pig, beef, tongue and *patés*, with wines and liquors of various sorts, and coffee. A large supply had been provided, but after everybody was served, there was not much remaining. The ladies began to leave about two o'clock, but when I came away, an hour later, the dance was still going on with spirit.

The members met this morning at the usual hour, to perform the last duty that remained to them—that of signing the Constitution. They were all in the happiest humor, and the morning was so bright and balmy that no one seemed disposed to call an organization. Mr. Semple was sick, and Mr. Steuart, of San Francisco, therefore called the meeting to order by moving Capt. Sutter's appointment in his place. The Chair was taken by the old pioneer, and the members took their seats around the sides of the hall, which still retained the pine-trees and banners, left from last night's decorations. The windows and doors were open, and a delightful breeze came in from the Bay, whose blue waters sparkled in the distance. The view from the balcony in front was bright and inspiring. The town below—the shipping in the harbor—the pine-covered hills behind—were mellowed by the blue October haze, but there was no cloud in the sky, and I could plainly see, on the northern horizon, the mountains of Santa Cruz and the Sierra de Gavilan.

After the minutes had been read, the Committee appointed to draw up an Address to the People of California was called upon to report, and Mr. Steuart, Chairman, read the Address. Its tone and sentiment met with universal approval, and it was adopted without a dissenting voice. A resolution was then offered to pay Lieut. Hamilton, who is now engaged in engrossing the Constitution upon parchment, the sum of $500 for his labor. This magnificent price, probably the highest ever paid for a similar service, is on a par with all things else in California. As this was their last session, the members were not disposed to find fault with it, especially when it was stated by one of them that Lieut. Hamilton had written day and night to have it ready, and was still working upon it, though with a lame and swollen hand. The sheet for the signers' names was ready, and the Convention decided to adjourn for half an hour and then meet for the purpose of signing.

I amused myself during the interval by walking about the town. Everybody knew that the Convention was about closing, and it was generally understood that Capt. Burton had loaded the guns at the fort, and would fire a salute of thirty-one guns at the proper moment. The citizens, therefore, as well as the members, were in an excited mood. Monterey never before looked so bright, so happy, so full of pleasant expectation.

About one o'clock the Convention met again ; few of the members, indeed, had left the hall. Mr. Semple, although in feeble health, called them to order, and, after having voted Gen. Riley a salary of $10,000, and Mr. Halleck, Secretary of State, $6,000 a year, from the commencement of their respective offices, they proceeded to affix their names to the completed Constitution. At this moment a signal was given ; the American colors ran up the flag-staff in front of the Government buildings, and streamed out on the air. A second afterward the first gun boomed from the fort, and its stirring echoes came back from one hill after another, till they were lost in the distance.

All the native enthusiasm of Capt. Sutter's Swiss blood was aroused; he was the old soldier again. He sprang from his seat, and, waving his hand around his head, as if swinging a sword, exclaimed: "Gentlemen, this is the happiest day of my life. It makes me glad to hear those cannon : they remind me of the time when I was a soldier. Yes, I am glad to hear them—this is a great day for California!" Then, recollecting himself, he sat down, the tears streaming from his eyes. The members with one accord, gave three tumultuous cheers, which were heard from one end of the town to the other. As the signing went on, gun followed gun from the fort, the echoes reverberating grandly around the bay, till finally, as the loud ring of the *thirty-first* was heard, there was a shout : "That's for California!" and every one joined in giving three times three for the new star added to our Confederation.

There was one handsome act I must not omit to mention. The Captain of the English bark Volunteer, of Sidney, Australia, lying in the harbor, sent on shore in the morning for an American flag. When the first gun was heard, a line of colors ran fluttering up to the spars, the stars and stripes flying triumphantly from the main-top. The compliment was the more marked, as some of the American vessels neglected to give any token of recognition to the event of the day.

The Constitution having been signed and the Convention dissolved, the members proceeded in a body to the house of Gen. Riley. The visit was evidently unexpected by the old veteran. When he made his appearance Captain Sutter stepped forward and having shaken him by the hand, drew himself into an erect attitude, raised one hand to his breast as if he were making a report to his commanding officer on the field of battle, and addressed him as follows :

"GENERAL : I have been appointed by the Delegates, elected by the people of California to form a Constitution, to address you in their names and in behalf of the whole people of California, and express the thanks of the Convention for the aid and cooperation they have received from you in the discharge of the responsible duty of creating a State Government. And, sir, the Convention, as you will perceive from the official records, duly appreciates the great and important services you have rendered to our common country, and especially to the people of California, and entertains the confident belief that you will receive from the whole of the people of the United States, when you retire from your official duties here, that verdict so grateful to the heart of the patriot : ' Well done, thou good and faithful servant.' "

Gen. Riley was visibly affected by this mark of respect, no less appropriate than well deserved on his part. The tears in his eyes and the plain, blunt sincerity of his voice and manner, went to the heart of every one present. " Gentlemen :" he said, " I never made a speech in my life. I am a soldier—but I can *feel ;* and I do feel deeply the honor you have this day conferred upon me. Gentlemen, this is a prouder day to me than that on which my soldiers cheered me on the field of Contreras. I thank you all from my heart. I am satisfied now that the people have done right in selecting Delegates to frame a Constitution. They have chosen a body of men upon whom our country may look with pride : you have framed a Constitution worthy of California. And I have no fear for California while her people choose their Representatives so wisely. Gentlemen, I congratulate you upon the successful conclusion of your arduous labors ; and I wish you all happiness and prosperity."

The General was here interrupted with three hearty cheers

which the members gave him, as Governor of California, followed by three more, " as a gallant soldier, and worthy of his country's glory." He then concluded in the following words : " I have but one thing to add, gentlemen, and that is, that my success in the affairs of California is mainly owing to the efficient aid rendered me by Capt. Halleck, the Secretary of State. He has stood by me in all emergencies. To him I have always appealed when at a loss myself; and he has never failed me."

This recognition of Capt. Halleck's talents and the signal service he has rendered to our authorities here, since the conquest, was peculiarly just and appropriate. It was so felt by the members, and they responded with equal warmth of feeling by giving three enthusiastic cheers for the Secretary of State. They then took their leave, many of them being anxious to start this afternoon for their various places of residence. All were in a happy and satisfied mood, and none less so than the native members. Pedrorena declared that this was the most fortunate day in the history of California. Even Carillo, in the beginning one of our most zealous opponents, displayed a genuine zeal for the Constitution, which he helped to frame under the laws of our Republic.

Thus closes the Convention ; and I cannot help saying, with Capt. Sutter, that the day which sees laid the broad and liberal foundation of a free and independent State on the shores of the Pacific, is a great day for California. As an American, I feel proud and happy—proud, that the Empire of the West, the commerce of the great Pacific, the new highway to the Indies, forming the last link in that belt of civilized enterprise which now clasps the world, has been established under my country's flag ; and happy, that in all the extent of California, from the glittering snows of the Shaste to the burning deserts of the Colorado, no slave shall ever lift his arm to make the freedom of that flag a mockery.

The members of the Convention may have made some blunders in the course of their deliberations; there may be some objectionable clauses in the Constitution they have framed. But where was there ever a body convened, under such peculiar circumstances?—where was ever such harmony evolved out of so wonderful, so dangerous, so magnificent a chaos? The elements of which the Convention was composed were no less various, and in some respects antagonistic, than those combined in the mining population. The questions they had to settle were often perplexing, from the remarkable position of the country and the absence of all precedent. Besides, many of them were men unused to legislation. Some had for years past known no other life than that of the camp; others had nearly forgotten all law in the wild life of the mountains; others again were familiar only with that practiced under the rule of a different race. Yet the courtesies of debate have never been wantonly violated, and the result of every conflict of opinion has been a quiet acquiescence on the part of the minority. Now, at the conclusion, the only feeling is that of general joy and congratulation.

Thus, we have another splendid example of the ease and security with which people can be educated to govern themselves. From that chaos whence, under the rule of a despotism like the Austrian, would spring the most frightful excesses of anarchy and crime, a population of freemen peacefully and quietly develops the highest form of civil order—the broadest extent of liberty and security. Governments, bad and corrupt as many of them are, and imperfect as they all must necessarily be, nevertheless at times exhibit scenes of true moral sublimity. What I

have to-day witnessed has so impressed me ; and were I a believer in omens, I would augur from the tranquil beauty of this
evening—from the clear sky and the lovely sunset hues on the
waters of the bay—more than all, from the joyous expression of
every face I see—a glorious and prosperous career for the STAT
OF CALIFORNIA !

CHAPTER XVII.

SHORE AND FOREST.

No one can be in Monterey a single night, without being startled and awed by the deep, solemn crashes of the surf as it breaks along the shore. There is no continuous roar of the plunging waves, as we hear on the Atlantic seaboard; the slow, regular swells—quiet pulsations of the great Pacific's heart—roll inward in unbroken lines and fall with single grand crashes, with intervals of dead silence between. They may be heard through the day, if one listens, like a solemn undertone to all the shallow noises of the town, but at midnight, when all else is still, those successive shocks fall upon the ear with a sensation of inexpressible solemnity. All the air, from the pine forests to the sea, is filled with a light tremor and the intermitting beats of sound are strong enough to jar a delicate ear. Their constant repetition at last produces a feeling something like terror. A spirit worn and weakened by some scathing sorrow could scarcely bear the reverberation.

When there has been a gale outside, and a morning of dazzling clearness succeeds a night of fog and cold wind, the swells are loudest and most magnificent. Then their lines of foam are flung upward like a snowy fringe along the dark-blue hem of the sea, and a light, glittering mist constantly rises from the hollow curve of the shore. One quiet Sunday afternoon, when the uproar was such as to be almost felt in the solid earth, I walked out along the sand till I had passed the anchorage and could look on the open Pacific. The surface of the bay was comparatively calm ; but within a few hundred yards of the shore it upheaved with a slow, majestic movement, forming a single line more than a mile in length, which, as it advanced, presented a perpendicular front of clear green water, twelve feet in height. There was a gradual curving-in of this emerald wall—a moment's waver—and the whole mass fell forward with a thundering crash, hurling the shattered spray thirty feet into the air. A second rebound followed ; and the boiling, seething waters raced far up the sand with a sharp, trampling, metallic sound, like the jangling of a thousand bars of iron. I sat down on a pine log, above the highest wave-mark, and watched this sublime phenomenon for a long time. The sand-hills behind me confined and redoubled the sound, prolonging it from crash to crash, so that the ear was constantly filled with it. Once, a tremendous swell came in close on the heels of one that had just broken, and the two uniting, made one wave, which shot far beyond the water-line and buried me above the knee. As far as I could see, the shore was white with the subsiding deluge. It was a fine illustration of the magnificent language of Scripture : " He maketh the deep to boil like a pot ; he maketh the sea like a pot of ointment ; one would think the deep to be hoary."

The pine forest behind the town encloses in its depths many spots of remarkable loneliness and beauty. The forest itself had a peculiar charm for me, and scarcely a day passed without my exploring some part of its solemn region. The old, rugged trees, blackened with many fires, are thickly bearded with long gray moss, which gives out a hoarse, dull sound as the sea-wind sweeps through them. The promontory of Monterey is entirely covered with them, excepting only the little glens, or cañadas, which wind their way between the interlocking bases of the hills. Here, the grass is thick and luxuriant through the whole year ; the pines shut out all sight but the mild, stainless heaven above their tops ; the air is fragrant with the bay and laurel, and the light tread of a deer or whirr of a partridge, at intervals, alone breaks the delicious solitude. The far roar of the surf, stealing up through the avenues of the forest, is softened to a murmur by the time it reaches these secluded places. No more lovely hermitages for thought or the pluming of callow fancies, can be found among the pine-bowers of the Villa Borghese.

After climbing all of the lesser heights, and barking my hand on the rough bark of a branchless pine, in the endeavor to climb it for a look-out, I started one afternoon on an expedition to the top of a bald summit among the hills to the southward. It was apparently near at hand and easy of access, but after I had walked several miles, I saw, from the top of a ridge, that a deep valley— a chasm, almost—was to be passed before I could reach even its foot. The side seemed almost precipitous and the loose stones slid under my feet ; but by hanging to the low limbs of trees, I succeeded in getting to the bottom. The bed of the valley, not more than a hundred yards in breadth, was one matted mass of wild vines, briars and thorny shrubs. I trusted to the strength of my corduroys for defence against them, and to a good horse-pistol should I stumble on some wild beast's lair—and plunged in. At the first step I sank above my head, without touching the bottom. The briars were woven so closely that it was impossible to press through or creep under them ; I could only flounder along, draw-

ing myself up by the greatest exertions, to sink into another gulf
a few inches in advance. My hands and clothes were torn, my
mouth filled with dry and bitter pollen from the withered vines
that brushed my face, and it was only after an hour's labor that I
reached the other side, completely exhausted.

I climbed the opposite hill, thinking my object nearly attained,
when lo ! another, a deeper and rougher chasm still intervened.
The sun was already down and I gave up the journey. From the
end of the ridge I had attained, I overlooked all the circumference
of the bay. Behind the white glimmer of the town the forest rose
with a gradual sweep, while before me lay a wide extent of undu-
lating hills, rolling off to the Salinas Plains, which appeared beyond—

> " Dim tracts and vast, robed in the lustrous gloom
>   Of leaden-colored even, and fiery hills
>   Mingling their flames with twilight, on the verge
>   Of the remote horizon."

Taking another road, I wandered home in the dusk, not without
some chance of losing myself among the frequent hollows and
patches of chapparal. I lay in wait half an hour for two deer, a
glimpse of whom I had caught in the woods, but as I had not the
keen sight of a Kentucky hunter, I was obliged to go home without them.

The opposite shore of the promontory contains many striking
and picturesque points, to which the Montereyans often resort on
parties of pleasure. One of the most remarkable of these is *Punta
de los Cipreses*, or Cypress Point, which I visited several times.
One of my most memorable days, while at Monterey, was spent
there in company with my friend, Ross Browne. We started
early in the morning, carrying with us a loaf of bread and a piece

of raw beef, as materials for dinner. After threading the mazes of the forest for several miles, we came upon the bleak sand-hills piled like snow-drifts between the forest and the beach. The bare tongue of land which jutted out beyond them was covered with a carpet of maritime plants, among which I noticed one with a beautiful star-like flower : another, with succulent, wax-like leaves, bears a fruit which is greatly relished by the Californians.

The extremity of the Point is a mass of gray rock, worn by the surf into fantastic walls and turrets. The heavy swells of the open sea, striking their bases with tremendous force, fill their crevices with foaming spray, which pours off in a hundred cataracts as the wave draws back for another shock. In the narrow channels between the rocks, the pent waters roll inland with great force, flooding point after point and flinging high into the air the purple flags and streamers of sea-weed, till they reach the glassy, sheltered pools, that are quietly filled and emptied with every pulsation of the great sea without. A cold mist hung over the sea, which heightened the wildness and bleakness of the scene and made it inspiring. Flocks of sea-gulls uttered their shrill, piping cry as they flew over us, and a seal now and then thrust up his inquisitive head, outside of the surf.

We collected the drift-wood which lay scattered along the shore, and made a roaring fire on the rocks. After having sliced and spitted our meat and set our bread to toast, we crept into the crevices that opened to the sea, and at the momentary risk of being drenched, tore off the muscles adhering to them. When well roasted, their flesh is tender and nearly as palatable as that of an oyster ; it is of a bright orange color, with a little black beard at one end, which is intensely bitter and must be rejected. We seasoned our meat by dipping it into the sea, and when our meal was ready, ate it from the pearly shells of the *avelone*, which strewed the sand. It was a rare dinner; that, with its grand accompaniment of surf-music and the clanging sea-gulls as our attendants. On our way home we came suddenly on a pack of seven black wolves, who had been feeding on the body of a large stranded fish. They gave a howl of surprise and started off at full speed, through the bushes, where I attempted to follow them, but my legs were no match for their fleetness.

I rode to Point Pinos one afternoon, in company with Major Hill. Our way was through the Pine Forest; we followed no regular path, but pushed our horses through chapparal, leaped them over trees that had been uprooted in the last winter's storms, and spurred them at a gallop through the cleared intervals. A narrow ridge of sand intervenes between the pines and the sea. Beyond it, the Point—a rugged mass of gray sandstone rock, washed into fantastic shapes, juts out into the Pacific. The tide was at its ebb, but a strong wind was blowing, and the shock and foam of the swells was magnificent. We scrambled from ledge to ledge till we gained the extremity of the Point, and there, behind the last rock that fronts the open sea, found a little sheltered cove, whose sides and bottom were covered with star-fish, avelones, muscles, and polypi of brilliant colors. There were prickly balls of purple, rayed fish of orange and scarlet, broad flower-like animals of green and umber hue, and myriads of little crabs and snails, all shining through the clear green water. The avelone, which is a univalve, found clinging to the sides of rocks, furnishes the finest mother-of-pearl. We had come provided with a small iron bar, which was more than a match for their suction power, and in a short space of time secured a number of their beautiful shells. Among the sand-hills and even in some parts of the forest, the earth is strewed with them. The natives were formerly in the habit of gathering them into large heaps and making lime therefrom.

The existence of these shells in the soil is but one of the facts which tend to prove the recent geological formation of this part of the coast. There is every reason to believe that a great part of the promontory on which Monterey is built, was at no very remote period of time covered by the sea. A sluggish salt lagoon, east of the Catholic Church, was not more than twenty years ago a part of the bay, from which it is now separated by a sandy meadow, quarter of a mile in breadth. According to an Indian tradition, of comparatively modern origin, the waters of San Francisco Bay once communicated with the bay of Monterey by the valley of San José and the Rio del Pajaro. I should think a level of fifty feet, or perhaps less—above the present one, would suffice to have effected this. The other Indian tradition, that the outlet of the Golden Gate was occasioned by violent disruption of the hills, through the means of an earthquake, is not based on natural evidence. The sloughs and marshes in the valley of San Joaquin, and around the Tularé Lakes, present every appearance of having been left by the drainage of a subsiding ocean. A thorough geological exploration of California would undoubtedly bring to light many strange and interesting facts connected with her physical formation.

On our way home, we discovered a sea-otter, basking on an isolated rock. Major Hill crept stealthily to within about fifty yards of him, took good aim and fired. He gave a convulsive leap and tumbled into the sea, evidently badly wounded, if not killed. His boady floated out on the waves, and a flock of sea-mews, attracted by the blood, flew round him, uttering their piping cry and darting down to the water.   The otter is rare on this part of the coast, and the skin of one is valued at $40.

I shall notice but one other ramble about the forests and shores of Monterey.   This was a visit to the ex-Mission of Carmel and Point Lobos, which I made in company with Mr. Lyon, one of the Secretaries of the Convention.   A well-traveled road, leading over the hills, conducted us to the Mission, which is situated on the Pacific side of the promontory, at the head of a shallow bay.   The beautiful but deserted valley in which it stands is threaded by the Rio de Carmel, whose waters once gave unfailing fertility to its now neglected gardens.   The Mission building is in the form of a hollow Square, with a spacious court-yard, overlooked by a heavy belfry and chapel-dome of sun-dried bricks.   The out-buildings of the Indian retainers and the corrals of earth that once herded thousands of cattle are broken down and tenantless.   We climbed into the tower and struck the fine old Spanish bells, but the sound called no faces into the blank windows.

We bribed a red-headed boy, who was playing with two or three younger children in the court-yard, to bring us the keys of the church.   His father—an American who had been many years in the country and taken unto himself a native wife—followed, and opened for us the weather-beaten doors.   The interior of the Church was lofty, the ceiling a rude attempt at a Gothic arch, and the shrine a huge, faded mass of gilding and paint, with some monkish portraits of saints.   A sort of side-chapel near the entrance was painted with Latin mottos and arabesque scrolls which exhibited a genuine though uncultivated taste for adornment. The walls were hung with portraits of saints, some black and some white, some holding croziers, some playing violins and some baptizing Indians.   Near the altar is the tomb of Padre Junipero

Serra, the founder of Monterey and the zealous pioneer in the settlement and civilization of California.

We reached Point Lobos, which is three miles beyond the Mission, by a ride along the beach. It is a narrow, bluff headland, overgrown with pines nearly to its extremity. The path brought us to the brink of a stony declivity, shelving down to the sea. Off the Point, and at the distance of not more than two hundred yards, is a cluster of low rocks, some of which are covered with a deposit of guano. As we reined up on the edge of the bluff, a most extraordinary sound met our ears—a mingled bellowing, groaning and snorting, unlike anything I had ever heard. The rocks seemed to be in motion at the first glance, and one might readily have imagined that the sound proceeded from their uneasy heaving on the waves. But, on looking more closely, I saw that their visible surface was entirely covered with the huge bodies of the seals and sea-lions who had congregated there—great, unwieldy, wallowing creatures, from eight to fifteen feet in length, rolling to and fro among each other and uttering their peculiar bellowing cry. Occasionally, a group of them would slip off into the water, and attracted by their curiosity, approach the shore. The sea-lions, with their broad heads, rough manes and square fronts, showed some resemblance to the royal beast, when viewed in front. They are frequently captured and killed by whalers for the sake of their blubber, which yields a considerable quantity of oil.

I attended the Catholic Church in Monterey one Sunday, to hear good old Padre Ramirez. The church is small and with scanty decorations; the nave and gallery were both crowded by the Californian families and Indians. Near the door hung opposite pictures of Heaven and Hell—the former a sort of pyramid

8*

inhabited by straight white figures, with an aspect of solemn distress; the latter enclosed in the expanded jaws of a dragon, swarming with devils who tormented their victims with spears and pitchforks. The church music was furnished by a diminutive parlor-organ, and consisted of a choice list of polkas, waltzes and fandango airs. Padre Ramirez preached a very excellent sermon, recommending his Catholic flock to follow the example of the Protestants, who, he said, were more truly pious than they, and did much more for the welfare of their church. I noticed that, during the sermon, several of the Californians disappeared through a small door at the end of the gallery. Following them, out of curiosity, I found them all seated in the belfry and along the coping of the front, composedly smoking their cigars.

There was a little gold excitement in Monterey during my visit, on account of the report that a washing of considerable richness had been discovered near the Mission of San Antonio, among the Coast Mountains, sixty miles to the southward. According to the accounts which reached us, a number of people had commenced working there, with fair success, and traders were beginning to send their teams in that direction. Gold was also said to exist in small quantities near the Mission of Carmel, where, indeed, there were strong geological indications of it. These discoveries, however, were too slight to affect the repose of the town, which a much greater excitement could scarcely have shaken.

CHAPTER XVIII.

THREE or four weeks of my stay in Monterey were principally passed in the office of the Civil Government, where I was employed in examining all the records relating to land titles and Mission property in California. Notwithstanding the apparent dryness of the subject, I found the documents curious and interesting. The smoky *papel sellado* on which they were written— the naïve and irregular orthography—the rude drawings and maps which accompanied them and the singular laws and customs of which they gave evidence, had a real charm to any one possessing the slightest relish for the odor of antiquity. Most interesting of all was a box of records, brought from La Paz, Lower California, where many similar boxes, equally precious, were used for the wadding of Castro's cannon. Among its contents were letters of instruction from the Viceroy Galvez, original letters of Padre Junipero Serra and mandates from the Bishops of Mexico to the Missionaries in Sonora and California. I was never tired of hearing Capt. Halleck, the Secretary of State, whose knowledge of the early history of California is not equalled by any one in the country, talk of those marvellous times and make clear the misty meaning of the rare old papers.

The extensive history of Vanegas, an abridgment of which has been introduced by Mr. Forbes into his work on California, is the most complete of all which have been written. It is mainly confined, however, to the settlement of the Peninsula, and throws no light on the after decay and ruin of the Missions of Alta California. These establishments, to which solely are owing the settlement and civilization of the country, have now entirely fallen from their former supremacy, and are of no further importance in a civil view. Some facts concerning the manner of their downfall, which I learned during my labors among the archives, may be not inappropriately given here. Henceforth, under the ascendancy of American institutions, they have no longer an existence : shall we not, therefore, now that their day is over, take one backward glance over the places they have filled and the good or evil they have accomplished ?

The history of their original foundation is one of remarkable interest. Through the perseverance and self-denying labors of a few Catholic Priests alone, the natives, not only of the Peninsula and the Coast, as far north as San Francisco Bay, but the extensive provinces of Sonora and Sinaloa, were taught the arts of civilized life and subjected to the dominion of Spain. The lives of Padres Kino, Salvatierra and Ugarte exhibit instances of danger, adventure and heroic endurance scarcely inferior to those of Cortez and Coronado. The great work they accomplished on the Peninsula and in the Northern Provinces of Mexico, in the beginning of the last century, was followed fifty years later by Padre Junipero Serra, who in 1769 founded the Mission of San Diego, the first settlement in Alta California. In the succeeding year he landed at Monterey, and by a solemn mass which was performed under an oak-tree still standing near the fort, took posses-

sion of the spot. After laboring for thirteen years with indefati-
gable zeal and activity, during which time he founded nine missions,
the good Padre died in 1784, and was buried in the grave-yard of
Carmel. His successors continued the work, and by the year
1800 had increased the number of Missions to sixteen. Since
that time only three more have been added. The Missions are
named and located as follows : San Rafael and San Francisco Solano, north of San Francisco Bay; Dolores, near San Francisco;
Santa Clara and San José, near Pueblo San José; San Juan,
Santa Cruz and Carmel, near Monterey ; Soledad, San Antonio
and San Miguel, in the Valley of Salinas River ; San Luis Obispo ;
La Purisima, Santa Ynez, Santa Barbara and San Buenaventura,
near Santa Barbara; San Gabriel and San Fernando, near Los
Angeles; and San Luis Rey, San Juan Capistrano and San
Diego, on the coast, south of Los Angeles.

The wealth and power in the possession of these Missions naturally excited the jealousy of Government, after California was
organized into a territory.   The padres, however, had been granted
almost unlimited privileges by the earlier Viceroys, and for a long
time no authority could be found to dispossess them.   A decree
of the Spanish Cortes, in 1813, relating to the Missions of South
America, was made the basis of repeated attempts to overthrow
the temporal power of the padres, but without effect, and from 1800
to 1830, they revelled securely in the full enjoyment of their
wealthy establishments.

That, indeed, was *their* age of gold—a right bounteous and prosperous time, toward which many of the Californian and even of the
old American residents, look back with regret.   Then, each Mission was a little principality, with its hundred thousand acres, and
its twenty thousand head of cattle.   All the Indian population,

.except the " Gentiles" of the mountains, were the subjects of the
padres, cultivating for them their broad lands and reverencing
them with the same devout faith as they did the patron saint of the
settlement. The spacious galleries, halls and courtyards of the
Missions exhibited every sign of order and good government, and
from the long rows of adobe houses flanking them an obedient
crowd came forth, at the sound of morning and evening chimes.
The tables of the padres were laden with the finest fruits and
vegetables from their thrifty gardens and orchards, and flasks of
excellent wine from their own vineyards. The stranger who came
that way was entertained with a lavish hospitality for which all recompense was proudly refused, and on leaving, was welcome to
exchange his spent horse for his pick out of the caballada. Nearly
all the commerce of the country with other nations was in their
hands. Long habits of management and economy gave them a
great aptitude for business of all kinds, and each succeeding year
witnessed an increase of their wealth and authority.

The first blow given to their privileges, was a decree of the Supreme Government of Mexico, dated August 17, 1833, by which
the Missions of Upper and Lower California were secularized and
became public property. They were converted by law into
parishes, and the padres, from being virtual sovereigns of their
domains, became merely curates, possessing only spiritual powers
over their former subjects. Instead of managing the revenue of
the estates, they were paid from $2,000 to $2,500, at the option
of Government. The church was still kept for religious purposes,
and the principal building for the curate's house, while other portions of the establishment were appropriated to the purposes of
court-houses and schools.

This law of course emancipated the Indians from the authority of the padres, and likewise absolved the latter from their obligations to maintain them. To provide for their support, therefore, the Government granted to every head of a family a lot from one to four hundred varas square, which was assigned to the use of themselves and their descendants, but could not be sold by them under penalty of the land reverting back to the public domain. The temporal affairs of each Mission were placed under the charge of an Ayuntamiento, who was commissioned to explain to the Indians the new relations, and put them in possession of the land. A portion of the revenue was applied to their benefit, and in return therefor they were obliged to assist in cultivating the common lands of the new pueblos or parishes. By a further decree, in 1840, Governor Alvarado substituted majordomos in place of the ayuntamientos, giving them power to manage the temporal affairs of the Missions, but not to dispose of the revenues or contract debts without the permission of Government.

These decrees put a stop to the prosperity of the Missions. The Padres, seeing the establishments taken out of their hands, employed themselves no longer in superintending their cultivation ; while the Indians, though free, lost the patient guidance and encouragement they had received, and relapsed into their hereditary habits of sloth and stupidity. Many of them scattered from their homes, resuming a roving life among the mountains, and very soon several of the Missions almost ceased to have an existence. Gov. Micheltorena, therefore, in 1843, in a pompous proclamation setting forth his loyalty to the Catholic Faith, attempted to restore the former state of things by delivering twelve of the Missions into the hands of the priests. He declared, at the same time, that all the cattle and property should be given up to them, but that those portions of the Mission estates which had been granted to individuals should

still remain in possession of the latter. The proclamation, so far
as I can learn, never went into effect, and the chasing of Micheltorena from the country soon put an end to his plans.

In the year 1845 Governor Pio Pico completed the obliteration
of the Missions. By a Government decree he directed that the
Missions of San Juan, Carmel, San Francisco Solano and San
Juan Capistrano should be sold at auction on a specified day.
One month's notice was given to the Indian neophytes of the
Missions of San Rafael, Dolores, Soledad, San Miguel and La
Purisima to return to the cultivation and occupancy of the lands
assigned them by Government, otherwise the same should be declared unoccupied and disposed of like the preceding. All the
remaining Missions, except the Episcopal Mansion at Santa Barbara, were to be rented. Of the proceeds of these sales and leases
one-third was to be used for the support of the resident priests,
one-third for the benefit of the Indians, and the remaining third
constituting the Pious Fund of California to be applied to purposes
of education and beneficence.

The Indian neophytes of the five last-named Missions having
neglected to assemble, Pico, by a decree in October, 1845, ordered that they should be sold to the highest bidder ; and at the
same time, that those of San Fernando, Buenaventura, Santa
Barbara and Santa Ynez, should be rented for the term of nine
years. This was the last valid decree touching the Missions.
The remaining Missions of Santa Clara, San José, Santa Cruz,
San Antonio, San Luis Obispo, San Gabriel and San Diego were
therefore thrown immediately into the hands of the United States
after possession had been taken by our troops ; and all Mission
property not legally granted or sold under the laws of California,
becomes part of the public domain.

I endeavored to obtain some statistics of the land, cattle and other property belonging to the various Missions. The data on record, however, partake of the same indefinite character as the description of lands for which grants are asked. I found, it is true, an account of the boundaries of most of the Missions, with the quality of the land embraced by them, but the particulars, notwithstanding they were given by the resident padres themselves, are very unsatisfactory. The lands are described as lying between certain hills and rivers, or embracing certain plains; sometimes they are spoken of as *cañadas* or *llanos* only. Some are of great extent; the Mission lands of San Antonio contain two hundred and twenty-five square leagues and those of San Miguel five hundred and thirty-two. The others vary from twenty to one hundred square leagues. At a rough guess, I should compute the original Mission lands at about eight millions of acres; probably four to five millions of acres have since been disposed of by sales and grants. The remaining three millions of acres, comprising the finest lands in California, are the property of the United States. As much of it has been cultivated, or is capable of immediate adaptation for the planting of orchards, gardens and vineyards, the sale or disposal of it would seem to require different regulations from those which govern other portions of the public domain.

The Mission buildings now are but wrecks of their former condition. The broken walls, deserted corrals, and roofless dwellings which surround them, are but melancholy evidences of their ancient prosperity. Their character for wealth and hospitality has passed away with the rule of the padres and the vassalage of the Indians. They have had their day. They have fulfilled (and nobly, too, be it acknowledged) the purpose of their creation. I see no cause for lamenting, as many do, over their downfall. The spirit of enterprise which has now taken firm root in the soil, will make their neglected gardens blossom again, and deck their waste fields with abundant harvests.

A subject of more direct interest to the California emigrants, is that of the character and validity of the grants made to settlers previous to the acquisition of the country. The extravagant pitch to which land speculation has risen, and the uncertain tenure by which many of the best locations along the coast are held, render some official examination and adjustment very necessary. The amount of speculation which has already been done on an insecure basis, will give rise to endless litigation, when the proper tribunal shall have been established. Meanwhile, a brief account of the character of the grants, derived partly from Capt. Halleck's admirable Report on California Affairs and partly from an examination of the grants themselves, may not be without its interest and uses.

The first general decree for the granting of lands bears date of June, 1779, when Governor Neve, then established at Monterey, drew up a series of regulations, which were approved by the King of Spain, and for more than forty years remained in force, with little modification, throughout the territory. To each *poblador* (settler) was granted a bounty of $116 44 per annum for the first two years, and $60 per annum for the three following, with the loan of horses, cattle and farming utensils from the Government supplies. Settlers in pueblos, or towns, had likewise the privilege of pasturing their stock on the lands belonging to the town. Many of the minor regulations established in this decree of Gov. Neve, are sufficiently amusing. For instance, no poblador is allowed to sell any of his animals, until he shall possess fifteen mares and one stallion, fifteen cows and one bull, and so on, down to cocks and hens. He must then sell his extra stock to the Government, which of course pays its own price.

These regulations, designed only for the first rude stage of colonization, were superseded by the decree of the Mexican Republic for the colonization of its Territories, dated Aug. 18, 1824, which was further limited and defined by a series of regulations, dated Nov. 21, 1828. Up to the time when California passed into the hands of the United States, no modifications were made to these acts, and they consequently remain in force. Their most important provisions are as follows:

The Governor of the Territory is empowered to make grants of lands to contractors (for towns or colonies) and individuals or heads of families. Grants of the first-named class require the approval of the Supreme Government to make them valid. For the latter the ratification of the Territorial Assembly is necessary; but in no case can the Governor make grants of any land lying within ten leagues of the sea-coast or within twenty leagues of the boundaries of any foreign power, without the previous approval of the Supreme Government. The authorities of towns, however, are allowed to dispose of lands lying within the town limits, the proceeds to be paid into the municipal fund. The maximum extent of a single grant is fixed at one square league of irrigable land, four of *temporal*, or land where produce depends on the seasons, and six of land for pasturing and rearing cattle— eleven square leagues (about fifty thousand acres) in all. The minimum extent is two hundred varas square (a vara is a little less than a yard) of irrigable land, eight hundred of temporal, and twelve hundred of pasturage. The size of a house lot in any of the pueblos is fixed at one hundred varas. The irregular spaces and patches lying between the boundaries of grants throughout the country are to be distributed among the colonists who occupy the adjoining land, or their children, preference being given to those who have distinguished themselves by their industry and moral deportment.

All grants not made in accordance with these regulations, from the time of their adoption up to July 7, 1846, when the American flag was raised at Monterey and the Departmental Junta broken up, are not strictly valid, according to Mexican law. The restrictions against lands within ten leagues of the sea-coast were never removed. The only legal grant of such land, was that made to Captain Stephen Smith, of the port of Bodega, which received the approval of the Supreme Government. In the Macnamara Colonization Grant, made by Pio Pico, only four days before the occupation of Monterey by our forces, it is expressly stated that the consent of the Mexican Government is necessary to make it valid. Yet, in spite of this distinct provision, large tracts of this coast, from San Francisco to San Diego, were granted to citizens and colonists by Figueroa, Alvarado and other Governors. All these acts, having never received the sanction of the Supreme Government, would, by a literal construction of the law, be null and void. The Supreme Government of Mexico always reserved to itself the right of using any portion of the coast, promontories, harbors or public land of the interior, for the purpose of erecting forts, arsenals or national storehouses.

There are on file in the archives about five hundred and eighty grants, made by various Governors between 1828 and 1846. Probably one hundred of these lack the full requirements of the Mexican law—exclusive of those located on the sea-coast. Some are complete and satisfactory in all respects, to the signature of the Governor, but the concurrence of the Territorial Assembly is wanting. In others the final concession is withheld for the purpose of procuring further information. Others again, appear to have been neglected by the proper authorities, and a few, on further testimony, have been denied. As the owners of such lands, in many instances, are entirely unaware of the imperfect nature of their titles, many sales and transfers have been made in good faith, which will hereafter be invalidated. Some individuals have acted in a more reprehensible manner, by making sales of lands to which they had no legal claim.

In settling the boundaries of grants, which are sound in every respect, there will nevertheless be some difficulty. Much of the land was never surveyed, the locality and character being rudely sketched on paper by the petitioner, sometimes without any specified extent, and sometimes with a guess at the quantity, which is often very wide of the mark. Such sketch, or topographical outline is, I believe, required by law, and the collection embraced in the number of grants and applications on file, exhibits a most curious variety of attempts at drawing. In the absence of any further clue, it would be difficult to find many of the localities or anything in the least resembling them. The boundaries are frequently given as included within certain hills, arroyos, rivers and marshes, but the space so designated frequently contains double the amount of land asked for.

On the lands throughout the country, known and recognized as belonging to the United States, a number of emigrants have established themselves, making choice of advantageous locations, and trusting to obtain possession by right of preëminence as settlers. Nearly all of the fords on the Sacramento and San Joaquin and their tributaries—the springs and meadow lands at the bases of the mountains—and all sites which seem calculated

for future towns or villages—have been appropriated in like manner. The discovery of gold has rendered any bounty unnecessary, to promote emigration.

I endeavored to ascertain the exact extent of granted land in
California, as well as the amount which will remain to the United
States ; but owing to the indefinite character of many of the
grants, and the absence of correct statistical information, was
unable fully to succeed. The geographical limits within which
the grants are embraced, are more easily traced. By referring to
Frémont's Map of California, a line drawn from the mouth of
Russian River, on the Pacific, north of Bodega, to the mouth of
Rio Chico, a tributary of the Sacramento, and continued to the
Sierra Nevada, would comprise the northern limit. From this line
to the Oregon boundary—a region two hundred and fifty miles in
length by two hundred in breadth—belongs to the public domain.
The land about the mouths of the Sacramento and San Joaquin,
with some tracts on the Rio Americano, Cosumne, Calaveras
and Mariposa, is included in various grants, but the remainder
of the settled land as you go southward, is upon the western side
of the Coast Range, and all of it within ninety miles of the
sea. The best agricultural districts—those of Napa, San José
and Los Angeles—are already settled and cultivated, but the
upper portion of the Sacramento country, the valleys of Trinity
River and Russian River, and the lower slopes of the Sierra Nevada, embrace a great deal of arable land of excellent quality.
The valleys of the Coast Range north of San Francisco Bay have
been but partially explored.

The entire gold district of the Sierra Nevada belongs to the
United States, with the exception of Johnson's Ranche on Bear
Creek, Sutter's possessions on the Rio Americano, a grant on the

Cosumne, and Alvarado's Ranche on the Mariposa, now in possession of Col. Fremont. Some anxiety is felt among the mining
population, as to the disposition which the Government will make
of these vast storehouses of wealth. The day before the adjournment of the Convention, a resolution was offered, requesting Congress not to dispose of any part of the gold region, but to suffer it
to remain free to all American citizens. It was defeated by a
bare majority, but many of those voting nay, avowed themselves
in favor of the spirit of the resolution, objecting to its adoption on
the ground of propriety alone. The population, generally, is opposed to the sale of gold land for the reason that it would probably fall into the hands of speculators, to the disadvantage of the
mining class. The lease of land would present the same objec-
tions, besides being but an uncertain privilege. The fairest and
most satisfactory course would be the imposition of a small per
centage on the amount of gold actually dug or washed out by
each individual or company. The miners would not object to
this ; they only oppose any regulation which would give speculators a chance to elbow them out of their ' bars' and ' pockets.'

CHAPTER XIX.

AFTER the adjournment of the Convention, Monterey relapsed into its former quiet, and I soon began to feel the old impatience and longing for motion and change. The season was waning, and barely time enough remained for the accomplishment of my de-sign of a journey to the head of the Sacramento Valley. My friend, Lieut. Beale, with whom I had beguiled many an hour in tracing out plans for overland journeys and explorations, which should combine a spice of bold adventure with the acquisition of permanently useful knowledge, had left a week previous, in com-pany with Col. Frémont and his family. A heavy fog had for several days lain like a bar across the mouth of the bay, and we feared that the anxiously-awaited steamer from Panama would pass without touching. This was a question of interest, as there had been no mail from the Atlantic States for more than two months, and the general impatience on that account was painful to witness. Under these circumstances, I grew tired of looking on the fresh, sparkling, intense blue of the bay and the dewy-violet shadows of the mountains beyond it, and so one fine morn-ing thrust my few moveables into my knapsack and rolled up my sarape for a start.

I had a better reliance than my own feet, in making the journey Mr. Semple, ex-President of the Convention, with his son and two of the ex-Clerks, were about leaving, and I was offered the means of conveyance as far as Pueblo San José. Mr. Semple was barely recovering from a severe attack of typhoid fever, and was obliged to be conveyed in an army ambulance, which was furnished by Capt. Kane, of the Quartermaster's Department. We started at noon, under a hot, bright sun, though the entrance to the bay was still covered by the bar of dark fog. The steamer Unicorn was anxiously expected, and as a gun had been heard during the night, Gen. Riley ordered a shot to be fired from the fort every half-hour, as a guide for the steamer, should she be outside. Had there been any certainty of her arrival, our haste to receive the long-delayed mail would have induced us to postpone the journey.

We toiled through the desolate sand-hills to the Salinas River, and lanched again upon its broad, level plains. Our team consisted of four Californian horses, neither of which had ever been a week in harness, and consequently were not broken of the dashing gait to which they had been accustomed. The driver was an emigrant who arrived two months previous, by the Gila route, after suffering the most terrible privations. We had all our provisions, blankets and camping utensils stowed in the ambulance, and as it was not large enough to contain our bodies likewise, two of the party followed in a light wagon. Under the steady gallop at which our fiery horses drew us, the blue ridges of the Sierra de Gavilan soon rose high and bleak before us, and the timbered shores of the plain came in sight. Our crossing of the arroyos would have startled even an Alleghany stage-driver. When one of these huge gullies yawned before us, there was no check of our speed. We dashed sheer off the brink at an angle of fifty de-grees ; there was a giddy sensation of falling for an instant, and in the next our heavy vehicle regained the level, carried half-way up the opposite steep by the momentum of our descent. The excitement of such a plunge was delightful : the leaping of a five-barred gate on an English hunter would have been tame to it.

On the skirt of the timber Mr. Semple pointed out the scene of a battle between the Californian and American troops, during the war. Foster, a scout belonging to the company of Emigrant Vo-lunteers, while reconnoitering along the bases of the mountains, discovered a body of two hundred Californians on the plain. He immediately sent word to Burrows' company of Americans, then at the Mission San Juan, and in the meantime attacked them with the small force accompanying him. The fight was carried on among the trees. When the Americans—sixty-six in all—arrived on the field, they found Foster dead, with eleven wounds on his body. Four Americans and seven Californians were shot in the fight, which resulted in the defeat of the latter and their retreat up the plains to their post at the Mission of Soledad. Foster was buried where he fell, under a large oak, near the road.

We entered the mountains, and encamped about dusk in a sheltered glen, watered by a little stream. Some benevolent pre-decessor had left us a good stock of wood, and in a short time the ruddy lights of our fire were dancing over the gnarled oak-boughs, and their streamers of grey moss. I tried my hand, for the first time, at making coffee, while the others spitted pieces of meat on long twigs and thrust them into the blaze. My coffee was approved by the company, and the seasoning of the keen mountain air was not lost on our meal. The pipe of peace—never omitted by the genuine trapper or mountaineer—followed ; after which we spread our blankets on the ground and looked at the stars through the chinks of the boughs, till we dropped asleep.   There is no rest so sweet as that taken on the hard bosom of Mother Earth.   I slept soundly in our spacious bed-chamber, undisturbed even by the continued barking whine of the coyotes.   The cool, sparkling dawn called us up betimes, to rekindle the fire and resume cooking. When the sun made his appearance above the hills, our driver said : " There comes old Hannah, to open the shutters of our house and let in the light"—the most ludicrous combination of scullionish and poetical ideas it was ever my lot to hear.   I must acknowledge, however, that " Old Hannah" did her office well, giving our house the most cheery illumination.

As we wound through the lonely passes of the mountains, Mr. Semple pointed out many spots where he had hidden on his night-rides as messenger between San Francisco and Monterey during the war.   From some of the heights we looked down valleys that stretched away towards Santa Cruz, and could discern the dark lines of redwood timber along their border.   The forest near the Mission contains the largest specimens of this tree to be found in California, some of the trunks, as I was credibly informed, measuring fifteen feet in diameter.   Captain Graham, an old settler, had five saw-mills in operation, which he leased to speculators at the rate of fifty dollars per day for each.   The timber is soft and easily worked, susceptible of a fine polish, and when kept dry, as in the interior of buildings, will last for centuries.

Midway down one of the long descents, we met Messrs. Marcy and Tefft, who had been to San Francisco to attend to the printing of the Constitution, bundles of which, in English and Spanish, were strapped to their saddles.   Our next incident was the discovery of three grizzly bears, on the side of a cañada, about a quarter of a mile distant. Mr. Semple, who, with the keen sight of one accustomed to mountain life, was on the alert for game, first espied them. They were moving lazily among a cluster of oaks; their bodies were, apparently, as large as that of a mule, but an experienced eye could at once detect the greater thickness and shortness of their legs. We had no other arms than pistols and knives, and no horses of sufficient fleetness to have ventured an attack with safety ; so we passed on with many a wistful and lingering look, for the gray hide of one of those huge beasts would have been a trophy well worth the capture. Indeed, the oldest hunter, when he meets a grizzly bear, prefers making a boy's bargain—" If you'll let me alone, I'll let you alone." They are rarely known to attack a man when unprovoked, but when wounded no Indian tiger is more formidable.

Towards noon we reached the Mission San Juan. The bands of emigrants from the South had stripped all the fruit-trees in its gardens, but at a *tienda* in the Mission building, we were supplied with pears at the rate of three for a real—plump, luscious fruit, with russet peel, and so mellow that they would scarcely bear handling. While we were idling an hour in the warm corridor, trying to maintain a conversation in Spanish with some of the natives, a brother of Mr. Semple, who had come from Benicia to meet him, rode up to the inn. He had a gray horse, whose trot was remarkably rough, and at his request I changed places, giving up to him my seat in the ambulance. We dashed out on the plain of San Juan at a full gallop, but my perverse animal soon lagged behind. He was what is called a " Snake horse," of the breed owned by the Snake Indians in Oregon, whence, in fact, he had been brought, still retaining the steady, deliberate pace at which he had been accustomed to haul lodge-poles. His trot was racking, and as a final resort to procure a gallop, I borrowed a pair of very sharp spurs from our driver. At the first touch the old Snake started ; at the second he laid his ears flatly back, gave a snort and sprang forward with galvanic energy, taking me far in advance of the flying ambulance. It was so long since he had traveled such a pace that he seemed as much astonished as I was at the effect of my spurs.

The ambulance at last reached the Pajaro River, which flowed between deep and precipitous banks. The four horses plunged down the declivity ; the ambulance followed with a terrible shock, which urged it into the middle of the stream, where it stuck, the king-bolt having been snapped off. We partly stripped, and after working an hour with the ice-cold water above our knees, succeeded in fastening with chains the fragment of the bolt. It was now dinner-time, and we soon had a blaze among the willows and a pot of coffee boiling before it. The beverage, which never tasted more refreshing, sent a fine glow into our benumbed nether limbs, and put us into traveling humor again. The Pajaro Plains, around the head of the river, are finely watered, and under proper culti- vation would produce splendid crops. From the ridge descending to the valley of San José we overlooked their broad expanse. The meadows were still green, and the belts of stately sycamore had not yet shed a leaf. I hailed the beautiful valley with pleasure, although its soil was more parched and arid than when I passed before, and the wild oats on the mountains rolled no longer in waves of gold. Their sides were brown and naked to desolation ; the dead umber color of the landscape, towards sunset, was more cheerless than a mid-November storm. A traveler seeing Cali- fornia only at this season, would never be tempted to settle.

As we journeyed down the valley, flocks of wild geese and

brant, cleaving the air with their arrow-shaped lines, descended to their roost in the meadows. On their favorite grounds, near the head of Pajaro River, they congregated to the number of millions, hundreds of acres being in many places actually hidden under their dense ranks. They form in columns as they alight, and their stations at roost are as regularly arranged as in any military camp. As the season advances and their number is increased by new arrivals, they become so regardless of human presence that the rancheros kill large quantities with clubs. The native children have a curious method of entrapping them while on the wing. They tie two bones at the ends of a string about a yard in length, which they hurl into the air so skilfully that in falling it forms an arch. As the geese fly low, this instrument, dropping into a flock, generally takes one of them across the neck ; the bones fall on each side and drag the goose to the earth, where he is at once seized and dispatched.

We passed Murphy's Ranche and the splendid peak of El Toro and reached Fisher's Ranche as the blaze of camp-fires under the sycamores was beginning to show through the dusk. Here we found Major Hill, who, with Mr. Durivage and Midshipman Carnes, with six men from the wreck of the propeller Edith, had left Monterey the day before ourselves. Their fire was kindled, the cooking implements in order, and several of the party employed in the task of picking three wild geese and preparing them for the pan. While at supper, one of Capt. Fisher's men excited the sporting propensities of some of our party by describing a lake in the valley, where the geese roosted in immense quantities. As it was not more than a mile distant, muskets were got ready and four of the sportsmen set out by moonlight. They found some difficulty, however, in fishing out the geese after they were shot, and only brought two with them at midnight. I, who was fatigued with my management of the Snake horse, crept into a cart-bed near the Ranche, laid a raw-hide over the top and was soon floating adrift on a sea of dreams.

We had harnessed and were off before the daybreak brightened into sunrise. As we passed the last mountain headland and the mouth of the valley lay wide before us, I noticed a dim vapor over the place where the Pueblo San José should stand. The reason of this was explained when we reached the entrance of the town. We were met by a hurricane of dust which for several minutes prevented our advancing a step; the adobe houses on each side were completely hidden, and we could only breathe by covering our faces with the loose folds of our jackets. Some wind intended for San Francisco had got astray among the mountains, and coming on San José unawares, had put in motion all the dust that had been quietly accumulating during the summer.

The two weeks which had elapsed since San José had been made a capital, were sufficient to have created a wonderful change. What with tents and houses of wood and canvas, in hot haste thrown up, the town seemed to have doubled in size. The dusty streets were thronged with people; goods, for lack of storage room, stood in large piles beside the doors; the sound of saw and hammer, and the rattling of laden carts, were incessant. The Legislative Building—a two-story adobe house built at the town's expense—was nearly finished. Hotels were springing up in all quarters; French *restaurateurs* hung out their signs on little one-story shanties; the shrewd Celestials had already planted themselves there, and summoned men to meals by the sound of their barbaric gongs. Our old stopping-place, the " Miner's Home," was converted into a " City Hotel," and when we drew up before the door, we were instantly surrounded by purveyors from rival establishments, offering to purchase the two wild geese which hung at the wagon-tail. The roads to Monterey, to Stockton, to San Francisco, and to the Embarcadero, were stirring with continual travel. The price of lots had nearly doubled in consequence of this change, so that the town lost nothing by its gift of the legislative building to Government.

The ambulance, carrying Mr. Semple, set out for Benicia along the eastern shore of San Francisco Bay. Those of us who were bound for San Francisco made search for other conveyances. Hearing that a launch was about starting, I walked down to the Embarcadero, about seven miles distant, where I found a dozen vessels anchored in an estuary which ran up among the tulé. One of them was to leave that night at ten o'clock ; the fare was $10, and the time dependent on the wind, but usually varying from two to four days. I gave up the chance at once, and retracing my steps to the nearest ford, crossed Coyote River and struck across the meadows towards Whisman's Ranche, which I reached after two hours' walk. Evening came on while I was journeying alone in the midst of the boundless landscape—boundless, but for the shadowy mountain-piles which lay along the horizon, seeming, through the haze, like the hills of another planet which had touched the skirts of the globe on its journey through space. Long lines of geese and brant sailed through the air, and the white crane, from his covert on the edge of the marsh, uttered at intervals his strong, guttural cry. As the sunset gathered to a blaze, the mountains across the bay were suffused with a rosy purple tint, while those against the western sky stood in deep violet shadow. At last, the sounds of animal life died away on the plain, and the stars were gradually kindled in the cloudless firmament.

By this time I had approached a fine old grove, detached from the shore of timber. The sound of musket shots and the braying of mules told that a party had encamped there. No sooner had I reached the shadow of the trees than my name was shouted, and I recognized Major Hill and my other friends of his party. I threw down my sarape, took a seat among them and employed myself on the breast of a goose. We sat cross-legged around a glowing fire, passing the pans and cups from hand to hand, and using fingers or knives according to the toughness of the meat. The mules were picketed among the oats which grew knee-deep under the trees, and a few paces off, around a still larger fire, the sailors and teamsters brewed their bucket of tea and broiled their huge slices of beef. Our meal over, we lighted our *puros* and stretched out at full length on the grass, enjoying to the full the quiet of the place and the soothing influence of the weed. And then came rest—rest delicious anywhere, but doubly so under the broad arms of the evergreen oak, with the full clear flood of moonlight broken into a thousand minute streams on the turf. It was a long time before I could compose myself to sleep. The solemn repose of the grove—the deep shadows of the trees—the far, misty, silvery glimpses of plain through the openings—wrought powerfully on my imagination and kept every faculty keenly alive. Even in sleep the impression remained, and when I awoke in the night, it was with a happy thrill at opening my eyes on the same maze of moonlight and foliage.

The next day I accompanied the party on foot, taking an occasional lift with the sailors in the wagon. The jolly tars were not at home on dry land, and seemed impatient to see the end of the journey. The driver was enjoined to keep a good look-out from the fore-top (the saddle-mule.) "Breakers ahead!" shouted

9*

Jack, when we came to an arroyo ; " hard up !" was the answer.
" Take a reef in the aft wheel !" was the order of the driver.
The lock was clapped on, and we rode in triumph into a smoother
sea. We nooned at Sanchez' Ranche, reached the Mission Dolores
at dusk, and started over the sand-hills in the moonlight. The
jaded team stalled at the foot of a steep hill but was afterwards
got off by unloading the wagon. I pushed on ahead, hearing the
bustle and mingled sounds of the town, long before I reached it.
I struck the suburbs half a mile sooner than on my previous return, and from the first rise in the sand had an indistinct view of
a place twice as large as I had left. I was too weary, however to
take a long survey, but went directly to the Post Office, where I
found Mr. Moore and his sons as cheerful, active and enterprising
as ever, and was again installed in a comfortable nook of the
garret.

CHAPTER XX.

DURING my absence in Monterey, more than four thousand emigrants by sea had landed in San Francisco. The excitement relative to gold-digging had been kept up by new discoveries on the various rivers ; the rage for land speculation had increased ; and to all this was added the gathering heat of political conflict. San Francisco was something of a whirlpool before, but now it had widened its sweeps and seemed to be drawing everything into its vortex.

The morning after I arrived, I went about the town to note the changes and improvements. I could scarcely believe my eyes. The northern point, where the Bay pours its waters into the Golden Gate, was covered with houses nearly to the summit— many of them large three-story warehouses. The central and highest hill on which the town is built, was shorn of its chapparal and studded with tents and dwellings ; while to the eastward the streets had passed over the last of the three hills, and were beginning to encroach on the Happy Valley. The beautiful crescent of the harbor, stretching from the Rincon to Fort Montgomery, a distance of more than a mile, was lined with boats, tents and warehouses, and near the latter point, several piers jutted into the water. Montgomery street, fronting the Bay, had undergone a marvellous change. All the open spaces were built up, the canvas houses replaced by ample three-story buildings, an Exchange with lofty sky-light fronted the water, and for the space of half a mile the throng of men of all classes, characters and nations, with carts and animals, equaled Wall street before three o'clock.

In other parts of the town the change was equally great. Tents and canvas houses had given place to large and handsome edifices, blanks had been filled up, new hotels opened, market houses in operation and all the characteristics of a great commercial city fairly established. Portsmouth Square was filled with lumber and house frames, and nearly every street in the lower part of the city was blocked up with goods. The change which had been wrought in all parts of the town during the past six weeks seemed little short of magic. At first I had difficulty in believing that what I looked upon was real, so utterly inadequate seemed the visible means for the accomplishment of such wonderful ends.

On my way to call upon Col. Frémont, whom I found located with his family in the Happy Valley, I saw a company of Chinese carpenters putting up the frame of a Canton-made house. In Pacific street another Celestial restaurant had been opened, and every vessel from the Chinese ports brought a fresh importation. An Olympic circus, on a very handsome scale, had been established, and a company of Ethiopian serenaders nightly amused the public. "Delmonico's" was the fashionable eating-house, where you had boiled eggs at seventy-five cents each, and dinner at $1 50 to $5, according to your appetite. A little muslin shed rejoiced in the title of "Irving House." A number of fine billiard rooms and bowling alleys had been opened, and all other devices for spending money brought into successful operation.

The gamblers complained no longer of dull prospects ; there were hundreds of monte, roulette and faro tables, which were crowded nightly until a late hour, and where the most inveterate excesses of gaming might be witnessed. The rents of houses had increased rather than fallen. I might give hundreds of instances, but it would be only a repetition of the stories I have already told. Money brought fourteen per cent. monthly, on loan. A gentleman of Baltimore, who came out in the Panama, sold for $15,000 a steam engine which cost him $2,000. Some drawing paper, which cost about $10 in New York, brought $164. I found little change in the prices of provisions and merchandise, though the sum paid for labor had diminished. Town lots were continually on the rise ; fifty vara lots in the Happy Valley, half a mile from town, brought $3,500. I met with a number of my fellow passengers, nearly all of whom had done well, some of them having already realized $20,000 and $30,000.

The population of San Francisco at that time, was estimated at fifteen thousand ; a year before it was about five hundred. The increase since that time had been made in the face of the greatest disadvantages under which a city ever labored ; an uncultivated country, an ungenial climate, exorbitant rates of labor, want of building materials, imperfect civil organization—lacking everything, in short, but gold dust and enterprise. The same expense, on the Atlantic coast, would have established a city of a hundred thousand inhabitants. The price of lumber was still $300 to $400 per thousand feet. In addition to the five saw-mills at Santa Cruz, all the mills of Oregon were kept going, lumber, even there, bringing $100 per thousand. There was no end to the springs of labor and traffic, which that vast emigration to Cali-

fornia had set in motion, not only on the Pacific Coast, but throughout all Polynesia and Australia.

The activity throughout the mining region during the fall season, gave rise to a thousand reports of golden discoveries, the
effect of which was instantly seen on the new-comers. Their
highest anticipations of the country seemed realized at once, and
their only embarrassment was the choice of so many places of
promise. The stories told were marvellous even to Californians;
what wonder, then, that the green emigrants, who devoutly swallowed them whole, should be disappointed and disgusted with the
reality ? The actual yield on most of the rivers was, nevertheless, sufficiently encouraging. The diggers on the forks of the
American, Feather and Yuba Rivers, met with a steady return
for their labors. On the branches of the San Joaquin, as far as
the Tuolumne, the big lumps were still found. Capt. Walker,
who had a company on the Pitiuna—a stream that flows into the
Tularè Lakes—was in Monterey, buying supplies at the time I
left. His company was alone in that desolate region, and working
to advantage, if one might judge from the secrecy which attended
their movements. The placers on Trinity River had not turned
out so well as was expected, and many of the miners were
returning disappointed to the Sacramento. Several companies
had been absent among the higher ridges of the Sierra Nevada, for
a month or more, and it was suspected that they had discovered
diggings somewhere on the eastern side.

The sickly season on the Sacramento and its tributaries, was
nearly over, but numbers of pale, emaciated frames, broken down
by agues and diarrhœas, were daily arriving in the launches and
steamers. At least one-third of the miners suffered more or less
from these diseases, and numbers of men who had landed only a

few months before, in the fulness of hale and lusty manhood, were walking about nearly as shrunken and bloodless as the corpses they would soon become. One of the most pitiable sights I ever beheld was one of these men, who had just been set ashore from a launch. He was sitting alone on a stone beside the water, with his bare feet purple with cold, on the cold, wet sand. He was wrapped from head to foot in a coarse blanket, which shook with the violence of his chill, as if his limbs were about to drop in pieces. He seemed unconscious of all that was passing; his long, matted hair hung over his wasted face; his eyes glared steadily forward, with an expression of suffering so utterly hopeless and wild, that I shuddered at seeing it. This was but one out of a number of cases, equally sad and distressing. The exposure and privations of a miner's life soon sap a frame that has not previously been hardened by the elements, and the maladies incident to a new country assail with double force the constitutions thus prepared to receive them.

I found the climate of San Francisco vastly improved during my absence. The temperature was more genial and equable, and the daily hurricanes of the summer had almost entirely ceased. As a consequence of this, the streets had a more active and pleasant aspect, and the continual whirl of business was enlivened by something like cheerfulness. Politics had taken root in this appropriate hot-bed of excitement, and was flourishing with a rapidity and vigor of growth which showed that, though an exotic plant, it would soon be native in the soil. Meetings were held nearly every night at Denison's Exchange, where the rival parties —for the different personal interests were not slow in arraying themselves against each other—had their speeches, their huzzas and their drinks. The Congressional candidates bore the brunt of the struggle, since three or four of them were residents; but the Senatorship gave rise to the most deep-laid and complicated machinations. The principal candidates, T. Butler King, Col. Frémont and Dr. Gwin, had each his party of devoted adherents, who occupied the two weeks intervening between the nomination and election, in sounding and endeavoring to procure the votes of the candidates for the State Legislature, on whom the choice of Senators depended.

Col. Frémont was residing at the time in the Happy Valley, in a Chinese house, which he had erected on one of his lots. Mr. King was at Sonoma, where he had gone to recruit, after an illness which was near proving fatal. His friends, however, called a meeting in his favor, which was held in Portsmouth Square—an injudicious movement, as the consequence proved. Dr. Gwin was making an electioneering tour through the mining districts, for the purpose of securing the election of the proper Delegates to the State Senate and Assembly. It was curious how soon the American passion for politics, forgotten during the first stages of the State organization, revived and emulated the excitement of an election in the older States.

A day or two after my arrival, the Steamer Unicorn came into the harbor, being the third which had arrived without bringing a mail. These repeated failures were too much for even a patient people to bear; an indignation meeting in Portsmouth Square was called, but a shower, heralding the rainy season, came on in time to prevent it. Finally, on the last day of October, on the eve of the departure of another steamer down the coast, the Panama came in, bringing the mails for July, August and September all at once! Thirty-seven mail-bags were hauled up to the little Post-Office that night, and the eight clerks were astounded by the receipt of forty-five thousand letters, besides uncounted bushels of newspapers. I was at the time domiciled in Mr. Moore's garret and enjoying the hospitalities of his plank-table ; I therefore offered my services as clerk-extraordinary, and was at once vested with full powers and initiated into all the mysteries of counting, classifying and distributing letters.

The Post-Office was a small frame building, of one story, and not more than forty feet in length. The entire front, which was graced with a narrow portico, was appropriated to the windows for delivery, while the rear was divided into three small compartments —a newspaper room, a private office, and kitchen. There were two windows for the general delivery, one for French and Spanish letters, and a narrow entry at one end of the building, on which faced the private boxes, to the number of five hundred, leased to merchants and others at the rate of $1,50 per month. In this small space all the operations of the Office were carried on. The rent of the building was $7,000 a year, and the salaries of the clerks from $100 to $300 monthly, which, as no special provision had been made by Government to meet the expense, effectually confined Mr. Moore to these narrow limits. For his strict and conscientious adherence to the law, he received the violent censure of a party of the San Franciscans, who would have had him make free use of the Government funds.

The Panama's mail-bags reached the Office about nine o'clock. The doors were instantly closed, the windows darkened, and every preparation made for a long siege. The attack from without commenced about the same time. There were knocks on the doors, taps on the windows, and beseeching calls at all corners of the house. The interior was well lighted ; the bags were emptied on the floor, and ten pairs of hands engaged in the assortment and distribution of their contents. The work went on rapidly and noiselessly as the night passed away, but with the first streak of daylight the attack commenced again. Every avenue of entrance was barricaded; the crowd was told through the keyhole that the Office would be opened that day to no one : but it all availed nothing. Mr. Moore's Irish servant could not go for a bucket of water without being surrounded and in danger of being held captive. Men dogged his heels in the hope of being able to slip in behind him before he could lock the door.

We labored steadily all day, and had the satisfaction of seeing the huge pile of letters considerably diminished. Towards evening the impatience of the crowd increased to a most annoying pitch. They knocked ; they tried shouts and then whispers and then shouts again ; they implored and threatened by turns ; and not seldom offered large bribes for the delivery of their letters. " Curse such a Post-Office and such a Post-Master !" said one ; " I'll write to the Department by the next steamer. *We'll* see whether things go on in this way much longer." Then comes a messenger slyly to the back-door : " Mr. —— sends his compliments, and says you would oblige him very much by letting me have his letters ; he won't say anything about it to anybody." A clergyman, or perhaps a naval officer, follows, relying on a white cravat or gilt buttons for the favor which no one else can obtain. Mr. Moore politely but firmly refuses ; and so we work on, unmoved by the noises of the besiegers. The excitement and anxiety of the public can scarcely be told in words. Where the source that governs business, satisfies affection and supplies intelligence, had been shut off from a whole community for three months, the rush from all sides to supply the void, was irresistible.

In the afternoon, a partial delivery was made to the owners of

private boxes. It was effected in a skillful way, though with some
danger to the clerk who undertook the opening of the door. On
account of the crush and destruction of windows on former occasions, he ordered them to form into line and enter in regular order.
They at first refused, but on his counter-refusal to unlock the door,
complied with some difficulty. The moment the key was turned,
the rush into the little entry was terrific ; the glass faces of the
boxes were stove in, and the wooden partition seemed about to
give way. In the space of an hour the clerk took in postage to
the amount of $600 ; the principal firms frequently paid from $50
to $100 for their correspondence.

We toiled on till after midnight of the second night, when the
work was so far advanced that we could spare an hour or two for
rest, and still complete the distribution in time for the opening of
the windows, at noon the next day. So we crept up to our blankets in the garret, worn out by forty-four hours of steady labor.
We had scarcely begun to taste the needful rest, when our sleep,
deep as it was, was broken by a new sound. Some of the besiegers, learning that the windows were to be opened at noon,
came on the ground in the middle of the night, in order to have
the first chance for letters. As the nights were fresh and cool,
they soon felt chilly, and began a stamping march along the portico, which jarred the whole building and kept us all painfully
awake. This game was practised for a week after the distribution
commenced, and was a greater hardship to those employed in the
Office than their daily labors. One morning, about a week after
this, a single individual came about midnight, bringing a chair with
him, and some refreshments. He planted himself directly opposite
the door, and sat there quietly all night. It was the day for dis-
patching the Monterey mail, and one of the clerks got up about

four o'clock to have it in readiness for the carrier. On opening
the door in the darkness, he was confronted by this man, who,
seated solemnly in his chair, immediately gave his name in a loud
voice : " John Jenkins !"

When, finally, the windows were opened, the scenes around the
office were still more remarkable. In order to prevent a general
riot among the applicants, they were recommended to form in
ranks. This plan once established, those inside could work with
more speed and safety. The lines extended in front all the way
down the hill into Portsmouth Square, and on the south side
across Sacramento street to the tents among the chapparal ; while
that from the newspaper window in the rear stretched for some
distance up the hill. The man at the tail of the longest line
might count on spending six hours in it before he reached the
window. Those who were near the goal frequently sold out their
places to impatient candidates, for ten, and even twenty-five dollars ; indeed, several persons, in want of money, practised this
game daily, as a means of living ! Venders of pies, cakes and
newspapers established themselves in front of the office, to supply
the crowd, while others did a profitable business by carrying cans
of coffee up and down the lines.

The labors of the Post Office were greatly increased by the
necessity of forwarding thousands of letters to the branch offices
or to agents among the mountains, according to the orders of the
miners. This part of the business, which was entirely without
remuneration, furnished constant employment for three or four
clerks. Several persons made large sums by acting as agents,
supplying the miners with their letters, at $1 each, which in-
cluded the postage from the Atlantic side. The arrangements

for the transportation of the inland mail were very imperfect, and these private establishments were generally preferred.

The necessity of an immediate provision for the support of all branches of Government service, was, (and still remains, at the time I write,) most imminent. Unless something be speedily done, the administration of many offices in California must become impossible. The plan of relief is simple and can readily be accomplished—in the Civil Department, by a direct increase of emolument, in the Military and Naval, by an advance in the price of rations, during service on the Pacific Coast. Our legislators appear hardly to understand the enormous standard of prices, and the fact that many years must elapse before it can be materially lessened. Men in these days will not labor for pure patriotism, when the country is so well able to pay them.

CHAPTER XXI.

SACRAMENTO RIVER AND CITY.

THE change of temperature following the heavy shower which fell the day after my arrival at San Francisco, seemed to announce the near approach of the rainy season. I made all haste, therefore, to start on my tour through the northern placers, fearing lest it might be made impossible by a longer delay. The schooner James L. Day was advertised to leave for Sacramento City about the time we had finished distributing the mail, and as no preparation is required for a journey in California, I took my sarape and went down to Clark's Point, which is to San Francisco what Whitehall is to New York. The fare was $14, which included our embarkation—a matter of some little consequence, when $5 was frequently paid to be rowed out to a vessel. There were about seventy passengers on board, the greater part of whom had just arrived in the steamer Panama. The schooner was a trim, beautiful craft, that had weathered the gales of Cape Horn. A strong wind was blowing from the south, with a rain coming up, as we hove anchor and fired a parting gun. We passed the islands of Yerba Buena and Alcatraz, looked out through the Golden Gate on the Pacific, and dashed into the strait connecting the Bay of San Francisco with Pablo Bay, before a ten-knot breeze. This strait, six miles in length and about three in breadth, presents a constant variety of scene, from the irregularity of its mountain-shores. In the middle of it stands an island of red volcanic rock, near which are two smaller ones, white with guano, called The Brothers. At the entrance of Pablo Bay are two others, The Sisters, similar in size and form.

Pablo Bay is nearly circular, and about twelve miles in diameter. The creeks of Napa, Petaluma and San Rafael empty into it on the northern side, opposite Mare Island, so called from a wild mare who was formerly seen at the head of a band of elk, galloping over its broad meadows. We had but a dim glimpse of the shore through the rain. Our schooner bent to the wind, and cut the water so swiftly, that it fairly whistled under her sharp prow. The spray dashed over the deck and the large sails were motionless in their distension, as we ran before the gale, at a most exhilarating speed. A very good dinner at $1, was served up in the eight-by-ten cabin and there was quite a run upon the cook's galley, for pies, at $1 apiece.

We speedily made the entrance to the Straits of Carquinez, where the mountains approach to within three-quarters of a mile. Several of the newly-arrived emigrants expressed themselves delighted with the barren shores and scanty patches of chapparal. It was their first view of the inland scenery of California. The rain had already brought out a timid green on the hills, and the soil no longer looked parched and dead. "Ah!" said one of the company, "what beautiful mountains! this California is really a splendid country." "Very well," thought I, "but if you dig less gold than you anticipate, catch the ague or fail in speculation, what will you say then? Will not the picture you draw be as dark and forbidding as it is now delightful?"

We passed a small sail-boat, bound for Sacramento and filled with emigrants. Half of them were employed in bailing out the scud thrown over the gunwale by every surge. We shot by them like a flash, and came in sight of Benicia, once thought to be a rival to San Francisco. In a glen on the opposite shore is the little town of Martinez. Benicia is a very pretty place ; the situation is well chosen, the land gradually sloping back from the water, with ample space for the spread of the town. The anchorage is excellent, vessels of the largest size being able to lie so near shore as to land goods without lightering. The back country, including the Napa and Sonoma valleys, is one of the finest agricultural districts of California. Notwithstanding these advantages, Benicia must always remain inferior, in commercial importance, both to San Francisco and Sacramento City. While in the country, I was much amused in reading the letters respecting it, which had been sent home and published, many of them predicting the speedy downfall of San Francisco, on account of the superior advantages of the former place. On the strength of these letters vessels had actually cleared for Benicia, with large cargoes. Now, anchorage is one thing, and a good market another ; a ship may lie in greater safety at Albany, but the sensible merchant charters his vessel for New York. San Francisco is marked by Nature and Fate (though many will disagree with me in the first half of the assertion) for the great commercial mart of the Pacific, and whatever advantages she may lack will soon be amply provided for by her wealth and enterprise.

Benicia—very properly, as I think—has been made the Naval and Military Station for the Bay. Gen. Smith and Commodore Jones both have their head quarters there. The General's house and the military barracks are built on a headland at the entrance of Suisun Bay—a breezy and healthy situation. Monte Diablo, the giant of the Coast Range, rises high and blue on the other side of the strait, and away beyond the waters of the Bay, beyond the waste marshes of tulé and the broad grazing plains, and above the low outlines of many an intermediate chain, loom up faint and far and silvery, the snows of the Sierra Nevada.

We came-to off New-York-of-the-Pacific in four hours after leaving San Francisco—a distance of fifty miles. The former place, with its aspiring but most awkward name, is located on a level plain, on the southern shore of Suisun Bay, backed by a range of barren mountains. It consists of three houses, one of which is a three-story one, and several vessels at anchor near the shore. The anchorage is good, and were it not for the mosquitos, the crews might live pleasantly enough, in their seclusion. There never will be a large town there, for the simple reason that there is no possible cause why there *should* be one. Stockton and Sacramento City supply the mines, San Francisco takes the commerce, Benicia the agricultural produce, with a fair share of the inland trade, and this Gotham-of-the-West, I fear, must continue to belie its title.

We anchored, waiting for the steamer Sacramento, which was to meet the schooner and receive her passengers. She came along side after dark, but owing to the violence of the rain, did not leave until midnight. She was a small, light craft, not more than sixty feet in length, and had been shipped to San Francisco around Cape Horn. She was at first employed to run between Sacramento City and San Francisco, but proved insufficient to weather the rough seas of the open Bay. The arrival of the steamer McKim, which is a good sea-boat and therefore adapted to the navigation of the Bay, where the waves are little less violent than in the Pacific, drove her from the route, but she still continued to run on the Sacramento River. Many small steamers, of similar frail construction, were sent around the Horn, the speculators imagining they were the very thing for inland navigation. The engine of the Sacramento was on deck, as also was her den of a cabin—a filthy place, about six feet by eight. A few berths, made of two coarse blankets laid on a plank, were to be had at $5 each; but I preferred taking a camp-stool, throwing my sarape over my shoulders and sleeping with my head on the table, rather than pay such an unchristian price.

As the day dawned, gloomy and wet, I went on deck. We were near the head of "The Slough," a broad navigable cut-off, which saves twenty miles in making the trip. The banks are lined with thickets, behind which extends a narrow belt of timber, principally oak and sycamore. Here and there, in cleared spots, were the cabins of the woodmen, or of squatters, who intend claiming preëmption rights. The wood, which brings $12 or $15 a cord, is piled on the bluff banks, and the steamers back up to it, whenever they are obliged to "wood up." At the junction of the slough with the river proper, there is a small village of Indian huts, built of dry tulé reeds.

The Sacramento is a beautiful stream. Its width varies from two to three hundred yards, and its banks fringed with rich foliage, present, by their continuous windings, a fine succession of views. In appearance, it reminded me somewhat of the Delaware. The foliage, washed by the rain, glistened green and freshly in the morning; and as we advanced the distant mountains on either hand were occasionally visible through gaps in the timber. Before reaching the town of Sutter, we passed a ranche, the produce of which, in vegetables alone, was said to have returned the owner

—a German, by the name of Schwartz—$25,000 during the season. Sutter is a town of some thirty houses, scattered along the bank for half a mile. Three miles above this we came in sight of Sacramento City. The forest of masts along the embarcadero more than rivalled the splendid growth of the soil. Boughs and spars were mingled together in striking contrast ; the cables were fastened to the trunks and sinewy roots of the trees ; sign-boards and figure-heads were set up on shore, facing the levee, and galleys and deck-cabins were turned out " to grass," leased as shops, or occupied as dwellings. The aspect of the place, on landing, was decidedly more novel and picturesque than that of any other town in the country.

The plan of Sacramento City is very simple. Situated on the eastern bank of the Sacramento, at its junction with the Rio Americano, the town plot embraces a square of about one and a-half miles to a side. It is laid out in regular right-angles, in Philadelphia style, those running east and west named after the alphabet, and those north and south after the arithmetic. The limits of the town extended to nearly one square mile, and the number of inhabitants, in tents and houses, fell little short of ten thousand. The previous April there were just four houses in the place ! Can the world match a growth like this ?

The original forest-trees, standing in all parts of the town, give it a very picturesque appearance. Many of the streets are lined with oaks and sycamores, six feet in diameter, and spreading ample boughs on every side. The emigrants have ruined the finest of them by building camp-fires at their bases, which, in some instances, have burned completely through, leaving a charred and blackened arch for the superb tree to rest upon. The storm which occurred a few days previous to my visit, snapped asunder

several trunks which had been thus weakened, one of them crushing to the earth a canvas house in which a man lay asleep. A
heavy bough struck the ground on each side of him, saving his
life. The destruction of these trees is the more to be regretted,
as the intense heat of the Summer days, when the mercury stands
at 120°, renders their shade a thing of absolute necessity.

The value of real estate in Sacramento City is only exceeded by
that of San Francisco. Lots twenty by seventy-five feet, in the
best locations, brought from $3,000 to $3,500. Rents were on
a scale equally enormous. The City Hotel, which was formerly a
saw-mill, erected by Capt. Sutter, paid $30,000 per annum. A
new hotel, going up on the levee, had been already rented at
$35,000. Two drinking and gaming-rooms, on a business street,
paid each $1,000, monthly, invariably in advance. Many of the
stores transacted business averaging from $1,000 to $3,000 daily.
Board was $20 per week at the restaurants and $5 per day at the
City Hotel. But what is the use of repeating figures? These
dead statistics convey no idea of the marvellous state of things in
the place. It was difficult enough for those who saw to believe,
and I can only hope to reproduce the very faintest impression of
the pictures I there beheld. It was frequently wondered, on this
side of the Rocky Mountains, why the gold dust was not sent out
of the country in larger quantities, when at least forty thousand
men were turning up the placers. The fact is, it was required as
currency, and the amount in circulation might be counted by millions. Why, the building up of a single street in Sacramento
City (J street) cost *half a million*, at least! The value of all
the houses in the city, frail and perishing as many of them were,
could not have been less than $2,000,000.

It must be acknowledged there is another side to the picture.

Three-fourths of the people who settle in Sacramento City are visited by agues, diarrhœas and other reducing complaints. In Summer the place is a furnace, in Winter little better than a swamp ; and the influx of emigrants and discouraged miners generally exceeds the demand for labor. A healthy, sensible, wide-awake man, however, cannot fail to prosper. In a country where Labor rules everything, no sound man has a right to complain. When carpenters make a strike because they only get *twelve dollars* a day, one may be sure there is room enough for industry and enterprise of all kinds.

The city was peopled principally by New-Yorkers, Jerseymen and people from the Western States. In activity and public spirit, it was nothing behind San Francisco ; its growth, indeed, in view of the difference of location, was more remarkable. The inhabitants had elected a Town Council, adopted a City Charter and were making exertions to have the place declared a port of entry. The political waters were being stirred a little, in anticipation of the approaching election. Mr. Gilbert, of the Alta California, and Col. Steuart, candidate for Governor, were in the city. A political meeting, which had been held a few nights before, in front of the City Hotel, passed off as uproariously and with as zealous a sentiment of patriotism as such meetings are wont to exhibit at home. Among the residents whom I met during my visit, was Gen. Green, of Texas, known as commander of the Mier Expedition.

The city already boasted a weekly paper, the *Placer Times*, which was edited and published by Mr. Giles, formerly of the Tribune Office. His printers were all old friends of mine—one of them, in fact, a former fellow-apprentice—and from the fraternal feeling that all possess who have ever belonged to the craft, the place became at once familiar and home-like. The little paper, which had a page of about twelve by eighteen inches, had a circulation of five hundred copies, at $12 a year ; the amount received weekly for jobs and advertising, varied from $1,000 to $2,000. Tickets were printed for the different political candidates, at the rate of $20 for every thousand. The compositors were paid $15 daily. Another compositor from the Tribune Office had established a restaurant, and was doing a fine business. His dining saloon was an open tent, unfloored ; the tables were plank, with rough benches on each side ; the waiters rude Western boys who had come over the Rocky Mountains—but the meals he furnished could not have been surpassed in any part of the world for substantial richness of quality. There was every day abundance of elk steaks, unsurpassed for sweet and delicate flavor ; venison, which had been fattened on the mountain acorns ; mutton, such as nothing but the wild pastures of California could produce ; salmon and salmon-trout of astonishing size, from the Sacramento River, and now and then the solid flesh of the grizzly bear. The salmon-trout exceeded in fatness any fresh-water fish I ever saw ; they were between two and three feet in length, with a layer of pure fat, quarter of an inch in thickness, over the ribs. When made into chowder or stewed in claret, they would have thrown into ecstacies the most inveterate Parisian gourmand. The full-moon face of the proprietor of the restaurant was accounted for, when one had tasted his fare ; after living there a few days, I could feel my own dimensions sensibly enlarged.

The road to Sutter's Fort, the main streets and the levee fronting on the Embarcadero, were constantly thronged with the teams of emigrants, coming in from the mountains. Such worn, weather-beaten individuals I never before imagined. Their tents were pitched by hundreds in the thickets around the town, where they rested a few days before starting to winter in the mines and elsewhere. At times the levee was filled throughout its whole length by their teams, three or four yoke of oxen to every wagon. The beasts had an expression of patient experience which plainly showed that no roads yet to be traveled would astonish them in the least. After tugging the wagons for six months over the salt deserts of the Great Basin, climbing passes and cañons of terrible asperity in the Sierra Nevada, and learning to digest oak bark on the arid plains around the sink of Humboldt's River, it seemed as if no extremity could henceforth intimidate them. Much toil and suffering had given to their countenances a look of almost human wisdom. If their souls should hereafter, according to the theory of some modern philosophers, reäppear in human frames, what a crowd of grave and reverend sages may not California be able to produce ! The cows had been yoked in with the oxen and made to do equal duty. The women who had come by the overland route appeared to have stood the hardships of the journey remarkably well, and were not half so loud as the men in their complaints

The amount of gambling in Sacramento City was very great, and the enticement of music was employed even to a greater extent than in San Francisco. All kinds of instruments and tunes made night discordant, for which harrowing service the performers were paid an ounce each. Among the many drinking houses, there was one called " The Plains," which was much frequented by the emigrants. Some western artist, who came across the country, adorned its walls with scenic illustrations of the route, such as Independence Rock, The Sweet-Water Valley, Fort Laramie, Wind River Mountains, etc. There was one of a pass in the Sierra Nevada, on the Carson River route. A wagon and team

were represented as coming down the side of a hill, so nearly perpendicular that it seemed no earthly power could prevent them
from making but a single fall from the summit to the valley.
These particular oxen, however, were happily independent of gravi-
tation, and whisked their tails in the face of the zenith, as they
marched slowly down.

I was indebted for quarters in Sacramento City, to Mr. De
Graw, who was installed in a frame house, copper-roofed, fronting
the levee. I slept very comfortably on a pile of Chinese quilts,
behind the counter, lulled by the dashing of the rain against the
sides of the house. The rainy season had set in, to all appear-
ances, though it was full a month before the usual time. The
sky was bleak and gray, and the wind blew steadily from the
south, an unfailing sign to the old residents. The saying of the
Mexicans seemed to be verified, that, wherever *los Yankis* go,
they take rain with them.

It was therefore the more necessary that I should start at once
for the mountains. In a few weeks the roads would be impassable, and my only chance of seeing the northern rivers be cut off.
The first requisite for the journey was a good horse, to procure
which I first attended the horse-market which was daily held towards the bottom of K street. This was one of the principal sights
in the place, and as picturesque a thing as could be seen anywhere.
The trees were here thicker and of larger growth than in
other parts of the city; the market-ground in the middle of the
street was shaded by an immense evergreen oak, and surrounded
by tents of blue and white canvas. One side was flanked by a
livery-stable—an open frame of poles, roofed with dry tulé, in
which stood a few shivering mules and raw-boned horses, while the
stacks of hay and wheat straw, on the open lots in the vicinity,

offered feed to the buyers of animals, at the rate of $3 daily for each head.

When the market was in full blast, the scene it presented was grotesque enough. There were no regulations other than the fancy of those who had animals to sell; every man was his own auctioneer, and showed off the points of his horses or mules. The ground was usually occupied by several persons at once,—a rough tawny-faced, long-bearded Missourian, with a couple of pack mules which had been starved in the Great Basin; a quondam New York dandy with a horse whose back he had ruined in his luckless "prospecting" among the mountains; a hard-fisted far-mer with the wagon and ox-team which had brought his family and household gods across the continent; or, perhaps, a jocky trader, who understood all the arts of depreciation and recom-mendation, and invariably sold an animal for much more than he gave. The bids were slow, and the seller would sometimes hang for half an hour without an advance; in fact, where three or four were up at once, it required close attention in the buyer to know which way the competition was running.

I saw a lean sorrel mule sold for $55; several others, of that glossy black color and clean make which denote spirit and endu-rance, were held at $140, the owner refusing to let them go for less. The owner of a bay horse, which he rode up and down the market at a brisk pace, could get no bid above $45. As the ani-mal was well made and in good condition, I was about to bid, when I noticed a peculiar glare of the eye which betrayed suffer-ing of some kind. "What kind of a back has he?" I inquired. "It is a very little scratched on the top," was the answer; "but he is none the worse for that." "He'll not do for me," I thought, but I watched the other bidders to see how the buyer would be

10*

satisfied with his purchase. The horse was finally knocked off at
$50 : as the saddle was not included the new owner removed it,
disclosing a horrible patch of raw and shrinking flesh. An alter-
cation instantly arose, which was not settled when I left to seek a
horse elsewhere.

The owner of a stack of hay near at hand desired to sell me a
mule out of a number which he had in charge. But one which
he recommended as a fine saddle-mule would not go at all, though
he wounded her mouth with the cruel bit of the country in the
effort to force her into a trot; another, which was declared to be
remarkably gentle, stumbled and fell with me, and a third, which
seemed to be really a good traveler, was held at a price I did not
desire to pay. At last, the proprietor of a sort of tavern adjoining the market, offered to sell me a gray mare for $100. Now, as
the gray mare is said to be the better horse, and as, on trial, I
found her to possess a steady and easy gait, though a little lazy, I
determined to take her, since, among so many worn-out and used-
up animals, it seemed a matter of mere luck whether I would
have selected a good one. The mare was American, but the
owner assured me she had been long enough in the country, to travel
unshod and keep fat on dry grass. As saddles, blankets, and other
articles were still necessary, my outfit was rather expensive. I procured a tolerable saddle and bridle for $10 ; a lariat and saddle-
blanket for $5 ; a pair of sharp Mexican spurs for $8, and blankets
for $12. With a hunting-knife, a pair of pistols in my pocket, a
compass, thermometer, note-book and pencil, I was prepared for
a tour of any length among the mountains.

BAYARD TAYLOR.

THE VOLCANO DIGGINGS.

NEW YORK, GEO. P. PUTNAM.

LITH. OF SARONY & MAJOR, N.Y.

CHAPTER XXII.

I WAITED another day for the rain to subside, but the wind still blew up the river and the sky remained hopelessly murk and lowering. I therefore buttoned up my corduroy coat, thrust my head through the centre of my sarape, and set out in the teeth of the gale. Leaving the muddy streets, swamped tents and shivering population of Sacramento City, a ride of a mile and a half brought me to Sutter's Fort, built on a slight rise in the plain. It is a large quadrangular structure, with thick adobe walls, and square bastions at each corner. Everything about it showed signs of dilapidation and decay. The corrals of earth had been trampled down ; doors and gateways were broken through the walls, and all kinds of building materials carried away. A two story wooden building, with flag-staff bearing the American colors, stood in the centre of the court-yard, and low ranges of buildings around the sides were variously occupied as hospitals, stores, drinking and gaming shops and dwellings. The hospital, under the charge of Drs. Deal and Martin, was said to be the best regulated in the district. It was at the time filled with fever patients, who received nursing and medical attendance for $100 per week.

Behind the fort, at the distance of quarter of a mile, flows the

Rio Americano, with several fine grazing ranches on its banks. The view on all sides is over a level plain, streaked with lines of timber, and bounded on the east and west, in clear weather, by the distant ranges of the Coast Mountains and the Sierra Nevada. Three or four houses have sprung up on the low ground in front of the fort during the summer. Riding up to a large unfinished frame building to make inquiries about the road, I was answered by a man whom I afterwards learned was the notorious Keysburg, the same who came out with the emigration of 1846, and lived all winter among the mountains on the dead bodies of his companions. He was of a stout, large frame, with an exceedingly coarse, sensual expression of countenance, and even had I not heard his revolting history, I should have marked his as a wholly animal face. It remains in my memory now like that of an ogre, and I only remember it with a shudder. One of those who went out to the Camp of Death, after the snows were melted, described to me the horrid circumstances under which they found him—seated, like a ghoul, in the midst of dead bodies, with his face and hands smeared with blood, and a kettle of human flesh boiling over the fire. He had become a creature too foul and devilish for this earth, and the forbearance with which the men whose children he had devoured while they were toiling back to his succor through almost fathomless snows, refrained from putting him to death, is to be wondered at. He had not the plea of necessity in the use of this revolting food ; for the body of an ox, which had been thawed out of the snow, was found untouched near his cabin. He spoke with a sort of fiendish satisfaction, of the meals he had made, and the men were obliged to drag him away from them by main force, not without the terrible conviction that some of the victims had been put to a violent death,

to glut his appetite.   There is no creation in the whole range of
fiction, so dark and awful in its character, as this man.

After passing the first belt of timber, I was alone on the plains,
which looked strikingly bleak and desolate under the dark and
rainy sky.   The road was filled with pools of mud and water, by
which, when night came down on the changeless waste, I was
enabled to find my way.   The rain set in again, adding greatly to
the discomfort of such travel.   My gray mare, too, lagged more
than I liked, and I began to calculate my chances of remaining
all night on the plain.   About two hours after dark, however, a
faint light glimmered in the distance, and I finally reached the
place of my destination—Murphy's Ranche on the Cosumne
River.   An Indian boy tied my horse to a haystack, and Mrs.
Murphy set about baking some biscuit in a pan, and roasting a
piece of beef for me on a wooden spit.   A company of gold-diggers, on their way from the Yuba to winter on the Mariposa, had
possession of one end of the house, where they lay rolled in their
blankets, their forms barely discernible through the smoke sent
out by the rain-soaked wood of which their fire was made.   I
talked an hour with them about the prospects of mining on the
different rivers, and then lay down to sleep on the clay floor.

The next morning the sky was as thick, heavy and gray as a
Mackinaw blanket, with a precocious drizzle, betokening a storm.
Nevertheless, I saddled and started for Hick's Ranche, a day's
journey distant, in the edge of the mountains.   I forded the
Cosumne River, (almost universally pronounced *Mokosumé*,) at
this place a clear, swift stream, bordered by dense thickets.   It
was already up to my saddle-skirts, and rapidly rising.   Two or
three tulé huts stood on the opposite bank, and a number of dirty,
stupid Indian faces stared at me through the apertures.   Taking

a dim wagon-trail, according to directions, I struck out once more on the open plains. The travel was very toilsome, my horse's feet sinking deeply into the wet, soft soil. The further I went the worse it became. After making five miles, I reached some scattering oak timber, where I was forced to take shelter from the rain, which now beat down drenchingly. Cold and wet, I waited two hours in that dismal solitude for the flood to cease, and taking advantage of the first lull, turned about and rode back to the ranche. All that night it rained hard, and the second morning opened with a prospect more dreary than ever.

My companions in that adobe limbo were the miners, who had been spending the Summer on the upper bars of the Yuba. According to their accounts, the average yield of the Yuba diggings was near two ounces for each man. Those who had taken out claims of eight paces square in the beginning of the season, frequently made $10,000 and upwards. Owing to the severity of the Winter in that region, the greater portion o the miners were moving southward until the Spring. Several companies came up in the course of the day, but as the ranche was full, they were constrained to pitch their tents along the banks of the swollen Cosumne. Mr. Murphy, I found, was the son of the old gentleman whose hospitalities I had shared in the valley of San José. He had been living three years on the river, and his three sturdy young sons could ride and throw the lariat equal to any Californian. There were two or three Indian boys belonging to the house, one of whom, a solid, shock-headed urchin, as grave as if he was born to be a "medicine-man," did all the household duties with great precision and steadiness. He was called "Billy," and though he understood English as well as his own language, I never heard him speak. My only relief, during the wearisome detention, was in watching his deliberate motions, and wondering what thoughts, or whether any thoughts stirred under his immoveable face.

The afternoon of the second day the clouds lifted, and we saw the entire line of the Sierra Nevada, white and cold against the background of the receding storm. As the sun broke forth, near its setting, peak after peak became visible, far away to north and south, till the ridge of eternal snow was unbroken for at least a hundred and fifty miles. The peaks around the head-waters of the American Fork, highest of all, were directly in front. The pure white of their sides became gradually imbued with a rosy flame, and their cones and pinnacles burned like points of fire. In the last glow of the sun, long after it had set to us, the splendor of the whole range, deepening from gold to rose, from rose to crimson, and fading at last into an ashy violet, surpassed even the famous " Alp-glow," as I have seen it from the plains of Piedmont.

An old hunter living on the ranche came galloping up, with a fat, black-tailed doe at the end of his lariat. He had first broken the hind leg of the poor beast with a ball, and then caught her running. The pleading expression of her large black eyes was almost human, but her captor coolly drew his knife across her throat, and left her to bleed to death. She lay on the ground, uttering a piteous bleat as her panting became thick and difficult, but not until the last agony was wholly over, did the dull film steal across the beauty of her lustrous eyes.

On the third morning I succeeded in leaving the ranche, where I had been very hospitably entertained at four dollars a day for myself and horse. The Cosumne was very much swollen by the rains, but my gray mare swam bravely, and took me across with but a slight wetting. I passed my previous halting-place, and was

advancing with difficulty through the mud of the plains, when, on
climbing a small "rise," I suddenly found myself confronted by
four grizzly bears—two of them half-grown cubs—who had possession of a grassy bottom on the other side.   They were not more
than two hundred yards distant.   I halted and looked at them,
and they at me, and I must say they seemed the most unconcerned
of the two parties.   My pistols would kill nothing bigger than a
coyote, and they could easily have outrun my horse ; so I went
my way, keeping an eye on the most convenient tree.   In case of
an attack, the choice of a place of refuge would have been a delicate matter, since the bears can climb up a large tree and gnaw
down a small one.   It required some skill, therefore, in selecting
a trunk of proper size.   At Murphy's, the night previous, they
told me there had been plenty of " bear-sign" along the river, and
in the " pockets" of solid ground among the tulé.   As the rainy
season sets in they always come down from the mountains.

After traveling eight or ten miles the wagon trails began to
scatter, and with my imperfect knowledge of prairie hieroglyphics,
I was soon at fault.   The sky was by this time clear and bright ;
and rather than puzzle myself with wheel-tracks leading everywhere, and cattle-tracks leading nowhere, I guessed at the location
of the ranche to which I was bound and took a bee-line towards it.

The knowledge of tracks and marks is a very important part of
the education of a woodsman.   It is only obtained by unlearning,
or forgetting for the time, all one's civilized acquirements and recalling the original instincts of the animal.   An observing man,
fresh from the city, might with some study determine the character
of a track, but it is the habit of observing them rather than the
discriminating faculty, which enables the genuine hunter to peruse
the earth like a volume, and confidently pronounce on the number

and character of all the animals and men that have lately passed over its surface. Where an inexperienced eye could discern no mark, he will note a hundred trails, and follow any particular one through the maze, with a faculty of sight as unerring as the power of scent in a dog. I was necessitated, during my journey in the interior of California, to pay some attention to this craft, but I never got beyond the rudiments.

Another necessary faculty, as I had constant occasion to notice, is that of observing and remembering the form, color and character of animals. This may seem a simple thing; but let any one, at the close of a ride in the country, endeavor to describe all the horses, mules and oxen he has seen, and he will find himself at fault. A Californian will remember and give a particular description of a hundred animals, which he has passed in a day's journey, and be able to recognize and identify any one of them. Horses and mules are to him what men, newspapers, books and machinery are to us; they are the only science he need know or learn. The habit of noticing them is easily acquired, and is extremely useful in a country where there are neither pounds nor fences.

The heavy canopy of clouds was lifted from the plain almost as suddenly as the cover from a roast turkey at a hotel dinner, when the head waiter has given the wink. The snows of the Nevada shone white along the clear horizon; I could see for many a league on every side, but I was alone on the broad, warm landscape. Over wastes of loose, gravelly soil, into which my horse sank above the fetlocks—across barren ridges, alternating with marshy hollows and pools of water, I toiled for hours, and near sunset reached the first low, timbered hills on the margin of the plain. I dismounted and led my weary horse for a mile or two, but as it grew dark, was obliged to halt in a little glen—a most bear-ish looking place, filled with thick chapparal. A fallen tree supplied me with fuel to hand, and I soon had a glowing fire, beside which I spread my blankets and lay down. Getting up at midnight to throw on more logs, I found my horse gone, and searched the chapparal for an hour, wondering how I should fare, trudging along on foot, with the saddle on my shoulders. At last I found her in a distant part of the wood, with the lariat wound around a tree. After this I slept no more, but lay gazing on the flickering camp-fire, and her gray figure as she moved about in the dusk. Towards dawn the tinkle of a distant mule-bell and afterwards the crowing of a cock gave me welcome signs of near habitation ; and, saddling with the first streak of light, I pushed on, still in the same direction, through a thick patch of thorny chapparal, and finally reached the brow of a wooded ridge just as the sun was rising.

Oh, the cool, fresh beauty of that morning! The sky was deliciously pure and soft, and the tips of the pines on the hills were kindled with a rosy flame from the new-risen sun. Below me lay a beautiful valley, across which ran a line of timber, be- traying, by its luxuriance, the water-course it shaded. The reaches of meadow between were green and sparkling with dew ; here and there, among the luxuriant foliage, peeped the white top of a tent, or rose the pale-blue threads of smoke from freshly- kindled camp-fires. Cattle were grazing in places, and the tinkle of the bell I had heard sounded a blithe welcome from one of the groups. Beyond the tents, in the skirts of a splendid clump of trees stood the very ranche to which I was bound.

I rode up and asked for breakfast. My twenty-four hours' fast was broken by a huge slice of roast venison, and coffee sweetened with black Mexican sugar, which smacks not only of the juice of the cane, but of the leaves, joints, roots, and even the unctuous

soil in which it grows. For this I paid a dollar and a half, but no
money could procure any feed for my famishing horse. Leaving
the ranche, which is owned by a settler named Hicks, my road led
along the left bank of Sutter's Creek for two miles, after which it
struck into the mountains. Here and there, in the gulches, I
noticed signs of the gold-hunters, but their prospecting did not
appear to have been successful. The timber was principally pine
and oak, and of the smaller growths, the red-barked madrono and
a species of *esculus*, with a fruit much larger than our Western
buckeye. The hills are steep, broken and with little apparent
system. A close observation, however, shows them to have a
gradual increase of elevation, to a certain point, beyond which
they fall again. As in the sea the motion of the long swells is
seen through all the small waves of the surface, so this broken
region shows a succession of parallel ridges, regularly increasing
in height till they reach the Sierra Nevada—the " tenth wave,"
with the white foam on its crest.

About noon, I came down again upon Sutter's Creek in a little
valley, settled by miners. A number of tents were pitched along
the stream, and some log houses for the winter were in process of
erection. The diggings in the valley were quite profitable during
the dry season, especially in a cañon above. At the time I passed,
the miners were making from half an ounce to an ounce per day.
I procured a very good dinner at Humphrey's tent, and attempted
to feed my famishing gray with Indian meal at half a dollar the
pound ; but, starving as she was, she refused to eat it. Her pace
had by this time dwindled to a very slow walk, and I could not
find it in my heart to use the spur. Leaving the place immediately after dinner, I crossed a broad mountain, and descended to
Jackson's Creek, where a still greater number of miners were

congregated. Not the Creek only, but all the ravines in the mountains around, furnished ground for their winter labors. A little knoll in the valley, above the reach of floods, was entirely covered with their white tents. The hotel tent was kept by an Oregonian named Cosgrove, and there was in addition a French restaurant.

From Jackson's Creek I took a footpath to the Mokelumne. After scaling the divide, I went down into a deep, wild ravine, where the path, notched along its almost perpendicular sides, threatened to give way beneath my horse's feet. Further down, the bottom was completely turned over by miners, a number of whom were building their log cabins. The rains had brought at last a constant supply of water, and pans and cradles were in full operation among the gravel; the miners were nearly all Frenchmen, and appeared to be doing well. The ravine finally *debouched* upon the river at the Middle Bar. I found the current deep and swollen by the rains, which had broken away all the dams made for turning it. The old brush town was nearly deserted, and very few persons were at work on the river banks, the high water having driven all into the gulches, which continued to yield as much as ever.

I forded the river with some difficulty, owing to the deep holes quarried in its channel, which sometimes plunged my horse down to the neck. On turning the point of a mountain a mile below, I came again in sight of the Lower Bar, and recognized the features of a scene which had become so familiar during my visit in August. The town was greatly changed. As I rode up the hill, I found the summer huts of the Sonorians deserted and the inhabitants gone; Baptiste's airy hotel, with its monte and dining tables, which had done us service as beds, was not to be found.

I feared that all of my friends were gone, and I had made the journey in vain. The place was fast beginning to wear a look of desolation, when as I passed one of the tents, I was hailed by a rough-looking fellow dressed in a red flannel shirt and striped jacket. Who should it be but Dr. Gillette, the sharer of my grotesque ride to Stockton in the summer. After the first salutations were over, he conducted me to Mr. James' tent, where I found my old comrade, Col. Lyons, about sitting down to a smoking dinner of beef, venison and tortillas. Dr. Gwin, one of the candidates for U. S. Senator, had just arrived, and was likewise the guest of Mr. James. I joined him in doing execution at the table, with the more satisfaction, because my poor mare had about a quart of corn—the last to be had in the place—for her supper.

After dinner, Mr. Morse, of New Orleans, candidate for Congress, and Mr. Brooks, of New York, for the Assembly, made their appearance. We had a rare knot of politicians. Col. Lyons was a prominent candidate for the State Senate, and we only lacked the genial presence of Col. Steuart, and the jolly one of Capt. McDougal (who were not far off, somewhere in the diggings,) to have had all the offices represented, from the Governor downwards. After dinner, we let down the curtains of the little tent, stretched ourselves out on the blankets, lighted our cigars and went plump into a discussion of California politics. Each of the candidates had his bundle of tickets, his copies of the Constitution and his particular plans of action. As it happened there were no two candidates for the same office present, the discussion was carried on in perfect harmony and with a feeling of good-fellowship withal. Whatever the politics of the different aspirants, they were, socially, most companionable men. We will not disclose the mysteries of the conclave, but simply remark that every

one slept as soundly on his hard bed as though he were dreaming
of a triumphant election.

The flood in the river, I found, had proved most disastrous to
the operations on the bar. Mr. James' company, which, after
immense labor and expense, had turned the channel for three
hundred yards, and was just beginning to realize a rich profit from
the river-bed, was suddenly stopped. The last day's washing
amounted to $1,700, and the richest portion of the bed was yet
to be washed. The entire expense of the undertaking, which
required the labor of forty men for nearly two months, was more
than twenty thousand dollars, not more than half of which had
been realized. All further work was suspended until the next
summer, when the returns would probably make full amends for
the delay and disappointment. The rich gulch was filled with
miners, most of whom were doing an excellent business. The
strata of white quartz crossing the mountains about half way up
the gulch, had been tried, and found to contain rich veins of gold.
A company of about twelve had commenced sinking a shaft to
strike it at right angles. In fact, the metal had increased, rather
than diminished in quantity, since my former visit.

\

CHAPTER XXIII.

My first care in the morning was to procure forage for my mare. The effects of famine were beginning to show themselves in her appearance. She stood dejectedly beside the pine stump to which she was tethered, now and then gnawing a piece of the bark to satisfy the cravings of her stomach. Her flanks were thin and her sides hollow, and she looked so wistfully at me with her dull, sunken eyes, that I set out at once in the endeavor to procure something better than pine-bark for her breakfast. The only thing I could find in all the village was bread, five small rolls of which I bought at half a dollar apiece, and had the satisfaction of seeing her greedily devour them. This feed, however, was far too expensive, and rather than see her starve outright, I gave her to Gen. Morse, for the ride back to Sacramento City, his own horse having broken loose during the night. The grass, which had already begun to sprout, was not more than quarter of an inch in height, and afforded no sustenance to cattle. I therefore reluctantly decided to shorten my journey, and perform the remainder of it on foot.

The same night of my arrival on the river, I heard many stories about " The Volcano"—a place some twenty miles further into

the heart of the mountains, where, it was said, a very rich deposit of gold had been found, near the mouth of an extinct crater.
I made due allowance for the size which gold lumps attain, the
farther they roll, but a curiosity to see some of the volcanic ap-
pearances which are said to become frequent as you approach the
snowy ridge, induced me to start in the morning after having seen
my horse's head turned again towards the region of hay.

Dr. Gillette kindly offered to accompany me on the trip—an
offer the more welcome, on account of the additional security it
gave me against hostile Indians.   The entire mountain district,
above the Upper Bar (about four miles from the Lower Bar)—
and particularly at the Forks of the Mokelumne—was overrun
with Indians, some of whom were of the tribe of the old chief,
Polo, and others of a tribe lately made hostile to the Americans
by an affray at the Volcano.   Polo, it was rumored had been
shot; but I gave no credit to the report.   He was much too
cautious and cunning, to be entrapped.   To the miners about
that region, he was as much of a will-o'-the-wisp as Abdel-
Kader was to the French.   More than once he visited the diggings in disguise, and no small company, prospecting above the
Forks, was safe from having a brush with his braves.

We took care to provide ourselves with a good double-barreled
rifle before starting.   Our route lay up the river to the Middle
Bar.   Climbing the mountain behind that place, we took a line
for the Butte, a lofty, isolated peak, which serves as a landmark
for the country between the Cosumne and the Mokelumne.   Descending through wild, wooded ravines, we struck an Indian trail,
with fresh tracks upon it.   The thick chapparal, here and there,
made us think of ambuscades, and we traveled more cautiously and
silently than was actually needful.   In the deep nooks and re-

cesses of the mountains we noticed ruined huts and the ashes of deserted camp-fires. The gulches in all directions had been dug up by gold-hunters during the summer. One, in particular, at the foot of the Butte, showed—as we ascended it, for more than a mile—scarcely a foot of soil untouched. The amount of gold obtained from it must have been very great. The traces of these operations, deep in the wilderness, accounted for the fact of miners becoming suddenly rich, after disappearing from the Bars for a few days.

We climbed to the level of the mountain region, out of which the Butte towered a thousand feet above us. Our trail led eastward from its foot, towards the Sierra Nevada, whose shining summits seemed close at hand. The hills were dotted with forests of pine and oak, many specimens of the former tree rising to the height of two hundred and fifty feet. The cones, of a dark red color, were fully eighteen inches in length. The madrono, which rises to a stately tree in the mountains near Monterey, was here a rough shrub, looking, with its blood-red arms and lifeless foliage, as if it had been planted over a murderer's grave. The ground, in the sheltered hollows, was covered with large acorns, very little inferior to chesnuts in taste; the deer and bear become very fat at this season, from feeding upon them. They form the principal subsistence of the Indian tribes during the winter. In one of the ravines we found an "Indian wind-mill," as the miners call it—a flat rock, with half a dozen circular holes on its surface, beside each of which lay a round stone, used in pulverizing the acorns. We passed one or two inhabited camps a short distance from the trail, but were apparently unobserved. Further on, in the forest, we came suddenly upon two young Indians, who were going on a trail leading towards the Forks. They started at first to run, but stopped when we hailed them ; they understood neither English nor Spanish, but some tobacco which the doctor gave them was very joyfully received.

The stillness and beauty of the shaded glens through which we traveled were very impressive. Threaded by clear streams which turned the unsightly holes left by the miners into pools of crystal, mirroring the boughs far above, their fresh, cool aspect was very different from the glowing furnaces they form in summer. The foliage was still very little changed ; only the leaves of the buck-eye had fallen, and its polished nuts filled the paths. The ash was turned to a blazing gold, and made a perpetual sunset in the woods. But the oak here wore an evergreen livery ; the grass was already shooting up over all the soil, and the Winter at hand was so decked in the mixed trappings of Summer Autumn and Spring, that we hardly recognized him.

Late in the afternoon we accidentally took a side trail, which led up a narrow ravine and finally brought us to an open space among the hills, where a company of prospecters were engaged in pitching their tent for the winter. They were seven in number, mostly sailors, and under the command of a Virginian named Woodhouse. Their pack-mules had just arrived with supplies from their former camp, and a half-naked Indian was trying to get some flour. On learning the scarcity of the article on the river, they refused to sell him any. He importuned them some time, but in vain : " Very well," said he, " you shall be driven off to-morrow," and went away. We were very hungry, and employed the cook of the company to get us something to eat. He built a fire, fried some salt pork, and made us a dish of pancakes. I could not help admiring the dexterity with which he tossed the cake in the air and caught it on the other side as it came down into the pan. We ate with an animal voracity, for the usual California appetite—equal to that of three men at home—was sharpened by our long walk.

It was now beginning to grow dark, and a rain coming on. We were seven miles from the Volcano, and would have preferred remaining for the night, had the miners given any encouragement to our hints on the subject. Instead of this, it seemed to us that they were suspicious of our being spies upon their prospecting, so we left them and again plunged into the forest. Regaining the proper trail we went at a rapid rate through gloomy ravines, which were canopied by thick mist. It grew darker, and the rain began to fall. We pushed on in silence, hoping to reach some place of shelter, but the trail became more and more indistinct, till at last we kept it with our feet rather than our eyes. I think we must have walked in it a mile after we ceased entirely to see it. Once or twice we heard yells in the distance, which we took to be those of a party of the hostile Indians. The air grew pitchy dark, and the rain fell so fast, that we lost the trail and determined to stop for the night. We had just crossed a sort of divide, and our position, as near as we could tell in the gloom, was at the entrance of a deep ravine, entirely covered with forests, and therefore a tolerably secure covert. I had two or three matches in my pocket, from which we struck a flame, at the foot of a pine tree. We fed it daintily at first with the dry needles and filaments of bark, till it grew strong enough and hungry enough to dry its own fuel. Swinging with our whole weight to the ends of the boughs, we snapped off sufficient to last for the night, and then lay down on the dark side of the tree, with our arms between us to keep them dry. The cold, incessant rain, pouring down through the boughs, soon drenched us quite, and we crawled around to the other side.

The Indians, like Death, love a shining mark ; and the thought of an arrow sent out of the gloom around us, made our backs feel uncomfortable as we stood before the fire. Lying in the rain, however, without blankets, was equally unpleasant ; so we took alternate half-hours of soaking and drying.

Salt pork and exercise combined, gave us an intolerable thirst, to allay which we made torches of cedar bark and went down to the bottom of the ravine for water. There was none to be found ; and we were about giving up the search when we came to a young pine, whose myriad needles were bent down with their burden of rain-drops. No nectar was ever half so delicious. We caught the twigs in our mouths and drained them dry, then cut down the tree and carried it back in triumph to our fire, where we planted it and let the rain fill up its aromatic beakers. The night seemed interminable. The sound of the rain was like stealthy footsteps on the leaves ; the howling of wolves and the roar of water-falls at a distance, startled us. Occasionally, the tread of some animal among the trees—possibly a deer, attracted by the flame—put all our senses on the alert. Just before daybreak the storm ceased, and in ten minutes afterwards the sky was without a cloud.

The morning broke brightly and cheeringly. We resumed the path, which led into a grassy meadow about a mile long, at the further end of which we struck a wagon trail. A saucy wolf came down to the edge of the woods, and barked at us most impertinently, but we did not think him worth the powder. The air was fragrant with the smell of cedar—a species of the *thuya*—which here grows to the height of two hundred feet. Its boles are perfectly straight and symmetrical, and may be split with the axe into boards and shingles. Many of the trees had been felled for this purpose, and lay by the roadside. From the top of a little ridge we looked down into the valley of the Volcano, and could see the smoke rising from the tents. The encampment is in a deep basin, surrounded by volcanic hills, several of which contain extinct craters. A small stream flows through the midst. The tents and cabins of the miners are on the lower slopes of the hills, and the diggings are partly in the basin and partly in gulches which branch off from its northern side. The location is very beautiful, and more healthy than the large rivers.

Descending into the valley, we stopped at a tent for breakfast, which was got ready by the only female in the settlement—a woman from Pennsylvania, whose husband died on the journey out. A number of the miners were from the same place. Maj. Bartlett of Louisiana, with his company, were also at work there ; and in another valley, beyond the wooded ridge to the north-east, Capt. Jones of Illinois was located, with a company of about sixty men. The whole number of persons at this digging was nearly one hundred and fifty, and they had elected an Alcalde and adopted laws for their government. The supplies on hand were very scanty, but they had more on the way, which the first favorable weather would enable them to receive.

In addition to my motives of curiosity, in visiting the Volcano, I was empowered with a political mission to the diggers. The candidates on the Mokelumne gave me letters to some of them, and packages of tickets which I was enjoined to commend to their use. On delivering the letters, I found I was considered as having authority to order an election—a power which was vested only in the Prefect of the District or his special agents. At the suggestion of some of the miners I went with them to the Alcalde, in order to have a consultation. I disclaimed all authority in the matter, but explained to them the mode in which the elections were to be held on the river, and recommended them to adopt a similar action. Owing to the short time which elapsed between the Governor's proclamation and the day of election, it was impossible for the Prefect of each district to notify all the organized communities. The only plan, therefore, was to meet on the appointed day, publicly elect Judges and Inspectors, and hold the election in all other respects according to the requirements of the Constitution. This was agreed to by the law-givers of the Volcano as the most advisable mode of action. But behold how easy it is, in a primitive community like this, to obtain the popular favor ! There was, on one of the tickets in the San Joaquin district, a candidate for the State Senate, whose surname was the same as mine, and the Volcanics, as I afterwards learned, took me to be the same individual. " We will vote for him," said they, " because he came here to see us, and because he appears to understand the law." Accordingly, the whole vote of the place was given to my namesake, but intended for me. Had I known this fact sooner, I might have been tempted to run for Alcalde, at least.

Major Bartlett went with us to examine the diggings. The alluvial soil of the basin contains little gold, but has been dug up very extensively by the miners, in search of the clay stratum ; beside which the gold is found in coarse grains, mixed with sand and gravel. There is, however, no regularity in the stratum ; everything bears marks of violent change and disruption. In holes dug side by side, I noticed that the clay would be reached eighteen inches below the surface in one, and perhaps eight feet in the other. This makes the digging something of a lottery, those who find a deposit always finding a rich one, and those who find none making nothing at all. In the gulches the yield is more certain. A Mexican had lately taken twenty-eight pounds out of a single "pocket;" another miner, having struck a rich spot, dug $8,000 in a few days. Many made three, four and five ounces daily for several days. In the upper valley the average was about an ounce a day. From my hasty examination of the place, I should not think the gold was thrown up by the craters in a melted state, as the miners imagine. The fact of its being found with the layer of clay would refute this idea. From the strata, water-courses, and other indications, it is nevertheless evident that large slides from the hills, occasioned by earthquakes or eruptions, have taken place.

I climbed the hills and visited two of the craters, neither of which appeared to be the main opening of the volcano. On the contrary, I should rather judge them to be vents or escape-holes for the confined flame, formed in the sides of the mountain. The rocks, by upheaval, are thrown into irregular cones, and show everywhere the marks of intense heat. Large seams, blackened by the subterranean fire, run through them, and in the highest parts are round, smooth holes, a foot in diameter, to some of which no bottom can be found. These are evidently the last flues through which the air and flame made their way, as the surface hardened over the cooling volcano. The Indian traditions go back to the time when these craters were active, but their chronology is totally indefinite, and I am not geologist enough to venture an opinion. Pines at least a century old, are now growing on the rim of the craters. Further up the mountain, the miners informed me, there are large beds of lava, surrounding craters of still larger dimensions.

We took dinner at Major Bartlett's tent, and started on our return accompanied by Dr. Carpentier, of Saratoga, N. Y. Before leaving, I took pains to learn the particulars of the recent fight with the Indians at the Volcano. The latter, it seems, first discovered the placer, and were digging when the whites arrived. They made room for them at once, and proposed that they should work peaceably together. Things went on amicably for several days, when one of the miners missed his pick. He accused the Indians of stealing it; the chief declared that if it was in their camp it should be returned, and started to make inquiries. Instead of walking he ran; upon which one of the whites raised his rifle and shot him. The Indians then armed at once. The miners called up the remaining white men from the placer, and told them that they had been attacked and one of their number killed. The consequence of this false information was a general assault upon the Indians who were at once driven off, and had not returned up to the time of my visit. The same day a man named Aldrich, from Boston, was found in the meadow on the trail by which we came, pierced with three arrows. The neighborhood of the Volcano was considered dangerous ground, and no one thought of venturing into the mountains, unless well armed. It is due to the miners to say, that on learning the true state of the quarrel, they banished the scoundrels whose heartless cruelty had placed the whole community in peril.

We retraced our steps, saw the snows of the Nevada turned by the sunset to a brighter gold than any hidden in its veins, and reached the camp of the prospecters in a starry and beautiful twilight. As we approached through the trees, in the gathering gloom, they shouted to us to keep off, taking us for Indians, but allowed us to approach, when we answered in English. We were kindly received, and again procured an excellent supper. The men were better than we imagined. They had been anxious about our safety the previous night, and fired their rifles as signals to

us.   After we had grown tired of talking around the blazing camp-
fire about grizzly bears, Mexicans, Gila deserts and gulches whose
pockets were filled with gold, they gave us a corner in their tent
and shared their blankets with us.   I took their kindness as a re-
buke to my former suspicions of their selfishness, and slept all
the better for the happiness of being undeceived.

It was a model morning that dawned upon us.   The splash of
a fountain in the sun, the gloss of a white dove's wing, the wink-
ing of the beaded bubbles on Keats' cool draught of vintage, could
not have added a sparkle to its brightness.   The sky was as blue
and keen as a Damascus blade, and the air, filled with a resinous
odor of pine, cedar and wild bay, was like the intoxication of new
life to the frame.   We were up and off with the dawn, and walked
several miles before breakfast.   On reaching the foot of the Butte,
Dr. G. and myself determined to make the ascent.   Its ramparts
of red volcanic rock, bristling with chapparal, towered a thousand
feet above us, seemingly near at hand in the clear air.   We believed we should be the first to scale its summit.   The miners do
not waste time in climbing peaks, and the Indians keep aloof, with
superstitious reverence, from the dwelling-places of spirits.

After a toilsome ascent, at an angle of 45°, we reached the
summit.   Here, where we supposed no human foot had ever been,
we found on the crowning stone—the very apex of the pyramid—
the letters " D. B." rudely cut with a knife.   Shade of Daniel
Boone ! who else but thou could have been pioneer in this far
corner of the Farthest West ! As the buried soldier is awakened
by the squadron that gallops to battle over his grave, has the
tramp of innumerable trains through the long wilderness called
thee forth to march in advance, and leave thy pioneer mark on
every unexplored region between sea and sea ?

Nevertheless we gave the name of Polo's Peak to the Butte—
in honor of the dauntless old chief who presided over the country
round about. Before I left the region, the name was generally
adopted by the miners, and I hope future travelers will remember
it. The view from the top is remarkably fine. Situated about
half-way between the plain and the dividing ridge of the Sierra
Nevada, the Peak overlooks the whole mountain country. The
general appearance is broken and irregular, except to the east,
where the ranges are higher. The mountains within ten miles of
us had snow on their crests, and the Nevada—immaculate and
lustrous in its hue—was not more than thirty miles distant. The
courses of the Calaveras, Mokelumne and Cosumne, with the
smaller creeks between them, could be distinctly traced. In the
nearer region at our feet, we could see the miners at work felling
logs and building their winter cabins, and hear the far whoop of
Indians, from their hidden rancherias. On the west, the horizon
was bounded by the Coast Range, Monte Diablo in the centre and
Suisun Bay making a gap in the chain. Between that blue wall
and the rough region at our feet lay the great plains of Sacramento and San Joaquin, fifty miles in breadth, and visible for at
least one hundred and fifty miles of extent. The sky was perfectly clear, and this plain alone, of all the landscape, was covered
with a thick white fog, the upper surface of which, as we looked
down upon it, was slowly tossed to and fro, moving and shifting
like the waves of an agitated sea.

We enjoyed this remarkable prospect for an hour, and then
made our way down the opposite side of the Peak, following bear
and deer trails through patches of thorny chapparal and long
slopes of sliding stones. We tarried for Dr. Carpentier in one of
the glens, eating the acorns which lay scattered under the trees.

As he did not appear, however, we climbed the river hills and came down on the Upper Bar, reaching our starting-point in time for a dinner to which we did full justice.

END OF VOL. I.

BAYARD TAYLOR.

LITH. OF SARONY & MAJOR. N.Y.

SAN FRANCISCO IN NOVEMBER 1849.

NEW YORK. GEO. P. PUTNAM.

VOLUME I I

LIST OF ILLUSTRATIONS.

CONTENTS OF VOL. II.

A

CHAPTER I.

On my arrival at the Lower Bar, I found Mr. Raney, of Stockton, who had made the journey with the greatest difficulty, the roads being almost impassable. The rainy season had now fairly set in, and as it came a month earlier than usual, the miners, in most cases, were without their winter supplies. Provisions of all kinds had greatly advanced in price, and the cost of freight from Stockton ran up at once to 75 cts. per lb. Flour was sold on the river at $1 per lb. and other articles were in the same proportion. Much anxiety was felt lest the rains should not abate, in which case there would have been a great deal of suffering on all the rivers.

The clouds gradually lowered and settled down on the topmost pines. Towards evening a chill rain came on, and the many gullies on the hill-sides were filled with brown torrents that brawled noisily on their way to the swollen Mokelumne. The big drops splashed dismally on our tent, as we sat within, but a double cover kept us completely dry and the ditch dug inside the pins turned off the streams that poured down its sides. During the night, however, the wind blew violently down the ravines, and the skirts of our blankets nearest the side of the tent were thoroughly soaked. My boots stood under a leaky part of the canvas, and as I hastened to put them on next morning, without examination, I thrust my foot into about three inches of water

The Election Day dawned wet and cheerlessly. From the folds of our canvas door, we looked out on the soaked and trickling hills and the sodden, dripping tents. Few people were stirring about the place, and they wore such a forlorn look that all idea of getting up a special enthusiasm was at once abandoned. There was no motion made in the matter until towards noon, as the most of the miners lay dozing in their tents. The Alcalde acted as Judge, which was the first step; next there were two Inspectors to be appointed. I was requested to act as one, but, although I had been long enough in the country to have held the office, I declined to accept until after application had been made to some of the inhabitants. The acquiescence of two of the resident traders relieved me of the responsibility. The election was held in the largest tent in the place, the Inspectors being seated behind the counter, in close proximity to the glasses and bottles, the calls for which were quite as frequent as the votes. I occupied a seat next the Alcalde, on a rough couch covered with an India-rubber blanket, where I passed the day in looking on the election and studying the singular characters present.

As there were two or three candidates for State offices in the place, the drumming up of voters gave one a refreshing reminiscence of home. The choosing of candidates from lists, nearly all of whom were entirely unknown, was very amusing. Names, in many instances, were made to stand for principles; accordingly, a Mr. Fair got many votes. One of the candidates, who had been on the river a few days previous, wearing a high-crowned silk hat,

with narrow brim, lost about twenty votes on that account. Some
went no further than to vote for those they actually knew. One
who took the opposite extreme, justified himself in this wise:—
"When I left home," said he, "I was determined to *go it blind*.
I went it blind in coming to California, and I'm not going to stop
now. I voted for the Constitution, and I've never seen the Constitution. I voted for all the candidates, and I don't know a
damned one of them. I'm going it blind all through, I am." The
Californians and resident Mexicans who were entitled to vote, were
in high spirits, on exercising the privilege for the first time in
their lives. It made no difference what the ticket was; the fact
of their having voted very much increased their self-importance,
for the day at least.

The votes polled amounted to one hundred and five, all of which
were "For the Constitution." The number of miners on the
Bar, who were entitled to vote, was probably double this number,
but those who were at work up among the gulches remained in
their tents, on account of the rain. A company on the other side
of the river was completely cut off from the polls by the rise of
the flood, which made it impossible for them to cross. The Inspectors were puzzled at first how far to extend the privilege of
suffrage to the Mexicans. There was no copy of the Treaty of
Queretaro to be had, and the exact wording of the clause referring
to this subject was not remembered. It was at last decided, however, that those who had been residing in the country since the
conquest, and intended to remain permanently, might be admitted
to vote; and the question was therefore put to each one in turn.
The most of them answered readily in the affirmative, and seemed
delighted to be considered as citizens. " *Como no* ?" said a fat,
good-humored fellow, with a ruddy olive face, as he gave his

sarape a new twirl over his shoulder : " *Como no ? soy Americano ahora.*" (Why not ? I am now an American.) The candidates, whose interest it was to search out all delinquents, finally exhausted the roll, and the polls were closed. The returns were made out in due form, signed and dispatched by a messenger to the Double Spring, to await the carrier from the Upper Bar, who was to convey them to Stockton.

During the few days I spent on the Mokelumne, I had an opportunity of becoming acquainted with many curious characteristics and incidents of mining life. It would have been an interesting study for a philosopher, to note the different effects which sudden enrichment produced upon different persons, especially those whose lives had previously been passed in the midst of poverty and privation. The most profound scholar in human nature might here have learned something which all his previous wisdom and experience could never teach. It was not precisely the development of new qualities in the man, but the exhibition of changes and contrasts of character, unexpected and almost unaccountable. The world-old moral of gold was completely falsified. Those who were unused to labor, whose daily ounce or two seemed a poor recompense for weary muscles and flagging spirits, might carefully hoard their gains ; but they whose hardy fibre grappled with the tough earth as naturally as if it knew no fitter play, and made the coarse gravel and rocky strata yield up their precious grains, were as profuse as princes and as open-hearted as philanthropists. Weather-beaten tars, wiry, delving Irishmen, and stalwart foresters from the wilds of Missouri, became a race of sybarites and epicureans. Secure in possessing the " Open Sesamé" to the exhaustless treasury under their feet, they gave free rein to every whim or impulse which could possibly be gratified.

It was no unusual thing to see a company of these men, who had never before had a thought of luxury beyond a good beef-steak and a glass of whiskey, drinking their champagne at ten dollars a bottle, and eating their tongue and sardines, or warming in the smoky camp-kettle their tin canisters of turtle-soup and lobster-salad. It was frequently remarked that the Oregonians, though accustomed all their lives to the most simple, solid and temperate fare, went beyond every other class of miners in their fondness for champagne and all kinds of cordials and choice liquors. These were the only luxuries they indulged in, for they were, to a man, cautious and economical in the use of gold.

One of the most amusing cases I saw was that of a company of Englishmen, from New South Wales, who had been on the Moke-lumne about a week at the time of my visit. They had only landed in California two weeks previous, and this was their first experience of gold-digging. One of them, a tall, strong-limbed fellow, who had served seven years as a private of cavalry, was unceasing in his exclamations of wonder and delight. He repeated his story from morning till night, and in the fullness of his heart communicated it to every new face he saw. "By me soul, but this is a great country!" he would exclaim ; " here a man can dig up as much goold in a day as he ever saw in all his life. Hav'n't I got already more than I know what to do with, an' I've only been here a week. An' to think 'at I come here with never a single bloody farthing in my pocket! An' the Frenchman, down the hill there, him 'at sells wittles, he wouldn't trust me for a piece of bread, the devil take him ! ' If ye 've no money, go an' dig some ;' says he ; ' people dig here o' Sundays all the same.' ' Ill dig o' Sundays for no man, ye bloody villain ;' says I, ' I'll starve first.' An' I did'nt, an' I had a hungry belly, too. But o'

Monday I dug nineteen dollars, an' o' Tuesday twenty-three, an' o'
Friday two hundred an' eighty-two dollars in one lump as big as
yer fist; an' all for not workin' o' Sundays. Was there ever
sich a country in the world!" And, as if to convince himself
that he actually possessed all this gold, he bought champagne, ale
and brandy by the dozen bottles, and insisted on supplying every
body in the settlement.

There was one character on the river, whom I had met on my
first visit in August and still found there on my return. He possessed sufficient individuality of appearance and habits to have
made him a hero of fiction; Cooper would have delighted to have
stumbled upon him. His real name I never learned, but he was
known to all the miners by the cognomen of "Buckshot"—an
appellation which seemed to suit his hard, squab figure very well.
He might have been forty years of age or perhaps fifty; his face
was but slightly wrinkled, and he wore a heavy black beard which
grew nearly to his eyes and entirely concealed his mouth. When
he removed his worn and dusty felt hat, which was but seldom, his
large, square forehead, bald crown and serious gray eyes gave him
an appearance of reflective intellect;—a promise hardly verified
by his conversation. He was of a stout and sturdy frame, and
always wore clothes of a coarse texture, with a flannel shirt and
belt containing a knife. I guessed from a slight peculiarity of his
accent that he was a German by birth, though I believe he was not
considered so by the miners.

The habits of "Buckshot" were still more eccentric than his
appearance. He lived entirely alone, in a small tent, and seemed
rather to shun than court the society of others. His tastes were
exceedingly luxurious; he always had the best of everything in
the market, regardless of its cost. The finest hams, at a dollar

and a half the pound; preserved oysters, corn and peas, at six dollars a canister; onions and potatoes, whenever such articles made their appearance; Chinese sweetmeats and dried fruits, were all on his table, and his dinner was regularly moistened by a bottle of champagne. He did his own cooking, an operation which cost little trouble, on account of the scarcity of fresh provisions. When particularly lucky in digging, he would take his ease for a day or two, until the dust was exhausted, when he would again shoulder his pick and crowbar and commence burrowing in some lonely corner of the rich gulch. He had been in the country since the first discovery of the placers, and was reported to have dug, in all, between thirty and forty thousand dollars,—all of which he had spent for his subsistence. I heard him once say that he never dug less than an ounce in one day, and sometimes as much as two pounds. The rough life of the mountains seemed entirely congenial to his tastes, and he could not have been induced to change it for any other, though less laborious and equally epicurean.

Among the number of miners scattered through the different gulches, I met daily with men of education and intelligence, from all parts of the United States. It was never safe to presume on a person's character, from his dress or appearance. A rough, dirty, sunburnt fellow, with unshorn beard, quarrying away for life at the bottom of some rocky hole, might be a graduate of one of the first colleges in the country, and a man of genuine refinement and taste. I found plenty of men who were not outwardly distinguishable from th inveterate trapper or mountaineer, but who, a year before, ha been patientless physicians, briefless lawyers and half-starved editors. It was this infusion of intelligence which gave the gold-hunting communities, notwithstanding their barbaric exterior and mode of life, an order and individual security which at first sight seemed little less than marvellous.

Since my first visit, the use of quicksilver had been introduced on the river, and the success which attended its application to gold-washing will bring it henceforth into general use. An improved rocker, having three or four lateral gutters in its bottom, which were filled with quicksilver, took up the gold so perfectly, that not the slightest trace of it could be discovered in the refuse earth. The black sand, which was formerly rejected, was washed in a bowl containing a little quicksilver in the bottom, and the amalgam formed by the gold yielded four dollars to every pound of sand. Mr. James, who had washed out a great deal of this sand, evaporated the quicksilver in a retort, and produced a cake of fine gold worth nearly five hundred dollars. The machines sold at one thousand dollars apiece, the owners having wisely taken the precaution to have them patented.

There is no doubt that, by means of quicksilver, much of the soil which has heretofore been passed by as worthless, will give a rich return. The day before my departure, Dr. Gillette washed out several panfuls of earth from the very top of the hills, and found it to contain abundance of fine grains of gold. A heap of refuse earth, left by the common rocker after ten thousand dollars had been washed, yielded still another thousand to the new machine. Quicksilver was enormously high, four dollars a pound having been paid in Stockton. When the mines of Santa Clara shall be in operation, the price will be so much reduced that its use will become universal and the annual golden harvest be thereby greatly increased. It will be many years before all the placers or gold deposits are touched, no matter how large the emigration to California may be. The region in which all the mining operations are now carried on, extending from the base of the proper Sierra Nevada to the plains of Sacramento and San Joaquin, is upwards of five hundred miles in length by fifty in breadth. Towards the head of the Sacramento River gold is also found in the granite formation, and there is every reason to believe that it exists in the valleys and cañons of the great snowy ridge.

I was strongly tempted to take hold of the pick and pan, and try my luck in the gulches for a week or two. I had fully intended, on reaching California, to have personally tested the pleasure of gold-digging, as much for the sake of a thorough experience of life among the placers as from a sly hope of striking on a pocket full of big lumps. The unexpected coming-on of the rainy season, made my time of too much account, besides adding greatly to the hardships of the business. Two or three days' practice is requisite to handle the implements properly, and I had no notion of learning the manipulations without fingering the gold. Once, indeed, I took a butcher-knife, went into one of the forsaken holes in the big gulch, lay on my back as I had seen the other miners do, and endeavored to pick out some yellow grains from the crevices of the crumbling rock. My search was vain, however, and I was indebted to the kindness of some friends for the only specimens I brought away from the Diggings.

CHAPTER II.

I LEFT the Mokelumne River the afternoon following Election Day, and retraced my path to Jackson's Creek, which I reached at dark. Being unhorsed, I resumed my old plodding gait, " packing" my blankets and spurs. I was obliged to walk to the Upper Bar, in order to cross the Mokelumne, whose current was now very deep and rapid. A man named Bills, who kept a brush hotel with a canvas roof, had set up an impromptu ferry, made by nailing a few planks upon four empty barrels, lashed together. This clumsy float was put over by means of a rope stretched from bank to bank. The tendency of the barrels to roll in the swift current, made it very insecure for more than two persons. The same morning, four men who were crossing at once, overbore its delicate equilibrium and were tipped into the water, whence they were rescued with some difficulty. A load of freight met with the same luck just before I reached the ferry. The banks were heaped with barrels, trunks, crates of onions and boxes of liquor, waiting to be taken over, and some of the Mexican arrieros were endeavoring to push their pack-mules into the water and force them to swim. I took my place on the unsteady platform with some doubts of a dry skin, but as we were all careful to keep a plumb line, the passage was made in safety.

I toiled up the windings of a deep gulch, whose loneliness, after I had passed the winter huts of the gold-diggers, was made very impressive by the gathering twilight. The gray rocks which walled it in towards the summit looked dim and spectral under the eaves of the pines, and a stream of turbid water splashed with a melancholy sound into the chasm below. The transparent glimmer of the lighted tents on Jackson's Creek had a cheery look as seen at the bottom of the gulch on the other side of the mountain. I stopped at Cosgrove's tent, where several travelers who had arrived before me were awaiting supper. We sat about the fire and talked of gold-digging, the election and the prospect of supplies for the winter. When Mrs. Cosgrove had finished frying her beef and boiling her coffee, we rolled to the table all the casks, boxes and logs we could find, and sat down to our meal under the open stars. A Chinook Indian from Oregon acted as waiter—an attendance which we would rather have dispensed with. I was offered a raw-hide in one corner of a small storage-tent, and spread my blanket upon it ; the dampness of the earth, however, striking through both hide and blankets, gave me several chills and rheumatic pains of the joints, before morning. The little community established on the knoll numbered about sixty persons. They were all settled there for the winter, though the gold dug did not average more than half an ounce to each man, daily.

Next morning, I crossed the hills to Sutter's Creek, where I found the settlement increased by several new arrivals. From this place my path branched off to the north, crossing several mountain ridges to Amador's Creek, which, like the streams I had already passed, was lined with tents and winter cabins. I questioned several miners about their profits, but could get no satisfactory answer. Singularly enough, it is almost impossible to learn

from the miners themselves, unless one happens to be a near acquaintance, the amount of their gains. If unlucky, they dislike
to confess it ; if the contrary, they have good reason for keeping it
secret. When most complaining, they may be most successful.
I heard of one, who, after digging fruitlessly for a week, came
suddenly on a pocket, containing about three hundred dollars.
Seeing a friend approaching, he hastily filled it up with stones, and
began grubbing in the top soil. " Well, what luck ?" inquired
his friend. " Not a damned cent," was the answer, given with a
mock despondency, while the pale face and stammering voice betrayed the cheat at once. Nobody believes you are not a gold-
hunter. He must be a fool, they think, who would go to the
mountains for any other purpose. The questions invariably asked
me were : " Where have you been digging ?" and " Where do
you winter ?" If I spoke of going home soon, the expression
was : " Well, I s'pose you've got your pile ;" or, " You've been
lucky in your prospecting, to get off so soon."

Leaving Amador's Creek, a walk of seven miles took me to
Dry Creek, where I found a population of from two to three hundred, established for the winter. The village was laid out with
some regularity, and had taverns, stores, butchers' shops and
monte tables. The digging was going on briskly, and averaged
a good return. The best I could hear of, was $114 in two
days, contrasted with which were the stories of several who had
got nothing but the fever and ague for their pains. The amount
of sickness on these small rivers during the season had been very
great, and but a small part of it, in my opinion, was to be ascribed
to excesses of any kind. All new countries, it is well known,
breed fever and ague, and this was especially the case in the gold
region, where, before the rains came on, the miner was exposed

to intense heat during the day and was frequently cold under double blankets at night. The water of many of the rivers occasions diarrhœa to those who drink it, and scarcely one out of a hundred emigrants escapes an attack of this complaint.

At all these winter settlements, however small, an alcalde is chosen and regulations established, as near as possible in accordance with the existing laws of the country. Although the authority exercised by the alcalde is sometimes nearly absolute, the miners invariably respect and uphold it. Thus, at whatever cost, order and security are preserved ; and when the State organization shall have been completed, the mining communities, for an extent of five hundred miles, will, by a quiet and easy process, pass into regularly constituted towns, and enjoy as good government and protection as any other part of the State. Nothing in California seemed more miraculous to me than this spontaneous evolution of social order from the worst elements of anarchy. It was a lesson worth even more than the gold.

The settlement on Dry Creek is just on the skirts of the rough mountain region—the country of cañons, gulches, cañadas and divides ; terms as familar in the diggings as " per cent" in Wall-street. I had intended to strike directly across the mountains to the American Fork. The people represented this route to be impracticable, and the jagged ridges, ramparted with rock, which towered up in that direction, seemed to verify the story, so I took the trail for Daly's Ranche, twenty-two miles distant. After passing the Willow Springs, a log hut on the edge of a swamp, the road descended to the lower hills, where it was crossed by frequent streams. I passed on the way a group of Indians who were skinning a horse they had killed and were about to roast. They were well armed and had probably shot the horse while it was grazing. I greeted them with a " buenas dias," which they sullenly returned, adding an " ugh ! ugh !" which might have expressed either contempt, admiration, friendship or fear.

In traveling through these low hills, I passed several companies of miners who were engaged in erecting log huts for the winter. The gravelly bottoms in many places showed traces of their prospecting, and the rocker was in operation where there was sufficient water. When I inquired the yield of gold I could get no satisfactory answer, but the faces of the men betrayed no sign of disappointment. While resting under a leafless oak, I was joined by a boy of nineteen who had been digging on the Dry Creek and was now returning to San Francisco, ague-stricken and penniless. We walked on in company for several hours, under a dull gray sky, which momentarily threatened rain. The hot flush of fever was on his face, and he seemed utterly desponding and disinclined to talk. Towards night, when the sky had grown darker, he declared himself unable to go further, but I encouraged him to keep on until we reached a cabin, where the miners kindly received him for the night.

I met on the road many emigrant wagons, bound for the diggings. They traveled in companies of two and three, joining teams whenever their wagons stuck fast in the mire. Some were obliged to unload at the toughest places, and leave part of their stores on the Plain until they could return from their Winter quarters. Their noon camps would be veritable treasures for my friend Darley, the artist, if he could have seen them. The men were all gaunt, long-limbed Rip Van Winkles, with brown faces, matted hair and beards, and garments which seemed to have grown up with them, for you could not believe they had ever been taken off. The women, who were somewhat more tidy, had suffered less from the journey, but there were still many fine subjects for the pencil among them. In the course of the day I passed about thirty teams.

At night, after a toilsome journey, I reached the Cosumne River, two miles below the diggings. I was wet from the swamps I crossed and the pools I had waded, weary in body, and thoroughly convinced of the impossibility of traveling on the Plains during the rainy season. One would think, from the parched and seamed appearance of the soil in summer, that nothing short of an absolute deluge could restore the usual moisture. A single rain, however, fills up the cracks, and a week of wet weather turns the dusty plain into a deep mire, the hollows into pools, and the stony arroyos into roaring streams. The roads then become impassable for wagons, killing to mules, and terribly laborious for pedestrians. In the loose, gravelly soil on the hilltops, a horse at once sinks above his knees, and the only chance of travel is by taking the clayey bottoms. Where, a month before there had been a *jornada* of twenty miles, arid as the desert, my path was now crossed by fifty streams.

Where the trail struck the river I came upon a small tent, pitched by the roadside, and was hailed by the occupants. They were two young men from Boston, who came out in the summer, went to the North-Fork of the American, prospered in their digging, and were going southward to spend the winter. They were good specimens of the sober, hardy, persevering gold-digger —a class who never fail to make their " piles." I willingly accepted their invitation to spend the night, whereupon they threw another log on the camp-fire, mixed some batter for slap-jacks, and put a piece of salt pork in the pan. We did not remain long about the fire, after my supper was finished. Uniting our store of blankets, we made a bed in common for all three, entirely filling the space covered by the little tent. Two or three showers fell during the night, and the dash of rain on the canvas, so near my head, made doubly grateful the warmth and snugness of our covert.

The morning brought another rain, and the roads grew deeper and tougher. At Coates's Ranche, two miles further, I was ferried across the Cosumne in a canoe. The river was falling, and teams could barely pass. The day previous a wagon and team had been washed several hundred yards down the stream, and the owners were still endeavoring to recover the running works which lay in a deep hole. Several emigrant companies were camped on the grassy bottoms along the river, waiting a chance to cross. At the ranche I found breakfast just on the table, and to be had at the usual price of a dollar and a half; the fare consisted of beef broiled in the fire, coarse bread, frijoles and coffee. The landlady was a German emigrant, but had been so long among the American settlers and native rancheros, that her talk was a three-stranded twist of the different languages. She seemed quite unconscious that she was not talking in a single tongue, for all three came to serve her thought with equal readiness.

I stood in the door some time, deliberating what to do. The sky had closed in upon the plain with a cheerless drizzle, which made walking very uncomfortable, and I could find no promise of a favorable change of weather. My intention had been to visit Mormon Island and afterwards Culloma Mill, on the American Fork. The former place was about thirty miles distant, but the trail was faint and difficult to find; while, should the rain increase, I could not hope to make the journey in one day. The walk to Sacramento presented an equally dispiriting aspect, but after some questioning and deliberation, I thought it possible that General Morse might have left my gray mare at some of the ranches further down the river, and resolved to settle the question before going further. Within the space of two or three miles I visited three, and came at last to a saw-mill, beyond which there was no habitation for ten miles. The family in an adjoining house seemed little disposed to make my acquaintance; I therefore took shelter from the rain, which was now pouring fast, in a mud cabin, on the floor of which lay two or three indolent vaqueros They were acquainted with every animal on all the ranches, and unhesitatingly declared that my mare was not among them.

When the rain slacked, I walked back to one of the other ranches, where I found several miners who had taken shelter in a new adobe house, which was partially thatched. We gathered together in a room, the floor of which was covered with wet tulé and endeavored to keep ourselves warm. The place was so chill that I went into the house inhabited by the family, and asked permission to dry myself at the fire. The occupants were two women, apparently sisters, of the ages of eighteen and thirty; the younger would have been handsome, but for an expression of habitual discontent and general contempt of everything. They made no answer to my request, so I took a chair and sat down near the blaze. Two female tongues, however, cannot long keep silent, and presently the elder launched into a violent anathema against all emi*grants*, as she called them. I soon learned that she had been in the country three years; that she had at first been living on Bear Creek; that the overland emigrants, the previous year, having come into the country almost destitute, appropriated some of the supplies which had been left at home while the family was absent gold-hunting; and, finally, that the fear of being in future

plundered of their cattle and wheat had driven them to the banks
of the Cosumne, where they had hoped for some security.   They
were deceived, however ; the emi*grants* troubled them worse than
ever, and though they charged a dollar and a half a meal and
sometimes cleared fifty dollars a day, still their hatred was not
abated.

Most especially did the elder express her resentment against
the said emigrants, on account of their treatment of the Indians.
I felt disposed at first to agree with her wholly in their condem-
nation, but it appeared that she was influenced by other motives
than those of humanity.   " Afore these here emi*grants* come,"
said she ; " the Injuns were as well-behaved and bidable as could
be ; I liked 'em more 'n the whites.   When we begun to find gold
on the Yuber, we could git 'em to work for us day in and day out,
fur next to nothin'.   We told 'em the gold was stuff to whitewash
houses with, and give 'em a hankecher for a tin-cup full ; but after
the emi*grants* begun to come along and put all sorts of notions
into their heads, there was no gettin' them to do nothin'."

I took advantage of a break in this streak of " chain lightning,"
to inquire whether Dr. Gwin and Gen. Morse had recently passed
that way ; but they did not know them by name.   " Well," said
I, " the gentlemen who are trying to get elected."   " Yes," rejoined the elder, " *them* people *was* here.   They stuck their heads
in the door one night and asked if they might have supper and
lodgin'.   I told 'em no, I guessed they couldn't.   Jist then Mr.
Kewen come along; he know'd 'em and made 'em acquainted.
Gosh! but I was mad.   I *had* to git supper for 'em *then ;* but if
't'd 'a bin *me*, I'd 'a had more spunk than to eat, after I'd bin
told I could'n't."   It had been difficult for me to keep a serious
countenance before, but now I burst into a hearty laugh, which

they took as a compliment to their " spunk." One of the household, a man of some education, questioned me as to the object of
my emigration to California, which I explained without reserve.
This, however, brought on another violent expression of opinion
from the same female. " That's jist the way," said she ; " *some*
people come here, think they've done great things, and go home
and publish all sorts of lies ; but they don't know no more'n nothin' in God A'mighty's world, as much as *them* people that's bin
here three years." After this declaration I thought it best to
retreat to the half-finished adobe house, and remain with my companions in misery. Towards evening we borrowed an axe, with
which we procured fuel enough for the night, and built a good
fire. A Mexican, driven in by the rain, took out his cards and set
up a monte bank of ten dollars, at which the others played with
shillings and quarters. I tried to read an odd volume of the
" Scottish Chiefs," which I found in the house, but the old charm
was gone, and I wondered at the childish taste which was so fascinated with its pages.

We slept together on the earthen floor. All night the rain pat-
tered on the *tulé* thatch, but at sunrise it ceased. The sky was
still lowering, and the roads were growing worse so rapidly, that
instead of starting across the plains for Mormon Island, the nearest point on the American Fork where the miners were at work,
I turned about for Sacramento City, thinking it best to return
while there was a chance. A little experience of travel over the
saturated soil soon convinced me that my tour in the mountains
was over. I could easily relinquish my anticipations of a visit to
the mining regions of the American Fork, Bear and Yuba Rivers,
for life at the different diggings is very much the same, and the
character of the gold deposits does not materially vary ; but there

had ever been a shining point in the background of all my former dreams of California—a shadowy object to be attained, of
which I had never lost sight during my wanderings and from
which I could not turn away without a pang of regret and disappointment. This was, a journey to the head of the Sacramento
Valley, a sight of the stupendous Shaste Peak, which stands like
an obelisk of granite capped with gleaming marble, on the borders of Oregon, and perhaps an exploration of the terrific cañons
through which the river plunges in a twenty-mile cataract, from
the upper shelf of the mountains. The fragments of description
which I had gathered from Oregonians, emigrants and " prospecters" who had visited that region, only made my anticipations
more glowing and my purpose more fixed. I knew there was
grandeur there, though there might not be gold. Three weeks of
rough travel, had the dry season extended to its usual length,
would have enabled me to make the journey ; but, like most of
the splendid plans we build for ourselves, I was obliged to give it
up on the eve of fulfilment. A few days of rain completely washed
it out of my imagination, and it was long before I could fill the
blank.

I was accompanied by one of the "Iowa Rangers," from Du-
buque, Iowa. He had been at work at the Dry Diggings on Weaver's Creek. He was just recovering from the scurvy, and could
not travel fast, but was an excellent hand at wading. Before
reaching the timber of the American Fork, we crossed thirty or
forty streams, many of which were knee-deep. Where they were
so wide as to render a leap impossible, my plan was to dash through
at full speed, and I generally got over with but a partial satura-
tion : the broad, shallow pools obliged us to stop and pull off our
boots. It was one form of the water-cure I did not relish. " If

this be traveling in the rainy season," thought I, " I'll have none of it."

On the banks of the American Fork we found a sandy soil and made better progress. Following that beautiful stream through the afternoon, we came at dusk to Sutter's Fort, which was surrounded by a moat of deep mud. I picked my way in the dark to Sacramento City, but was several times lost in its tented labyrinths before I reached Capt. Baker's store—under whose hospitable roof I laid down my pack and took up my abode for several days.

CHAPTER III.

SACRAMENTO CITY was one place by day and another by night; and of the two, its night-side was the most peculiar. As the day went down dull and cloudy, a thin fog gathered in the humid atmosphere, through which the canvas houses, lighted from within, shone with a broad, obscure gleam, that confused the eye and made the streets most familiar by daylight look strangely different. They bore no resemblance to the same places, seen at mid-day, under a break of clear sunshine, and pervaded with the stir of business life. The town, regular as it was, became a bewildering labyrinth of half-light and deep darkness, and the perils of traversing it were greatly increased by the mire and frequent pools left by the rain.

To one, venturing out after dark for the first time, these perils were by no means imaginary. Each man wore boots reaching to the knees—or higher, if he could get them—with the pantaloons tucked inside, but there were pit-falls, into which had he fallen, even these would have availed little. In the more frequented streets, where drinking and gambling had full swing, there was a partial light, streaming out through doors and crimson window-curtains, to guide his steps. Sometimes a platform of plank re-

BAYARD TAYLOR.

SACRAMENTO CITY, FROM THE SOUTH.

NEW YORK. GEO. P. PUTNAM.

LITH OF SARONY & MAJOR.

ceived his feet; sometimes he skipped from one loose barrel-stave to another, laid with the convex-side upward; and sometimes, deceived by a scanty piece of scantling, he walked off its further end into a puddle of liquid mud. Now, floundering in the stiff mire of the mid-street, he plunged down into a gulley and was " brought up" by a pool of water; now, venturing near the houses, a scaffold-pole or stray beam dealt him an unexpected blow. If he wandered into the outskirts of the town, where the tent-city of the emigrants was built, his case was still worse. The briery thickets of the original forest had not been cleared away, and the stumps, trunks and branches of felled trees were distributed over the soil with delightful uncertainty. If he escaped these, the la- riats of picketed mules spread their toils for his feet, threatening entanglement and a kick from one of the vicious animals; tent- ropes and pins took him across the shins, and the horned heads of cattle, left where they were slaughtered, lay ready to gore him at every step. A walk of any distance, environed by such dangers, especially when the air was damp and chill, and there was a pos- sibility of rain at any moment, presented no attractions to the weary denizens of the place.

A great part of them, indeed, took to their blankets soon after dark. They were generally worn out with the many excitements of the day, and glad to find a position of repose. Reading was out of the question to the most of them when candles were $4 per lb. and scarce at that; but in any case, the preternatural activity and employment of mind induced by the business habits of the place would have made impossible anything like quiet thought. I saw many persons who had brought the works of favorite authors with them, for recreation at odd hours, but of all the works thus brought, I never saw one read. Men preferred—or rather it grew,

involuntarily, into a custom—to lie at ease instead, and turn over
in the brain all their shifts and manœuvres of speculation, to see
whether any chance had been left uutouched. Some, grouped
around a little pocket-stove, beguile an hour or. two over their
cans of steaming punch or other warming concoction, and build
schemes out of the smoke of their rank Guayaquil *puros*—for the
odor of a genuine Havana is unknown. But, by nine o'clock at
farthest, nearly all the working population of Sacramento City are
stretched out on mattrass, plank or cold earth, according to the
state of their fortunes, and dreaming of splendid runs of luck or
listening to the sough of the wind in the trees.

There is, however, a large floating community of overland emigrants, miners and sporting characters, who prolong the wakeful-
ness of the streets far into the night. The door of many a gam-
bling-hell on the levee, and in J and K streets, stands invitingly
open ; the wail of torture from innumerable musical instruments
peals from all quarters through the fog and darkness. Full bands,
each playing different tunes discordantly, are stationed in front of
the principal establishments, and as these happen to be near together, the mingling of the sounds in one horrid, ear-splitting,
brazen chaos, would drive frantic a man of delicate nerve. All
one's old acquaintances in the amateur-music line, seem to have
followed him. The gentleman who played the flute in the next
room to yours, at home, has been hired· at an ounce a night to
perform in the drinking-tent across the way ; the very French
horn whose lamentations used to awake you dismally from the first
sweet snooze, now greets you at some corner ; and all the squeak-
ing violins, grumbling violincellos and rowdy trumpets which have
severally plagued you in other times, are congregated here, in
loving proximity. The very strength, loudness and confusion of

the noises, which, heard at a little distance, have the effect of one great scattering performance, marvellously takes the fancy of the rough mountain men.

Some of the establishments have small companies of Ethiopian melodists, who nightly call upon " Susanna !" and entreat to be carried back to Old Virginny. These songs are universally popular, and the crowd of listeners is often so great as to embarrass the player at the monte tables and injure the business of the gamblers. I confess to a strong liking for the Ethiopian airs, and used to spend half an hour every night in listening to them and watching the curious expressions of satisfaction and delight in the faces of the overland emigrants, who always attended in a body. The spirit of the music was always encouraging ; even its most doleful passages had a grotesque touch of cheerfulness—a mingling of sincere pathos and whimsical consolation, which somehow took hold of all moods in which it might be heard, raising them to the same notch of careless good-humor. The Ethiopian melodies well deserve to be called, as they are in fact, the national airs of America. Their quaint, mock-sentimental cadences, so well suited to the broad absurdity of the words—their reckless gaiety and irreverent familiarity with serious subjects—and their spirit of antagonism and perseverance—are true expressions of the more popular sides of the national character. They follow the American race in all its emigrations, colonizations and conquests, as certainly as the Fourth of July and Thanksgiving Day. The penniless and half-despairing emigrant is stimulated to try again by the sound of " It 'll never do to give it up so !" and feels a pang of home-sickness at the burthen of the " Old Virginia Shore."

At the time of which I am writing, Sacramento City boasted the only theatre in California. Its performances, three times a

week, were attended by crowds of the miners, and the owners
realized a very handsome profit.   The canvas building used for
this purpose fronted on the levee, within a door or two of the City
Hotel ; it would have been taken for an ordinary drinking-house,
but for the sign : " EAGLE THEATRE," which was nailed to the
top of the canvas frame.   Passing through the bar-room we arrive at the entrance ;   the prices of admission are : Box, $3 ;
Pit, $2.   The spectators are dressed in heavy overcoats and felt
hats, with boots reaching to the knees.   The box-tier is a single
rough gallery at one end, capable of containing about a hundred
persons ; the pit will probably hold three hundred more, so that
the receipts of a full house amount to $900.   The sides and roof
of the theatre are canvas, which, when wet, effectually prevents
ventilation, and renders the atmosphere hot and stifling.   The
drop-curtain, which is down at present, exhibits a glaring landscape, with dark-brown trees in the foreground, and lilac-colored
mountains against a yellow sky.

The overture commences ; the orchestra is composed of only
five members, under the direction of an Italian, and performs with
tolerable correctness.   The piece for the night is " The Spectre
of the Forest," in which the celebrated actress, Mrs. Ray, " of the
Royal Theatre, New Zealand," will appear.   The bell rings ; the
curtain rolls up ; and we look upon a forest scene, in the midst of
which appears Hildebrand, the robber, in a sky-blue mantle.   The
foliage of the forest is of a dark-red color, which makes a great
impression on the spectators and prepares them for the bloody
scenes that are to follow.   The other characters are a brave
knight in a purple dress, with his servant in scarlet ; they are
about to storm the robber's hold and carry off a captive maiden.
Several acts are filled with the usual amount of fighting and ter-

rible speeches ; but the interest of the play is carried to an awful height by the appearance of two spectres, clad in mutilated tent-covers, and holding spermaceti candles in their hands.   At this juncture Mrs. Ray rushes in and throws herself into an attitude in the middle of the stage : why she does it, no one can tell.   This movement, which she repeats several times in the course of the first three acts, has no connection with the tragedy ; it is evidently introduced for the purpose of showing the audience that there is, actually, a female performer.   The miners, to whom the sight of a woman is not a frequent occurrence, are delighted with these passages and applaud vehemently.

In the closing scenes, where Hildebrand entreats the heroine to become his bride, Mrs. Ray shone in all her glory.   " No !" said she, " I'd rather take a basilisk and wrap its cold fangs around me, than be clasped in the hembraces of an 'artless robber."   Then, changing her tone to that of entreaty, she calls upon the knight in purple, whom she declares to be " me 'ope—me only 'ope !"   We will not stay to hear the songs and duetts which follow ; the tragedy has been a sufficient infliction.   For her " 'art-rending" personations, Mrs. Ray received $200 a week, and the wages of the other actors were in the same proportion.   A musical gentle-man was paid $96 for singing " The Sea ! the Sea !" in a deep bass voice.   The usual sum paid musicians was $16 a night.   A Swiss organ-girl, by playing in the various hells, accumulated $4000 in the course of five or six months.

The southern part of Sacramento City, where the most of the overland emigrants had located themselves, was an interesting place for a night-ramble, when one had courage to undertake threading the thickets among which their tents were pitched.   There, on fallen logs about their camp-fires, might be seen groups that had

journeyed together across the Continent, recalling the hardships
and perils of the travel. The men, with their long beards,
weather-beaten faces and ragged garments, seen in the red, flickering light of the fires, made wild and fantastic pictures. Sometimes four of them might be seen about a stump, intent on re-
viving their ancient knowledge of "poker," and occasionally a
more social group, filling their tin cups from a kettle of tea or
something stronger. Their fires, however, were soon left to
smoulder away; the evenings were too raw and they were too
weary with the day's troubles to keep long vigils.

Often, too, without playing the eavesdropper, one might mingle
unseen with a great many of their companies gathered together
inside the tents. The thin, transparent canvas revealed the shadows of their forms, and was no impediment to the sound of their
voices; besides, as they generally spoke in a bold, hearty tone,
every word could be overheard at twenty yards' distance. The
fragments of conversation which were caught in walking through
this part of the city made a strange but most interesting medley.
There were narratives of old experience on the Plains; notes
about the passage of the mountains compared; reminiscences of
the Salt Lake City and its strange enthusiasts; sufferings at the
sink of Humboldt's River and in the Salt Desert recalled, and
opinions of California in general, given in a general manner.
The conversation, however, was sure to wind up with a talk
about home—a lamentation for its missed comforts and frequently
a regret at having forsaken them. The subject was inexhaustible,
and when once they commenced calling up the scenes and incidents of their life in the Atlantic or Mississippi world, everything
else was forgotten. At such times, and hearing snatches of these
conversations, I too was carried home by an irresistible longing,

and went back to my blankets and dreams of grizzly bear, discouraged and dissatisfied.

Before I left the place, the number of emigrants settled there for the winter amounted to two or three thousand. They were all located on the vacant lots, which had been surveyed by the original owners of the town and were by them sold to others. The emigrants, who supposed that the land belonged of right to the United States, boldly declared their intention of retaining possession of it. Each man voted himself a lot, defying the threats and remonstrances of the rightful owners. The town was greatly agitated for a time by these disputes ; meetings were held by both parties, and the spirit of hostility ran to a high pitch. At the time of my leaving the country, the matter was still unsettled, but the flood which occurred soon after, by sweeping both squatters and speculators off the ground, balanced accounts for awhile and left the field clear for a new start.

In the gambling-hells, under the excitement of liquor and play, a fight was no unusual occurrence. More than once, while walking in the streets at a late hour, I heard the report of a pistol ; once, indeed, I came near witnessing a horrid affray, in which one of the parties was so much injured that he lay for many days blind, and at the point of death. I was within a few steps of the door, and heard the firing in time to retreat. The punishment for these quarrels, when inflicted—which was very rarely done—was not so prompt and terrible as for theft ; but, to give the gambling community their due, their conduct was much more orderly and respectable than it is wont to be in other countries. This, however, was not so much a merit of their own possessing, as the effect of a strong public sentiment in favor of preserving order.

I must not omit to mention the fate of my old gray mare, who

2*

would have served me faithfully, had she been less lazy and better provided with forage. On reaching Sacramento City I found that Gen. Morse had been keeping her for me at a livery stable, at a cost of $5 a day. She looked in much better spirits than when I saw her eating pine-bark on the Mokclumne, and in riding to the town of Sutter, I found that by a little spurring, she could raise a very passable gallop. The rains, however, by putting a stop to travel, had brought down the price of horses, so that after searching some time for a purchaser I could get no offer higher than $50. I consented to let her go; we went into a store and weighed out the price in fine North Fork gold, and the new owner, after trotting her through the streets for about an hour, sold her again for $60. I did not care to trace her fortunes further.

CHAPTER IV.

SACRAMENTO CITY was the goal of the emigration by the northern routes. From the beginning of August to the last of December scarcely a day passed without the arrival of some man or company of men and families, from the mountains, to pitch their tents for a few days on the bank of the river and rest from their months of hardship. The vicissitudes through which these people had passed, the perils they had encountered and the toils they had endured seem to me without precedent in History. The story of thirty thousand souls accomplishing a journey of more than two thousand miles through a savage and but partially explored wilderness, crossing on their way two mountain chains equal to the Alps in height and asperity, besides broad tracts of burning desert, and plains of nearly equal desolation, where a few patches of stunted shrubs and springs of brackish water were their only stay, has in it so much of heroism, of daring and of sublime endurance, that we may vainly question the records of any age for its equal. Standing as I was, at the closing stage of that grand pilgrimage, the sight of these adventurers as they came in day by day, and the hearing of their stories, each of which had its own peculiar and separate character, had a more fascinating, because more real interest than the tales of the glorious old travelers which so impress us in childhood.

It would be impossible to give, in a general description of the emigration, viewed as one great movement, a complete idea of its many wonderful phases.   The experience of any single man, which a few years ago would have made him a hero for life, becomes mere common-place, when it is but one of many thousands ; yet the spectacle of a great continent, through a region of one thousand miles from north to south, being overrun with these adventurous bands, cannot be pictured without the relation of many episodes of individual bravery and suffering.   I will not attempt a full account of the emigration, but, as I have already given an outline of the stories of those who came by the Gila route, a similar sketch of what those encountered who took the Northern route —the great overland highway of the Continent—will not be without its interest in this place.

The great starting point for this route was Independence, Mo., where thousands were encamped through the month of April, waiting until the grass should be sufficiently high for their cattle, before they ventured on the broad ocean of the Plains.   From the first of May to the first of June, company after company took its departure from the frontier of civilization, till the emigrant trail from Fort Leavenworth, on the Missouri, to Fort Laramie, at the foot of the Rocky Mountains, was one long line of mule-trains and wagons.   The rich meadows of the Nebraska, or Platte, were settled for the time, and a single traveler could have journeyed for the space of a thousand miles, as certain of his lodging and regular meals as if he were riding through the old agricultural districts of the Middle States.   The wandering tribes of Indians on the Plains —the Pawnees, Sioux and Arapahoes—were alarmed and bewildered by this strange apparition.   They believed they were about to be swept away forever from their hunting-grounds and graves.

As the season advanced and the great body of the emigrants got under way, they gradually withdrew from the vicinity of the trail and betook themselves to grounds which the former did not reach. All conflicts with them were thus avoided, and the emigrants passed the Plains with perfect immunity from their thievish and hostile visitations.

Another and more terrible scourge, however, was doomed to fall upon them. The cholera, ascending the Mississippi from New Orleans, reached St. Louis about the time of their departure from Independence, and overtook them before they were fairly embarked on the wilderness. The frequent rains of the early spring, added to the hardship and exposure of their travel, prepared the way for its ravages, and the first three or four hundred miles of the trail were marked by graves. It is estimated that about four thousand persons perished from this cause. Men were seized without warning with the most violent symptoms, and instances occurred in which the sufferer was left to die alone by the road-side, while his panic-stricken companions pushed forward, vainly trusting to get beyond the influence of the epidemic. Rough boards were planted at the graves of those who were buried near the trail, but there are hundreds of others lying unmarked by any memorial, on the bleak surface of the open plain and among the barren depths of the mountains. I have heard men tell how they have gone aside from their company to bury some old and cherished friend—a brother, it may often have been—performing the last rites alone and unaided, and leaving the remains where none but the wolf will ever seek their resting-place.

By the time the companies reached Fort Laramie the epidemic had expended its violence, and in the pure air of the elevated mountain region they were safe from its further attacks. Now, however, the real hardships of their journey began.　Up and down the mountains that hem in the Sweetwater Valley—over the spurs of the Wind River chain—through the Devil's Gate, and past the stupendous mass of Rock Independence—they toiled slowly up to the South Pass, descended to the tributaries of the Colorado and plunged into the rugged defiles of the Timpanozu Mountains. Here the pasturage became scarce and the companies were obliged to take separate trails in order to find sufficient grass for their teams.　Many, who, in their anxiety to get forward with speed, had thrown away a great part of the supplies that encumbered them, now began to want, and were frequently reduced, in their necessity, to make use of their mules and horses for food.　It was not unusual for a mess, by way of variety to the tough mule-meat, to kill a quantity of rattle-snakes, with which the mountains abounded, and have a dish of them fried, for supper.　The distress of many of the emigrants might have been entirely avoided, had they possessed any correct idea, at the outset of the journey, of its length and privations.

It must have been a remarkable scene, which the City of the Great Salt Lake presented during the summer.　There, a community of religious enthusiasts, numbering about ten thousand, had established themselves beside an inland sea, in a grand valley shut in by snow-capped mountains, a thousand miles from any other civilized spot, and were dreaming of rebuilding the Temple and creating a New Jerusalem.　Without this resting-place in mid-journey, the sufferings of the emigrants must have been much aggravated.　The Mormons, however, whose rich grain-lands in the Valley of the Utah River had produced them abundance of supplies, were able to spare sufficient for those whose stock was exhausted.　Two or three thousand, who arrived late in the season, remained in the Valley all winter, fearing to undertake the toilsome journey which still remained.

Those who set out for California had the worst yet in store for them. Crossing the alternate sandy wastes and rugged mountain chains of the Great Basin to the Valley of Humboldt's River, they were obliged to trust entirely to their worn and weary animals for reaching the Sierra Nevada before the winter snows. The grass was scarce and now fast drying up in the scorching heat of mid-summer. In the endeavor to hasten forward and get the first chance of pasture, many again committed the same mistake of throwing away their supplies. I was told of one man, who, with a refinement of malice and cruelty which it would be impossible to surpass, set fire to the meadows of dry grass, for the sole purpose, it was supposed, of retarding the progress of those who were behind and might else overtake him. A company of the emigrants, on the best horses which were to be obtained, pursued him and shot him from the saddle as he rode—a fate scarcely equal to his deserts.

The progress of the emigrants along the Valley of Humboldt's River is described as having been slow and toilsome in the extreme. The River, which lies entirely within the Great Basin,—whose waters, like those of the uplands of Central Asia, have no connexion with the sea—shrinks away towards the end of summer, and finally loses itself in the sand, at a place called the Sink. Here, the single trail across the Basin divides into three branches, and the emigrants, leaving the scanty meadows about the Sink, have before them an arid desert, varying from fifty to eighty miles in breadth, according to the route which they take. Many companies, on arriving at this place, were obliged to stop and recruit their exhausted animals, though exposed to the danger of being detained there the whole winter, from the fall of snow on the Sierra Nevada. Another, and very large body of them, took the upper route to Lawson's Pass, which leads to the head of the Sacramento Valley ; but the greater part, fortunately, chose the old traveled trails, leading to Bear Creek and the Yuba, by way of Truckee River, and to the head-waters of the Rio Americano by way of Carson's River.

The two latter routes are the shortest and best. After leaving the Sink of Humboldt's River, and crossing a desert of about fifty miles in breadth, the emigrant reaches the streams which are fed from the Sierra Nevada, where he finds good grass and plenty of game. The passes are described as terribly rugged and precipitous, leading directly up the face of the great snowy ridge. As, however, they are not quite eight thousand feet above the sea, and are reached from a plateau of more than four thousand feet, the ascent is comparatively short ; while, on the western side, more than a hundred miles of mountain country must be passed, before reaching the level of the Sacramento Valley. There are frequent passes in the Sierra Nevada which were never crossed before the summer of 1849. Some of the emigrants, diverging from the known trail, sought a road for themselves, and found their way down from the snows to the head waters of the Tuolumne, the Calaveras and Feather River. The eastern slope of the Sierra Nevada is but imperfectly explored. All the emigrants concurred in representing it to me as an abrupt and broken region, the higher peaks of barren granite, the valleys deep and narrow, yet in many places timbered with pine and cedar of immense growth.

After passing the dividing ridge,—the descent from which was rendered almost impossible by precipices and steeps of naked rock —about thirty miles of alternate cañons and divides lay between the emigrants and the nearest diggings. The steepness of the slopes of this range is hardly equalled by any other mountains in the world. The rivers seem to wind their way through the bottoms of chasms, and in many places it is impossible to get down to the water. The word cañon (meaning, in Spanish, a funnel,) has a peculiar adaptation to these cleft channels through which the rivers are poured. In getting down from the summit ridge the emigrants told me they were frequently obliged to take the oxen from the wagon and lower it with ropes ; but for the sheer descents which followed, another plan was adopted. The wheels were all locked, and only one yoke of oxen left in front ; a middling-sized pine was then cut down, and the butt fastened to the axle-tree, the branchy top dragging on the earth. The holding back of the oxen, the sliding of the locked wheels, and the resistance of the tree together formed an opposing power sufficient to admit of a slow descent ; but it was necessary to observe great care lest the pace should be quickened, for the slightest start would have overcome the resistance and given oxen, wagon and tree together a momentum that would have landed them at the bottom in a very different condition.

In August, before his departure for Oregon, Gen. Smith took the responsibility of ordering pack-mules and supplies to be provided at the expense of Government, and gave Major Rucker orders to dispatch relief companies into the Great Basin to succor the emigrants who might be remaining there, for want of provisions to advance further. In this step he was also warmly seconded by Gen. Riley, and the preparations were made with the least possible delay. Public meetings of the citizens of San Francisco were also held, to contribute means of relief. Major Rucker dispatched a party with supplies and fresh animals by way of the

Truckee River route to the Sink of Humboldt's River, while he took the expedition to Pitt River and Lawson's Pass, under his own command. The first party, after furnishing provisions on the road to all whom they found in need, reached the Sink, and started the families who were still encamped there, returning with them by the Carson River route and bringing in the last of the emigration, only a day or two before the heavy snows came on, which entirely blocked up the passes. But for this most timely aid, hundreds of persons must have perished by famine and cold.

Those who took the trail for Lawson's Pass fared even worse. They had been grossly deceived with regard to the route, which, instead of being a nearer passage into California, is actually two hundred miles longer than the other routes, and though there is no ridge of equal height to be crossed, the amount of rough mountain travel is even greater. The trail, after crossing the Sierra by a low gap, (which has lately been mentioned in connection with the Pacific Railroad,) enters the Valley of Pitt River, one of the tributaries of the Upper Sacramento. Following the course of this river for about ninety miles, it reaches a spur of the Sierra Nevada, which runs from the head waters of Feather River to near the Shaste Peak, closing up the level of the lower Sacramento Valley. These mountains are from five to six thousand feet in height and rugged in the extreme, and over them the weary emigrant must pass before the Land of Promise—the rich Valley of the Sacramento—meets his view.

At the time I returned to Sacramento City, Major Rucker had just returned from his expedition. He found a large body of emigrants scattered along Pitt River, many of them entirely destitute of provisions and others without their animals, which the predatory Indians of that region had stolen. Owing to the

large number who required his assistance, he was obliged to return to the ranches on Deer Creek and procure further supplies,
leaving Mr. Peoples to hurry them on meanwhile. Everything
was done to hasten their movement, but a strange and unaccountable apathy seemed to have taken possession of them. The season was late, and a single day added to the time requisite to get
them into the Sacramento Valley might prove ruinous to them
and their assistants. Whether the weary six months they passed
in the wilderness had had the effect of destroying all their active
energy and care for their own safety, or whether it was actual
ignorance of their true situation and contempt of counsel because
it seemed to wear the shape of authority, it is difficult to tell—but
the effect was equally dangerous. After having improvidently
thrown away, in the first part of the journey, the supplies so needful afterwards, they now held fast to useless goods, and refused to
lighten the loads of their tired oxen. But few of them appeared
to have a sense of the aid which was rendered them; instead
of willingly coöperating with those who had charge of the relief
party, they gave much unnecessary trouble and delayed the journey several days.

Of the companies which came by this route several small parties
struck into the mountains to the southward of Pitt River, hoping
to find an easy road to the diggings on Feather River. Of these,
some reached the river, after many days of suffering and danger ;
others retraced their steps and by making desperate efforts regained the companies on Pitt River, while some, who had not
been heard of at the time I left, were either locked up for the
winter in the midst of terrible snows, or had already perished from
hunger. I met with one or two who had been several days in the
mountains without food, and only escaped death by a miracle. A

company of six, who set out on the hunt of some Indians who had
stolen their cattle, never returned.

It happened to the emigrants as Major Rucker had forewarned
them.   A letter from Mr. Peoples, which he received during my
stay, gave a most striking account of the hardships to which they
had subjected themselves.   A violent storm came on while they
were crossing the mountains to Deer Creek, and the mules, unac-
customed to the severe cold, sank down and died one after another.
In spite of their remonstrances, Mr. Peoples obliged them to leave
their wagons and hurry forward with the remaining animals.   The
women, who seemed to have far more energy and endurance than
the men, were mounted on mules, and the whole party pushed on
through the bleak passes of the mountains in the face of a raging
storm.   By extraordinary exertions, they were all finally brought
into the Sacramento Valley, with the loss of many wagons and
animals.   On receiving this letter, Major Rucker set out for Lawson's Ranche on Deer Creek, where he saw the emigrants comfortably established for the winter.   They had erected log-houses
for shelter ; the flour supplied to them from the Government stores
and cattle from the large herds on the neighboring ranches, furnished them with the means of subsistence.   The return to Sacramento City, in the depth of the rainy season, was an almost impossible undertaking.

The greater part of those who came in by the lower routes,
started, after a season of rest, for the mining region, where many
of them arrived in time to build themselves log huts for the winter.
Some pitched their tents along the river, to wait for the genial
spring season ; while not a few took their axes and commenced
the business of wood-cutting in the timber on its banks.   When
shipped to San Francisco, the wood, which they took with the

usual freedom of Uncle Sam's nephews, brought $40 a cord ; the steamboats which called for it on their trips up and down, paid $15. By the end of December the last man of the overland companies was safe on the western side of the Sierra Nevada, and the great interior wilderness resumed its ancient silence and solitude until the next spring.

CHAPTER V.

THE ITALY OF THE WEST.

At the end of a week of rain, during which we had a few deceptive gleams of clear weather, I gave up all hope of getting to the Yuba and Feather Rivers, and took my passage in the steamer Senator, for San Francisco. The time for leaving was before sunrise, and the loud ringing of the first bell awoke me as I lay on my Chinese quilt in Capt. Baker's store. The weather had changed during the night, and when I went out of doors I found a keen, cloudless dawn, with the wind blowing down the river. Had the three weeks of dry season, so confidently predicted by the old settlers, actually commenced? I was not long in deliberating, though the remote chance of an opportunity for making my journey to the Shaste Peak, tempted me sorely; but the end proved that I decided aright, for on the second day after my arrival at San Francisco, the rains set in again worse than ever.

The steamer, which formerly ran between Boston and Eastport, was a strong, spacious and elegant boat. Notwithstanding the fare to San Francisco was $30, she rarely carried less than two hundred passengers. When I went on board, her decks were already filled, and people were hurrying down from all parts of the town, her bell tolling meanwhile with the quick, incessant stroke of a Hudson River boat, one minute before the time of starting. After my recent barbaric life, her long upper saloon, with its sofas and faded carpet, seemed splendid enough for a palace. As we sped down the Sacramento, and the well-known bell and sable herald made their appearance, requesting passengers to step to the Captain's office, I could scarcely believe that I was in California. On the hurricane deck I met with several persons who had been fellow-passengers on the Atlantic and Pacific. Some had been to the head of the Sacramento Valley; some on Feather River; some again on the famous Trinity, where they had got more fever than gold; but all, though not alike successful, seemed energetic and far from being discouraged.

After passing the town of Sutter, the bell rang for breakfast, and having previously procured a ticket for two dollars, I joined the anxious throng who were pressing down the cabin stairs. The long tables were set below in the same style as at home; the fare was abundant and well prepared; even on the Hudson it would have given rise to few grumblings. We steamed rapidly down the river, with Monte Diablo far before us. Owing to the twists and turns of the stream, it was but an uncertain landmark, now appearing on one side and now on the other. The cold snows of the Sierra Nevada were faintly seen in the eastern sky, but between the Sacramento and the mountains, the great plain stretched out in a sweep which to the north and south ran unbroken to the horizon. The banks, stripped now of their summer foliage, would have been dreary and monotonous, but for the tents and log-houses of the settlers and wood-cutters. I noticed in little spots where the thicket had been cleared away, patches of cabbages and other hardy vegetables, which seemed to have a thrifty growth.

We came at last to the entrance of the slough, the navigation

of which was a matter of considerable nicety. The current was
but a few feet wider than the steamer, and many of the bends
occasioned her considerable trouble. Her bow sometimes ran in
among the boughs of the trees, where she could not well be
backed without her stern going into the opposite bank. Much
time and part of the planking of her wheel-houses were lost in
getting through these narrow straits. The small craft on their
way up the river were obliged to run close under the limbs of the
trees and hug the banks tightly until we had passed. At last we
came out again in the real Sacramento, avoiding the numerous
other sloughs which make off into the tulé marshes, and soon
reached the city of Montezuma, a solitary house on a sort of headland projecting into Suisun Bay and fronting its rival three-house
city, New-York-of-the-Pacific. The bay was dancing to the fresh
northern breeze as we skimmed its waters towards Benicia; Monte
Diablo, on the other side, wore a blue mist over his scarred and
rocky surface, which looked deceptively near.

The three weeks of rain which had fallen since I passed up the
bay, had brought out a vivid green over all the hills. Those along
the water were no longer lifeless and barren, but covered with
sprouting vegetation. Benicia, as we approached it, appeared
like a child's toy town set out on a piece of green velvet. Contrasted with this gay color, the changeless hue of the evergreen
oaks appeared sombre almost to blackness; seen in unison with
a cloudless sky and the glittering blue of the bay, the effect
of the fresh green was indescribably cheerful and inspiring.
We touched but a few minutes at Benicia, whose streets
presented a quiet appearance, coming from the thronged avenues
of Sacramento City. The houses were mostly frame, of neat
construction; a church with a small white spire, at the upper

end of the town, stood out brightly against the green of the hills behind.

Beyond these hills, at the distance of thirty-five miles, is the pleasant little town of Sonoma, Gen. Vallejo's residence. In summer it is reached from Sacramento City by a trail of forty miles, but when the rains come on, the tulé marshes running up from the bay between the river and the mountains, are flooded, and a circuit of more than a hundred miles must be made to get around them. Two days' journey north of Sonoma is Lake Clear, a beautiful sheet of water, sixty miles in length, embosomed in the midst of grand mountain scenery.

Sunset came on as we approached the strait opening from Pablo Bay into the Bay of San Francisco. The cloudless sky became gradually suffused with a soft rose-tint, which covered its whole surface, painting alike the glassy sheet of the bay, and glowing most vividly on the mountains to the eastward. The color deepened every moment, and the peaks of the Coast Range burned with a rich vermilion light, like that of a live coal. This faded gradually into as glowing a purple, and at last into a blue as intense as that of the sea at noonday. The first effect of the light was most wonderful; the mountains stretched around the horizon like a belt of varying fire and amethyst between the two roseate deeps of air and water; the shores were transmuted into solid, the air into fluid gems. Could the pencil faithfully represent this magnificent transfiguration of Nature, it would appear utterly unreal and impossible to eyes which never beheld the reality. It was no transient spectacle, fading away ere one could feel its surpassing glory. It lingered, and lingered, changing almost imperceptibly and with so beautiful a decay, that one lost himself in the enjoyment of each successive charm, without regret for those which were over. The dark blue of the mountains deepened into their night-garb of dusky shadow without any interfusion of dead ashy color, and the heaven overhead was spangled with all its stars long before the brilliant arch of orange in the west had sunk below the horizon. I have seen the dazzling sunsets of the Mediterranean flush the beauty of its shores, and the mellow skies which Claude used to contemplate from the Pincian Hill; but, lovely as they are in my memory, they seem cold and pale when I think of the splendor of such a scene, on the Bay of San Francisco.

The approach to the city was very imposing in the dusk. The crowd of shipping, two or three miles in length, stretched along the water in front; the triple crown of the hills behind was clearly marked against the sky, and from the broad space covered with sparkling lights, glimmerings of tents and white buildings, and the sounds of active life, I half believed that some metropolis of a century's growth lay before me. On landing, notwithstanding I had only been absent three weeks, I had some difficulty in recognizing localities. The change appeared greater than at any previous arrival, on account of the removal of a great many of the old buildings and the erection of larger and more substantial edifices in their stead.

After a few days of violent rain, the sky cleared and we had a week of the most delicious weather I ever experienced. The temperature was at no time lower than 50°, and in the middle of the day rose to 70°. When the floating gauze of mist had cleared off the water, the sky was without a cloud for the remainder of the day, and of a fresh, tender blue, which was in exquisite relief to the pale green of the hills. To enjoy the delighful temperature and fine scenery of the Bay, I used frequently to climb a hill just in the rear of the town, whence the harbor, the strait into Pablo

Bay, the Golden Gate and the horizon of the Pacific could all be seen at one view. On the top of the hill are the graves of several Russians, who came out in the service of the Russian Company, each surmounted with a black cross, bearing an inscription in their language. All this ground, however, has been surveyed, staked into lots and sold, and at the same rate of growth the city will not be long in climbing the hill and disturbing the rest of the Muscovites.

In company with my friends, the Moores, I made many short excursions among the hills, during this charming season. Our most frequent trip was to Fresh Pond, in the neighborhood of the old Presidio. With a gray donkey—an invaluable beast, by the way—harnessed to a light cart, in which we had placed two or three empty barrels, we drove out to the place, a little basin shut in by the hills, and only divided by a narrow bushy ridge from the waters of the Golden Gate. Several tents were pitched on its margin ; the washmen and gardeners had established themselves there and were diligently plying their respective occupations. A little strip of moist bottom adjoining the pond had been cleared of its thickets and was partly ploughed, showing a rich black loam. The washerwomen, of whom there were a few, principally Mexicans and Indians, had established themselves on one side of the pond and the washmen on another. The latter went into the business on a large scale, having their tents for ironing, their large kettles for boiling the clothes and their fluted wash-boards along the edge of the water. It was an amusing sight to see a great, burly, long-bearded fellow, kneeling on the ground, with sleeves rolled up to the elbows, and rubbing a shirt on the board with such violence that the suds flew and the buttons, if there were any, must soon snap off. Their clear-starching and ironing were still more ludicrous ; but, notwithstanding, they succeeded fully as well as the women, and were rapidly growing rich from the profits of their business.   Where $8 a dozen is paid for washing clothes, it is very easy to earn double the wages of a Member of Congress.

The sunsets we saw from the hills as we drove slowly back with the barrels filled, were all of the same gorgeous character.   The air had a purity and sweetness which made the long hour of twilight enchanting, and we frequently lingered on the road till after dark.   We helped our patient donkey up the hill by pushing behind his cart—an aid he seemed fully to appreciate, for he pulled at such times with much more spirit.   He had many curious ways about him, the most remarkable of which was his capacity for digestion.   Cloth, canvas and shavings seemed as much his natural food as hay or green grass.   Whenever he broke loose during the night, which was not seldom, it was generally followed in the morning by a visit from some emigrant, claiming damages for the amount of tent-covering which had been chewed up.   Once, indeed, a man who had indulged rather freely in bad brandy, at twenty-five cents a glass, wandered in the dark to the place where the donkey was tethered, lay down at his feet and fell asleep. When he awoke in the morning, sobered by the coolness of his bed and foggy blankets, he found to his utter surprise and horror, that the ravenous beast had not only devoured his cap but cropped nearly all the hair from one side of his head !   As the man's hair happened to be glowing in color and coarse in texture, the mistake of the donkey in taking it to be swamp hay, is not so much to be wondered at.

The valley about the Mission Dolores was charmingly green and beautiful at this time.   Several of the former miners, in anticipation of the great influx of emigrants into the country and a consequent market for vegetables, pitched their tents on the best spots along the Mission Creek, and began preparing the ground for gardens. The valley was surveyed and staked into lots almost to the summit of the mountains, and the operation of squatting was performed even by many of the citizens of San Francisco, for the purpose of obtaining titles to the land. Some gentlemen of my acquaintance came into the possession of certain stone quarries, meadow lands and fine sheep-pastures, in this manner; whereupon a friend of mine, and myself, concluded to try the experiment, thinking the experience might, at least, be of some benefit. So, one fine morning we rode out to the Mission, where we found the surveyor on one of the hills, chopping up the chapparal into " hundred vara" lots. He received us cordially, and on looking over his map of the locality, found two adjoining lots of two hundred varas each, which were still unoccupied. They lay on the western side of the Valley, on the slope of the mountains. We hastened away, crossed two yawning arroyos and climbed the steep, where, truly enough, we found the stakes indicating the limits of the survey. I chose a little valley, scooped out between two peaks of the ridge, and watered by a clear stream which trickled down through its centre. My friend took a broader tract, which was not so well watered as mine; however, on examining the soil, we agreed that it would produce good crops of cabbages and turnips. Accordingly, we marched leisurely over the ground, ascended to its highest part, and took a seat on a boulder of gray rock, which stood exactly upon the line between our two territories. All the beautiful Valley lay beneath us, with the bay beyond, a part of the shipping of San Francisco, and Monte Diablo in the distance—a fine prospect for a squatter!

On our return to the city, we debated whether we should pro-

cure materials for a tent and take up an abode on the lofty lots ;
but, as it was not at all clear that any land could be granted, or
that it would be worth taking even if we should become bona fide
settlers, we finally determined to let the matter rest.   We did not
repeat our visit, and we learned soon afterwards that violent disputes had arisen between the inhabitants of the Mission and the
emigrants who had commenced gardening.   I, who never owned
a rood of land in my life, would nevertheless have accepted the
proprietorship of one of the bleak pinnacles of the Sierra Navada—
or better, the top of the Shaste Peak—could it have been given
me, for the mere satisfaction of feeling that there was one spot of
the Earth which I might claim as my own, down to its burning
centre.

PORTSMOUTH SQUARE, SAN FRANCISCO.

NEW YORK, GEO. P. PUTNAM.

CHAPTER VI.

OF all the marvellous phases of the history of the Present, the growth of San Francisco is the one which will most tax the belief of the Future. Its parallel was never known, and shall never be beheld again. I speak only of what I saw with my own eyes. When I landed there, a little more than four months before, I found a scattering town of tents and canvas houses, with a show of frame buildings on one or two streets, and a population of about six thousand. Now, on my last visit, I saw around me an actual metropolis, displaying street after street of well-built edifices, filled with an active and enterprising people and exhibiting every mark of permanent commercial prosperity. Then, the town was limited to the curve of the Bay fronting the anchorage and bottoms of the hills. Now, it stretched to the topmost heights, followed the shore around point after point, and sending back a long arm through a gap in the hills, took hold of the Golden Gate and was building its warehouses on the open strait and almost fronting the blue horizon of the Pacific. Then, the gold-seeking sojourner lodged in muslin rooms and canvas garrets, with a philosophic lack of furniture, and ate his simple though substantial fare from pine boards. Now, lofty hotels, gaudy with verandas and balconies, were met with in all quarters, furnished with home luxury, and aristocratic restaurants presented daily their long bills of fare, rich with the choicest technicalities of the Parisian cuisine. Then, vessels were coming in day after day, to lie deserted and useless at their anchorage. Now scarce a day passed, but some cluster of sails, bound *outward* through the Golden Gate, took their way to all the corners of the Pacific. Like the magic seed of the Indian juggler, which grew, blossomed and bore fruit before the eyes of his spectators, San Francisco seemed to have accomplished in a day the growth of half a century.

When I first landed in California, bewildered and amazed by what seemed an unnatural standard of prices, I formed the opinion that there would be before long a great crash in speculation. Things, it appeared then, had reached the crisis, and it was pronounced impossible that they could remain stationary. This might have been a very natural idea at the time, but the subsequent course of affairs proved it to be incorrect. Lands, rents, goods and subsistence continued steadily to advance in cost, and as the credit system had been meanwhile prudently contracted, the character of the business done was the more real and substantial. Two or three years will pass, in all probability, before there is a positive abatement of the standard of prices. There will be fluctuations in the meantime, occasioning great gains and losses, but the fall in rents and real estate, when it comes, as it inevitably must in the course of two or three years, will not be so crushing as I at first imagined. I doubt whether it will seriously injure the commercial activity of the place. Prices will never fall to the same standard as in the Atlantic States. Fortunes will always be made by the sober, intelligent, industrious, and energetic ; but no one who is either too careless, too spiritless or too ignorant to succeed at home, need trouble himself about emigrating. The same general rule holds good, as well here as elsewhere, and it is all the better for human nature that it is so.

Not only was the heaviest part of the business conducted on cash principles, but all rents, even to lodgings in hotels, were required to be paid in advance. A single bowling-alley, in the basement story of the Ward House—a new hotel on Portsmouth-Square—prepaid $5,000 monthly. The firm of Findley, Johnson & Co. sold their real estate, purchased a year previous, for $20,000, at $300,000 ; $25,000 down, and the rest in monthly instalments of $12,500. This was a fair specimen of the speculations daily made. Those on a lesser scale were frequently of a very amusing character, but the claims on one's astonishment were so constant, that the faculty soon wore out, and the most unheard-of operations were looked upon as matters of course. Among others that came under my observation, was one of a gentleman who purchased a barrel of alum for $6, the price in New York being $9. It happened to be the only alum in the place, and as there was a demand for it shortly afterwards, he sold the barrel for $150. Another purchased all the candle-wick to be found, at an average price of 40 cts. per lb., and sold it in a short time at $2 25 per lb. A friend of mine expended $10,000 in purchasing barley, which in a week brought $20,000. The greatest gains were still made by the gambling tables and the eating-houses. Every device that art could suggest was used to swell the custom of the former. The latter found abundant support in the necessities of a large floating population, in addition to the swarm of permanent residents.

For a month or two previous to this time, money had been very scarce in the market, and from ten to fifteen per cent. monthly, was paid, with the addition of good security. Notwithstanding the quantity of coin brought into the country by emigrants, and the millions of gold dust used as currency, the actual specie basis was very small compared with the immense amount of business transacted. Nevertheless, I heard of nothing like a failure ; the principal firms were prompt in all their dealings, and the chivalry of Commerce—to use a new phrase—was as faithfully observed as it could have been in the old marts of Europe and America. The merchants had a 'Change and News-room, and were beginning to cooperate in their movements and consolidate their credit. A stock company which had built a long wharf at the foot of Sacra-ento-st. declared a dividend of ten per cent. within six weeks after the wharf was finished. During the muddy season, it was the only convenient place for landing goods, and as the cost of con-structing it was enormous, so were likewise the charges for wharf-age and storage.

There had been a vast improvement in the means of living since my previous visit to San Francisco. Several large hotels had been opened, which were equal in almost every respect to houses of the second class in the Atlantic cities. The Ward House, the Graham House, imported bodily from Baltimore, and the St. Francis Hotel, completely threw into the shade all former establishments. The rooms were furnished with comfort and even luxury, and the tables lacked few of the essentials of good living, according to a ' home' taste. · The sleeping apartments of the St. Francis were the best in California. The cost of board and lodging was $150 per month—which was considered unusually cheap. A room at the Ward House cost $250 monthly, without board. The principal restaurants charged $35 a week for board, and there were lodging houses where a berth or " bunk" —one out of fifty in the same room—might be had for $6 a week.

The model of these establishments—which were far from being " model lodging-houses"—was that of a ship. A number of state-rooms, containing six berths each, ran around the sides of a large room, or cabin, where the lodgers resorted to read, write, smoke and drink at their leisure. The state-rooms were consequently filled with foul and unwholesome air, and the noises in the cabin prevented the passengers from sleeping, except between midnight and four o'clock.

The great want of San Francisco was society. Think of a city of thirty thousand inhabitants, peopled by men alone! The like of this was never seen before. Every man was his own housekeeper, doing, in many instances, his own sweeping, cooking, washing and mending. Many home-arts, learned rather by observation than experience, came conveniently into play. He who cannot make a bed, cook a beefsteak, or sew up his own rips and rents, is unfit to be a citizen of California. Nevertheless, since the town began to assume a permanent shape, very many of the comforts of life in the East were attainable. A family may now live there without suffering any material privations ; and if every married man, who intends spending some time in California, would take his family with him, a social influence would soon be created to which we might look for the happiest results.

Towards the close of my stay, the city was as dismal a place as could well be imagined. The glimpse of bright, warm, serene weather passed away, leaving in its stead a raw, cheerless, south-east storm. The wind now and then blew a heavy gale, and the cold, steady fall of rain, was varied by claps of thunder and sudden blasts of hail. The mud in the streets became little short of fathomless, and it was with difficulty that the mules could drag their empty wagons through. A powerful London dray-horse, a very giant in harness, was the only animal able to pull a good load ; and I was told that he earned his master $100 daily. I saw occasionally a company of Chinese workmen, carrying bricks and mortar, slung by ropes to long bamboo poles. The plank side-walks, in the lower part of the city, ran along the brink of pools and quicksands, which the Street Inspector and his men vainly endeavored to fill by hauling cart-loads of chapparal and throwing sand on the top ; in a day or two the gulf was as deep as ever. The side-walks, which were made at the cost of $5 per foot, bridged over the worst spots, but I was frequently obliged to go the whole length of a block in order to get on the other side. One could not walk any distance, without getting at least ancle-deep, and although the thermometer rarely sank below 50°, it was impossible to stand still for even a short time without a death-like chill taking hold of the feet. As a consequence of this, coughs and bronchial affections were innumerable. The universal custom of wearing the pantaloons inside the boots threatened to restore the knee-breeches of our grandfathers' times. Even women were obliged to shorten their skirts, and wear high-topped boots. The population seemed to be composed entirely of dismounted hussars. All this will be remedied when the city is two years older, and Portsmouth Square boasts a pavé as elegant as that on the dollar side of Broadway.

The severe weather occasioned a great deal of sickness, especially among those who led an exposed life. The city overflowed with people, and notwithstanding buildings were continually growing up like mushrooms, over night, hundreds who arrived were obliged to lodge in tents, with which the summits of the hills were covered. Fever-and-ague and dysentery were the prevailing complaints, the great prevalence of which was owing undoubtedly to

exposure and an irregular habit of life. An association was formed to relieve those in actual want, many of the wealthiest and
most influential citizens taking an honorable part in the matter.
Many instances of lamentable destitution were by this means
brought to light. Nearly all the hospitals of the place were soon
filled, and numbers went to the Sandwich Islands to recruit. The
City Hospital, a large, well ventilated and regulated establishment, contained about fifty patients. The attending physician
described to me several cases of nearly hopeless lunacy which had
come under his care, some of them produced by disappointment
and ill-luck, and others by sudden increase of fortune. Poor
human nature!

In the midst of the rains, we were greeted one morning with a
magnificent spectacle. The wind had blown furiously during the
night, with violent falls of rain, but the sun rose in a spotless sky,
revealing the Coast Mountains across the bay wrapped in snow
half-way down their sides. For two days they wore their dazzling
crown, which could be seen melting away hour by hour, from their
ridges and cloven ravines. This was the only snow I saw while in
San Francisco; only once did I notice any appearance of frost.
The grass was green and vigorous, and some of the more hardy
plants in blossom; vegetables, it is well known, flourish with equal
luxuriance during the winter season. At one of the restaurants,
I was shown some remarkable specimens of the growth of California soil—potatoes, weighing from one to five pounds each; beets
and turnips eight inches in diameter, and perfectly sweet and
sound; and large, silver-skinned onions, whose delicate flavor the
most inveterate enemy of this honest vegetable could not but have
relished. A gentleman who visited the port of Bodega, informed
me that he saw in the garden of Capt. Smith, the owner of the

place, pea-vines which had produced their third crop from the same root in one summer.

As the rains drove the deer and other animals down from the mountains, game of all kinds became abundant. Fat elks and splendid black-tailed does hung at the doors of all the butcher-shops, and wild geese, duck and brant, were brought into the city by the wagon-load. " Grizzly bear steak," became a choice dish at the eating-houses ; I had the satisfaction one night of eating a slice of one that had weighed eleven hundred pounds. The flesh was of a bright red color, very solid, sweet, and nutritious; its flavor was preferable to that of the best pork. The large native hare, a specimen of which occasionally found its way to the restaurants, is nowise inferior to that of Europe. As an illustration of the money which might be spent in procuring a meal no better than an ordinary hotel-dinner at home, I may mention that a dinner for fifteen persons, to which I was invited, at the " Excelsior," cost the giver of it $225.

The effect of a growing prosperity and some little taste of luxury was readily seen in the appearance of the business community of San Francisco. The slouched felt hats gave way to narrow-brimmed black beavers ; flannel shirts were laid aside, and white linen, though indifferently washed, appeared instead ; dress and frock coats, of the fashion of the previous year in the Atlantic side, came forth from trunks and sea-chests ; in short, a San Francisco merchant was almost as smooth and spruce in his outward appearance as a merchant anywhere else. The hussar boot, however, was obliged to be worn, and a variation of the Mexican sombrero—a very convenient and becoming head-piece—came into fashion among the younger class.

The steamers which arrived at this time, brought large quantities of newspapers from all parts of the Atlantic States. The speculation which had been so successful at first, was completely overdone ; there was a glut in the market, in consequence whereof newspapers came down to fifty and twenty-five cents apiece. The leading journals of New-York, New-Orleans and Boston were cried at every street-corner. The two papers established in the place issued editions " for the Atlantic Coast," at the sailing of every steamer for Panama. The offices were invaded by crowds of purchasers, and the slow hand-presses in use could not keep pace with the demand. The profits of these journals were almost incredible, when contrasted with their size and the amount of their circulation. Neither of them failed to count their gains at the rate of $75,000 a year, clear profit.

My preparations for leaving San Francisco, were made with the regret that I could not remain longer and see more of the wonderful growth of the Empire of the West. Yet I was fortunate in witnessing the most peculiar and interesting stages of its progress, and I took my departure in the hope of returning at some future day to view the completion of these magnificent beginnings. The world's history has no page so marvellous as that which has just been turned in California.

CHAPTER VII.

SOCIETY IN CALIFORNIA.

THERE are some features of Society in California, which I have hitherto failed to touch upon in my narrative, but which deserve a passing notice before I take my final leave of that wonderful land. The direct effect of the state of things growing out of the discovery of the placers, was to develop new qualities and traits of character, not in single individuals, but in every individual of the entire community—traits frequently most unlooked-for in those who exhibited them in the most marked degree. Society, therefore, was for the time cast into new forms, or, rather, deprived of any fixed form. A man, on coming to California, could no more expect to retain his old nature unchanged, than he could retain in his lungs the air he had inhaled on the Atlantic shore.

The most immediate and striking change which came upon the greater portion of the emigrants was an increase of activity, and proportionately, of reckless and daring spirit. It was curious to see how men hitherto noted for their prudence and caution took sudden leave of those qualities, to all appearance, yet only prospered the more thereby. Perhaps there was at bottom a vein of keen, shrewd calculation, which directed their seemingly heedless movements ; certain it is, at least, that for a long time the rashest speculators were the most fortunate. It was this fact, no doubt, that seemed so alarming to persons newly-arrived, and gave rise to unnumbered predictions of the speedy and ruinous crash of the whole business fabric of San Francisco. But nothing is more contagious than this spirit of daring and independent action, and the most doleful prophets were, ere long, swallowed up in the same whirlpool against which they had warned others.

The emigrants who arrive in California, very soon divide into two distinct classes. About two-thirds, or possibly three-fourths of them are active, hopeful and industrious. They feel this singular intoxication of society, and go to work at something, no matter what, by which they hope to thrive. The remaining portion see everything " through a glass, darkly." Their first bright anticipations are unrealized ; the horrid winds of San Francisco during the dry season, chill and unnerve them : or, if they go to the placers, the severe labor and the ill success of inexperienced hands, completes their disgust. They commit a multitude of sins in the shape of curses upon every one who has written or spoken favorably of California. Some of them return home without having seen the country at all, and others, even if they obtain profitable situations, labor without a will. It is no place for a slow, an over-cautious, or a desponding man. The emigrant should be willing to work, not only at one business, but many, if need be ; the grumbler or the idler had far better stay at home.

It cannot be denied that the very activity of California society created a spirit of excitement which frequently led to dangerous excesses. The habits of the emigrants, never, even at home, very slow and deliberate, branched into all kinds of wild offshoots, the necessary effect of the sudden glow and expansion which they experienced Those who retained their health seemed to revel in an exuberance of animal spirits, which carried them with scarce a jar over barriers and obstacles that would have brought others to a full stand. There was something exceedingly hearty, cordial and encouraging in the character of social intercourse. The ordinary forms of courtesy were flung aside with a bluntness of good-fellowship infinitely preferable, under the circumstances. I was constantly reminded of the stories of Northern History—of the stout Vikings and Jarls who exulted in their very passions and made their heroes of those who were most jovial at the feast and most easily kindled with the rage of battle. Indeed, it required but little effort of the imagination to revive those iron ages, when the rugged gold-diggers, with their long hair and unshorn beards, were grouped around some mountain camp-fire, revelling in the ruddy light and giving full play to a mirth so powerful and profound that it would not have shamed the Berserkers.

The most common excesses into which the Californians run, are drinking and gambling. I say drinking, rather than drunkenness, for I saw very little of the latter. But a single case came under my observation while I was in the gold region. The man's friends took away his money and deposited it in the hands of the Alcalde, then tied him to a tree where they left him till he became sober. The practice of drinking, nevertheless, was widely prevalent, and its effects rendered more destructive by the large amount of bad liquor which was sent into the country. Gambling, in spite of a universal public sentiment against it, grew and flourished ; the disappointment and ruin of many emigrants were owing to its existence. The gamblers themselves were in many instances men who had led orderly and respectable lives at home. I have heard some of them frankly avow that nothing would induce them to acquaint their friends and families with the nature of their occupation ; they would soon have enough, they said, and then they would wash their hands of the unclean stain, and go home to lead more honorable lives. But alas! it is not so easy to wash out the memory of self-degradation. If these men have in truth any sentiment of honor remaining, every coin of the wealth they have hoarded will awaken a shameful consciousness of the base and unmanly business by which it was obtained.

In spite, however, of all these dissipating and disorganizing influences, the main stock of society was sound, vigorous and progressive. The rank shoots, while they might have slightly weakened the trunk, only showed the abundant life of the root. In short, without wishing to be understood as apologizing in any degree for the evils which existed, it was evident that had the Californians been more cool, grave and deliberate in their temperament—had they lacked the fiery energy and impulsive spirit which pushed them irresistibly forward—the dangers which surrounded them at the outset would have been far more imminent. Besides, this energy did not run at random ; it was in the end directed by an enlightened experience, and that instinct of Right, which is the strength and security of a self-governed People. Hundreds of instances might be adduced to show that the worst passions of our nature were speedily developed in the air of California, but the one grand lesson of the settlement and organization of the country is of a character that ennobles the race.

The unanimity with which all united in this work—the frankness with which the old prejudices of sect and party were disclaimed—the freshly-awakened pride of country, which made every citizen jealously and disinterestedly anxious that she should acquit herself honorably in the eyes of the Nation at large—formed a spectacle which must claim our entire admiration. In view of the splendid future which is opening for California, it insures her a stable foundation on which to build the superstructure of her wealth and power.

After what has been said, it will appear natural that California should be the most democratic country in the world. The practical equality of all the members of a community, whatever might be the wealth, intelligence or profession of each, was never before thoroughly demonstrated. Dress was no guage of respectability, and no honest occupation, however menial in its character, affected a man's standing. Lawyers, physicians and ex-professors dug cellars, drove ox-teams, sawed wood and carried luggage ; while men who had been Army privates, sailors, cooks or day laborers were at the head of profitable establishments and not infrequently assisted in some of the minor details of Government. A man who would consider his fellow beneath him, on account of his appearance or occupation, would have had some difficulty in living peaceably in California. The security of the country is owing, in no small degree, to this plain, practical development of what the French reverence as an abstraction, under the name of *Fraternité*. To sum up all in three words, LABOR IS RESPECTABLE : may it never be otherwise, while a grain of gold is left to glitter in Californian soil !

I have dwelt with the more earnestness on these features of Society because they do not seem to be fully appreciated on this side of the Continent. I cannot take leave, in the regular course of my narrative, of a land where I found so much in Nature to admire and enjoy, without attempting to give some general, though imperfect view of Man, as he appeared under those new and wonderful influences.

CHAPTER VIII.

THE rainy season, by rendering further travel very unsatisfactory and laborious, if not impossible, put an end to my wanderings in California, which, in fact, had already extended beyond the period I had originally fixed for my stay. I was therefore anxious to set out on my homeward journey through Mexico, to which I looked forward with glowing anticipations. Rather than wait for the steamer of Jan. 1st., I decided to take one of the sailing packets up for Mazatlan, as the trip down the coast is usually made in from ten to fifteen days. The most promising chance was that of a Peruvian brigantine belonging to a German house, which I was assured would sail on the 15th of December. A heavy gale coming up at the time put this out of the question. I waited until the 17th, when I went on board, determined to set foot no more in San Franciscan mud. The brigantine—which bore the name of Iquiqueña, from the Peruvian port of Iquiqua—was a small, rakish craft, built at the Island of Chiloë for a smuggler in the opium trade; having been afterwards purchased by a house in Callao, she still retained the Peruvian colors.

In her low, confined cabin, containing eight berths, which were reached by a dark and crooked well, opening on the deck near the rudder, seven passengers were crowded—Americans, Mexicans and Venezuelans—besides the captain, mate, supercargo and steward, who were Germans, as were likewise the greater part of the crew. To complete the circle that met around our little table to discuss the invariable daily dinner of rice soup and boiled beef, I must not omit mentioning a Chinese dog, as eccentric in his behavior as the Celestials on shore. The captain and crew did nothing to falsify the national reputation for tardiness and delay. In our case the *poco tiempo* of the Chagres boatmen was outdone. Seven days were we doomed to spend in the Bay, before the almost hopeless conjunction of wind, tide, crew, passengers and vessel started us from our anchorage. On getting aboard, the captain declared everything to be in readiness, except the wood and water, which would be forthcoming next day. Having some experience of German deliberation, I at once resigned myself to three days' delay. The next day was stormy and rough; on the second, two casks of water were brought on board; the third was stormy; the wood was purchased on the fourth; and on the fifth, the sailors quarreled about their pay and refused to go to sea.

While we thus lay in the harbor, just inside the Rincon, trying to bear with patience a delay so vexatious, one of the terrible south-east gales came on. The wind gradually rose through the night, and its violence was heard and felt in the whistle of the rigging and the uneasy roll of our brigantine. When morning dawned, the sky was as gray and cold as an arch of granite, except towards the south-east, where a streak of dun light seemed like the opening through which the whole fury of the blast was poured upon the bay. The timbers of the shipping creaked as they were tossed about by the lashed and driven waters; the rigging hummed and roared till the ropes were ready to snap with the violence of their vibrations. There was little rain accompanying the gale, but every drop stung like a shot. Seen under a sky and through an atmosphere from which all sensation of light and warmth was gone, the town and hills of San Francisco appeared as if cast in bronze, so cold, dark, and severe were their outlines. The blackest thunder-gusts I ever saw, had nothing so savage and relentless in their expression. All day and night, having dragged our anchor and drifted on the shoals, we lay thumping heavily with every swell, while a large barque, with three anchors out, threatened to stave in our bows. Towards morning the rain increased, and in the same proportion the gale abated. During its prevalence five or six vessels were injured, and two or three entirely lost.

The sailors having been pacified, the supercargo taken on board, and the brig declared ready for sea, we were detained another day on account of the anchor sticking fast in the mud, and still another through lack of a favorable wind. Finally, on the eighth day after going on board, the brig was warped through the crowded vessels, and took the first of the ebb tide, with a light breeze, to run out of the harbor.

I went on deck, in the misty daybreak, to take a parting look at the town and its amphitheatric hills. As I turned my face shoreward, a little spark appeared through the fog. Suddenly it shot up into a spiry flame, and at the same instant I heard the sound of gongs, bells and trumpets, and the shouting of human voices. The calamity, predicted and dreaded so long in advance, that men ceased to think of it, had come at last—San Francisco was on fire! The blaze increased with fearful rapidity. In fifteen minutes, it had risen into a broad, flickering column, making all the shore, the misty air and the water ruddy as with another sunrise. The sides of new frame houses, scattered through the town, tents high up on the hills, and the hulls and listless sails of vessels in the bay, gleamed and sparkled in the thick atmosphere. Meanwhile the roar and tumult swelled, and above the clang of gongs and the cries of the populace, I could hear the crackling of blazing timbers, and the smothered sound of falling roofs. I climbed into the rigging and watched the progress of the conflagration. As the flames leaped upon a new dwelling, there was a sudden whirl of their waving volumes—an embracing of the frail walls in their relentless clasp—and, a second afterwards, from roof and rafter and foundation-beam shot upward a jet of fire, steady and intense at first, but surging off into spiral folds and streamers, as the timbers were parted and fell.

For more than hour, while we were tacking in the channel between Yerba Buena Island and the anchorage, there was no apparent check to the flames. Before passing Fort Montgomery, however, we heard several explosions in quick succession, and conjectured that vigorous measures had been taken to prevent further destruction. When at last, with a fair breeze and bright sky, we were dashing past the rock of Alcatraz, the red column had sunk away to a smouldering blaze, and nothing but a heavy canopy of smoke remained to tell the extent of the conflagration. The Golden Gate was again before us, and I looked through its mountain-walls on the rolling Pacific, with full as pleasant an excitement as I had looked inwards, four months before, eager to catch the first glimpse of the new Eldorado.

The breeze freshened, the swell increased, and as the breakers of the entrance receded behind us, we entered the rough sea left by a recent gale. In trying to haul close to the wind, the captain discovered that the rudder was broken. Immediately afterwards, there was a cry of " a leak !" and from the terror on the faces of the mate and sailors, I thought that nothing less than a dozen blankets could stop the opening. The pumps were rigged in haste, but little water was found in the hold, and on examination it appeared that the leak, which was in the bow, was caused by the springing apart of the planking from a violent blow on the rocks, which the brig had received a short time previous. The captain decided at once to return, much to our disappointment, as the wind was fair for Mazatlan. We were twenty miles from the entrance, and after beating up until next morning found ourselves just as far off as ever. The wind continuing fair, the captain at length listened to us, and turned again towards Mazatlan. A change of wind again changed his mind, and all that day and the next we tacked back and forth—sometimes running out towards the Farellones, sometimes close under the lee of the Punta de Los Reyes, and again driven down the coast as far, on the other side of the entrance What our brig gained in tacking, she lost in leeway, and as the rudder hung by a single pintle, she minded her helm badly. On the afternoon of the third day we were becalmed, but drifted into the entrance of the Gate with the flood-tide, in company with fifteen vessels, that had been waiting outside. A light southern breeze springing up, enabled us to reach the anchorage west of Clark's Point in the night ; so that next morning, after landing on the beach and walking through a mile of deep mud, I was once more in San Francisco.

I hastened immediately to Portsmouth Square, the scene of the conflagration. All its eastern front, with the exception of the Delmonico Restaurant at the corner of Clay-st. was gone, together with the entire side of the block, on Washington-st. The Eldorado, Parker House, Denison's Exchange and the United States

Coffee House—forming, collectively, the great rendezvous of the city, where everybody could be found at some time of the day—were among the things that had been.   The fronts of the Verandah, Aguila de Oro, and other hells on Washington-st. were blackened and charred from the intense heat to which they were subjected, and from many of the buildings still hung the blankets by means of which they were saved.   Three days only had elapsed since the fire, yet in that time all the rubbish had been cleared away, and the frames of several houses were half raised.   All over the burnt space sounded one incessant tumult of hammers, axes and saws.   In one week after the fire, the Eldorado and Denison's Exchange stood completely roofed and weatherboarded, and would soon be ready for occupation.   The Parker House was to be re-built of brick, and the timbers of the basement floor were already laid.   The Exchange had been contracted for at $15,000, to be finished in two weeks, under penalty of forfeiting $150 for every additional day.   In three weeks from the date of the fire, it was calculated that all the buildings destroyed would be replaced by new ones, of better construction.   The loss by the conflagration was estimated at $1,500,000—an immense sum, when the number and character of the buildings destroyed, is considered.   This did not include the loss in a business way, which was probably $500,000 more.   The general business of the place, however, had not been injured.   The smaller gambling hells around and near Portsmouth Square were doing a good business, now that the head-quarters of the profession were destroyed.

Notwithstanding there was no air stirring at the time, the progress of the fire, as described by those who were on the spot, had something terrific in its character.   The canvas partitions of rooms shrivelled away like paper in the breath of the flames, and the dry, resinous wood of the outer walls radiated a heat so intense that houses at some distance were obliged to be kept wet to prevent their ignition. Nothing but the prompt measures of the city authorities and a plentiful supply of blankets in the adjacent stores, saved all the lower part of the city from being swept away. The houses in the path of the flames were either blown up or felled like trees, by cutting off the ground timbers with axes, and pulling over the structure with ropes fastened to the roof. The Spanish merchants on Washington street, and others living in adobe houses in the rear, were completely stupified by the danger, and refused to have their buildings blown up. No one listened to them, and five minutes afterwards, adobes, timbers and merchandize went into the air together.

A very few persons, out of the thousands present, did the work of arresting the flames. At the time of the most extreme danger, hundreds of idle spectators refused to lend a hand, unless they were paid enormous wages. One of the principal merchants, I was told, offered a dollar a bucket for water, and made use of several thousand buckets in saving his property. All the owners of property worked incessantly, and were aided by their friends, but at least five thousand spectators stood idle in the plaza. I hope their selfish indifference is not a necessary offshoot of society here. It is not to be disputed, however, that constant familiarity with the shifting of Fortune between her farthest extremes, blunts very much the sympathies of the popular heart.

The German house of whom I had obtained a passage for Mazatlan, was burned out, but the supercargo soon discovered its whereabouts. A committee of sea-captains, appointed to examine the brigantine, reported that she could be made ready for sea in three or four days. Under these circumstances, the owners refused to refund more than half the passage-money, which was $75, to those of us who chose to leave the vessel. My time was now growing precious, and I had no doubt the three days spoken of would be extended to as many weeks. I therefore went to the office of the Pacific Mail Steamship Company, where, as I expected, every ticket had been taken weeks before, and neither love, money nor entreaty seemed likely to procure one. Mr. Robinson, the Agent, however, with a prompt kindness I shall not soon forget, gave me a passage to Mazatlan, with the understanding that I would have no berth and probably little sleeping-room.

The steamer was to sail on the first of January, at daybreak. After coming upon my friends like an apparition—they having supposed me to be far out at sea—I spent two days on shore, housed up from rain and mud, and finally took a boat for the steamer on the last evening of the year 1849. It was during the prevalence of the spring-tides, and no boat could be had to go from the Long Wharf to the anchorage off the Rincon, for less than $4. I had two oarsmen for myself and blankets; it was near the middle of the ebb-tide, and we ran inside the shelter of the point till we were abreast of the steamer. She was now about three-quarters of a mile distant, but a foaming, raging flood was between us. Several large boats, manned by four and six oarsmen were struggling in the midst of the current, and borne away in spite of themselves. One of my men was discouraged, and wanted to turn back, but there was a majority against him. I took good hold of the tiller-ropes, the men stripped to their flannel shirts, planted their feet firmly against the ribs of the boat, and we dashed into the teeth of the tide. We were thrown and tossed about like a toy ; the spray flew over us, and the strongest efforts of the men did not seem to move us an inch. After half an hour of hard work, during which we continually lost ground, we came alongside of a vessel and made fast. At least a dozen other craft could be seen struggling out after us, but they all fell away, some of them drifting two or three miles before they could make a halt. We lay for nearly two hours, waiting for the height of the ebb to pass, but the flood still foamed and rushed, dashing against the prows of vessels and boiling around their sterns, with an incessant roar. At last, another boat with two passengers came down upon us in the darkness; we joined crews, leaving one of the boats behind, and set out again with four oars. It was pitchy dark, with a rain dashing in our faces. We kept on, towards the light of the steamer, gaining about a yard a minute, till we reached her lee gangway.

I unrolled my blankets and put in a preëmption claim for one end of the cabin-table. Several other berthless persons occupied the benches on either hand and the iron grating below, which printed their sides like a checker-board; and so we passed the night. The last boat-loads came out in the morning; the parting gun echoed back from the Island of Yerba Buena; the paddles moved; San Francisco slid away from us, and the Golden Gate opened again; the swells of the Pacific rolled forward to meet us; the coast wheeled around and fronted our larboard side; rain and fog were behind us, and a speck of clear blue far ahead—and so we sped southward, to the tropics, and homeward!

The Oregon's freight, both of gold and passengers, was the most important which had ever left San Francisco. Of the former, we had about two millions of dollars on board; of the latter, the Congressmen and Senators elect, Col. Frémont, Dr. Gwin, Gilbert and Wright, together with a score of the prominent merchants and moneyed men of San Francisco, and several officers

of the Army and Navy. Mr. Butler King was returning from
his survey of the country; Major Rucker, whom I have already
mentioned in connection with the overland emigration, and Major
Cross, recently from Oregon, were also on board. The character
of our little community was very different from that which came
up on the Panama; the steamer was under better regulations, and
at meal-time, especially, there was no disgraceful exhibition of
(for want of a better word) swinishness, such as I witnessed on the
former boat. We had a mild and spring-like temperature during
the trip, and blue skies, after doubling Cape Conception.

We touched at Santa Barbara on the third morning out. The
night had been foggy, and we ran astray in the channel between
the Island of Santa Rosa and the mainland, making the coast about
twenty-five miles south of the town. I did not regret this, as it
gave me an opportunity of seeing the point where the Coast Mountains come down to the sea, forming a narrow pass, which can only
be traveled at low tide, between the precipice and the surf. It is
generally known as the Rincon, or Corner—a common Spanish
term for the jutting end of a mountain; in a Californian ballad
(written before seeing the country,) I had made it the scene of an
imaginary incident, giving the name of *Paso del Mar*—the Pass
of the Sea—to the spot. I was delighted to find so near a corre-
spondence between its crags of black rock, its breakers and reaches
of spray-wet sand, and the previous picture in my imagination.
The village of Santa Barbara is charmingly situated, on a warm
slope above the roadstead, down to which stretch its fields of wheat
and barley. Behind it, on a shelf of the mountain, stands the
Mission, or Episcopal Residence of Santa Barbara, its white
arched corridors and tall square towers brightly relieved against the
pine forests in the distance. Above and beyond all, the Moun-

tain of Santa Ynez lifts its bold and sterile ramparts, like an unscaleable barrier against the inland.

We lay-to in the road for several hours, shipping supplies. The shore was so near that we could watch the vaqueros, as they galloped among the herds and flung their lariats over the horns of the doomed beeves. An immense whale lay stranded on the beach like the hull of some unlucky vessel. As we steamed down the coast, in the afternoon, we had a magnificent view of the snowy range which divides the rich vine-land of Los Angeles from the Tulare Plains. At daybreak the next morning we were in the harbor of San Diego, which was little changed since my visit in August; the hills were somewhat greener, and there were a few more tents pitched around the hide-houses. Thence away and down the rugged Peninsula—past the Bay of Sebastian Viscaino, the headland of San Lorenzo and the white deserts of sand that stretch far inland—around the jagged pyramids and hollow caverns of Cape San Lucas—beyond the dioramic glimpse of San José, and into the mouth of the Californian Gulf, where we were struck aback by a norther that strained our vessel's sinews and troubled the stomachs of her passengers. The next morning we groped about in the fog, hearing a breaker here and seeing a rock there, but the captain at last hit upon the right clue and ran us out of the maze into a gush of dazzling sunshine and tropic heat, which lay upon the islands and palmy shores of Mazatlan Harbor.

CHAPTER IX.

MAZATLAN.

I took leave of my friends and mess-mates, receiving many gloomy predictions and warnings of danger from the most of them, and went ashore with the captain, in the ship's boat. The water is very shallow, from within a mile of the landing, and abounds with rocks which rise nearly to the surface. Two of these are called The Turtles, from an incident which is told at the expense of an officer of the British Navy. He had just reached Mazatlan, and on his first visit to the shore, knowing that the waters contained turtle, had provided himself with rope and harpoon, and took his station in the bow of the boat. The men rowed for some time without interruption, but suddenly, at a whisper from the officer, backed their oars and awaited the throw. The harpoon was swung quickly to give it impetus ; the water flew as it descended ; " hit !" shouted the officer. And it *was* hit—so hard that the harpoon banged back again from the round face of the rock.

We landed on the beach, where we were instantly surrounded with the peons of the Custom House, in white shirts and pantaloons. The baggage was carried under the portico of an adobe house opposite the landing, where it was watched by one of the officials. Mr. Mott, of Mazatlan, who came passenger in the Ore-

MAZATLAN.

NEW YORK, GEO. P. PUTNAM.

gon, was well-known to all the authorities of the place, and I
found, after losing much time in getting a permit to have my luggage passed, that it had all been sent to his house without examination. My next care was to find a lodging-place. There was
the *méson*, a sort of native caravanserai; the *Ballo de Oro*,
(Golden Ball,) a tavern after the Mexican fashion, which is
comfortless enough ; and finally the *Fonda de Canton*, a Chinese
hotel, kept by Luën-Sing, one of the most portly and dignified of
all the Celestials. His broad face, nearly equal in circumference
to the gong which Chin-Ling, the waiter, beat three times a day
at the door, beamed with a paternal regard for his customers.
His oblique eyes, in spite of all their twinklings after the main
chance, looked a good-natured content, and his capacious girth
spoke too well of fat living to admit of a doubt about the quality
of his table. There was no resisting the attractions of Luën-
Sing's hotel, as advertised in his own person, and thither, accordingly, I went.

The place was overrun by our passengers, who nearly exhausted
the supplies of eggs, milk and vegetables in the market. The
Fonda de Canton was thronged ; all the rooms were filled with
tables, and gay groups, like children enjoying a holiday, were clustered in the palm-shaded court-yard. Chin-Ling could not half
perform the commands ; he was called from every side and scolded
by everybody, but nothing could relax the gravity of his queer
yellow face. The sun was intensely hot until near evening, and I
made myself quite feverish by running after luggage, permits and
passports. I was not sorry when the gun of the steamer, at dusk,
signalized her departure, and I was left to the company and hospitalities of my friend Luën-Sing. After the monte players had
closed their bank in one of the rooms and the customers had with-

drawn, Chin-Ling carried in a small cot, and made me a very good bed, on which I slept nearly as soundly as if it had been soft plank.

I took a ramble about the city in the clear coolness of the morning. Its situation is very peculiar and beautiful. Built at the foot of a bold hill, it stands on the neck of a rocky, volcanic headland, fronting the sea on each side, so that part of the city looks up the Californian Gulf and part down the coast towards San Blas. The houses are stone, of a white, pink or cream-color, with heavy arched entrances and cool court-yards within. The contrast of their clear, bright fronts, with the feathery tops of the cocoa-palm, seen under a dazzling sky, gives the city a rich oriental character, reminding me of descriptions of Smyrna. The houses are mostly a single story in height, but in the principal street there are several magnificent buildings of two stories, with massive cornices and large balconied windows. The streets are clean and cheerful, and the principal shops are as large, showy and tastefully arranged as those of Paris or New York. At night, especially, when they are brilliantly lighted and all the doors and windows are opened, displaying the gaudy shawls, scarfs and sarapes within; when the whole population is out to enjoy the pleasant air, the men in their white shirts and the women in their bewitching rebosas; when some native band is playing, just far enough distant to drown the discordance; when the paper lanterns of the fruit-venders gleam at every corner, and the aristocratic señoritas smoke their paper cigars in the balconies above—Mazatlan is decidedly the gayest and liveliest little city on the Continent.

But I was speaking of my morning stroll. The sun was already shining hotly in the streets, and the mellow roar of the surf on the northern side of the promontory tempted my steps in that direction. I threaded the narrow alleys in the suburbs of the town, lined with cactus hedges, behind which stood the thatched bamboo huts of the natives, exactly similar to those on the Isthmus. Gangs of men, naked to the waist, were at work, carrying on their heads large faggots of dye-wood, with which some of the vessels in the harbor were being freighted. I reached a shaded cove among the rocks, where I sat and looked out on the dark-blue expanse of the Gulf. The air was as transparent as crystal and the breakers rolled in with foam and delightful freshness, to bathe the shelly sand at my feet. Three craggy islands off the shore looked to be within gunshot, owing to the purity of the atmosphere, yet their scarred sides and ragged crests were clothed in the purple of distance. The region about the mouth of the Gulf of California enjoys an unvarying clearness of climate, to which there is probably no parallel on the earth. At Cape San Lucas, the rising and setting of a star is manifest to the naked eye. Two or three years frequently pass without a drop of rain. There is, however, a season of about a week's duration, occurring in some of the winter months, when the soil is kept continually moist from the atmosphere. Not a cloud is to be seen ; the sun is apparently as bright as ever ; yet a fine, gauzy film of moisture pervades the air, settles gradually on the surface of the earth and performs the service of rain.

I saw an interesting picture one evening, in front of the Theatre. A large band was stationed near the door, where they performed waltzes and polkas in excellent style—an idea no doubt derived from " Scudder's Balcony" or the gambling-hells of San Francisco. It had the effect, at least, to draw a dense crowd of the lower orders to the place, and increase the business of the traders in fruits and drinks. A military band, of trumpets alone, marched

up and down the principal street, blowing long blasts of piercing
sound that affected one like the shock of an electro-galvanic battery. Soldiers were grouped around the door of the Theatre, with
stacked arms, and the tables of dealers in fruit and provisions were
ranged along the walls. Over their braziers of charcoal simmered
the pans of *manteca*, (lard,) near which stood piles of tortillas and
dishes of fowl mixed with *chili colorado*, ready to be served up at
a medio the plate. Bundles of sugar-cane were heaped upon the
ground, and oranges, bananas, and other fruits spread upon mats
beside which their owners sat. There were tables covered with
porous earthern jars, containing cool and refreshing drinks made
of orange juice, cocoa milk, barley flour, and other wholesome in-
gredients.

The market-place presents a most picturesque appearance,
whether by day or night. It is a small square, on the steep side
of the hill, reached by narrow alleys, in which are to be found all
the articles most in demand by the lower classes—earthenware
after the old Aztec fashion, flaming calicoes, sarapes, rebosas and
broad Guayaquil sombreros. The place is filled with square,
umbrella-like stands or canopies of palm-leaves, under which are
spread on the ground all kinds of vegetables, fruit and grain that
grow in the vicinity, to be had at low prices. Among the fruits I
noticed a plump green berry, with a taste like a strawberry and
gooseberry combined; they were called by the natives, *arellanes*.
At night, the square was lighted by flaring lamps or torches of
some resinous wood.

The proximity of California had increased in a striking manner
the growth and activity of Mazatlan. Houses were going up in
all parts of the towns, and the prices of articles in the shops were
little below the San Francisco standard. At a tailoring establish-

ment I was asked $20 for a pair of Mexican calzoneros, and $25 for a cloth traveling jacket—sums entirely above my reach. I purchased a good Panama hat for $5, and retaining my suit of corduroy and shirt of blue flannel, set about hunting for a mule. There were about fifty emigrants in the place, who had come in a few days previous, from Durango ; but their animals had all been disposed of to the Mexican traders, at very low prices. I was directed to the *méson*, where I found a number for sale, in the corral. The owners offered to sell me a *caballo sillado* (a saddled and bridled horse) for $100, or a tolerable mule for $80, but seemed to think I would prefer a *frisone*, (an American horse,) at $100, unsaddled. After riding a number of mules around the corral, I made choice of a small brown one, for which $45 was asked, but which I obtained for $30. One of the emigrants sold me his saddle and bridle for $5 ; I added a good lariat and blanket, and was thoroughly equipped for the journey.

It now remained to have my passport arranged, for which the signature of the President of the City Council was requisite. After a great deal of search, I found the proper place, where a sort of Alcalde, who was settling a dispute between two Indians, wrote a *visto*, and directed me to call on the President, Don Luis Abioli. This second visit cost me several hours, but at last I succeeded in discovering Don Luis, who was busily engaged behind the counter of his grocery store, in a little building near the market-place. He stopped weighing sugar to affix his signature to the passport, received my " *mil gracias !*" with a profound bow and turned again to his customers.

The emigrants expressed great astonishment at my fool-hardiness, as they termed it, in undertaking the journey through to Vera Cruz. These men, some of whom had come overland from

Chihuahua and some from Matamoras, insisted most strenuously
that I should not start alone. The Mexicans, they said, were
robbers, to a man ; one's life, even, was not safe among them, and
their bitter hostility to Americans would subject me to continual
insult. " Would you believe it ?" said a tall, raw-boned Yankee ;
" they actually *rocked* us !" This gentle proceeding, I found, on
further inquiry, had been occasioned by the emigrants breaking
their contract with their guide. I therefore determined to follow
the plan I had adopted in California, and to believe nothing that I
had not seen with my own eyes. " I've traveled in the country,
and I know all about it," was the remark with which I was constantly greeted ; " you'll very soon find that I was right." To
escape from the annoyance of these counsels and warnings, I hastened my preparations, and was ready for departure on the second
morning after my arrival.

Luën-Sing, who had traveled over the road once, as far as Tepic, told me I should find it toilsome but safe. The Celestials
assisted me in packing my scanty luggage behind the saddle, and
enjoined on me the promise of patronizing the *Fonda de Canton*,
when I returned to Mazatlan. I took my final cup of chocolate
on the old table in the corridor, had a last talk with Chin-Ling
about the gold-diggings, shook hands with the whole yellow-faced,
long-eyed crew, mounted my mule and started up the main street,
in the breathless heat of a noonday sun. I doubled the corner of
the hill, passing the *Plaza de Toros*, (an arena for bull-fights,)
and the scattering huts of the suburbs, till I reached the *garita*,
near the sea. Here, an officer of the customs, who was lounging in
the shade, pointed out the road to the old Presidio of Mazatlan,
which I took, feeling very warm, very lonely and a little dispirited
at the ride of twelve hundred miles which lay before me.

CHAPTER X.

It was a cloudless noon. The sun burned down on the sand and quivering sea, and the three islands in the Gulf seemed vitrifying in the blue heat of the air. Riding slowly down to the arid level of a dried-up marsh, over which my path lay, I met an arriero, of whom I asked the distance to the Presidio. " *No llega hoy*," said he ; " *la mula no anda nada ; es muy flojo.*" (You'll not get there to-day ; your mule don't go at all ; " he's very lazy.") My heart misgave me for a moment, for his criticism of the mule was true ; but, seeing that my spur had as yet drawn no blood, I broke a stick from the thicket and belabored him with hand and foot. I passed a few plantations, with fenced fields, near the town, and afterwards took to the sandy chapparal near the sea.

The foliage of a tropical winter, on this coast, is not very attractive. There is a season when the growth is suspended—when the bud closes, the leaf falls and the bough gathers sap for a long time of splendid bloom. Only the glossy green of the lemon, mango and sycamore remains ; the rest of the wood takes a grayish cast from its many half-clothed boughs, among which rise the strange, gloomy pillars of the *cereus giganteus*, often more than forty feet in height. After making the circuit of a spacious bay, I came to a cluster of fishing huts on the shore, about three leagues from Mazatlan. Beyond these the road turned among low hills, covered with the gray, wintry woods, as far as eye could reach. Gaudy parrots flew screaming among the boughs ; large brown birds, with hooked bills sat musing by the road, and in the shady spots, I heard the tender coo of the dove—the sweet emblem of peace and domestic affection, to which no clime is alien—which haunts all lands and all zones, where beats the human heart whose softer emotions it typifies.

I was toiling along in the heat, torturing my conscience as much as the mule's flanks, when a couple of rancheros, riding behind me, came up with a good-humored greeting and proposed joining company. The foremost, a merry old native, of mixed blood, commenced using his whip on my mule's back and I soon found that the latter could keep up a sharp trot for an hour, without trouble. Thanks to my self-constituted *mozo*, I reached the banks of the Rio Mazatlan, opposite the Presidio, two hours before sunset. The old man invited me to pass the night at his ranche, which was near to hand, and I willingly complied. He turned his own beast loose, and started to a neighboring ranche, for an armful of *oja* (the fodder of maize) for my mule. Meanwhile, I walked down to the river, to refresh myself with a bath. The beauty of the scene kept me from the water for a long time. On the opposite bank the old walls of the Presidio towered above the trees ; the valley, stretching away to the eastward, to a far-off line of mountains, out of a notch in which the river found its way, was spotted with plantations of maize, bananas and melons. The rancheros were out at work, ploughing and sowing their grain. The fervor of the day was over, and a warm, tempered light was poured over the landscape. As I lay, clasped in the soft-flowing crystal of the river, the thought of another bath, on that very day four years before, came suddenly into my mind. It was my birth-day; but on that other anniversary I had baptized my limbs in the sparkling surf of the Mediterranean, on the shore of the Roman Campagna. I went back to the ranche with that sensation of half-pain, half-joy, which we feel when the mind and body are in different places.

My mule was fed and the old man gave me a dish of frijoles, with three tortillas in lieu of knife and fork. Then we sat down in the delicious twilight, amid the beautiful repose of Nature, and I answered, as well as I could, the questions prompted by their simple curiosity. I told them about my country and its climate, and the long journey I must yet make to reach it, which they heard with evident interest and wonder. They were anxious to know how a steamboat could move against the wind, for they had been told this was the case, by their friends in Mazatlan. The nearest idea of it which I could give them, was by describing it as a *sea-cart*, with broad wheels rolling on the water. At last the twilight deepened into night, and I unrolled my blankets to make my bed. " You must sleep to-night *en el seréno*," said the old man ; and a beautiful, star-lit *Seréno* it was. " Ah," said his wife, " what fine blankets ! you will sleep better than the Arch-bishop !" They then went to their hammocks in the hut, and I lay down on the earth, thanking God that the dismal forebodings which accompanied me out of Mazatlan had been so happily falsi-fied.

My kind host asked nothing in payment, when I saddled in the morning, but I insisted on giving him a trifle. " *Vaya con Dios !*" said he, as we shook hands, " and if you go to California, bring me a little piece of gold when you come back." I forded the river and passed through old Mazatlan—a miserable village of huts with a massive presidio and church in ruins. The morning was fresh and cool, and the road lay in shade for several miles. My mule, having no whip behind him, was as lazy as ever and made me the subject of remark from all the natives who passed. A ranchero, carrying an escopette and three live turkeys slung to the saddle, before him, offered his horse in exchange. I refused to trade, but an hour later, met an arriero, with a train of horses, laden with *oja*. He made the same proposition and unloaded the mountainous stack under which one of his horses was buried, that I might try him. "*Es muy caminador*," (a great traveler,) said the owner ; but he was crooked-legged, sore-backed and terribly thin in withers and flanks. Looking at him in front, he seemed to have no breadth ; he was like a horse carved out of plank, and I was almost afraid to mount, for fear I should pull him over. Nevertheless, he started off briskly ; so without wasting words, I made an even exchange. Nothing was gained however, in point of dignity, for my brisk lean horse occasioned quite as many remarks as my fat lazy mule.

Towards noon I reached a little village called Santa Fe, where I got a breakfast of frijoles and chopped sausage, mixed with red-pepper—a dish called *chorisa*—for a real. The country I passed was hilly and barren, with a range of broken mountains between me and the sea. Crossing a ridge beyond Santa Fe, I came upon extensive fields of aloes, cultivated for the vinous drink called *mescal*, which is made of their juice. In the midst of them stood the adobe town of Agua Caliente—a neat though scattering place, with a spacious church. I journeyed on for leagues in the burning sun, over scorched hills, without water or refreshing verdure. My *caminador*, too, lost the little spirit he had displayed, and jogged along at a snail's pace. I suffered greatly from thirst for several hours, till I reached a broad arroyo crossing the road, where I found a little muddy water at the bottom of a hole. Some Indians who were seated in the shade, near a sort of camp-fire, put me on the right trail for Potrerillos, the village where I expected to pass the night. A pleasantly shaded path of a league took me thither by sunset.

Mr. Brown—my old friend on the Rio Mazatlan told me I could stop wherever I chose, on the road; no ranchero would refuse to receive me. I accordingly rode up to the first house, and inquired; "Can I stay here to-night?" "Si Señor," was the ready answer. The place was small, and the people appeared impoverished, so I asked whether there was a *posada* in the place. "Go to Don Ipolito," said the man; "that is where the *estranjeros* stay," Don Ipolito was a Frenchman, who had an adobe hut and corral for mules, in the centre of the village. He was about starting for Mazatlan, but gave directions to the women and *mozos* to furnish me with supper, and my horse with corn and *oja*. His instructions were promptly obeyed; I had a table set with chorisa and frijoles, under the thatched portico; then a cup of black coffee and a *puro*, which I enjoyed together, while trying to comprehend the talk of a very pretty girl of fifteen and a handsome young ranchero, evidently her lover, who sat near me on a low adobe wall. They were speaking of marriage—that I found at once; but another ranchero—perhaps a rival suitor—named Pio, formed their principal topic. "*Es sin verguënza, Pio*" (He's a shameless fellow, that Pio,) was frequently repeated by both of them.

My bed-time was not long in coming. A boy was sent into the loft of the hut for a frame made of woven cane, which was placed

on the portico, and covered with a coarse matting. I threw my
blankets on it, using my coat for a pillow, and was sound asleep
in five minutes. Half an hour might have elapsed, when I was
suddenly aroused by a sound like the scream of a hundred fiends.
The frame on which I lay was rocked to and fro, and came near
overturning; I sprang up in alarm, finding my bed in the midst of
a black, moving mass, from which came the horrid sound. It
proved to be a legion of hogs, who had scented out a few grains of
corn in a basket which had held my horse's feed, and was placed
under the bed. The door of the hut opened, and the hostess appeared with a lamp. At sight of her, the beasts gave a hasty
grunt, cleared the wall at one bound, and disappeared. " *Santa
Maria !*" shrieked the woman; "*son demonios—son hijos del
diablo !* " (they are demons—they are children of the devil !) I
feared that another descent upon me would be made after she had
gone back to her hammock; but I was not molested again.

I arose in the morning, fed my horse, saddled, and was off by
sunrise. The town of El Rosario was but four leagues distant,
and the road was full of young rancheros in their holiday dresses,
riding thither to mass. Three of them joined company with me,
and tried to sell me one of their horses. " You'll never reach
Tepic with that horse," said they, " look at ours !" and away
they would gallop for a hundred yards, stopping with one bound,
to wait for my slow-paced *caminador*. They drew out their
tobacco and tinder-boxes, as we rode along; one of them, a spruce
young fellow, with a green silk sash around his waist, rolled his
cigarito in corn-husk, smoked about one-third of it and presented
me with the remainder, that I might see how much better it
tasted than paper. The flavor was indeed mild and delightful; I
puffed away an inch of it, and then returned him the stump. A

naked boy, basking in the sun at the door of a hut, called out "*Yanki!*" as I passed.

El Rosario is built on a beautiful site, in a broad valley, surrounded by blue and jagged peaks. It has several streets of spacious stone houses, for the most part ruined, and a church with a fine stone tower a hundred and fifty feet in height. I had to cross the plaza, which was filled with the rancheros of the neighborhood, waiting for the hour of mass; my caminador was the subject of general notice, and I was truly rejoiced when I had hidden his raw bones from sight in the court-yard of a *fonda*. The house was kept by a good-natured old lady, and three large parrots, who, (the parrots) sat each on a different perch, continually repeating: "*chiquito perriquito, bonito, blanquito!*"—the only phrase I ever heard a Mexican parrot utter, and which may be thus translated: "very little, pretty little, white-little parrotling!" I ate my breakfast of beans and red-peppers, chatting the while with the old lady, who was loud in her praises of Tepic, whither I told her I was bound. "*Es mi pais,*" said she, "*es un pais precioso.*" She scolded me good-humoredly at starting, for having left my horse where he might have been stolen, and bade me beware of the robbers; but, thought I, who would take such a horse?

Crossing the river of Rosario, I took a path embowered in green thickets, through which glided multitudes of macaws and tufted birds of gay plumage. At noon I came into a lovely valley among the mountains, and followed a stream shaded by splendid sycamores and palms. Little patches of meadow land slept like still lakes among the woods, with thatched ranches spotting their shores. I rode up to one of these for a drink of water, which an old man brought me in a calabash, standing bare-headed till I had

finished drinking. The trails soon after scattered, and I found
that I had lost the main road. In this emergency I met a ranchero, who told me I had wandered far from the right track, but
that he would act as guide. I promised him a reward, if he would
accompany me, whereupon he ran to his hut for a lariat, caught a
horse and sprang on his unsaddled back. We rode for more than
two hours in a foot-path through the depths of the tangled forest,
before striking the road. The impervious screen of foliage above
our heads kept off the sun and turned the daylight into an emerald
gloom. Taking leave of my guide, I emerged from these lonely
and enchanting shades upon the burnt upland, where the tall fan-
palms rustled drearily in the hot wind. As the afternoon wore
away, another green level of billowy foliage appeared ahead ; the
hills lay behind me, and far away to the right I saw the sea-blink
along the edges of the sky.

Notwithstanding the unsurpassed fertility of soil and genial
character of climate, this region is very scantily settled, except in
the broad river-bottoms opening towards the sea. There, under
the influence of a perpetual summer, the native race becomes indolent and careless of the future. Nature does everything for
them ; a small patch of soil will produce enough maize and bananas
for a family, with which, and the eternal frijoles, they have abundance for life's wants. The saplings of the woods furnish them
with posts, rafters and ridge-poles, the palm and the cane with
thatch and bedding. They are exempt from all trouble as to
their subsistence ; the blue ramparts of the Sierra Madre on one
side, and the silver streak of the sea on the other, enclose their
world. They grow up lithe and agile in the free air, mate, wax
old and die, making never a step out of the blind though contented
round which their fathers walked before them. I do not believe

that a more docile or kindly-disposed people exists than these rancheros.   In all my intercourse with them I was treated with unvarying honesty, and with a hospitality as sincere as it was courteous and respectful.   During all my travels in the Tierra Caliente, I was never imposed upon as a stranger nor insulted as an American.

My resting-place the third night was the village of Escuinapa, where I found a *méson*, kept, or at least managed by a lady whose kindness and cheerfulness were exactly in proportion to her size ; that is, they were about as broad as they were long.   She was a fast friend of the Americans, and spoke with rapture of the promptness with which all the emigrants whom she had entertained, had paid their bills.   Her own countrymen, she said, were slippery cus-tomers ; they frequently ran off without paying a *claco*.   She talked of going to California ; she thought if she were to establish a *méson* in the diggings, all the emigrants who had passed through Escuinapa would patronize her.   " They are all good people," said she ; " I like them as well as if they were my brothers, and I am sure they would come to visit me."   An old man, who seemed to be her husband, sat swinging in the hammock, lifting his feet high enough that his blue velvet calzoneros should not be soiled on the floor.   I had an excellent dinner of eggs, fish and chocolate, finishing with a delicate *cigarito* which the corpulent hostess pre-pared for me.   Two or three Mexican travelers arrived for the night and took possession of the cane bed-frame and benches in the room, leaving me only the cold adobe floor.   " Will you take out your saddle and bridle ?" requested the old lady ; " *los señores* are going to sleep here."   " But where am I to sleep ?" I asked. " *Con migo !*" was the immediate answer.   " *Como ?*" said I, surprised and alarmed ; I was horror-struck and must have looked so, for she seemed amused at my bewilderment. "Come!" she replied, and took up the lamp. I shouldered the saddle, and followed to a dark, windowless closet, in the rear of the house. It was just large enough to hold two frames, covered with matting, and some bags of maize and barley. "This is your bed," said she, pointing to one of them, "and this is ours. I hope you do not object to our sleeping in the same room." I laid my saddle on the frame indicated, put my head on it, and slept soundly till the early dawn shone through the cracks of the door.

Leaving Escuinapa, a day's journey of fifty miles lay before me, through an uninhabited country. I doubted the powers of my *caminador*, but determined to let him have a fair trial, so I gave him a good feed of corn, drank a cup of chocolate, slung a pineapple to my saddle-bow, and rode out of the village in the morning dusk. At first the trail led through pleasant woods, with here and there a ranche, but diverging more and more to the east, it finally came out on a sandy plain bordering the leagues of salt marsh on the side towards the sea. On the left the mountain chain of the Sierra Madre rose high and abrupt, showing in its natural buttresses and ramparts of rock a strong resemblance to the peaks of the Gila country. A spur of the chain ran out towards the sea, far in front, like the headland of a bay. The wide extent of salt marsh reaching from near El Rosario to La Bayona—a distance of seventy-five miles, showed the same recession of the Pacific, as I had already observed at Panama and Monterey. The ancient sea-margins may still be traced along the foot of the mountains.

I jogged steadily onward from sunrise till blazing noon, when, having accomplished about half the journey, I stopped under a palm-tree and let my horse crop a little grass, while I refreshed myself with the pine-apple. Not far off there was a single ranche, called Piedra Gorda—a forlorn-looking place, where one cannot remain long without being tortured by the sand-flies. Beyond it, there is a natural dome of rock, twice the size of St. Peters, capping an isolated mountain. The broad intervals of meadow between the wastes of sand were covered with groves of the beautiful fan-palm, lifting their tufted tops against the pale violet of the distant mountains. In lightness, grace and exquisite symmetry, the Palm is a perfect type of the rare and sensuous expression of Beauty in the South. The first sight of the tree had nearly charmed me into disloyalty to my native Pine ; but when the wind blew, and I heard the sharp, dry, metallic rustle of its leaves, I retained the old allegiance. The truest interpreter of Beauty is in the voice, and no tree has a voice like the Pine, modulated to a rythmic accord with the subtlest flow of Fancy, touched with a human sympathy for the expression of Hope and Love and Sorrow, and sounding in an awful undertone, to the darkest excess of Passion.

Making the circuit of the bay, the road finally doubled the last mountain-cape, and plunged into dark green thickets, fragrant with blossoms. I pushed on hour after hour, the pace of my caminador gradually becoming slower, and sunset approached without any sign of " Bayona's hold." Two Indians, mounted on small horses, came down by a winding trail from the hills, and rode a little in advance of me. " *No tiene uste miedo de viajar solo?*" (Are you not afraid to travel alone ?) said one of them. "What should I be afraid of ?" I asked in return. " The robbers." " I should like to see them ;" I said. " *Tiene mucho valor,*" remarked one to the other. They then spoke of my tired horse, and looked admiringly at my blankets, asking me first to make a gift of them, then to sell them, and, finally, to let them carry them behind their own saddles. I refused them very decidedly, and they trotted in advance. At the next bend of the road, however, I saw through the trees that they waited till I nearly overtook them, when they slowly moved forward. The repetition of this roused my suspicions; taking off a heavy pair of gloves, I pulled out my pistol, put on a fresh cap, and kept it in my right hand. I believe they must have been watching my motions, for instead of waiting as usual, they dashed off suddenly at a gallop.

The sun went down ; the twilight faded, and the column of the zodiacal light shortened to the horizon, as I walked behind my caminador, looking for La Bayona. At last I came to a river, with two or three ranches on its banks; in front of them was a large fire, with several men standing about it. One of them offered to accompany me to the town, which was near. On the way, he expatiated on the great number of rabbits in the neighborhood, and lamented that he had no powder to shoot them, winding up with: "Perhaps, Señor, you might give me a little ; you can easily buy more when you reach Acaponeta." I poured out half the contents of my flask into a corner of his shirt, which he held up to receive it; he then pointed out the fording-place, and I crossed to La Bayona, where my poor horse had rest and good feed after his hard day's journey. There was a dirty little *mèson* in the place, a bare room. In which was given me for two reales, and a supper of tortillas and frijoles for a medio (6¼ cents.)

The landlord and one of his friends talked with me a long while about the United States. "Tell me," said the latter, "is it true what Don Carlos, an American that was here last spring, told me—that there is a machine in your country in which you look at the moon, and it seems to be twenty feet long?" I assured him it was perfectly true, for I had often seen the moon in it. "Is it also true," he continued, "that in the United States a man pays only one dollar a year, and sends all his children to school for nothing?—and, then, when they have gone twelve years to school, they are fit for any business? Ah, how grand that is! how much better than here! Now, I do not know how to read at all. Why is it that everything is so fortunate in the United States?" "Because," said the other, "it is a nation *muy poderosa*." "I have heard that there are several millions of people in it." "That is true," rejoined the other, "and that is the reason why all the Americans we see are so much wiser than we are." I was deeply interested in their naïve remarks. In fact, not only here, but throughout all western Mexico, I found none of the hostility to Americans which had been predicted for me, but on the reverse, a decided partiality. In speaking of us, the natives exhibited (and I say it not with any feeling of national pride,) the liking which men bear to their superiors. They acknowledged our greater power and intelligence as a nation, without jealousy, and with an anticipation rather than a fear, that our rule will one day be extended over them.

The next morning I rode to Acaponeta, four leagues distant, by a pleasant road over low hills. The scenery was highly picturesque ; the town lies in the lap of a wide valley, nearly encircled by mountains which rise one above another, the farthest still the highest, like the seats in an amphitheatre. Their sides are cloven by tremendous chasms and ravines, whose gloom is concealed by perpetual verdure, but the walls of white rock, dropping sheer down many hundreds of feet from the summit, stand out distinctly in the vaporless atmosphere. Except the church and a few low adobe buildings around the plaza, Acaponeta is formed entirely of cane huts. I stopped at the *Méson del Angel*, gave a basket of corn to my horse, and ordered eggs, beefsteak, and chocolate for breakfast. The *cocinera* and her daughter were two hours in preparing it, and meanwhile I sat in the shade of an orange tree, beside a cool well in the court-yard. The women were very talkative, and amused themselves greatly with my bad Spanish. The daughter was preparing a quantity of empty egg-shells for the Carnival, by filling them with finely-minced paper of different colors and sealing the ends again. In order to show me how these were used, they bade me take off my hat. Each then took an egg and approached me, saying, "*tu es mi bien amorado*,"—at the same time breaking the shells on my head. My hair was completely filled with their many-colored contents, and it was several days before it was clear of this testimony of affection.

I crossed another large river at Acaponeta, and went on through embowered paths,

"Under a shade perpetual, which never
Ray of the sun let in, nor moon.

Gay parrots and macaws glanced in and out amid the cool green shawdows; lovely vistas opened between the boughs into the faery heart of the wilderness; the trees were laced each to each, by vines each more luxuriant than themselves; subtile odors pervaded the air, and large, yellow, bell-shaped flowers swung on their long stems like cups of gold, tremulous in the chance rays of sunshine. Here and there, along the ledges of the mural mountains on my left, I noted the smoke of Indian camp-fires, which, as night approached, sparkled like beacons. I intended to have stopped at a ranche called San Miguel, but passed it unknowingly, and night found me on the road. A friendly ranchero pointed out to me a path which led to a hut, but I soon lost it, and wandered about at random on the dark fenceless meadows. At last I heard a dog's bark—the sure sign of habitation—and, following the sound, came to a small ranche.

I was at once given permission to stay, and the women went to work on the tortillas for my supper. I swung off my fatigue in a hammock, and supped by starlight on the food of the Aztecs—the everlasting tortilla, which is a most nourishing and palatable cake when eaten fresh from the hot stone on which it is baked. There were several dogs about the ranche, and the biggest of them showed a relentless hostility towards me. "El Chucho don't like you," said the ranchero; "he'll bite if he can get hold of you; you had better climb up there and sleep," and he pointed to a sort of cane platform used for drying fruit, and raised on poles about twelve feet from the ground. I took my blankets, climbed up to the frail couch, and lay down under the stars, with Taurus at the zenith. El Chucho took his station below; as often as I turned on my airy bed during the night, the vile beast set up his howl and all the dog-herd howled in concert.

The next day I breakfasted at the hacienda of Buena Vista and rode about six leagues further, to the town of Rosa Morada. (The Violet Rose.) Just before reaching the place I caught sight of a mountain very far to the south, and recognized its outline as that of the *Silla de San Juan* (Saddle of St. John,) which rises behind the roadstead of San Blas. This was a welcome sight, for it marked the first step of my ascent to the Table-Land. I was growing tired of the Tierra Caliente; my face was blistered with the heat, and my skin so punctured by musquitos, fleas, sand-flies and venomous bugs that I resembled a patient in the last stage of small-pox. There was no *méson* in Rosa Morada, but a miserable *posada*, where I found three Frenchmen, two of whom were fresh from Bordeaux and on their way to California. They were all engaged about the kitchen fire, concocting their dinner, which they invited me to share with them. The materials they picked up in the village were not slighted in the cooking, for better vermicelli I never ate. They likewise carried their beds with them and stretched their cot-frames on the airy portico. I lay down on the adobes and slept "like a brick."

I was off at daylight, riding over an elevated plain towards the Rio Santiago. Two arrieros, on their way to Tepic, shared their tortillas with me and proposed we should join company. They stopped two hours to noon, however, and I left them. Urging forward my despairing horse, I crossed one branch of the river at San Pedro and reached Santiago, on the main branch, an hour before sunset. In descending to the Rio Santiago—or, more properly, the Rio Tololotlan, its ancient Aztec apellation—I came upon plantations of bananas and plantains, heavy with ripening fruit. The country showed signs of wealth and culture; the houses were large and well built and the fields divided by strong fences of palm logs. All up and down the broad banks of the river were scattered arrieros, mules and rows of pack-saddles, while half a dozen large canoes were plying backwards and forwards with their loads. I got into the first vacant one with my saddle, bridle and blankets, taking a turn of the lariat round my horse's nose. An arriero who had passed me the day previous, with a horse as worn-out as my own, was the other passenger. The river is about sixty yards wide, and very deep and swift. Our horses swam bravely behind us, and I believe were much the better for the bath.

I took an instant liking to the arriero for two reasons : firstly, he had a dark, melancholy, intellectual eye ; secondly, he was the only traveler I saw on the road, whose horse was so woeful an animal as mine. We started in company, and soon grew strongly attached. At dusk, we reached a village called Las Verritas. The inhabitants were all gone to Tepic, except an old man and a little boy who were selling *oja* to a company of muleteers squatted around a fire in the middle of the street. Nothing was to be had to eat, except some cheeses which one of the latter carried in a wicker pack. I could get no tortillas for money, nor exactly for love, but compassion helped me. The wife of one of the men came quietly to me as I sat by my saddle, and slipping two tortillas into my hand, said in a whisper : " now, when you buy the cheese, you'll have something to eat with it." With a cheese for two reals, my sworn friend and I made a hearty supper. He did for me many kind little offices, with a sort of meek fidelity, that touched me exceedingly. After our meal was finished, he went into the woods and brought me a calabash of water, standing uncovered while I drank it. I lay upon the ground, but all the fleas in the village, who had been without sustenance for two days, pounced in upon me in swarms. Added to this, every exposed part of the body was attacked by legions of musquitos, so that, with such enemies without and within, I never passed a more terrible night.

CHAPTER XI.

I was lying upon my back, with my handkerchief over my face, trying to imagine that I was asleep, when the welcome voice of the arriero shouted in my ear: "Ho! *Placero!* up and saddle!—the morning is coming and we must reach Tepic to-day." We fed our horses and sat on the ground for an hour before the first streak of dawn appeared. Three or four leagues of travel through a rich meadow-land brought us to the foot of the first ascent to the table-land. Our horses were fast failing, and we got off to walk up the stony trail. "I think we had better keep very close together," said my friend; " these woods are full of robbers, and they may attack us." Our path was fenced in by thorny thickets and tall clumps of cactus, and at every winding we were careful to have our arms in readiness. We climbed the first long ascent to a narrow plain, or shelf, from which we ascended again, finding always higher ridges above us. From the Abrevadero, a sort of inn or hospice standing alone in the woods, the hot, low country we left was visible nearly as far as Acaponeta; to one going towards Mazatlan, its dark-blue level might easily be mistaken for the sea. The Silla de San Juan was now to the west of us, and stood nearly five thousand feet in height. From the top of every successive ridge we overlooked a great extent of country, broken and cloven in all downward directions by the agency of some pre-Adamite flood, yet inclosing in many sheltered valleys and basins spots of singular fertility and beauty, which are watered through whole year from the cisterns of the mountains. It was truly, as the old lady at El Rosario said, "*un pais precioso.*"

We reached at noon a village called El Ingenio, about twelve leagues from Tepic. It lies in a warm valley planted with bananas and sugar-cane; the mountain streams are made to turn a number of mills, from which the place probably derives its name. Here the road from San Blas runs up through a narrow gorge and joins that from Mazatlan. We walked behind our horses all the afternoon, but as mine held out best, I gradually got ahead of the arriero. I halted several times for him to come up, but as he did not appear, I thought it advisable to push on to a good place of rest. My caminador had touched the bottom of his capability, and another day would have broken him down completely. Nevertheless, he had served me faithfully and performed miracles, considering his wasted condition. I drove him forward up ravines, buried in foliage and fragrant with blossoms; the golden globes of the oranges spangled the " embalméd darkness," as twilight settled on the mountains. Two leagues from Tepic, I reached the hacienda of La Meca, and quartered myself for the night. One of the rancheros wished to purchase my horse, and after some chaffering, I agreed to deliver him in Tepic for four dollars! The owner of the hacienda, on learning this, was greatly disappointed that I had not bargained with him, and urged me very strongly to break my word and sell him the horse for three dollars and a half! I told him I would not sell the animal for

5*

eight dollars, after having made a bargain ; he was enraged at this, but, as I could plainly see, respected me the more for it.

The young rancheros belonging to the hacienda amused themselves very much at my expense. A demon of fun seemed to possess them, and the simple sentences in my Spanish phrase-book excited them to yells of laughter. They were particularly curious to know my tastes and preferences, and on learning that I had never drank *mescal*, invited me to go with them and try it. We went down the road to a little hut, where a shelf with a bottle and two glasses upon it swinging under the thatched portico, signified " Liquor for Sale," to the passing arrieros. We entered and sat down among the family, who were at their scanty supper of rice and tortillas. The poor people offered me their own plates with a most genuine unsophisticated hospitality ; the rancheros told them whence I came, and they seemed anxious to learn something about my country. I tasted the *mescal*, which is stronger than brandy, and has a pungent oily flavor ; I should think its effects most pernicious if habitually drank. The people were curious to know about our Free School System of which they had heard by some means. None of them knew how to read, and they lamented most bitterly that education in Mexico was so difficult for their class. I was deeply touched by the exclamation of an old man, whose eyes trembled with tears as he spoke : " Ah, how beautiful a thing it is to be able to read of God !" then adding, in a softened tone, as if speaking to himself : " but I cannot read—I cannot read." I found many such persons among those ignorant rancheros—men who were conscious of their inferiority and desired most earnestly to be enlightened and improved.

Tepic is built on the first plateau of the table-land, and about half-way between the Silla de San Juan and an extinct volcano called San Guénguéy, which lifts its blackened brow high into the eastern sky. The plain, about fifteen miles in breadth, is for the most part moist meadow-land, threaded by several small streams. The city is girdled by pleasant gardens which hide everything from view on approaching, except the towers and dome of its cathedral. It is a solid well-built town of massive adobe houses mostly of one story, and divided by streets running at right angles. The general aspect of the place is dull and monotonous, with the exception of the plaza, which is one of the most beautiful in Mexico. A row of giant plane-trees runs around the four sides, shading the arched corridors of stone in which the traders display their fruits, trinkets, and articles of dress. There is an old stone fountain in the centre, around which, under canopies of grass-matting, are heaped piles of yellow bananas, creamy chirimoyas, oranges, and the scarlet, egg-like fruit of the Chinese pomegranate. All the gayety of the city seems to concentrate in the plaza, and, indeed, there is nothing else worth the traveler's notice, unless he is interested in manufactures—in which case he should visit the large cotton mills of Barron and Forbes in the vicinity. It is mainly through these mills that Tepic is known in the United States.

I had been directed to call at the posada of Doña Petra, but no one seemed to know the lady. Wandering about at random in the streets, I asked a boy to conduct me to some méson. As I rode along, following him, a group of tailors sitting at a street-corner, sewing, called out : " Americano !" " *No tiene ustéd cuidado,*" said the boy, " *son mal criados*" (Don't mind them ; they have bad manners.) I followed him into the court-yard of a large building, where I was received by the *patron*, who gave my done-over horse to the charge of the mozo, telling me I was just in time for breakfast. My name was suddenly called from the opposite corridor; I turned about in surprise, and recognised the face of Mr. Jones of Guadalajara, whom I had met in Mazatlan. He had likewise just arrived, and was deep in the midst of a tempting salad and omelette, where I soon joined him. I had been in the house but a few minutes, when a heavy shower began, and continued several hours without cessation; it was the first of the *cabañuelos*, a week of rainy weather, which comes in the middle of the dry season. The purchaser of my horse did not make his appearance, notwithstanding I was ready to fulfil my part of the bargain. As soon as the rain was over, I went the round of the different mésons, to procure another horse, and at last made choice of a little brown mustang that paced admirably, giving my caminador and twenty dollars for him. I made arrangements to leave Tepic the next morning, for the journey from Mazatlan had cost me eight days, and nine hundred miles still lay between me and Vera Cruz, where I was obliged to be on the 16th of February.

Leaving the méson on a bright Sunday noon, I left the city by the Guadalajara road. The plaza was full of people, all in spotless holiday dress; a part of the exercises were performed in the portals of the cathedral, thus turning the whole square into a place of worship. At the tingle of the bell, ten thousand persons dropped on their knees, repeating their *aves* with a light, murmuring sound, that chimed pleasantly with the bubbling of the fountain. I stopped my horse and took off my sombrero till the prayer was over. The scenery beyond Tepic is very picturesque; the road crosses the plateau on which the city is built, and rounds the foot of San Guëngüëy, whose summit, riven into deep gulfs between its pinnacles of rock, was half-hidden in clouds as I passed. I came into a pretty valley, surrounded on all sides by rugged hills ; fields of cane and rice dotted its surface, but the soil was much less fertile than in the rich bottoms of the Tierra Caliente.

My *priéto*—the Mexican term for a dark-brown horse—paced finely, and carried me to the village of San Lionel, ten leagues from Tepic, two hours before nightfall. I placed him securely in the corral, deposited my saddle in an empty room, the key of which, weighing about four pounds, was given into my possession for the time being, and entered the kitchen. I found the entire household in a state of pleased anticipation ; a little girl, with wings of red and white gauze, and hair very tightly twisted into ropy ringlets, sat on a chair near the door. In the middle of the little plaza, three rancheros, with scarfs of crimson and white silk suspended from their shoulders and immense tinsel crowns upon their heads, sat motionless on their horses, whose manes and tails were studded with rosettes of different colored paper and streamers of ribbons. These were, as I soon saw, part of the preparations for a sacred dramatic spectacle—a representation, sanctioned by the religious teachers of the people.

Against the wing-wall of the Hacienda del Mayo, which occupied one end of the plaza, was raised a platform, on which stood a table covered with scarlet cloth. A rude bower of cane-leaves, on one end of the platform, represented the manger of Bethlehem ; while a cord, stretched from its top across the plaza to a hole in the front of the church, bore a large tinsel star, suspended by a hole in its centre. There was quite a crowd in the plaza, and very soon a procession appeared, coming up from the lower part of the village. The three kings took the lead ; the Virgin, mounted on an ass that gloried in a gilded saddle and rose-besprinkled mane and tail, followed them, led by the angel ; and

several women, with curious masks of paper, brought up the rear.
Two characters of the harlequin sort—one with a dog's head on
his shoulders and the other a bald-headed friar, with a huge hat
hanging on his back—played all sorts of antics for the diversion
of the crowd.   After making the circuit of the plaza, the Virgin
was taken to the platform, and entered the manger.   King Herod
took his seat at the scarlet table, with an attendant in blue coat
and red sash, whom I took to be his Prime Minister.   The three
kings remained on their horses in front of the church ; but between
them and the platform, under the string on which the star was to
slide, walked two men in long white robes and blue hoods, with
parchment folios in their hands.   These were the Wise Men of
the East, as one might readily know from their solemn air, and
the mysterious glances which they cast towards all quarters of the
heavens.

In a little while, a company of women on the platform, concealed behind a curtain, sang an angelic chorus to the tune of " O
pescator dell'onda."   At the proper moment, the Magi turned
towards the platform, followed by the star, to which a string was conveniently attached, that it might be slid along the line.   The three
kings followed the star till it reached the manger, when they dismounted, and inquired for the sovereign whom it had led them to
visit.   They were invited upon the platform and introduced to
Herod, as the only king ; this did not seem to satisfy them, and,
after some conversation, they retired.   By this time the star had
receded to the other end of the line, and commenced moving forward again, they following.   The angel called them into the manger, where, upon their knees, they were shown a small wooden
box, supposed to contain the sacred infant ; they then retired,
and the star brought them back no more.   After this departure,

King Herod declared himself greatly confused by what he had witnessed, and was very much afraid this newly-found king would weaken his power. Upon consultation with his Prime Minister, the Massacre of the Innocents was decided upon, as the only means of security.

The angel, on hearing this, gave warning to the Virgin, who quickly got down from the platform, mounted her bespangled donkey and hurried off. Herod's Prime Minister directed all the children to be handed up for execution. A boy, in a ragged sarape, was caught and thrust forward; the Minister took him by the heels in spite of his kicking, and held his head on the table. The little brother and sister of the boy, thinking he was really to be decapitated, yelled at the top of their voices, in an agony of terror, which threw the crowd into a roar of laughter. King Herod brought down his sword with a whack on the table, and the Prime Minister, dipping his brush into a pot of white paint which stood before him, made a flaring cross on the boy's face. Several other boys were caught and served likewise; and, finally, the two harlequins, whose kicks and struggles nearly shook down the platform. The procession then went off up the hill, followed by the whole population of the village. All the evening there were fandangos in the méson, bonfires and rockets on the plaza, ringing of bells, and high mass in the church, with the accompaniment of two guitars, tinkling to lively polkas.

I left San Lionel early in the morning. The road, leaving the valley, entered the defiles of the mountains, crossing many a wild and rocky *barranca*. (A barranca nearly answers to the idea of our word "gulley," but is on a deeper and grander scale.) A beautiful species of pine already appeared, but in the warm hollows small plantations of bananas still flourished. I lost sight of San

Guënguëy, and after two hours of rough travel, came out on a mountain slope overlooking one of the most striking landscapes I ever beheld. In front, across a reach of high table-land, two lofty volcanic peaks rose far above the rim of the barren hills. To the left, away towards the east, extended a broad and lovely valley, dotted with villages and the green shimmer of fields, and hemmed in on all sides by mountains that touched the clouds. These lofty ranges—some of which were covered with trees to the summit, and some bleak and stony, despite their aerial hue of purple— make no abrupt transition from the bed of the valley : on the con- trary, the latter seems to be formed by the gradual flattening of their bases. The whole scene wore a distinct, vaporless, amethyst tint, and the volcano of Zurubuco, though several leagues distant, showed every jag in the cold and silent lips of its crater.

I rode thirty miles, to the village of Santa Ysabel, before break- fasting, and still had twenty-one miles to Ahuacatlan, my stopping- place for the night. My road led down the beautiful valley, between fields of the *agave americana.* Sunset came on as I reached the foot of Zurubuco, and struck on a rocky path across a projecting spur. Here a most wonderful region opened before me. The pleasant valley disappeared, with everything that reminded me of life, and I was surrounded, as far as the vision extended, with the black waves of a lava sea. It was terrible as the gates of Tartarus—a wild, inexorable place, with no gleam of light on its chaotic features. The road was hewn with difficulty through the surgy crests of rock, which had stiffened to adamant, while tossing in their most tempestuous rage. The only thing like vegetation, was a tree with a red and bloated trunk, the bark of which peeled off in shreds,—apparently a sort of vegetable elephan- tiasis, as disgusting as the human specimens I saw on the Isthmus.

I passed this region with a sensation bordering on fear, welcoming the dusky twilight of the shaded road beyond, and the bright moon under whose rays I entered Ahuacatlan.

At the méson I found no one but the hostess and her two little sons; but the latter attended to my wants with a childish courtesy, and gravity withal, which were charming. The little fellows gave me the key to a room, saw my *priéto* properly cared for, and then sat down to entertain me till the tortillas were made and the eggs fried. They talked with much naïveté and a wisdom beyond their years. After supper they escorted me to my room, and took leave of me with : "*pasa usté muy buena noche!*" I arose in the cloudless dawn, rode through the gay, spacious plaza of the village, crossed another barranca, and reached Iztlan in time for breakfast. This is a beautiful place, embosomed in gardens, from the midst of which the church lifts its white tower. Beyond Iztlan, a delicious valley-picture lay before me. The dark red mountains, bristling with rock, formed nearly an even circle, inclosing a bowl about ten miles in diameter. Further down their sides, the plantations of the agave, or aloe, made a belt of silvery gray, and deep in the fertile bosom of the plain, the gardens and orange groves, with sparkling glimpses of streams between the black loam, freshly ploughed, and the fields of young cane, of a pale golden green, basked in the full light of the sun. Far off, over the porphyry rim of the basin, a serrated volcanic peak stood up against the stainless blue of the sky. It was one of those rare chances in nature, when scenery, color, climate, and the sentiment of the spot, are in entire and exquisite harmony.

Leaving this valley, which was like a crystal or a piece of perfect enamel, buried in a region that Nature had left in the rough, I climbed a barren hill, which terminated at the brink of

the grand Barranca—a tremendous chasm, dividing two sections
of the table-land. Two thousand feet below, at the level of the
Tierra Caliente, lay a strip of Eden-like richness and beauty, but
the mountains which walled it on both sides were dark, sterile and
savage. Those opposite to me rose as far above the level of the
ledge on which I stood, as their bases sank below it. Their appearance was indescribably grand; for the most perfect and sublime effect of a mountain is to be had neither from base nor
summit, but a station midway between the two and separated from
it. The road descending to Plan de Barranca, a little village at
the bottom of the chasm, is built with great labor along the very
verge of giddy precipices, or notched under the eaves of crags which
threaten to topple down upon it. The ascent of the opposite
steep is effected by a stony trail, barely large enough for two
mules to pass, up the side of a wide crevice in the mountain-wall.
Finally, the path appears to fail; the precipice falls sheer on one
side; the bare crag rises on the other. But a sudden twist
around the corner of a rock reveals a narrow cleft, terminating in
the lower shelf of the table-land above. Looking back after I
had scaled this, an *atajo* of mules which followed me, appeared
to be emerging from the bowels of the earth. The road crossing
the barranca is nearly fifteen miles in length. Large numbers of
workmen are engaged in completing it for vehicles, and over the
deepest chasm a bridge is being constructed by the State of Jalisco.
Five years, however, is the shortest period named for the completion of the work, up to which time the barranca will remain
impassable except for mules. The line of stages to Tepic, which
is greatly demanded by the increase of travel, cannot therefore be
perfected before that time; but Señor Zurutuza, the proprietor of
the diligence lines, proposes opening a communication immediately,

by means of a mule-post across the barranca. From Tepic to San Blas is but a day's journey, so that the chain of comfortable travel will then reach nearly from ocean to ocean.

My *priéto* began to feel the effects of the hard hills and thin air of the upper region, and I therefore stopped for the night at the inn of Mochitilte, an immense building, sitting alone like a fortress among the hills. The key of a large, cheerless room, daubed with attempts at fresco ornament, was given to me, and a supper served up in a cold and gloomy hall. The wind blew chill from the heights on either side, and I found *priéto's* blanket a welcome addition to my own, in the matter of bedding.

CHAPTER XII.

I SLEPT soundly in my frescoed chamber, fed *priéto*, and was off by sunrise. The road ascended the valley for several leagues, to the rim of the table-land, with high, barren mountains on either hand. Before crossing its edge I turned to look down into the basin I had left. A few streaks of dusky green varied its earthen hue; far off, in its very bottom, the front of the méson of Mochitilte shone like a white speck in the sunrise, and the blue walls of the barranca filled up the farthest perspective. I now entered on a broad, barren plain, bordered by stony mountains and holding in its deepest part a shallow lake, which appeared to be fast drying in the sun. The scenery strikingly resembled that of some parts of California, towards the end of the rainy season.

The little town of Magdalena, where I breakfasted, sits beside the lake, at the foot of a glen through which the road again enters the hills. The waters of a clear stream trickle down through its streets and keep green the gardens of splendid orange-trees which gleam behind the gray adobe walls. At the méson I gave priéto a sheaf of *oja* and two hours' rest before starting for the town of Tequila. " *No quiere ustè tomar ausilio ?—hay muchos ladrones en el camino ;*" (Don't you want a guard ?—the road is full of robbers,) asked the vaquero of the house. " Every traveler," he continued, " takes a guard as far as Tequila, for which he pays each man a dollar." I told him I had no particular fear of the robbers, and would try it alone. " You are very courageous," he remarked, " but you will certainly be attacked unless you take me as an *ausilio*."

Soon after leaving the town I met a *conducta* of a hundred soldiers, escorting about fifty specie-laden mules. The officers were finely mounted, but the men, most of whom had broad, swarthy Indian faces, trudged along in the dust. Some of them greeted me with : " *Como va, paisano* ?" some with " How do you do ?" and others with a round English oath, but all imagining, apparently, that they had made the same salutation. As I was passing, a tawny individual, riding with one of the officers, turned about and addressed me in English. He was an American, who had been several years in the country, and was now on his way to California, concerning which he wanted some information. Notwithstanding he was bound to San Blas and had all his funds packed on one of the mules, he seemed still undecided whether to embark for San Francisco, and like most of the other emigrants I met, insisted strongly on my opinion as to the likelihood of *his* success. The road now entered a narrow pass, following the dry bed of a stream, whose channel was worn about twenty feet deep in the earth. Its many abrupt twists and windings afforded unequalled chances for the guerillas, especially as the pass was nearly three leagues in length, without a single habitation on the road. My friend, Lieutenant Beale, was chased by a party of robbers, in this very place, on his express journey across Mexico, in the summer of 1848. I did not meet with a single soul, although it was not later than the middle of the afternoon. The recent passing of the *conducta* had probably frightened the robbers away from the vicinity.

After riding two hours in the hot afternoon sun, which shone down into the pass, a sudden turn disclosed to me a startling change of scenery. From the depths of the scorched hills, I came at once upon the edge of a bluff, several hundred feet high, down which the road wound in a steep and tortuous descent. Below and before me extended a plain of twenty miles in length, entirely covered with fields of the *maguey*. At my very feet lay the city of Tequila, so near that it seemed a stone might be thrown upon the square towers of its cathedral. The streets, the gardens, the housetops and the motley groups of the populace, were as completely unveiled to my observation as if Asmodeus had been my traveling companion. Around the plain, which now lay basking in the mellow light of the low sun, ran a circle of mural mountains, which, high and blue as they were, sank into nothing before the stupendous bulk of a black volcanic peak rising behind Tequila. The whole scene, with its warm empurpled hues, might have served, if not for the first circle of Dante's Paradise, at least for that part of Purgatory which lay next to it.

I rode down into the city, crossing several arroyos, which the floods gathered by the volcano had cut deeper into the plain. At the *Meson de San José*—the only inn in the place—I found a large company of soldiers quartered for the night. The inner *patio* or courtyard, with its stables, well, and massive trough of hewn stone, was appropriated to their horses, and groups of swarthy privates, in dusty blue uniforms, filled the corridors. I obtained a dark room for myself, and a corner of one of the stalls for *priéto*, where I was obliged to watch until he had finished his corn, and keep off his military aggressors. The women were all absent, and I pro-

cured a few tortillas and a cup of pepper-sauce, with some difficulty. The place looked bleak and cheerless after dark, and for
this reason, rather than its cut-throat reputation, I made but a
single stroll to the plaza, where a number of rancheros sat beside
their piles of fruit and grain, in the light of smoky torches, hoisted
on poles. The méson was full of fleas, who seemed to relish my
blood better than that of the soldiers, for I believe they all paid
me a visit in the course of the night.

When I arose, the sun, just above the hills, was shining down
the long street that led to Guadalajara. I had a journey of
eighteen leagues to make, and it was time to be on the road ; so,
without feeding my horse, I saddled and rode away. A little
more than four leagues across the plain, brought me to the town
of Amatitlan ; where, at a miserable mud building, dignified by the
name of a méson, I ordered breakfast, and a *mano de oja* for my
horse. There was none in the house, but one of the neighbors
began shelling a quantity of the ripe ears. When I came to pay,
I gave her a Mexican dollar, which she soon brought back, saying
that it had been pronounced counterfeit at a *tienda*, or shop, across
the way. I then gave her another, which she returned, with the
same story, after which I gave her a third, saying she must change
it, for I would give her no more. The affairs of a few hours
later caused me to remember and understand the meaning of this
little circumstance. At the *tienda*, a number of fellows in greasy
sarapes were grouped, drinking mescal, which they offered me. I
refused to join them : " *es la ultima vez*," (it is the last time,)
said one of them, though what he meant, I did not then know.

It was about ten in the forenoon when I left Amatitlan. The
road entered on a lonely range of hills, the pedestal of an abrupt
spur standing out from the side of the volcano. The soil was

covered with stunted shrubs and a growth of long yellow grass.
I could see the way for half a league before and behind; there
was no one in sight—not even a boy-arriero, with his two or three
donkeys. I rode leisurely along, looking down into a deep ravine
on my right and thinking to myself; " that is an excellent place
for robbers to lie in wait; I think I had better load my pistol"—
which I had fired off just before reaching Tequila. Scarcely had
this thought passed through my mind, when a little bush beside
the road seemed to rise up ; I turned suddenly, and, in a breath,
the two barrels of a musket were before me, so near and surely
aimed, that I could almost see the bullets at the bottom. The
weapon was held by a ferocious-looking native, dressed in a pink
calico shirt and white pantaloons ; on the other side of me stood
a second, covering me with another double-barreled musket, and
a little in the rear, appeared a third. I had walked like an un-
suspecting mouse, into the very teeth of the trap laid for me.

" Down with your pistols !" cried the first, in a hurried whisper.
So silently and suddenly had all this taken place, that I sat still a
moment, hardly realizing my situation. " Down with your pistols
and dismount !" was repeated, and this time the barrels came a
little nearer my breast. Thus solicited, I threw down my single
pistol—the more readily because it was harmless—and got off my
horse. Having secured the pistol, the robbers went to the rear,
never for a moment losing their aim. They then ordered me to
lead my horse off the road, by a direction which they pointed out.
We went down the side of the ravine for about a quarter of a mile
to a patch of bushes and tall grass, out of view from the road,
where they halted, one of them returning, apparently to keep
watch. The others, deliberately levelling their pieces at me,
commanded me to lie down on my face—" *la boca à tierra !*" I

cannot say that I felt alarmed : it had always been a part of my belief that the shadow of Death falls before him—that the man doomed to die by violence feels the chill before the blow has been struck. As I never felt more positively alive than at that moment, I judged my time had not yet come. I pulled off my coat and vest, at their command, and threw them on the grass, saying : " Take what you want, but don't detain me long." The fellow in a pink calico shirt, who appeared to have some authority over the other two, picked up my coat, and, one after the other, turned all the pockets inside out. I felt a secret satisfaction at his blank look when he opened my purse and poured the few dollars it contained into a pouch he carried in his belt. " How is it," said he, " that you have no more money ?" " I don't own much," I answered, " but there is quite enough for you." I had, in fact, barely sufficient in coin for a ride to Mexico, the most of my funds having been invested in a draft on that city. I believe I did not lose more than twenty-five dollars by this attack. " At least," I said to the robbers, " you'll not take the papers"—among which was my draft. " *No*," he replied, " *no me valen nada*." (They are worth nothing to me.)

Having searched my coat, he took a hunting-knife which I carried, (belonging, however, to Lieut. Beale,) examined the blade and point, placed his piece against a bush behind him and came up to me, saying, as he held the knife above my head : " Now put your hands behind you, and don't move, or I shall strike." The other then laid down his musket and advanced to bind me. They were evidently adepts in the art: all their movements were so carefully timed, that any resistance would have been against dangerous odds. I did not consider my loss sufficient to justify any desperate risk, and did as they commanded. With the end of my horse's lariat, they bound my wrists firmly together, and having me thus secure, sat down to finish their inspection more leisurely. My feelings during this proceeding were oddly heterogeneous—at one moment burning with rage and shame at having neglected the proper means of defence, and the next, ready to burst into a laugh at the decided novelty of my situation. My blanket having been spread on the grass, everything was emptied into it. The robbers had an eye for the curious and incomprehensible, as well as the useful. They spared all my letters, books and papers, but took my thermometer, compass and card-case, together with a number of drawing-pencils, some soap, (a thing the Mexicans never use,) and what few little articles of the toilette I carried with me. A bag hanging at my saddle-bow, containing ammunition, went at once, as well as a number of oranges and cigars in my pockets, the robbers leaving me *one* of the latter, as a sort of consolation for my loss.

Between Mazatlan and Tepic, I had carried a doubloon in the hollow of each foot, covered by the stocking. It was well they had been spent for *priéto*, for they would else have certainly been discovered. The villains unbuckled my spurs, jerked off my boots and examined the bottoms of my pantaloons, ungirthed the saddle and shook out the blankets, scratched the heavy guard of the bit to see whether it was silver, and then, apparently satisfied that they had made the most of me, tied everything together in a corner of my best blanket. " Now," said the leader, when this was done, " shall we take your horse ?" This question was of course a mockery; but I thought I would try an experiment, and so answered in a very decided tone : " No ; you shall not. I *must* have him ; I am going to Guadalajara, and I cannot get there without him. Besides, he would not answer at all for your business." He made no reply, but took up his piece, which I noticed was a splendid article and in perfect order, walked a short distance towards the road, and made a signal to the third robber. Suddenly he came back, saying: "Perhaps you may get hungry before night—here is something to eat;" and with that he placed one of my oranges and half a dozen tortillas on the grass beside me. "*Mil gracias*," said I, "but how am I to eat without hands?" The other then coming up, he said, as they all three turned to leave me : "Now we are going ; we have more to carry than we had before we met you ; adios !" This was insulting— but there are instances under which an insult must be swallowed.

I waited till no more of them could be seen, and then turned to my horse, who stood quietly at the other end of the lariat : "Now, *priéto*," I asked, "how are we to get out of this scrape ?" He said nothing, but I fancied I could detect an inclination to laugh in the twitching of his nether lip. However, I went to work at extricating myself—a difficult matter, as the rope was tied in several knots. After tugging a long time, I made a twist which the India-rubber man might have envied, and to the great danger of my spine, succeeded in forcing my body through my arms. Then, loosening the knots with my teeth, in half an hour I was free again. As I rode off, I saw the three robbers at some distance, on the other side of the ravine.

It is astonishing how light one feels after being robbed. A sensation of complete independence came over me ; my horse, even, seemed to move more briskly, after being relieved of my blankets. I tried to comfort myself with the thought that this was a genuine adventure, worth one experience—that, perhaps, it was better to lose a few dollars than have even a robber's blood on my head ; but it would not do. The sense of the outrage and

indignity was strongest, and my single desire was the unchristian
one of revenge. It is easy to philosophize on imaginary premises,
but actual experience is the best test of human nature. Once, it
had been difficult for me to imagine the feeling that would prompt
a man to take the life of another ; now, it was clear enough. In
spite of the threats of the robbers, I looked in their faces sufficiently to know them again, in whatever part of the world I might
meet them. I recognized the leader—a thick-set, athletic man,
with a short, black beard—as one of the persons I had seen
lounging about the *tienda*, in Amatitlan, which explained the
artifice that led me to display more money than was prudent. It
was evidently a preconceived plan to plunder me at all hazards,
since, coming from the Pacific, I might be supposed to carry a
booty worth fighting for.

I rode on rapidly, over broad, barren hills, covered with patches
of chapparal, and gashed with deep arroyos. These are the usual
hiding-places of the robbers, and I kept a sharp look-out, inspect-
ing every rock and clump of cactus with a peculiar interest.
About three miles from the place of my encounter, I passed a
spot where there had been a desperate assault eighteen months
previous. The robbers came upon a camp of soldiers and traders
in the night, and a fight ensued, in which eleven of the latter were
killed. They lie buried by the road-side, with a few black crosses
to mark the spot, while directly above them stands a rough
gibbet, on which three of the robbers, who were afterwards taken,
swing in chains. I confess to a decided feeling of satisfaction,
when I saw that three, at least, had obtained their deserts.
Their long black hair hung over their faces, their clothes
were dropping in tatters, and their skeleton-bones protruded
through the dry and shrunken flesh. The thin, pure air of the

table-land had prevented decomposition, and the vultures and buzzards had been kept off by the nearness of the bodies to the road. It is said, however, that neither wolves nor vultures will touch a dead Mexican, his flesh being always too highly seasoned by the red-pepper he has eaten. A large sign was fastened above this ghastly spectacle, with the words, in large letters: "ASI CASTIGA LA LEY EL LADRON Y EL ASESINO." (Thus the law punishes the robber and the assassin.)

Towards the middle of the afternoon, I reached a military station called La Venta, seven leagues from Guadalajara. Thirty or forty idle soldiers were laughing and playing games in the shade. I rode up to the house and informed the officer of my loss, mentioning several circumstances by which the robbers might be identified; but the zealous functionary merely shrugged his shoulders and said nothing. A proper distribution of half the soldiers who lay idle in this guard-house, would have sufficed to make the road perfectly secure. I passed on, with a feeling of indignation against the country and its laws, and hurried my priéto, now nearly exhausted, over the dusty plain. I had ascended beyond the tropical heats, and, as night drew on, the temperature was fresh almost to chilliness. The robbers had taken my cravat and vest, and the cold wind of the mountains, blowing upon my bare neck gave me a violent nervous pain and toothache, which was worse than the loss of my money. Priéto panted and halted with fatigue, for he had already traveled fifty miles; but I was obliged to reach Guadalajara, and by plying a stick in lieu of the abstracted spur, kept him to his pace. At dusk I passed through Sapopa, a small village, containing a splendid monastery, belonging to the monks of the order of Guadalupe. Beyond it, I overtook, in the moonlight, the family of a ranchero, jogging along on their mules and repeating paternosters, whether for protection against robbers or cholera, I could not tell. The plain was crossed by deep, water-worn arroyos, over which the road was bridged. An hour and a half of this bleak, ghostly travel brought me to the suburbs of Guadalajara—greatly to the relief of *priéto*, for he began to stagger, and I believe could not have carried me a mile further.

I was riding at random among the dark adobe houses, when an old padre, in black cassock and immense shovel-hat, accosted me. " *Estrangero?*" he inquired; " *Si, padre,*" said I. " But," he continued, "do you know that it is very dangerous to be here alone?" Several persons who were passing, stopped near us, out of curiosity. " Begone!" said he, " what business have you to stop and listen to us?"—then, dropping his voice to a whisper, he added : " Guadalajara is full of robbers; you must be careful how you wander about after night; do you know where to go?" I answered in the negative. " Then," said he, " go to the Méson de la Mercéd ; they are honest people there, and you will be perfectly safe; come with me and I'll show you the way." I followed him for some distance, till we were near the place, when he put me in the care of " Ave Maria Santissima," and left. I found the house without difficulty, and rode into the court-yard. The people, who seemed truly honest, sympathized sincerely for my mishap, and thought it a great marvel that my life had been spared   For myself, when I lay down on the tiled floor to pass another night of sleepless martyrdom to fleas and the toothache, I involuntarily said, with a slight variation of Touchstone's sage reflection : "Aye, now I am in Guadalajara; the more fool I; when I was at home I was in a better place; but travelers must be content."

CHAPTER XIII.

THREE DAYS IN GUADALAJARA.

WHEN I got off my horse at the Méson de la Mercéd, I told the host and the keeper of the *fonda* that I had been robbed, that I had no money, and did not expect to have any for two or three days. "*No hace nada*," said they, "you may stay as long as you like." So they gave my horse a sheaf of *oja* and myself a supper of tortillas and pepper-sauce. The old lady who kept the fonda was of half-Castilian blood, and possessed all the courtesy of her white ancestors, with the quickness and vivacity of the Indian. She was never tired of talking to me about the strangers who had stopped at the méson,—especially of one whom she called Don Julio, who, knowing little Spanish, frequently accosted her as "mule!" or "donkey!" for want of some other word. She would mimic him with great apparent delight. She had three daughters—Felipa, Mariquita and Concepcion—of whom the two former were very beautiful. They were employed in the manufacture of rebosas, and being quite skilful in tending the machines, earned a dollar a day—a considerable sum for Mexico. Concepcion was married, and had a son named Zenobio—a very handsome, sprightly little fellow, with dark, humid, lustrous eyes. The circumstance of my remembering and calling each one by name, seemed to please them highly, and always at meal-time they gathered around the table, asking me innumerable questions about my country and my travels.

My first move next morning was to find the Diligence Office. I went into the main plaza, which is a beautiful square, shaded by orange trees, and flanked on two sides by the picturesque front of the Cathedral and the Government Palace. As I was passing the latter building, one of the sentinels hailed me. Supposing it to be meant in derision, I paid no attention to it, but presently a sergeant, accompanied by two men, came after me. One of the latter accosted me in English, saying that it was so long since he had seen an American, he hoped I would stop and talk with him He was a Scotchman, who for some reason had enlisted for a year and had already served about half of his time. He complained bitterly of the bad treatment of the men, who, according to his story, were frequently on the point of starvation. The Mexican soldiers are not furnished with rations, but paid a small sum daily, on which they support themselves. As the supplies from head-quarters are very irregular, and a system of appropriation is practised by all the officers through whose hands they must come, the men are sometimes without food for a day or two, and never receive more than is barely sufficient for their wants. The poor Scotchman was heartily sick of his situation and told me he would have deserted long before, only that he had no other clothes in which to disguise himself.

At the office of the Diligence, I found the *administrador*, Don Lorenzo del Castaño, to whom I related my story and showed my draft. " *Es superior*," said he, after examining it, and then told me to call the next morning, as he would see a merchant in the meantime, who, he was sure, would pay me the amount. Drafts on the city of Mexico were at a premium of two per cent. and he had no difficulty in getting it accepted. The money, however, was paid to me in quarter-dollars, reals and medios, which it took me more than an hour to count. I went back to the office, with a heavy canvas-bag in each pocket, paid all the money to the administrador, who gave me a ticket for the next stage to Mexico, and an order for the residue on all the agents of the line. By exhibiting these orders at the different stopping-places on the road, the traveler receives credit for all his expenses, the amount at each place being endorsed at the bottom, and the remainder, if any, paid on his arrival at Mexico. By this means, he is saved the necessity of taking any money with him, and may verify the old Latin proverb by whistling in the face of the robber. I was thus led, perforce, to give up my original plan of traveling on horseback to Mexico, by way of Lake Chapala, Zamora, the ancient city of Morelia and the valley of Toluca. This route offered less of general interest than that of Lagos and Guanajuato, but had the attraction of being little traveled by strangers and little known. Perhaps I lost nothing by the change, for the hills near Zamora are robber-ground, and I had no desire to look into the barrels of three or four leveled muskets a second time.

I found Guadalajara in a state of terror and prayers. For a month previous the inhabitants had been expecting the arrival of the Cholera, now that its ravages in Durango and Zacatecas were over. The city authorities were doing everything in their power to hasten its approach, by prohibiting all public amusements and instituting solemn religious festivals. The Cathedral was at all times crowded with worshippers, the Host frequently carried through the streets, gunpowder burned and rockets sent up to propitiate the Virgin. As yet no case had been reported in the

6*

city, though there were rumors of several in the neighboring villages. The convicts were brought out every morning in long gangs, chained together, each man carrying a broom made of small twigs. Commencing with the centre of the city, they were kept sweeping the whole day, till all the principal streets were left without a particle of dust or filth. The clanking of their fetters was constantly heard in some part of the city; the officers who walked behind them carried short whips, with which they occasionally went up and down the lines, giving each man a blow. This daily degradation and abuse of criminals was cruel and repulsive. The men, low and debased as they were, could not have been entirely devoid of shame, the existence of which always renders reclamation possible; but familiarity with ignominy soon breeds a hardened indifference which meets the pride of honesty with an equal pride of evil.

Guadalajara is considered the most beautiful city in Mexico. Seated on a shelf of the table-land, between three and four thousand feet above the sea, it enjoys a milder climate than the capital, and while its buildings lack very little of the magnificence of the latter, its streets are a model of cleanliness and order. The block fronting on the north side of the plaza, is a single solid edifice of stone, called the *Cortal*, with a broad corridor, supported on stone arches, running around it. The adjoining block is built on the same plan, and occupied entirely by shops of all kinds. Shielded alike from rain and sun, it is a favorite promenade, and always wears a gay and busy aspect. The intervals between the pillars, next the street, are filled with cases of toys, pictures, gilt images of saints, or gaudy slippers, sarapes and rebosas. Here the rancheros may be seen in abundance, buying ornaments for the next festivals. Venders of fruit sit at the corners, their mats filled with fragrant and gleaming pyramids, and the long shelves of cool barley-water and *tepache*, ranged in glasses of alternate white and purple, attract the thirsty idler. Here and there a group is gathered around a placard pasted on the wall—some religious edict of the cholera-fearing authorities, a list of the fortunate tickets in the last lottery, or the advertisement of a magnificent cock-fight that is to come off in the old town of Uruàpan. The bulletin at the lottery-office is always surrounded ; rancheros, housemaids, padres and robbers come up, pull out their tickets from under their cassocks and dirty sarapes, compare the numbers and walk away with the most complete indifference at their ill luck. The shops belonging to different trades are always open ; tailors and shoemakers frequently sit in groups in the open corridor, with their work on their knees, undisturbed by the crowds that pass to and fro. I spent several hours daily in the *cortal*, never tiring of the picturesque life it exhibited.

It is remarkable how soon a man's misfortunes are made public. The second day of my stay in Guadalajara, I believe I was known to most of the inhabitants as " the American who was robbed." This, together with my rugged and dusty suit of clothing, (what was left of it,) made me the subject of general notice ; so, after selling my draft, I hastened to disguise myself in a white shirt and a pair of Mexican pantaloons. One benefit of this notoriety was, that it was the means of my becoming acquainted with two or three American residents, and through them, with several intelligent and agreeable citizens. I never entered a place under such woful auspices, nor passed the time of my stay more delightfully. In walking about the streets I was often hailed with the word " *uistli !*" by some of the lower class. From the sound I thought it might possibly be an old Aztec word of salutation ; but one day I met a

man, who, as he said it, held up a bottle of mescal, and I saw at
once that he meant *whiskey*. The fact that it was constantly repeated to me as an American, gave rather a curious inference
as to the habits of the emigrants who had passed through the city
before me.

The appearance of Guadalajara on Sunday morning was very
cheerful and beautiful. Everybody was in the streets, though not
more than half the shops were closed ; the bells rang at intervals
from the cathedral and different churches ; the rancheros flocked
in from the country, the men in snow-white shirts and blue calzoneros, the women in their best rebosas and petticoats of some
gay color ; and the city, clean swept by the convicts, and flooded
with warm sunshine, seemed to give itself up truly to a holiday. I
walked down along the banks of the little river which divides it
into two unequal parts. The pink towers of the Bishop's Palace
rose lightly in the air ; up a long street, the gateway of the Convent of San Francisco stood relieved against a shaded court-yard ;
the palms in some of the near gardens rustled in a slow breeze,
but the dark shafts of the cypress were silent and immovable.
Along the parapets of the bridges, the rancheros displayed their faggots of sugar-cane and bunches of bananas, chatting gaily with each
other, and with their neighbors who passed by on mules or asses.
I visited most of the churches during the time of service. Many
of them are spacious and might be made impressive, but they are
all disfigured by a tawdry and tasteless style of ornament, a profusion of glaring paint and gilding, ghastly statues, and shocking
pictures. The church of the Convent of San Francisco is partly
an exception to this censure ; in a sort of loggia it has a large
painting of the Last Supper, by a Mexican artist, which is truly a
work of great beauty. In the body of the church are several un-

doubted originals by Murillo, though not of his best period; I did not see them. The cathedral, more majestic in proportion, is likewise more simple and severe in its details; its double row of columns, forming three aisles, the central one supporting a low dome, have a grand effect when viewed from the entrance. It was constantly filled with worshippers, most of whom were driven thither by the approach of the cholera. Even in passing its door, as they crossed the plaza, the inhabitants uncovered or made the sign of the cross—an extent of devotion which I never witnessed out of Mexico.

I found great source for amusement in the carriages collected near the doors during mass-hour. They were all the manufacture of the country, and the most of them dated from the last century. The running works were of immense size, the four wheels sustaining a massive and elaborately carved frame, rising five or six feet from the ground, and about twelve feet in length. In the centre of this, suspended in some miraculous manner, hung a large wooden globe, with a door in each side—a veritable Noah's Ark in form and solidity, and capable of concealing a whole family (and the Mexican families are always large) in its hollow maw. These machines were frequently made still more ridiculous by the pair of dwarfed, starved mules, hitched to the tongue, so far in advance that they seemed to be running away from the mountain which pursued and was about to overwhelm them. I concluded, however, after some reflection, that they were peculiarly adapted to the country. In case of revolution they would be not only bullet but bomb proof, and as there are no good roads among the mountains, they would roll from top to bottom, or shoot off a precipice, without danger to the family within. There are several extensive carriage manufactories in Guadalajara, but the modern fabrics more nearly resemble those of our own cities, retaining only the heavy, carved frame-work, on which the body rests.

In the afternoon I went with some friends to make a *paseo* on the Alameda. This is a beautiful square on the border of the city, shaded with fine trees, and traversed by pleasant walks, radiating from fountains in the centre. It is surrounded by a hedge of roses, which bloom throughout the whole year, covering with a fragrant shade the long stone benches on which the citizens repose, Don and ranchero mingled together, smoking their puros and cigaritos. The drive is around the outside of the Alameda; I saw but a small part of the fashion of Guadalajara, as most of the families were remaining at home to invite the cholera. There were some handsome turn-outs, and quite a number of splendid horses, ridden in the Mexican style, which is perfection itself—horse and rider moving as one creature, and having, apparently, but one soul. The Mexican horses are all sprung from the Arabic and Andalusian stock introduced into the country by Cortez, and those large bands which run wild on the plains of San Joaquin and in the Camanche country, probably differ but slightly from the Arab horse of the present day.

A still more beautiful scene awaited us in the evening. The *paseo* is then transferred to the plaza, and all the fashionable population appears on foot—a custom which I found in no other Mexican city. I went there at nine o'clock. The full moon was shining down over the cathedral towers; the plaza was almost as distinct as by day, except that the shadows were deeper; the white arches and pillars of the *cortal* were defined brilliantly against the black gloom of the corridor, and the rows of orange trees, with their leaves glittering in the moonlight, gave out a rare and exquisite odor from their hidden blossoms. We sat down on one of the benches, so near the throng of promenaders passing around the plaza, that their dresses brushed our feet. The ladies were in full dress, with their heads uncovered, and there were many specimens of tropic beauty among them. The faint clear olive of their complexion, like a warm sunset-light on alabaster— the deep, dark, languishing eye, with the full drooping lid that would fain conceal its fire—the ripe voluptuous lip—the dark hair whose silky waves would have touched the ground had they been unbound—and the pliant grace and fullness of the form, formed together a type of beauty, which a little queenly ambition would have moulded into a living Cleopatra. A German band in front of the cathedral played "God save the King" and some of the melodies of the Fatherland. About ten o'clock, the throng began to disperse; we sat nearly an hour longer, enjoying the delicious moonlight, coolness and fragrance, and when I lay down again on the tiles, so far from thinking of Touchstone, I felt glad and grateful for having seen Guadalajara.

Among the Guadalajarans I met was Don Ramon Luna, a gentleman of great intelligence and refinement. His father emigrated from Spain as a soldier in the ranks, but by prudence, energy and native talent, succeeded in amassing a large fortune. Don Ramon spoke English and French with great fluency, and was, moreover, very enthusiastic on the subject of Mexican antiquities. At his ranche, a few leagues from Guadalajara, he had, as he informed me, a large number of ancient idols and fossil remains, which the workmen had collected by his order. I regretted that the shortness of my stay did not permit me to call on Padre Najar, of the Convent del Carmen, who formerly resided in Philadelphia, and published a very able work on the Otomai language.

The diligence was to start on Monday. On Saturday afternoon

I sold my horse to a sort of trader living in the méson, for seven dollars, as he was somewhat worn out, and horses were cheap in Guadalajara. The parting with my good hosts the next day was rather more difficult, and I was obliged to make a positive promise of return within three years, before they would consent that I should go. After I had obtained some money and paid them for my board, the old lady told me that thenceforth she would only charge half-price for every meal I chose to take in her house. " Thanks to the Supreme King," said she, " I have not been so much in need that I should treat friends and strangers both alike." After this, I only paid a medio for my dinner of eggs, frijoles, lantecas and chili colorado.   On Sunday night I rolled up my few possessions in my sarape, took leave of the family and went to the *Casa de Diligencias* to spend the night.   The old hostess threw her arms around me and gave me a hearty embrace, and the three daughters followed her example. I did not dislike this expression of friendship and regret, for they were quite beautiful. As I went down the court-yard, the voice of the mother followed me : " Go with Ave Maria Purisima, and do not forget Maria de la Ascencion Hidalgo !"

CHAPTER XIV.

THE mozo awoke me shortly after three o'clock, and before I had finished dressing, brought me a cup of foaming chocolate and a biscuit. The only other passenger was a student from Tepic, on his return to college, in Mexico. The stage already waited for us, and we had no sooner taken our seats on the leather cushions, than "*vamonos !*" cried the driver, the whip cracked and the wheels thundered along the silent, moonlit streets. The morning was chill, and there was little in the dim glimpses of adobe walls and blank fields on either hand, to interest us; so we lay back in the corners and took another nap.

The style of diligence travel in Mexico is preferable to that of any other country. The passenger is waked at three o'clock in the morning, has a cup of chocolate brought him, (and no one has drank chocolate who has not drank it there) takes his seat, and has nearly reached the end of the second post by sunrise. The heavy stage, of Troy manufacture, is drawn by six horses, four leaders abreast, who go at a dashing gallop as long as the road is level. About eleven o'clock a breakfast of six or eight courses is served up in good style, the coachman waiting until the last man has leisurely finished. There is no twanging of the horn and cry of

"All ready!" before one has bolted the first mouthful. Off again, there is no stoppage till the day's journey is over, which is generally about four o'clock, allowing ample time for a long walk and sight-seeing before dinner.

The second post brought us to the Rio Santiago, which I had crossed once between Mazatlan and Tepic. We got out to look at the old stone bridge and the mist of a cataract that rose above the banks, two or three hundred yards below. Our road lay across broad, stony tracts of country, diversified by patches of cactus; in the distance, the mountain parapet of a still higher table-land was to be seen. The third post, thirty miles from Guadalajara, was at the village of Zapotlanejo, where the cholera had already appeared. The groom who assisted in harnessing our fresh horses, informed us that twenty persons had died of it. The place looked quiet and half-deserted; many of the houses were studded with little wooden crosses, stuck into the chinks of the adobes. The village of Tepatitlan, which we passed during the forenoon, was likewise a cholera locality. We dashed through it and over a bare, bleak upland, many leagues in width, in the middle of which stood the Rancho de la Tierra Colorada, (Ranche of the Red Earth) our breakfast-place.

During the afternoon we crossed a very rough and stony barranca. The chasm at the bottom was spanned by a fine bridge, and eight cream-colored mules were in readiness to take us up the ascent. Even after reaching the level, the road was terribly rough, and the bounds which our stage made as it whirled along, threatened to disjoint every limb in our bodies. I received a stunning blow on the crown of my head, from being thrown up violently against the roof. We were truly rejoiced when, late in the afternoon, we saw the little town of San Miguel before us, in a hollow dip of the plain. We finished a ride of ninety miles as we drove into it, and found the stage from Lagos already before the hotel. The town did not boast a single " sight," so my companion and I took a siesta until dinner was announced.

The next morning our route lay over the dreary table-land, avoiding the many chasms and barrancas with which its surface was seamed : often running upon a narrow ridge, with a gaping hollow on each side. The rancheros were ploughing in some places, but the greater part of the soil seemed to be given up to pasturage. The fields were divided by walls of stone, but frequently, in the little villages, a species of cactus had been planted so as to form gardens and corrals, its straight, single pillars standing side by side, to the height of ten feet, with scarcely a crevice between. The people we met, were more hale and ruddy in their appearance than those of the Tierra Caliente. As they galloped alongside the stage, with their hats off, speaking with the driver, I thought I had never seen more lightly and strongly made forms, or more perfect teeth. When they laughed, their mouths seemed to blaze with the sparkling white rows exhibited. Towards noon, we saw, far ahead, the tops of two towers, that appeared to rise out of the earth. They belonged to the church of San Juan de Los Lagos, the place of the great Annual Fair of Mexico—a city of five thousand inhabitants, built at the bottom of a deep circular basin, whose rim is only broken on one side by a gash which lets out the waters it collects in the rainy season. Seen from the edge of the basin, just before you commence the descent, a more fantastic picture could scarcely be imagined. The towers of the church are among the tallest in Mexico. During the Fair, the basin is filled to its brim, and a tent-city, containing from three hundred thousand to half a million inhabitants, is

planted in it.   From Sonora to Oajaca, all Mexico is there, with
a good representation from Santa Fé, Texas and California.   We
descended by a zigzag road, of splendid masonry, crossed the gulley at the bottom by a superb bridge, and stopped at the Diligence
Hotel for breakfast.   The town was at prayers, on account of
cholera.   Five hundred people had already died, and the epidemic
was just beginning to abate.   I saw several of the ignorant populace issue from their huts on their knees, and thus climb their
painful way up the hill to the cathedral, saying paternosters as
they went.   Two attendants went before, spreading sarapes on
the stones, to save their knees, and taking them up after they had
passed.   We ate a hearty breakfast in spite of the terror around
us, and resuming our seats in the diligence, were whirled over
hill and plain till we saw the beautiful churches of Lagos in the
distance.   At the hotel, we found the stage from Zacatecas just
in, bringing passengers for Mexico.

I took an afternoon stroll through Lagos, visiting the market-
place and principal churches, but found nothing worthy of particular note.   We arose in the moonlight, chocolated in the *comedor*,
or dining-hall, and took our seats—seven in all—in the diligence.
We speedily left the neat, gay and pleasant city behind us, and
began a journey which promised to be similar to that of the two
preceding days—a view of barren table-land, covered with stone
fences and cactus hedges, on either side, and blue mountains ever
in far perspective.   With the sun, however, things looked more
cheerful, and soon after entering on the third post, we climbed a
stony *cerro*, from which opened a splendid view of the Valley of
Leon.   Far as the vision extended, the effect was still heightened
by a veil of thin blue vapor which arose from the broad leagues of
field and meadow below us.   In the centre of the picture rose the

spires of Villa de Leon, from the midst of green barley-fields and gardens of fruit trees. To the eastward, beyond the valley—which to the south melted into the sky without a barrier—ran the high and rocky ranges of the mineral mountains of Guanajuato. We had nearly crossed the table-land of the Pacific side of Mexico, and these hills were spurs from the spinal ridge of the Continent.

Our horses galloped into Leon—a large and lively town, which pleased me much better than Lagos. We had a capital breakfast of eight courses in the hall of the *Sociedad del Comercio*, and took in two fresh passengers, which just filled the diligence. Dashing out of the town, the road led over the level plain, between fields and gardens of great fertility. In the soft morning light, the animation and beauty of the scene were delightful. The peons were everywhere at work in the fields, watering the trees and vege-tables from wells, out of which they drew the water with long poles. At a bridge over the dry bed of a river near the town, I noticed a gang of about fifty ferocious fellows, in ragged sarapes. Several soldiers, well armed, paced up and down the road, and I after-wards learned that the diligence was frequently robbed there. Two long posts down the valley, made with horses going *à carrera*, brought us to Silao. While the grooms were changing teams, we supplied ourselves with oranges, bananas, *zapotes chicos* and *granaditas de China*. The latter fruit is about the size of an egg, with a brittle shell of a bright scarlet color, inside of which is a soft white sack. Breaking this open, the tender, fragrant pulp is revealed—the most dainty, exquisite thing that Nature ever compounded. We also bought an armful of sugar-cane, which we hung on the umbrella-hooks, and chopped up and chewed as thirst required.

From Silao to Guanajuato is but one post. Leaving the former place, we approached a cape of the mountains, and traveled for several miles over wild hills covered with immense cactus trees, the trunks of many of them measuring two feet in diameter. From the summit we looked down into a large mountain-basin, opening towards the south into the Valley of Leon. On its opposite side, among mountains whose summits are the more sterile from the glittering veins of precious ore within, we saw the walls of some of the mining establishments of Guanajuato.

Of all places in Mexico, the situation of this city is the most picturesque and remarkable. It lies like an enchanted city, buried in the heart of the mountains. Entering a rocky cañada, the bottom of which barely affords room for the road, you pass between high adobe walls, above which, up the steep, rise tier above tier of blank, windowless, sun-dried houses, looking as if they had grown out of the earth. You would take them to be a sort of cubic chrystalization of the soil. Every corner in the windings of the road is filled with the buildings of mining companies— huge fortresses of stone, ramparted as if for defence. The scene varies with every moment;—now you look up to a church with purple dome and painted towers ; now the blank adobe walls, with here and there a spiry cypress or graceful palm between them, rise far above you, along the steep ledges of the mountain ; and again, the mountain itself, with its waste of rock and cactus, is all you see. The cañada finally seems to close. A precipice of rock—out of a rift in which the stream flows—shuts up the passage. Ascending this by a twist in the road, you are in the heart of the city. Lying partly in the narrow bed of the ravine and partly on its sides and in its lateral branches, it is only by mounting to some higher eminence that one can realize its extent and position. At the farther end of the city the mountains form a *cul de sac.* The cañada is a blind passage, and you can only leave it by the road you came. The streets are narrow, crooked, and run up and down in all directions; there is no room for plazas nor alamedas. A little triangular space in front of the cathedral, however, aspires to the former title. The city reminded me of descriptions of the old Moorish towns of Spain—not as they now exist, but as they stood in the fourteenth century.

In the afternoon I took a walk through the city, climbing one of the hills to a cross planted on a small rocky point under the fortress of San Miguel. Thence I could look down on the twisted streets and flat house-tops, and the busy flood of life circulating through all. The churches, with their painted spires and domes, gave a bizarre and picturesque character to the scene. Off to the north, in the sides of the mountains, I could see the entrances to the silver mines, and the villages of the mining communities. Around Guanajuato there are more than a hundred mines, employing about seventy-five thousand workmen. The business of Guanajuato is now very flourishing, the mines having in 1849 yielded $8,400,000, or $600,000 more than the previous year. New mines have been opened on the rich vein of La Luz, which will soon be in a producing state, and promise much higher results. There is a fascination about the business, which is almost equal to that of play. The lucky discoverer of a new mine will frequently squander away the sudden wealth he has acquired in a week's dissipation. The wages of the common workmen vary from four reals to two dollars a day.

Before night I visited the cathedral and the churches of San Diego and San Felipe—the latter a dark old structure, covered with quaint, half-Gothic ornaments, its front shaded by several tall cypresses. In the church of San Diego, I saw a picture of

great beauty, of the Murillo school, but hardly, I think, an original of the renowned master of Spanish painting. After dinner,
while wandering about, looking at the fruit-stands, which were
lighted with a red glow by smoky torches, I witnessed a curious
ceremony. One of a band of robbers, who had been taken and
convicted, was to be shot the next morning. All the bells in the
city commenced tolling at sunset, and the incessant ding-dong
they kept up for nearly two hours, was enough to drive one frantic. I heard the sound of music, and saw the twinkling of wax
tapers ; I therefore pressed through the crowd into the middle of
the little plaza, to obtain a good view of the procession. First
came a company of soldiers, with a military band, playing dirges ;
after this the Bishop of the city bearing the Host, under a canopy
of white and silver, borne by priests, who also carried lanterns of
blue glass ; another company of soldiers followed, and after them
a long double line of citizens, each of whom held an immense
burning taper in his hand. With the clang of bells and the wail
of brazen instruments, they came towards us. The thousands in
the plaza dropped on their knees, leaving me standing alone in the
centre. A moment's reflection convinced me of the propriety of
following their example, so I sank down between a woman with a
very dirty rebosa and a black-bearded fellow, who might have been
the comrade of the condemned robber.

The procession, keeping a slow and measured pace, proceeded
to the prison, where the sacrament of extreme unction was administered to the criminal. It then returned to the cathedral, which
was brilliantly lighted, and filled with a dense throng of people.
The military band was stationed in the centre, under the dome,
and mingled its harmonies with those of the powerful organ. I
could get no further than the door-way, whence the whole interior

was visible as a lighted picture, framed in the gloomy arch under which I stood. The rise and swell of the choral voices—the deep, stunning peal of the bells in the tower—the solemn attitude of the crowd, and the blaze of light under which all these imposing ceremonies were seen—made a powerful impression on me. The people about me constantly repeated their paternosters, and seemed to feel a deep sympathy with the convicted. I remembered, that in the afternoon I had seen in the cathedral a man somewhat advanced in years, who was praying with an intensity of grief and supplication that made him for the time insensible to all else. His sobs and groans were so violent as to shake his whole frame ; I had never seen a more vehement expression of anguish. Thinking he might have been the robber's father, I began to have some compassion for the former, though now and then a wicked feeling of rejoicing would steal in, that another of the tribe was soon to be exterminated. The most curious feature of the scene was a company of small boys, carrying bundles of leaves on which was printed the " Last Dying Speech and Confession," in poetry, the burden being " *Adios, Guanajuato amado !*" These boys were scattered through the crowd, crying out : " Here you have my sentence, my confession, my death, my farewell to Guanajuato —all for a *cuartilla !*' The exercises were kept up so long, that finally I grew weary, and went to bed, where the incessant bells rang death-knells in my dreams.

In Guanajuato I tasted *pulque* for the first and last time. Seeing a woman at the corner of a street with several large jars of what I took to be barley-water, I purchased a glass. I can only liken the taste of this beverage to a distillation of sour milk (if there could be such a thing) strongly tinctured with cayenne pepper and hartshorn. Men were going about the streets with cans on their heads, containing ices made from tropical fruits, which were much more palatable.

They even have authors in Guanajuato. On the theatre bills I saw the announcement that an original tragedy entitled " *El Amor Conyugal*," by a young Guanajuatense, was in preparation. " The precious comedy of the Two Fernandos and the Two Pepas" was to be given as an afterpiece—probably a travesty of the " Comedy of Errors."

CHAPTER XV.

WE were roused in Guanajuato at three o'clock in the morning,
for the *jornada* of one hundred and ten miles to Queretaro. A
splendid moon was riding near the zenith, with her attendant star
at her side ; and by her light we drove down the ominous depths
of the cañada. The clumsy leaves of the cactus, along the ledges
of the hills, seemed in the uncertain light, like the heads of robbers
peering over the rocks; the crosses of the dead, here and there,
spread out their black arms, and we were not free from all ap-
prehensions of attack, until, after a post of three leagues, we
reached the level and secure land of the *Bajio*. Once, only, a
company of about twenty wild-looking men, whose weapons glittered in the moonlight, hooted at us as we passed ; we took them
to be a part of the robber-band, on their way to Guanajuato to
witness the execution of their comrade.

In five posts we reached the city of Salamanca, where breakfast was already on the table. No sooner had the final dish of frijoles and cup of coffee been dispatched, than the *cochero* summoned
us. The mozo drew away with a jerk the rope which held the
four leaders ; the horses plunged and pranced till the lumbering
mass of the diligence began to move, when they set off in a furious

gallop. For ten miles, over the level road, the speed was scarcely
slackened, till we drew up at the next post, and exchanged our
dusty and reeking steeds for a fresh team, as fiery and furious as
the first.

The country through which we passed, is one of the richest
regions in Mexico. It is called the *Bajio*, or Lowland, but is in
fact an extent of table-land, about four thousand feet above the
level of the sea, and only lower than the mountain-ridges which
enclose it and draw from the upper clouds the streams that give
it perpetual growth. From the city of Leon, near Lagos, it extends to San Juan del Rio, beyond Queretaro—a distance of
nearly two hundred miles. It is traversed by the Rio Lerma, the
stream which, rising in the Volcano of Toluca (the neighbor of
Popocatapetl) mingles with the waters of Lake Chapala, and afterwards—first as the Rio Blanco and then as the Rio Santiago—
finds its way into the Pacific at San Blas. This immense level is
all under fine cultivation and covered with thousand-acre fields of
wheat, maize and barley in different stages of growth. The white
fronts of haciendas gleamed from out their embowering gardens,
in the distance, and the spires of the country towns, rising at intervals, gave life and animation to the picture. In the afternoon
we passed the city of Zelaya, nearly smothered in clouds of dust
that rose from the dry soil.

As we reached the boundary of the State of Queretaro, eight
lancers, armed likewise with escopettes and holster-pistols, galloped out of the cactus on a wild, stony hill, and took their places
on each side of us. They constituted a military escort (at the
expense of the passengers,) to the gates of Queretaro. With their
red pennons fluttering in the wind and their rugged little horses
spurred into a gallop, they were very picturesque objects. Our

time was divided in watching their movements and looking out for the poles planted by the roadside as a sign that robbers had been taken and shot there. My Mexican fellow-travelers pointed to these tokens of unscrupulous punishment with evident satisfaction. A large tree near Queretaro, with a great many lateral branches, bears a sign with the words "*Por Ladrones,*" (For Robbers,) in large letters. It is probably used when a whole company is caught at once.

We drove into Queretaro after dark, and the only glimpse I had of the place was from the balcony of the hotel. I regretted not having arrived earlier, for the purpose of visiting the cotton manufactory of Don Gaetano Rubio, which is the largest in the Republic. Among the passengers in the diligence from Mexico, who joined us at the dinner-table, was a jovial padre, who talked constantly of the Monplaisir troupe of dancers and Cœnen, the violinist. In fact, he was more familiar with American and European theatricals than any one I had met for a long time, and gave me a ready account of the whereabouts of Cerito, Ellsler, Taglioni, and all the other divinities of the dance. He then commenced a dissertation upon the character of the different modern languages. The English, he said, was the language of commerce; the French, of conversation; the German, of diplomacy, because there were no words of double meaning in it!—and the Spanish, of devotion. With his conversation and delightful cigaritos, I passed the hour before bed-time very pleasantly. I never met a more lively and entertaining padre.

We drove to the town of San Juan del Rio, eleven leagues distant, for breakfast. A fresh escort was given us at every post, for which a fresh contribution of two reals was levied on each passenger. Towards evening, leaving the *Bajio,* we came upon a

large, arid *llano*, flat as a table, and lying at the foot of the
Mount of Capulalpan. A string of mules, carrying stone from the
mountains, stretched across it, till they almost vanished in the
perspective. One by one they came up out of the distance, emptied the stones, which were heaped upon their backs in rough
wicker frames, and turned about to repeat the journey. They
belonged to the estate of Señor Zurutuza, proprietor of the diligence lines of Mexico, who shows as much prudence and skill in
the cultivation of his lands as in the arrangement of his stages
and hotels. The estate which he purchased of the Mexican
Government, at a cost of $300,000, contains thirty-seven square
leagues, nearly all of which is arable land. The buildings stand
in a little valley, nine thousand feet above the sea. The principal
storehouse is two hundred feet square, and solid as a fortress. An
arched entrance, closed by massive gates, leads to a paved court-
yard, around which runs a lofty gallery, with pillars of oak resting
on blocks of lava. Under this shelter were stored immense piles
of wheat and chopped straw. On the outside, a number of persons were employed in removing the grain from a large circular
floor of masonry, where it had been trodden out by mules, and
separating it from the chaff by tossing it diligently in the wind.
The hotel for the accommodation of travelers, is a new and elegant structure, and a decided improvement on other buildings of
the kind in Mexico.

We slept soundly in the several rooms allotted to us, and by
daybreak next morning were on the summit of the Pass of Capulalpan, about eleven thousand feet above the sea. The air was
thin and cold ; the timber was principally oak, of a stunted and
hardy kind, and the general appearance of the place is desolate in
the extreme. Here, where the streams of the two oceans are

divided, the first view of Popocatapetl, at more than a hundred miles distance, greets the traveler. A descent of many miles, through splendid plantations, lying in the lap of the mountains, brought us to the old town of Tula, on the banks of the Tula River, which empties into the Gulf, at Tampico. Here we breakfasted, and then started on our last stage towards the capital. Crossing a low range of hills, we reached the Desagua, an immense canal, cut for the draining of the Valley of Mexico. The afternoon was hot and breezeless; clouds of dust enveloped and almost stifled us, rising as they rolled away till they looked like slender pillars, swayed from side to side by the vibrations of the air. We passed the towns of Guatitlan and Tanepantla, where we only stopped to get a drink of *tepache*, a most nourishing and refreshing beverage, compounded of parched corn, pineapple, and sugar. The road was hedged by immense aloes, some of which had leaves ten feet in length: they are cultivated in great quantities for the pulque, which is manufactured from their juice. A few hours of this travel, on the level floor of the Valley of Mexico, brought us to the suburbs, where we met scores of people in carriages and on horseback, going out to take their evening *paseo* around the Alameda. Rattling over the streets of the spacious capital, in a few minutes we were brought to a stand in the yard of the Casa de Diligencias.

A few minutes after my arrival, the Vera Cruz stage drove into the yard. The first person who jumped out was my friend Mr. Parrot, U. S. Consul at Mazatlan. Gov. Letcher, our Envoy to Mexico, came in the same stage, but was met at the Peñon Grande by a number of Americans in carriages, and brought into the city. It is a pleasant thing to have friends of your own size. I made my first appearance in the City of the Montezumas covered with dust and clad in the weather-beaten corduroys, which were all the robbers left me. Thanks to the kind offer of Mr. Parrot and Mr. Peyton, who accompanied him, I sat down to dinner in half an hour afterwards, looking and feeling much more like a member of civilized society.

CHAPTER XVI.

I SALLIED out, on the bright sunny morning after reaching Mexico, to make a survey of the city. The sky was cloudless except on the horizon, in the direction of Popocatapetl, and the air was charmingly cool and fresh. Its rarity, by accelerating the breathing, had a stimulating effect, but I found that a faster pace than ordinary exhausted me in a few minutes. Most of the shops were closed, and the people from the neighboring villages began to come in for the morning mass. The streets are broad, tolerably clean, and have an air of solidity and massive strength beyond that of any modern city. The houses are all of stone, with few windows on the streets, but an arched gateway in the centre, leading to a patio, or courtyard, where the only correct view of their size and magnificence may be obtained. The glimpses through these gateways, while passing, are often very beautiful—the richly-sculptured frame of stone enclosing a sunny picture of a fountain, a cluster of orange-trees, or the slender, graceful arches of the corridor. The buildings are painted of some light, fresh color, pink and white being predominant; some of them, indeed, are entirely covered with arabesque patterns in fresco. The streets run at right angles, with nearly Philadelphian

7*

regularity, but the system of naming them is very confusing to a
stranger. A name extends no farther than a single block, the
same street having sometimes as many as twenty different names
in different places. Thus, while there are several thousand names
of streets in the city, (all of them long and difficult to remember)
the actual number of streets is small.

I wandered about for some time, looking for the Grand Plaza,
and at last fell into the wake of the mass-going crowd, as the
surest way to find it. It is in the very centre of the city, though
the business quarter lies almost entirely on the western side. It
is one of the most imposing squares in the world, and still far inferior to what it might be made. It covers about fourteen.acres,
which are entirely open and unbroken, except by a double row of
orange-trees in front of the Cathedral. The splendid equestrian
statue of Charles IV. by the sculptor Tolsa, which formerly
stood in the centre, has been removed since the war of Independence, and the Government has never been able to replace it by
something more to its republican taste. The National Palace,
with a front of five hundred feet, occupies nearly the entire eastern
side of the plaza, while. the Cathedral, with a church adjoining,
fills the northern. Around the other sides runs a *cortal*, whose
arches are nearly blocked up by the wares and gay fabrics there
disposed for sale. One of the houses forming this cortal was built
by Cortez, and is still owned by his descendants. As in our own
cities, there is a row of hacks strung along one side of the plaza,
the drivers of which assail you with continual invitations to ride.

The Cathedral is grand and impressive from its very size, but
the effect of the front is greatly injured by its incongruous style of
architecture. There seems to have been no single design adopted,
but after half had been built, the architect changed his plan and

finished the remainder in a different style. The front, as high as the Cathedral roof, has a venerable appearance of age and neglect, while the two massive, square, unadorned towers rising from it, are as brilliantly white and fresh as if erected yesterday. The front of the church adjoining is embossed with very elaborate ornaments of sculpture, all showing the same disregard of architectural unity. The interior of the Cathedral is far more perfect in its structure. The nave, resting its lofty arch on pillars of a semi-Gothic character, with the gorgeous pile of the high-altar at its extremity, blazing with gold and silver and precious marbles, looks truly sublime in the dim, subdued light which fills it. The railing around the altar is solid silver, as well as the lamps which burn before it. In the shrines along the side aisles there are many paintings of fine character, but everywhere the same flash of gold and appearance of lavish treasure. The Cathedral was crowded to the very door by a throng of rancheros, Indians, stately ladies in silks and jewels, soldiers and *lepéros*, kneeling side by side. The sound of the organ, bearing on its full flood the blended voices of the choir, pealed magnificently through the nave. There were some very fine voices among the singers, but their performance was wanting in the grand and perfect unison which distinguishes the Italian chorus.

In the afternoon, there was a great fair or festival at Tacubaya, and half the population of the city went out to attend it. The stages in front of the Diligence Hotel, which bore the inscription on their sides: "*A Tacubaya, por 2 reales,*" were jammed with passengers. I preferred a quiet walk in the Alameda to a suffocating ride in the heat and dust, and so did my friend, Peyton. The Alameda is a charming place, completely shaded by tall trees, and musical with the plash of fountains.

Through its long avenues of foliage, the gay equipages of the aristocracy may be seen rolling to and from the *paseo*—President Herrera, in a light, open carriage, followed by a guard of honor, among them. We roamed through the cool, shaded walks, finding sufficient amusement in the curious groups and characters we constantly met until the afternoon shadows grew long and the sun had nearly touched the Nevada of Toluca. Then, joining the increasing crowd, we followed the string of carriages past a guard-house where a company of trumpeters shattered all the surrounding air by incessant prolonged blasts, that nearly tore up the paving-stones. A beautiful road, planted with trees, and flanked by convenient stone benches, extended beyond for about a mile, having a circle at its further end, around which the carriages passed, and took their stations in the return line. We sat down on one of the benches facing the ring, enjoying the tranquillity of the sunset and the animation of the scene before us. The towers of Mexico rose behind us, above the gardens which belt the city; the rock of Chapultepec was just visible in front, and far to the south-east, a snowy glimmer, out of the midst of a pile of clouds, revealed the cone of Popocatapetl. Among the equipages were some of great magnificence : that of Don Gaetano Rubio was perhaps the most costly. Large American horses are in great demand for these displays, and a thousand dollars a pair is frequently paid for them. The mixture of imported vehicles—English, French and American—with the bomb-proof arks and moveable fortifications of the country, was very amusing, though their contrast was not more marked than that of the occupants. The great ambition of a Mexican family is to ride in a carriage on all public occasions, and there are hundreds who starve themselves on tortillas and deny themselves every comfort but the cigarito, that they may pay the necessary hire.

I went one evening to the Teatro de Santa Anna, which is one of the finest theatres in the world. On this occasion, the performance might have honorably stood the ordeal of even Paris criticism. There was a ballet by the Monplaisir troupe, songs by the prima donna of the native opera and violin solos by Franz Coenen. The theatre is very large, having, if I remember rightly, five tiers of boxes, yet it was crowded in every part. There was a great display of costly dresses and jewelry, but I saw much less beauty than on the moonlit plaza of Guadalajara. The tendency of the Mexican women to corpulency very soon destroys the bloom and graces of youth ; indeed, their season of beauty is even more brief than in the United States. Between the acts the spectators invariably fell to smoking. The gentlemen lit their *puros*, the ladies produced their delicate boxes of cigaritos and their matches, and for some minutes after the curtain fell, there was a continual snapping and fizzing of brimstone all over the house. By the time the curtain was ready to rise, the air was sensibly obscured, and the chandeliers glimmered through a blue haze. At home, this habit of smoking by the ladies is rather graceful and pretty ; the fine paper cigar is handled with an elegance that shows off the little arts and courtesies of Spanish character, with the same effect as a fan or a bouquet ; but a whole congregation of women smoking together, I must admit, did take away much of the reverence with which we are wont to regard the sex. Because a lady may be a Juno in beauty, is no reason why she should thus retire into a cloud—nor is the odor of stale tobacco particularly Olympian.

The streets of Mexico are always an interesting study. Even

after visiting the other large cities of the Republic, one is here introduced to new and interesting types of Mexican humanity.
Faces of the pure Aztec blood are still to be found in the squares
and market-places, and the canal which joins Lakes Chalco and
Tezcuco is filled with their flat canoes, laden with fruits, vegetables
and flowers.   They have degenerated in everything but their hostility to the Spanish race, which is almost as strong as in the days
of Montezuma.   The *léperos* constitute another and still more disgusting class; no part of the city is free from them.   They im-
plore you for alms with bended knees and clasped hands, at every
turn ; they pick your pockets in broad daylight, or snatch away
your cloak if there is a good opportunity ; and if it be an object
with any one to have you removed from this sphere of being, they
will murder you for a small consideration.   The second night I
spent in Mexico, my pocket was picked in the act of passing a
corner where two or three of them were standing in a group.   I
discovered the loss before I had gone ten steps further ; but,
though I turned immediately, there was no one to be seen.   The
aguadores, or water-carriers, are another interesting class, as they
go about with heavy earthen jars suspended on their backs by a
band about the forehead, and another smaller jar swinging in
front to balance it, by a band over the top of the head.   The
priests, in their black cassocks and shovel hats with brims a yard
long, are curious figures ; the monasteries in the city send out
large numbers of fat and sensual friars, whose conduct even in public is a scandal to the respectable part of the community.   In all
the features of its out-door life, Mexico is quite as motley and
picturesque as any of the old cities of Spain.   The Republic
seems to have in no way changed the ancient order, except by

tearing down all the emblems of royalty and substituting the eagle and cactus in their stead.

The scarcity of all antiquities of the Aztec race, will strike travelers who visit the city. Not one stone of the ancient capital has been left upon another, while, by the gradual recession of the waters of the lakes, the present Mexico, though built precisely on the site of the ancient one, stands on dry ground. There are frequently inundations, it is true, caused by long-continued rains, which the mountain slopes to the north-east and south-west send into the valley, but the construction of the Desagua—an immense canal connecting Lake Tezcuco with the Rio Montezuma—has greatly lessened the danger. Of all the temples, palaces, and public edifices of the Aztecs, the only remains are the celebrated Calendar, built into one corner of the cathedral, the Sacrificial Stone and a collection of granite gods in the National Museum. The Calendar is an immense circular stone, probably ten feet in diameter, containing the divisions of the Aztec year, and the astronomical signs used by that remarkable people. The remaining antiquities are piled up neglectedly in the court-yard of the Museum, where the stupid natives come to stare at them, awed, yet apparently fascinated by their huge, terrible features. The Sacrificial Stone is in perfect preservation. It is like a great mill-stone of some ten or twelve feet diameter, with a hollow in the centre, from which a groove slants to the edge, to carry away the blood of the victim. Scattered around it on the pavement were idols of all grotesque forms, feathered serpents and hideous combinations of human and animal figures. The Aztec war-god, Quetzalcoatl, was the hugest and most striking of all. He was about fourteen feet in height, with four faces, and as many pairs of arms and legs, fronting towards the quarters of the compass; his mouth was open and tongue projecting, and in the hollow thus formed, the heart of the victim was thrust, while yet warm and palpitating. His grim features struck me with awe and something like terror, when I thought of the thousands of human hearts that had stained his insatiate tongues. Here, at least, the Aztecs had a truer conception of the Spirit of War than ourselves. We still retain the Mars of the poetic Greeks—a figure of strength and energy, and glorious ardor only—not the grand monster which all barbaric tribes, to whom war is a natural instinct, build for their worship.

There are some relics of the Spanish race in this museum, which I should not omit to mention. In one dusty corner, behind a little wooden railing, are exhibited the coats-of-mail of Cortez and Alvarado. The great Cortez, to judge from his helmet, breast-plate and cuishes, was a short, broad-chested and powerful man—the very build for daring and endurance. Alvarado was a little taller and more slight, which may account for his celebrated leap—the measure of which is still shown on a wall near the city, though the ditch is filled up. In the centre of the court-yard stands the celebrated equestrian statue of Charles IV., by the Mexican sculptor, Tolsa. It is of bronze, and colossal size. In the general spirit and forward action of the figures, it is one of the best equestrian statues in the world. The horse, which was modeled from an Andalusian stallion of pure blood, has been censured. It differs, in fact, very greatly from the perfect Grecian model, especially in the heavy chest and short round flank; but those who have seen the Andalusian horse consider it a perfect type of that breed. It is a work in which Mexico may well glory, for any country might be proud to have produced it.

CHAPTER XVII.

I SPENT one morning during my stay in Mexico, in visiting both Houses of the Mexican Congress, which were then in session, in the National Palace. I could not but regret, on approaching this edifice, that so fine an opportunity for architectural effect had been lost through a clumsy and incongruous plan of building. The front of five hundred feet, had it been raised another story, and its flat pink surface relieved by a few simple pilasters and cornices, would have equaled that of the Pitti Palace or the Royal *Residenz* in Munich. One of its court-yards, with a fountain in the centre and double gallery running around the four sides, is nevertheless complete and very beautiful. While looking out of the windows of the Palace on the magnificent square, the foremost picture in my mind's eye was not that of Cortez and Alvarado, battling their way back to Tlascala, after the " Noche Triste ;" not that of the splendid trains of the Viceroys of yet powerful Spain; but the triumphal entry of Scott, when the little army that had fought its way in from Chapultepec, greeted his appearance on the Plaza with huzzas that brought tears even into Mexican eyes. Think as one may of the character of the war, there are scenes in it which stir the blood and brighten the eye.

Mr. Belden, an American many years resident in Mexico, accompanied me to the Halls of Congress, and pointed out the principal characters present.   We first visited the Senate Chamber—a small elliptical room in the centre of the Palace.   There were no desks except for the Secretaries, the members being seated on a continuous bench, which ran around the room, with a rail in front of it.   Probably two-thirds of the Senators—fifteen or twenty in all—were present.   The best head among them is that of Otero, who, I think, was one of the Cabinet during the war.   He is a large, strongly-built man, with features expressing not only intelligence, but power.   At the end of the room sat Don Luis Cuevas, one of the Commissioners who signed the Treaty of Guadalupe Hidalgo—a man of polished bearing, and, from appearance, something of a *diplomat*.   Gen. Almonte, whose low forehead, broad cheek-bones and dark skin betray his Indian blood, occupied the seat next to Pedraza, the President of a few days during a revolution in 1828.   Almonte is the son of the Liberator Morelos, and that circumstance alone gave him an interest in my eyes.

The demeanor of the Senate is exceedingly quiet and grave. The speeches are short, though not, in consequence, always to the point.   On the contrary, I am told that any definite action on any subject is as difficult to be had as in our own Congress.   It is better, however, to do nothing decorously, than after a riotous fashion.

The Hall of Congress fronts on one of the inner courts of the Palace.   It is semi-circular in form, and lighted by windows of blue glass, near the top.   As in the Senate, the members have no desks, but are ranged along two semi-circular benches, the outer one raised a step from the floor.   The Speaker sits on a broad platform, in front of the centre of the chord, with two Secretaries on each hand. At each corner of the platform is a circular pulpit, just large enough to take in a spare man nearly to the armpits. They are used by the members for set harangues. Behind the Speaker's chair, and elevated above it, is a sort of throne with two seats, under a crimson canopy. Here, the President of the Republic and the Speaker of Congress take their seats, at the opening and close of each Session. Above the canopy, in a gilded frame, on a ground of the Mexican tricolor, hangs the sword of Iturbide. A picture of the Virgin of Guadalupe, with her blue mantle and silver stars, completes the decorations. Around the architrave of the pillars which form the semi-circle and across the cornice of the chord, are inscribed, in letters of gold, the names of the Mexican Chiefs of the War of Independence—conspicuous among them those of Morelos, Bravo, Victoria and Mina.

The Mexican Congress elects its Speaker monthly. The incumbent at the time, Portillo, was a young man, who presided with admirable dignity and decorum. As in the Senate, the members exhibit a grave and courteous demeanor; the etiquette of dignified legislation, I presume, is never violated. The only notable Representative present was Arrangoiz, whose name is well known in the United States. I was disappointed in not seeing Alaman, the head of the Monarchist faction, Editor of the *Universal*, and author of an excellent History of Mexico, then in the course of publication. Two or three short speeches were made during my visit, but I was not sufficiently versed either in the language or politics, to get more than the general drift of them. Congress appeared to be doing nothing satisfactory; the thinking population (a very small number) were discontented, and with reason. A short time previous, the Report of the Committee of Finance came up for discussion. After engaging the House for

several days, during which many warm speeches were made on
both sides, all seemed ready for a decision ; when, lo ! the members suddenly determined that *they had no right to vote upon it !*

One o'clock the same afternoon was the hour appointed for the
presentation of Mr. Letcher, the new Envoy from the United
States.   On coming out of the Senate Chamber we noticed that
the corridor leading to the rooms of the President was deserted by
the groups of officers in full uniform who had been lounging about
the door.   Entering the ante-chamber, we found that Mr. Letcher,
with Mr. Walsh, Secretary of Legation, had just passed into the
Hall of Audience.   Mr. Belden was well known to all the officers
of Government, and his company procured us admission at once.
We took our places among the Secretaries of the different Departments, about half way up the Hall.   Gen. Herrera, the President, was seated on a platform at the end of the room; under a
crimson canopy, having on his right hand Lacunza, Minister of
Foreign Affairs, and on his left Castañeda, Minister of Justice.
The other Ministers, with a number of officers of the General
Staff, were ranged at the foot of the platform.   Mr. Letcher had
just commenced his address as we entered.   He appeared slightly
embarrassed during the first phrases, but soon recovered the proper
composure.   I had no doubt, however, that he would have felt
much more at home in making a stump speech in his native Kentucky.   His address consisted mainly of expressions of good will
on the part of the United States, and a desire for more intimate
and amicable relations between the two Governments.   Gen. Herrera, on receiving the letters accrediting Mr. Letcher, replied in a
neat speech, cordially responding to the expressions of amity which
had been made, and invoking for both nations the same harmony

in their mutual relations as they already possessed in their constitutional forms.

After the interchange of a few compliments, Mr. Letcher took his leave, and immediately afterwards the President rose and left the hall, in company with his Ministers. He bowed to us in passing, probably recognizing us as Americans. He is a man of about sixty, of short stature, and with a countenance whose prominent expression is honesty and benevolence. This corresponds with the popular idea of his character. He is a man of excellent heart, but lacks energy and determination. His Government, though quiet and peaceful enough at present, is not sufficiently strong for Mexico. So long as the several States continue to defy and violate the Federal Compact, a powerful Head is needed to the General Government. The rule of Herrera met with no open opposition At the time of my visit, the country was perfectly quiet. The insurrection in the Sierra Madre had been entirely quelled, and the ravages of the Indians in Durango and Chihuahua appeared to have subsided for a time. Nevertheless, the Conservative party, whose tendency is towards a monarchy, was said to be on the increase—a fact no doubt attributable to the influence and abilities of Alaman, its avowed leader. The name of Santa Anna had been brought forward by his friends, as a candidate for Congress from the district of the Capital, though his success was scarcely a matter of hope.

The Government was still deeply embarrassed by its forced loans, and Congress took the very worst means to settle its difficulty. A committee, appointed to report some plan of settlement, made the following propositions, which I here give, as a curiosity in legislation:—1. That the Government be authorized to make an amicable arrangement with its creditors, within the space of forty days. (!) 2. That such arrangement cannot take effect without the approbation of Congress; (!!) and 3. That the Government be authorized to accept a further sum of $300,000 on the American indemnity. The resignation of Señor Elorriaga, the Minister of Finance, was fully expected, and took place, in fact, about three weeks after I left. Very few Ministers hold this office more than two or three months. The entire want of confidence between the Executive and Legislative Departments utterly destroys the efficiency of the Mexican Government. The Ministers wear a chain, which is sometimes so shortened by the caprice of Congress, that the proper exercise of their functions is rendered impossible.

Several of the States had a short time previous been taking singular liberties with the Constitution. For instance, the Legislatures of Zacatecas, Durango and Jalisco, had separately passed laws regulating the revenue not only on internal commerce, but foreign imports! The duties on many articles were enormous, as, for instance, in the State of Jalisco, 37 1-2 cents per lb. on tobacco, and 75 cents on snuff. Zacatecas, with a curious discrimination, imposed a duty of 12 1-2 per cent. on home manufactures, and 5 per cent. on foreign merchandise! In such a state of things one knows not which most to wonder at, the audacity of the States, or the patient sufferance of the Supreme Government.

I scanned with some curiosity the faces and forms of the chief officers of the Republic as they passed.

Herrera wore the uniform of a general—a more simple costume than that of the other officers present, whose coats were ornamented with red facings and a profusion of gold embroidery. The Ministers, except Arista, were dressed in plain suits of black.

Lacunza is a man of low stature and dark complexion, and a barely perceptible cast of shrewdness is mingled with the natural intelligence of his features. Castañeda, on the other hand, is tall, thin, with a face of which you are certain, at the first glance, that it knows how to keep its owner's secrets. The finest-looking man present was Gen. Arista, who is six feet high, and stout in proportion, with a large head, light hair closely cropped, fair complexion and gray eyes. From the cast of his features, one would take him to be a great overgrown Scotch boy, who had somehow blundered into a generalship. He is said to have the most influential hand in the Cabinet. Among the States of the North there is, as is well known, a powerful party devoted to his interests.

While in Mexico, I had the pleasure of meeting with Don Vicente Garcia Torres, the talented editor of the *Monitor Republicano*, as well as with several of the writers for *El Siglo Diez y Nueve*. To M. Réné Masson, the enterprising editor and proprietor of *Le Trait D'Union*, (the only foreign journal in Mexico,) I was also indebted for many courteous attentions. His paper is conducted with more industry and gives a more intelligible view of Mexican affairs than any of the native prints. The Count de la Cortina, the most accomplished writer in Mexico, and author of several works, was pointed out to me in the street one day. He possesses a princely fortune and the finest picture-gallery in America.

CHAPTER XVIII.

RIDES TO CHAPULTEPEC AND GUADALUPE.

No American, whatever be his moral creed or political sentiments, should pass through Mexico without a visit to the battle-fields in the Valley, where his country's arms obtained such signal triumphs. To me they had a more direct, thrilling interest than the remains of Aztec Empire or the Spanish Viceroyalty. I was fortunate in seeing them with a companion, to whom every rood of ground was familiar, and who could trace all the operations of Scott's army, from San Augustin to the Grand Plaza in the city. We started for Chapultepec one fine afternoon, with Mr. Belden, taking his carriage and span of black mules. We drove first to the Garita de Belén, where one of the aqueducts enters the city. Here a strong barricade was carried after the taking of Chapultepec by Pillow's division, while Worth, following down the line of the other aqueduct, got possession of the Garita de San Cosmé. The brick arches are chipped with shot, for the whole distance of three miles. The American troops advanced by springing from arch to arch, being exposed, as they approached the Garita, to a cross-fire from two batteries. The running battle of the Aqueducts, from Chapultepec to Mexico, a distance of three miles, was a brilliant achievement, and had not our forces been so flushed and excited with the storming of the height, and the spirit of the Mexicans proportionately lessened, the slaughter must have been terrible.

We followed the aqueduct, looking through its arches on the green wheat-fields of the Valley, the shining villages in the distance and sometimes the volcanoes, as the clouds grew thinner about their white summits. At last, we reached the gate of Chapultepec. Mr. Belden was known to the officer on guard, and we passed unchallenged into the shade of Montezuma's cypresses. Chapultepec is a volcanic hill, probably two hundred feet in height, standing isolated on the level floor of the valley. Around its base is the grove of cypress trees, known as Montezuma's Garden—great, gnarled trunks, which have been formed by the annual rings of a thousand years, bearing aloft a burden of heavy and wide-extending boughs, with venerable beards of gray moss. The changeless black-green of the foliage, the dull, wintry hue of the moss, and the gloomy shadows which always invest this grove, spoke to me more solemnly of the Past—of ancient empire, now overthrown, ancient splendor, now fallen into dust, and ancient creeds now forgotten and contemned,—than the shattered pillars of the Roman Forum or the violated tombs of Etruria. I saw them on a shaded, windless day, with faint glimmerings of sunshine between the black and heavy masses of cloud. The air was so still that not a filament of the long mossy streamers trembled ; the trees stood like giant images of bronze around the rocky foot of the hill. The father of the band, who, like a hoary-headed seneschal, is stationed at the base of the ascending carriage-way, measures forty-five feet in circumference, and there are in the grove several others of dimensions but little inferior. The first

8

onset of our troops, in storming Chapultepec, was made under cover of these trees.

Leaving our carriage and mules in charge of the old cypress, we climbed the hill on foot. The zigzag road still retains its embankment of adobes and the small corner-batteries thrown up in anticipation of the attack ; the marks of the cannon-balls from Tacubaya and the high ground behind Molino del Rey, are everywhere visible. The fortress on the summit of Chapultepec has been for many years used as a National Military Academy. We found a company of the cadets playing ball on a graveled terrace in front of the entrance. One of them escorted us to the private apartments of the commanding officer, which are built along the edge of a crag, on the side towards Mexico. Mr. Belden was well acquainted with the officer, but, unfortunately, he was absent. His wife, however, received us with great courtesy and sent for one of the Lieutenants attached to the Academy. A splendid Munich telescope was brought from the observatory, and we adjourned to the balcony for a view of the Valley of Mexico.

I wish there was a perspective in words—something beyond the mere suggestiveness of sound—some truer representative of color, and light, and grand aerial distance ; for I scarcely know how else to paint the world-wide panorama spread around me. Chapultepec, as I have said before, stands isolated in the centre of the Valley. The mountains of Toluca approach to within fifteen miles beyond Tacubaya, and the island-like hills of Guadalupe are not very distant, on the opposite side ; but in nearly every other direction the valley fades away for fifty or sixty miles before striking the foot of the mountains. The forms of the chains which wall in this little world are made irregular and wonderfully picturesque by the embaying curves of the Valley—now receding far and faint, now piled nearer in rugged and barren grandeur, now tipped with a spot of snow, like the Volcano of Toluca, or shooting far into the sky a dazzling cone, like cloud-girdled Popocatapel. But the matchless Valley—how shall I describe that ? How reflect on this poor page its boundless painting of fields and gardens, its silvery plantations of aloes, its fertilizing canals, its shimmering lakes, embowered villages and convents, and the many-towered capital in the centre—the boss of its great enameled shield ? Before us the aqueducts ran on their thousand arches towards the city, the water sparkling in their open tops ; the towers of the cathedral, touched with a break of sunshine shone white as silver against the cloud-shadowed mountains ; Tacubaya lay behind, with its palaces and gardens ; farther to the north Tacuba, with the lone cypress of the " Noche Triste," and eastward, on the point of a mountain-cape shooting out towards Lake Tezcuco, we saw the shrine of Our Lady of Guadalupe. Around the foot of our rocky watch-tower, we looked down on the heads of the cypresses, out of whose dark masses it seemed to rise, sundered by that weird ring from the warmth and light and beauty of the far-reaching valley-world.

We overlooked all the battle-grounds of the Valley, but I felt a hesitancy at first in asking the Lieutenant to point out the localities. Mr. Belden at length asked whether we could see the height of Padierna, or the *pedregal* (field of lava) which lies to the left of it. The officer immediately understood our wish, and turning the glass first upon the Peñon Grande, (an isolated hill near Ayotla,) traced the march of Gen. Scott's army around Lake Chalco to the town of San Augustin, near which the first hostilities commenced. We could see but a portion of the field of Padierna, more familiarly known as Contreras. It lies on the lower slopes of the Nevada of Toluca, and overlooking the scenes of the subse-

quent actions.   The country is rough and broken, and the crossing of the famed *pedregal*, from the far glimpse I had of the
ground, must have been a work of great labor and peril.   Nearly
east of this, on the dead level of the valley, is the memorable field
of Churubusco.   The *tête de pont*, where the brunt of the battle
took place, was distinctly visible, and I could count every tree in
the gardens of the convent.   The panic of the Mexicans on the
evening after the fight at Churubusco was described to me as having been without bounds.   Foreigners residing in the capital say
it might then have been taken with scarce a blow.

Beyond Tacubaya, we saw the houses of Miscoac, where the
army was stationed for some time before it advanced to the former
place.   Gen. Scott's head-quarters was in the Bishop's Palace at
Tacubaya, which is distinctly seen from Chapultepec and within
actual reach of its guns.   On an upland slope north of the village
and towards Tacuba the shattered walls of the Casa Mata were
pointed out.   Near at hand—almost at the very base of the
hill—rose the white gable of Molino del Rey.   The march of the
attacking lines could be as distinctly traced as on a map.   How
Chapultepec, which commands every step of the way, could be
stormed and carried with such a small force, seems almost miraculous.   Persons who witnessed the affair from Tacubaya told me
that the yells of the American troops as they ascended the hill in
the face of a deadly hail of grape-shot, were absolutely terrific ;
when they reached the top the Mexicans seemed to lose all thought
of further defence, pouring in bewildered masses out of the doors
and windows nearest the city, and tumbling like a torrent of water
down the steep rocks.   The Lieutenant, who was in Chapultepec
at the time, said that one thousand and fifty bombs fell on the
fortress before the assault ; the main tower, the battlements and

stairways are still broken and shattered from their effects. "Here," said he, as we walked along the summit terrace, "fifty of ours lie buried; and down yonder"—pointing to the foot of the hill—"so many that they were never counted." I was deeply moved by his calm, sad manner, as he talked thus of the defeat and slaughter of his countrymen. I felt like a participant in the injury, and almost wished that he had spoken of us with hate and reproach.

I do not believe, however, that Mexican enmity to the United States has been increased by the war, but rather the contrary. During all my stay in the country I never heard a bitter word said against us. The officers of our army seem to have made friends everywhere, and the war, by throwing the natives into direct contact with foreigners, has greatly abated their former prejudice against all not of Spanish blood. The departure of our troops was a cause of general lamentation among the tradesmen of Mexico and Vera Cruz. Nothing was more common to me than to hear Generals Scott and Taylor mentioned by the Mexicans in terms of entire respect and admiration. "If you should see General Taylor," said a very intelligent gentleman to me, "tell him that the Mexicans all honor him. He has never given up their houses to plunder; he has helped their wounded and suffering; he is as humane as he is brave, and they can never feel enmity towards him." It may be that this generous forgetfulness of injury argues a want of earnest patriotism, but it was therefore none the less grateful to me as an American.

We took leave of our kind guide and descended the hill. It was now after sunset; we drove rapidly through the darkening cypresses and across a little meadow to the wall of Molino del Rey. A guard admitted us into the courtyard, on one side of which loomed the tall structure of the mill; the other sides were flanked with low buildings, flat-roofed, with heavy parapets of stone along the outside. Crossing the yard, we passed through another gate to the open ground where the attack was made. This battle, as is now generally known, was a terrible mistake, costing the Americans eight hundred lives without any return for the sacrifice. The low parapets of the courtyard concealed a battery of cannon, and as our troops came down the bare, exposed face of the hill, rank after rank was mowed away by their deadly discharge. The mill was taken, it is true, but, being perfectly commanded by the guns of Chapultepec, it was an untenable position.

It was by this time so dark that we returned to the city by the route we came, instead of taking the other aqueduct and following the line of Gen. Worth's advance to the Garita of San Cosmé. Landing at Mr. Belden's residence, the Hotel de Bazar, we went into the Café adjoining, sat down by a marble table under the ever-blooming trees of the court-yard, and enjoyed a *chirimoya* ice —how delicious, may readily be imagined when I state that this fruit in its native state resembles nothing so much as a rich vanilla cream. The Café de Bazar is kept by M. Arago, a brother of the French astronomer and statesman, and strikingly like him in features. At night, the light Moorish corridors around his fountained court-yard are lighted with gay-colored lamps, and knots of writers, politicians or stray tourists are gathered there until ten o'clock, when Mexican law obliges the place to be closed.

Mr. Peyton and myself procured a pair of spirited mustangs and one morning rode out to the village of Guadalupe, three miles on the road to Tampico. It was a bright, hot day, and Iztaccihuatl flaunted its naked snows in the sun. The road was crowded with arrieros and rancheros, on their way to and from the city—suspicious characters, some of them, but we had left our purses at home and taken our pistols along. The shrine of the Virgin was closed at the time, but we saw the little chapel in which it was deposited and the flight of steps cut in the rock, which all devout Christians are expected to ascend on their knees. The principal church in the place is a large, imposing structure, but there is a smaller building entirely of blue and white glazed tiles, the effect of which is remarkably neat and unique. Half way up the hill, some rich Mexican who was saved from shipwreck by calling upon the Virgin of Guadalupe, has erected a votive offering in the shape of an immense mast and three sails, looking, at a distance, like part of an actual ship.

After a week in Mexico, I prepared to leave for Vera Cruz, to meet the British steamer of the 16th of February. The seats in the diligence had all been engaged for ten days previous, and I was obliged to take a place in the *pescante*, or driver's box, for which I paid $34. Again I rolled my sarape around my scanty luggage and donned the well-worn corduroy coat. I took leave of my kind friend Mr. Parrot, and lay down to pass my last night in the city of the Montezumas.

CHAPTER XIX.

THE BASE OF POPOCATAPETL.

WHEN we were called up by the mozo, at four o'clock, the air was dark, damp and chilly: not a star was to be seen. The travelers who gathered to take their chocolate in the dining-hall wore heavy cloaks or sarapes thrown over the shoulder and covering the mouth. Among them was my companion from Guanajuato, Don Antonio de Campos. I climbed to my seat in the *pescante*, above the driver and groom, and waited the order to start. At last the inside was packed, the luggage lashed on behind, and the harness examined by lanterns, to see that it was properly adjusted. "*Vamos!*" cried the driver; the rope was jerked from the leaders, and away we thundered down the silent streets, my head barely clearing the swinging lamps, stretched from corner to corner. We passed through the great plaza, now dim and deserted: the towers of the Cathedral were lost in mist. Crossing the canal, we drove through dark alleys to the barrier of the city, where an escort of lancers, in waiting among the gloomy court-yards, quietly took their places on either side of us.

A chill fog hung over all the valley. The air was benumbing, and I found two coats insufficient to preserve warmth. There are no gardens and fields of maguey on this side of the city, as on that of Tacubaya. Here and there, a plantation of maize interrupts the uniformity of the barren plains of grass. In many places, the marshy soil bordering on Lake Tezcuco, is traversed by deep ditches, which render it partially fit for cultivation. Leaving the shores of Tezcuco, we turned southward, changed horses at the little Peñon, (an isolated hill, between Lakes Chalco and Xochimilco) and drove on to Ayotla. This is the point where the American army under Gen. Scott left the main road to Mexico, turning around the Peñon Grande, south of the town, and taking the opposite shore of Lake Chalco. It is a small, insignificant village, but prettily situated beside the lake and at the foot of the towering Peñon; a little further, a road branches off to Ameca and the foot of Popocatapetl. Here we left the valley, and began ascending the barren slopes of the mountain. Clumps of unsightly cactus studded the rocky soil, which was cut into rough arroyos by the annual rains.

Slowly toiling up the ascent, we changed horses at a large hacienda, built on one of the steps of the mountains, whence, looking backward, the view of the valley was charming. The Peñon stood in front; southward, towards Ameca and Tenango, stretched a great plain, belted with green wheat-fields and dotted with the white towers of villages. The waters of Chalco were at our feet, and northward, through a gap in the hills, the broad sheet of Lake Tezcuco flashed in the sun. But it was not till we had climbed high among the pine forests and looked out from under the eaves of the clouds, that I fully realized the grandeur of this celebrated view. The vision seemed to embrace a world at one glance. The Valley of Mexico, nearly one hundred miles in extent, lay below, its mountain-walls buried in the clouds which hung like a curtain above the immense picture. But through a

8*

rift in this canopy, a broad sheet of sunshine slowly wandered over the valley, now glimmering on the lakes and brightening the green of the fields and gardens, and now lighting up, with wonderful effect, the yellow sides of the ranges of hills. Had the morning been clear, the view would have been more extended, but I do not think its broadest and brightest aspect could have surpassed in effect, the mysterious half-light, half-gloom in which I saw it.

The clouds rolled around us as I gazed, and the cold wind blew drearily among the pines. Our escort, now increased to twelve lancers, shortened their ascent by taking the mule paths. They looked rather picturesque, climbing in single file through the forest; their long blue cloaks hanging on their horses' flanks and their red pennons fluttering in the mist. The rugged defiles through which our road lay, are the most famous resort for robbers in all Mexico. For miles we passed through one continued ambush, where frequent crosses among the rocks hinted dark stories of assault and death. Our valorous lancers lagged behind, wherever the rocks were highest and the pines most thickly set; I should not have counted a single moment on their assistance, had we been attacked. I think I enjoyed the wild scenery of the pass more, from its perils. The ominous gloom of the day and the sound of the wind as it swept the trailing clouds through the woods of pine, heightened this feeling to something like a positive enjoyment.

When we reached the inn of Rio Frio, a little below the summit of the pass, on its eastern side, our greatest danger was over. Breakfast was on the table, and the eggs, rice, guisados and frijoles speedily disappeared before our sharp-set appetites. Luckily for our hunger, the diligence from Puebla had not arrived. The little valley of Rio Frio is hedged in by high, piny peaks, somewhat resembling the Catskills. Below it, another wild, dangerous pass of two or three miles opens upon the fertile and beautiful table-land of Puebla. The first object which strikes the eye on emerging from the woods, is the peak of Malinche, standing alone on the plain, about midway between the mountain ranges which terminate, on the Mexican side, in Popocatapetl, on the Vera Cruz side, in Orizaba. I looked into the sky, above the tree-tops, for the snows of Iztaccihuatl and Popocatapetl, but only a few white streaks on the side of the former volcano, could be seen. A violent snow-storm was raging along its summit, and upon Popocatapetl, which was entirely hidden from sight.

The table-land on which we entered, descends, with a barely perceptible slant, to Puebla—a distance of forty miles. Its surface, fenceless, and almost boundless to the eye, is covered with wheat and maize. Fine roads cross it; and the white walls of haciendas, half-buried in the foliage of their gardens, dot it, at intervals, to the feet of the distant mountains. The driver, an intelligent Mexican, pointed out to me the various points of interest, as we passed along. He professed to speak a little English, too, which he said he had picked up from passengers on the road; but as all his English amounted only to a choice vocabulary of oaths, it told badly for the character of his passengers.

All afternoon the clouds covered the summits of the volcanoes, and stretching like a roof across the table-land, rested on the broad shoulders of Malinche. As the sun descended, they lifted a little, and I could see the sides of Popocatapetl as far as the limit of the snow; but his head was still hooded. At last, through a break just above the pinnacle of his cone, the light poured in a full blaze, silvering the inner edges of the clouds with a sudden and splendid lustre. The snowy apex of the mountain, bathed in full radiance, seemed brighter than the sun itself—a spot of light so pure, so inconceivably dazzling, that though I could not withdraw my gaze, the eye could scarcely bear its excess. Then, as the clouds rolled together once more, the sun climbing through numerous rifts, made bars of light in the vapory atmosphere, reaching from the sides of Popocatapetl to their bases, many leagues away, on. the plain. It was as if the mountain genii who built the volcano had just finished their work, leaving these, the airy gangways of their scaffolding, still planted around it, to attest its marvellous size and grandeur.

The most imposing view of Popocatapetl is from the side towards Puebla. It is not seen, as from the valley of Mexico, over the rims of intermediate mountains, but the cone widens downward with an unbroken outline, till it strikes the smooth tableland. On the right, but separated by a deep gap in the range, is the broad, irregular summit of Iztaccihuatl, gleaming with snow. The signification of the name is the "White Lady," given by the Aztecs on account of a fancied resemblance in its outline to the figure of a reclining female. The mountain of Malinche, opposite to the volcanoes, almost rivals them in majestic appearance. It rises from a base of thirty miles in breadth, to a height of about thirteen thousand feet. I gazed long upon its cloudy top and wooded waist, which the sun belted with a beam of gold, for on its opposite side, on the banks of a river which we crossed just before reaching Puebla, stands the ancient city of Tlascala. The name of the volcano, Malinche, is an Aztec corruption of Mariana, the Indian wife of Cortez. I could not look upon it without an ardent desire to stand on its sides, and with Bernal Diaz in hand, trace out the extent of the territory once possessed by his brave and magnanimous allies.

On the other hand, between me and the sunset, stood a still more interesting memorial of the Aztec power. There, in full view, its giant terraces clearly defined against the sky, the topmost one crowned with cypress, loomed the Pyramid of Cholula! The lines of this immense work are for the most part distinctly cut; on the eastern side, only, they are slightly interrupted by vegetation, and probably the spoliation of the structure. Although several miles distant, and rising from the level of the plain, without the advantage of natural elevation, the size of the pyramid astonished me. It seems an abrupt hill, equal in height and imposing form to the long range in front of it, or the dark hill of Tlaloc behind. Even with Popocatapetl for a back-ground, its effect does not diminish. The Spaniards, with all their waste of gold on heavy cathedrals and prison-like palaces, have never equaled this relic of the barbaric empire they overthrew.

I do not know whether the resemblance between the outline of this pyramid and that of the land of Mexico, from sea to sea, has been remarked. It is certainly no forced similitude. There is the foundation terrace of the Tierra Caliente ; the steep ascent to the second broad terrace of the table-land ; and again, the succeeding ascent to the lofty, narrow plateau dividing the waters of the continent. If we grant that the forms of the pyramid, the dome, the pillar and the arch, have their antitypes in Nature, it is no fanciful speculation to suppose that the Aztecs, with that breadth of imagination common to intelligent barbarism, made *their world* the model for their temples of worship and sacrifice.

Cholula vanished in the dusk, as we crossed the river of Tlascala and entered the shallow basin in which stands Puebla. The many towers of its churches and convents showed picturesquely in the twilight. The streets were filled with gay crowds returning from the Alameda. Motley maskers, on horseback and on foot, reminded us that this was the commencement of Carnival. The great plaza into which we drove was filled with stands of fruit-venders, before each of which flared a large torch raised upon a pole. The cathedral is in better style, and shows to greater advantage than that of Mexico. So we passed to the Hotel de Diligencias, where a good dinner, in readiness, delighted us more than the carnival or the cathedral.

After the final dish of frijoles had been dispatched, I made a short night-stroll through the city. The wind was blowing strong and cold from the mountains, whistling under the arches of the cortal and flaring the red torches that burned in the market-place. The fruit-sellers, nevertheless, kept at their posts, exchanging jokes occasionally with a masked figure in some nondescript costume. I found shelter from the wind, at last, in a grand old church, near the plaza. The interior was brilliantly lighted, and the floor covered by kneeling figures. There was nothing in the church itself, except its vastness and dimness, to interest me; but the choral music I there heard was not to be described. A choir of boys, alternating with one of rich masculine voices, overran the full peal of the organ, and filled the aisle with delicious harmony. There was a single voice, which seemed to come out of the air, in the pauses of the choral, and send its clear, trumpet-tones directly to the heart. As long as the exercises continued, I stood by the door, completely chained by those divine sounds. The incense finally faded; the tapers were put out one by one; the worshippers arose, took another dip in the basin of holy water, and retired; and I, too, went back to the hotel, and tried to keep warm under cover of a single sarape.

The manufactures of Puebla are becoming important to Mexico

—the more so, from the comparative liberality which is now exercised towards foreigners. A few years ago, I was informed, a stranger was liable to be insulted, if not assaulted, in the streets ; but, latterly, this prejudice is vanishing. The table-land around the city is probably one of the finest grain countries in the world. Under a proper administration of Government, Puebla might become the first manufacturing town in Mexico.

CHAPTER XX.

RISING before three o'clock is no pleasant thing, on the high table-land of Puebla, especially when one has to face the cold from the foretop of a diligence ; but I contrived to cheat the early travel of its annoyance, by looking backward to Popocatapetl, which rose cold and unclouded in the morning twilight. We sped over fertile plains, past the foot of Malinche, and met the sunrise at the town of Amozoque, another noted robber-hold. In the arroyos which cross the road at its eastern gate a fight took place between the advanced guard of the American army and a body of Mexican soldiers, on the march to the capital.

From Amozoque the plain ascends, with a scarcely perceptible rise, to the summit of the dividing ridge, beyond Perote. The clouds, which had gathered again by this time, hid from our view the mountain barriers of the table-land, to the east and west. The second post brought us to Acajete, whose white dome and towers we saw long before reaching it, projected brightly against the pines of a steep mountain behind. One is only allowed time at the posts to stretch his legs and light a cigar. The horses—or mules, as the case may be—are always in readiness, and woe to the unlucky traveler who stands a hundred yards from the diligence when the rope is drawn away from the ramping leaders.

The insular mountain of Acajete shelters a gang of robbers among its ravines, and the road, bending to the left around its base, is hedged with ambush of the most convenient kind. The driver pointed out to me a spot in the thicket where one of the gang was shot not long before. Half-way up the acclivity, a thread of blue smoke rose through the trees, apparently from some hut or camp on a little shelf at the foot of a precipice. Further than this, we saw nothing which seemed to denote their propinquity. The pass was cleared, the horses changed at El Pinal—a large hacienda on the north side of the mountain—and we dashed on till nearly noon, when the spires of Nopaluca appeared behind a distant hill—the welcome heralds of breakfast!

Beyond this point, where a trail branches off to Orizaba, the character of the scenery is entirely changed. We saw no longer the green wheat-plains and stately haciendas of Puebla. The road passed over an immense llano, covered with short, brown grass, and swept by a furious wind. To the north, occasional peaks—barren, rocky and desolate in their appearance,—rose at a short distance from our path. On the other hand, the llano stretched away for many a league, forming a horizon to the eye before it reached the foot of the mountains. The wind frequently increased to such a pitch that all trace of the landscape was lost. Columns of dust, rising side by side from the plain, mingled as they whirled along, shrouding us as completely as a Newfoundland fog. The sun was at times totally darkened. My eyes, which were strongly blood-shotten, from too much gazing at the snows of Popocatapetl, were severely affected by this hurricane. But there is no evil without some accompanying good ; and the same wind

which nearly stifled me with dust, at last brushed away the clouds
from the smooth, gradual outline of Cofre de Perote, and revealed
the shining head of Orizaba.

Beyond La Venta de Soto, the road skirts a striking peak of
rock, whose outline is nearly that of an exact pyramid, several
thousand feet in height. The mozo called it Monte Pizarro.
From its dark ravines the robbers frequently sally, to attack travelers on the plain. At some distance from the road, I noticed
a mounted guard who followed us till relieved by another, planted
at short intervals. As the sunset came on, we reached a savage
volcanic region, where the only vegetation scattered over the ridgy
beds of black lava, was the yucca and the bristly cactus. There
were no inhabitants; some huts, here and there, stood in ruins;
and the solitary guard, moving like a shadow over the lava hills,
only added to the loneliness and increased the impression of danger. I have seen many wild and bleak spots, but none so absolutely Tartarean in its aspect. There was no softer transition of
scene to break the feeling it occasioned, for the nightfall deepened
as we advanced, leaving everything in dusky shadow, but the vast
bulk of Cofre de Perote, which loomed between me and the southern
stars. At last, lights glimmered ahead; we passed down a street
lined with miserable houses, across a narrow and dirty plaza, and
into a cramped court-yard. The worst dinner we ate on the
whole journey was being prepared in the most cheerless of rooms.
This was Perote.

I went out to walk after dinner, but did not go far. The
squalid look of the houses, and the villanous expression of the
faces, seen by the light of a few starving lamps, offered nothing
attractive, and the wind by this time was more piercing than ever.
Perote bears a bad reputation in every respect: its situation is

the bleakest in Mexico, and its people the most shameless in their depredations. The diligence is frequently robbed at the very gates of the town. We slept with another blanket on our beds, and found the addition of our sarapes still desirable. The mozo awoke us at half-past two, to coffee and chocolate in the cold. I climbed into the pescante and drew the canvas cover of the top around my shoulders. The driver—an American, who had been twenty years on the road—gave the word of starting, and let his eight mules have full rein. Five lancers accompanied us—two some distance in advance, one on each side and one bringing up the rear. The stars shone with a frosty lustre, looking larger and brighter in the thin air. We journeyed for two hours in a half darkness, which nevertheless permitted me to see that the country was worth little notice by daylight—a bleak region, ten thousand feet above the sea, and very sparsely inhabited.

About sunrise we reached the summit of the pass, and commenced descending through scattering pine woods. The declivity was at first gradual, but when we had passed the bevelled slope of the summit ridge, our road lay along the very brink of the mountains overlooking everything that lay between them and the Gulf of Mexico. Immediately north of the pass, the mountain chain turns eastward, running towards the Gulf in parallel ridges, on the summits of which we looked down. The beds of the valleys, wild, broken, and buried in a wilderness but little visited, were lost in the dense air, which filled them like a vapor. Beginning at the region of lava and stunted pine, the eye travels downward, from summit to summit of the ranges, catching, at intervals, glimpses of gardens, green fields of grain, orange orchards, groves of palm and gleaming towers, till at last it rests on the far-away glimmer of the sea, under the morning sun. Fancy yourself riding along the ramparts of a fortress ten thousand feet in height, with all the climates of the earth spread out below you, zone lying beyond zone, and the whole bounded at the furthest horizon to which vision can reach, by the illimitable sea! Such is the view which meets one on descending to Jalapa.

The road was broad and smooth, and our mules whirled us downward on a rapid gallop. In half an hour from the time when around us the hoar-frost was lying on black ridges of lava and whitening the tips of the pine branches, we saw the orange and banana, basking in the glow of a region where frost was unknown. We were now on the borders of paradise. The streams, leaping down crystal-clear from the snows of Cofre de Perote, fretted their way through tangles of roses and blossoming vines; the turf had a sheen like that of a new-cut emerald; the mould, upturned for garden land, showed a velvety richness and softness, and the palm, that true child of light, lifted its slender shaft and spread its majestic leaves against the serene blue of heaven. As we came out of the deep-sunken valleys on the brow of a ridge facing the south, there stood, distinct and shadowless from base to apex, the Mountain of Orizaba. It rose beyond mountains so far off that all trace of chasm or ledge or belting forest was folded in a veil of blue air, yet its grand, immaculate cone, of perfect outline, was so white, so dazzling, so pure in its frozen clearness, like that of an Arctic morn, that the eye lost its sense of the airy gulf between, and it seemed that I might stretch out my hand and touch it. No peak among mountains can be more sublime than Orizaba. Rising from the level of the sea and the perpetual summer of the tropics, with an unbroken line to the height of eighteen thousand feet, it stands singly above the other ranges with its spotless crown of snow, as some giant, white-haired

Northern king might stand among a host of the weak, effeminate
sybarites of the South. Orizaba dwells alone in my memory, as
the only perfect type of a mountain to be found on the Earth.
After two leagues of this enchanting travel we came to Jalapa,
a city of about twenty thousand inhabitants, on the slope of the
hills, half-way between the sea and the table-land, overlooking the
one and dominated by the other. The streets are as clean as a
Dutch cottage; the one-story, tiled houses, sparkling in the sun,
are buried in gardens that rival the Hesperides. Two miles before
reaching the town the odor of its orange blossoms filled the air.
We descended its streets to the Diligence Hotel, at the bottom,
where, on arriving, we found there would be no stage to Vera
Cruz for two days, so we gave ourselves up to the full enjoyment
of the spot. My fellow-passenger for Guanajuato, Don Antonio
de Campos, and myself, climbed into the tower of the hotel, and
sat down under its roof to enjoy the look-out. The whole landscape was like a garden. For leagues around the town it was one
constant alternation of field, grove and garden—the fields of the
freshest green, the groves white with blossoms and ringing with the
songs of birds, and the gardens loading the air with delicious perfume. Stately haciendas were perched on the vernal slopes, and
in the fields; on the roads and winding mule-paths of the hills we
saw everywhere a gay and light-hearted people. We passed the
whole afternoon in the tower; the time went by like a single pulsation of delight. I felt, then, that there could be no greater happiness than in thus living forever, without a single thought beyond
the enjoyment of the scene. My friend, Don Antonio, was busy
with old memories. Twenty years before, he came through Jalapa
for the first time, an ardent, aspiring youth, thinking to achieve
his fortune in three or four years and return with it to his native

Portugal; but alas! twenty years had barely sufficed for the fulfilment of his dreams—twenty years of toil among the barren
mountains of Guanajuato. Now, he said, all that time vanished
from his mind; his boyish glimpse of Jalapa was his Yesterday,
and the half-forgotten life of his early home lay close behind it.

After dinner, all our fellow-travelers set out for the Alameda,
which lies in a little valley at the foot of the town. A broad
paved walk, with benches of stone at the side and stone urns on
lofty pedestals at short intervals, leads to a bridge over a deep
chasm, where the little river plunges through a mesh of vines into
a large basin below. Beyond this bridge, a dozen foot-paths lead
off to the groves and shaded glens, the haciendas and orange
orchards. The idlers of the town strolled back and forth, enjoying
the long twilight and balmy air. We were all in the most joyous
mood, and my fellow-passengers of three or four different nations
expressed their delight in as many tongues, with an amusing
contrast of exclamations: " *Ah, que joli petit pays de Jalape !*"
cried the little Frenchwoman, who had talked in a steady stream
since leaving Mexico, notwithstanding she was going to France on
account of delicate lungs. " *Siente usté el aroma de las naran-
jas ?*" asked a dark-eyed Andalusian. " *Himmlische Luft !*"
exclaimed the enraptured German, unconsciously quoting Götz
von Berlichingen. Don Antonio turned to me, saying in
English: "My pulse is quicker and my blood warmer than for
twenty years; I believe my youth is actually coming back again."
We talked thus till the stars came out and the perfumed air was cool
with invisible dew.

When we awoke the next morning it was raining, and continued
to rain all day—not a slow, dreary drizzle, nor a torrent of heavy
drops, as rain comes to us, but a fine, ethereal, gauzy veil of mois-

ture that scarcely stirred the grass on which it fell or shook the
light golden pollen from the orange flowers. Every two or three
days such a shower comes down on the soil of Jalapa—

> " a perpetual April to the ground,
> Making it all one emerald."

We could not stroll among the gardens or sit under the urns of
the Alameda, but the towers and balconies were left us ; the landscape, though faint and blurred by the filmy rain, was nearly as
beautiful, and the perfume could not be washed out of the air.
So passed the day, and with the night we betook ourselves early
to rest, for the Diligence was to leave at three o'clock on the
morrow.

For two leagues after leaving Jalapa I smelt the orange blossoms in the starry morning, but when daylight glimmered on the
distant Gulf, we were riding between bleak hills, covered with
chapparal, having descended to the barren heats of the tropical winter, beyond the line of the mountain-gathered showers.
The road was rough and toilsome, but our driver, an intelligent
American, knew every stone and rut in the dark and managed his
eight mules with an address and calculation which seemed to me
marvellous. He had been on the road six years, at a salary of
$150 per month, from the savings of which he had purchased a
handsome little property in Jalapa. Don Juan, as the natives
called him, was a great favorite along the road, which his sturdy,
upright character well deserved. At sunrise we reached the
hacienda of El Encero, belonging to Santa Anna, as do most of
the other haciendas between Jalapa and Vera Cruz. The hill of
Cerro Gordo appeared before us, and a drive of an hour brought
us to the cluster of cane-huts bearing the same name.

The physical features of the field of Cerro Gordo are very interesting.   It is a double peak, rising from the midst of rough,
rolling hills, covered with a dense thicket of cactus and thorny
shrubs.   Towards Vera Cruz it is protected by deep barrancas
and passes, which in proper hands might be made impregnable.
Had Gen. Scott attempted to take it by advancing up the broad
highway, he must inevitably have lost the battle ; but by cutting
a road through the chapparal with great labor, making a circuit of
several miles, he reached the north-eastern slope of the hill—the
most accessible point, and according to the Mexican story, the side
least defended.   Having gained one of the peaks of the hill, the
charge was made down the side and up the opposite steep in the
face of the Mexican batteries.   The steady march of our forces
under this deadly hail, to the inspiriting blast of the Northern
bugles, has been described to me by officers who took part in the
fight, as the most magnificent spectacle of the war.   After taking
the battery, the guns were turned upon the Mexicans, who were
flying through the chapparal in all directions.   Many, overcome
by terror, leaped from the brink of the barranca at the foot of the
hill and were crushed to death in the fall.   Santa Anna, who
escaped at this place, was taken down by a path known to some
of the officers.   The chapparal is still strewn thickly with bleached
bones, principally of the mules and horses who were attached to
the ammunition wagons of the enemy.   The driver told me that
until recently there were plenty of cannon-balls lying beside the
road, but that every American, English or French traveler took
one as a relic, till there were no more to be seen.   A shallow
cave beside the road was pointed out as the spot where the Mexicans hid their ammunition.   It was not discovered by our troops,
but a Mexican who knew the secret, sold it to them out of re-

venge for the non-payment of some mules which he had furnished to his own army. The driver lay hidden in Jalapa for some days previous to the battle, unable to escape, and the first intelligence he received of what had taken place, was that furnished by the sight of the flying Mexicans. They poured through the town that evening and the day following, he said, in the wildest disorder, some mounted on donkeys, some on mules, some on foot, many of the officers without hats or swords, others wrapped in the dusty coat of a private, and all cursing, gesticulating and actually weeping, like men crazed. They had been so confident of success that the reverse seemed almost heart-breaking.

A few miles beyond Cerro Gordo we reached Plan del Rio, a small village of cane huts, which was burned down by order of Santa Anna, on the approach of the American forces. A splendid stone bridge across the river was afterwards blown up by the guerillas, in the foolish idea that they would stop an American specie-train, coming from Vera Cruz. In half a day after the train arrived there was an excellent road across the chasm, and the Mexicans use it to this day, for the shattered arch has never been rebuilt. From Plan del Rio to the Puente Nacional is about three leagues, through the same waste of cactus and chapparal. The latter place, the scene of many a brush with the guerillas during the war, is in a very wild and picturesque glen, through which the river forces its way to the sea. The bridge is one of the most magnificent structures of the kind on the continent. On a little knoll, at the end towards Jalapa, stands a stately hacienda belonging to Santa Anna.

We sped on through the dreary chapparal, now sprinkled with palms and blossoming trees. The country is naturally rich and productive, but is little better than a desert. The only inhabitants are a set of half-naked Indians, who live in miserable huts, supporting themselves by a scanty cultivation of maize, and the deer they kill in the thickets. Just before we reached the sea-shore, one of these people came out of the woods, with a little spotted fawn in his arms, which he offered to sell. The driver bought it for a dollar, and the beautiful little creature, not more than two weeks old, was given to me to carry. I shielded it from the cold sea-wind, and with a contented bleat it nestled down in my lap and soon fell fast asleep.

At sunset we drove out on the broad sands bordering the Gulf. A chill norther was blowing, and the waves thundered over the coral reefs with a wintry sound. Vera Cruz sat on the bleak shore, a league before us, her domes and spires painted on the gloomy sky. The white walls of San Juan d'Ulloa rose from the water beyond the shipping. Not a tree or green thing was to be seen for miles around the city, which looked as completely desolate as if built in the middle of Zahara. Nevertheless, I blessed the sight of it, and felt a degree of joy as I passed within its gates, for the long journey of twelve hundred miles across the Continent was safely accomplished

CHAPTER XXI.

I CANNOT say much of Vera Cruz. A town built and sustained by commerce alone, and that not the most flourishing, presents few points of interest to the traveler. Its physiognomy differs but little from that of the other Mexican cities I have described. There is the Plaza, flanked by the Cathedral,—the same pink mass of old Spanish architecture, picturesque only for its associations—the Diligence Hotel, with its arched corridor forming a *cortal* along one side—the dreary, half-deserted streets, with their occasional palaces of stone enclosing paved and fountained court-yards—the market, heaped with the same pyramids of fruit which have become so familiar to us—the dirty adobe huts, nearest the walls, with their cut-throat population—and finally, the population itself, rendered more active, intelligent and civilized by the presence of a large number of foreigners, but still comprised mainly of the half-breed, with the same habits and propensities as we find in the interior. The town is contracted ; standing in the plaza, one can see its four corners, bounded by the walls and the sea, and all within a few minutes' walk. Outside of the gates we come at once upon the deserts of sand.

On reaching Vera Cruz, there were no tidings of the steamer, which was due on the 4th. The U. S. schooner Flirt, Capt. Farren, was in port waiting for a norther to go down, to sail for New Orleans, but there was small chance of passage on board of her. On the morning of the 15th, the U. S. steamer Water-witch, Capt. Totten, made her appearance, bound homeward after a cruise to Havana, Sisal, Campeachy and Laguna. I had almost determined, in default of any other opportunity, to take passage in her, as a " distressed citizen," when, on rowing out to the Castle of San Juan d'Ulloa on the third morning, one of the boat-men descried a faint thread of smoke on the horizon. " *El vapor !*" was the general exclamation, and at least fifty dissatisfied persons recovered their good-humor.

My friend Don Antonio was acquainted with the Commandante of the Castle, Don Manuel Robles, by which means we obtained free admission within its coral walls. It is a place of immense strength, and in the hands of men who know how to defend it, need no more be taken than Gibraltar. We climbed to the top of the tower, walked around the parapets, shouted into the echoing wells sunk deep in the rock, and examined its gigantic walls. The spongy coral of which it is built receives the shot and shells that have been thrown upon it, without splintering ; here and there we noticed holes where they had imbedded themselves in it, rather adding to its solidity. We sat two or three hours in the tower, watching the approaching smoke of the steamer. As the chimes rang noon in Vera Cruz, a terrific blast of trumpets pealed through the courtyard of the Castle, below us. The yellow-faced soldiers, in their white shirts and straw hats with the word " Ulua" upon them, mustered along one side, and after a brief drill, had their dinner of rice, frijoles and coffee served to them. The force in

the Castle appeared very small ; the men were buried in its immense vaults and galleries, and at times, looking down from the
tower, scarcely a soul was to be seen. The Commandante invited
us to his quarters, and offered us refreshments, after we had made
the round of the parapets. Singularly enough, his room was hung
with American engravings of the battles of the late war

The most interesting object in Vera Cruz is an old church, in
the southern part of the city, which was built by Cortez, in 1531
—the oldest Christian church in the New World. Some miles
distant is the old town of Vera Cruz, which was abandoned for the
present site. I had not time to visit it, nor the traces of the
Americans among the sand-hills encircling the city. One Sunday
evening, however, I visited the *paseo*, a paved walk outside the
gate, with walls to keep off the sand and some miserable attempts
at trees here and there. As it was Carnival, the place was
crowded, but most of the promenaders appeared to be foreigners.
Beyond the paseo, however, stood a cluster of half-ruined buildings,
where the lower class of the native population was gathered at a
fandango. After the arrival of the steamer nothing was talked of
but our departure and nothing done but to pack trunks and contrive
ways of smuggling money, in order to avoid the export duty of six
per cent.

We left Vera Cruz on the morning of February 19th, and reached
Tampico Bar after a run of twenty-two hours. The surf was so
high after the recent norther, that we were obliged to wait three
days before the little river-steamer could come to us with her million of dollars. The Thames, however, was so spacious and pleasant a ship, that we were hardly annoyed by the delay. Coming
from semi-civilized Mexico, the sight of English order and the en-

joyment of English comfort were doubly agreeable. Among our passengers were Lady Emeline Stuart Wortley, returning from a heroic trip to Mexico ; Lord Mark Kerr, a gentleman of intelligence and refinement, and an amateur artist of much talent; and Mr. Hill, an English traveler, on his way home after three years spent in Russia, Siberia, Polynesia, and the interior of South America. My eight days spent on board the Thames, passed away rapidly, and on the afternoon of the 26th, we made the light-house on Mobile Point, and came-to among the shipping at the anchorage. I transferred myself and sarape to the deck of a high-pressure freight-boat, and after lying all night in the bay, on account of a heavy fog, set foot next morning on the wharf at Mobile.

Leaving the same afternoon, I passed two days on the beautiful Alabama River ; was whirled in the cars from Montgomery to Opelika, and jolted twenty-four hours in a shabby stage, over the hills of Georgia, to the station of Griffin, on the Central Railroad ; sped away through Atlanta and Augusta to Charleston ; tossed a night on the Atlantic, crossed the pine-barrens of Carolina and the impoverished fields of the Old Dominion ; halted a day at Washington to deliver dispatches from Mexico, a day at HOME, in Pennsylvania, and finally reached my old working-desk in the Tribune Office on the night of March 10th—just eight months and eight days from the time of my departure.

Thus closed a journey more novel and adventurous than any I hope to make again. I trust the profit of it has not been wholly mine, but that the reader who has followed me through the foregoing pages, may find some things in them, which to have read were not also to have forgotten.

APPENDIX.

APPENDIX.

‒‒‒‒‒‒‒‒‒‒‒‒‒‒‒‒

REPORT OF HON. T. BUTLER KING.

WASHINGTON, March 22, 1850.

SIR : In obedience to your instructions, dated the 3d of April last, I proceeded to California by way of the Isthmus of Panama, and arrived at San Francisco on the 4th day of June.

The steamer in which I took passage was the first conveyance that reached California with intelligence of the inauguration of President Taylor and the appointment of his Cabinet, and that Congress had failed to aid the Executive in providing a government for the people of that Territory. The greatest anxiety was naturally felt and manifested to ascertain the cause of this neglect on the part of the Government of the United States, and what steps duty to themselves required them to take, in the painful and embarrassing position in which they were placed, for their protection and welfare.

A brief sketch of their condition will explain the cause of this anxiety.

The discovery of the gold mines had attracted a very large number of citizens of the United States to that Territory, who had never been ac customed to any other than American law, administered by American courts. There they found their rights of property and person subject to the uncertain, and frequently most oppressive, operation of laws written in a language they did not understand, and founded on principles, in many respects, new to them. They complained that the alcaldes, or judges, most of whom had been appointed or elected before the immigration had commenced, were not lawyers by education or profession ; and, being Americans, they were, of course, unacquainted with the laws of Mexico, or the principles of the civil law on which they are founded.

As our own laws, except for the collection of Revenue, the transmission of the mails, and establishment of post offices, had not been extended over that Territory, the laws of Mexico, as they existed at the conclusion of the treaty of Guadalupe Hidalgo, regulating the relations of the inhabitants of California with each other, necessarily remained in force ;* yet, there was not a single volume containing those laws, as far as I know or believe, in the whole Territory, except, perhaps, in the Governor's office, at Monterey.

The magistrates, therefore, could not procure them, and the administration of justice was, necessarily, as unequal and fluctuating as the opinions of the judges were conflicting and variable.

There were no fee bills to regulate costs, and, consequently, the most cruel exactions, in many instances, were practised.

The greatest confusion prevailed respecting titles to property, and the decision of suits, involving the most important rights, and very large sums of money depended upon the dictum of the judge.

The sale of the Territory by Mexico to the United States had necessarily cut off or dissolved the laws regulating the granting or procuring titles to land ; and, as our own land laws had not been extended over it, the people were compelled to receive such titles as were offered to them, without the means of ascertaining whether they were valid or not.

Litigation was so expensive and precarious, that injustice and oppression were frequently endured, rather than resort to so uncertain a remedy.

Towns and cities were springing into existence—many of them without charters or any legal right to organize municipal authorities, or to tax property or the citizens for the establishment of a police, the erection of prisons, or providing any of those means for the protection of life and property which are so necessary in all civil communities, and especially among a people mostly strangers to each other.

* See American Insurance Company et al. *vs.* Canter. 1st Peters's Supreme Court Reports, 542.

Nearly one million and a half of dollars had been paid into the Custom Houses, as duties on imported goods, before our revenue laws had been extended over the country ; and the people complained bitterly that they were thus heavily taxed without being provided with a Government for their protection, or laws which they could understand, or allowed the right to be represented in the councils of the nation.

While anxiously waiting the action of Congress, oppressed and embarrassed by this state of affairs and feeling the pressing necessity of applying such remedies as were in their power and circumstances seemed to justify, they resolved to substitute laws of their own for the existing system, and to establish tribunals for their proper and faithful administration.

In obedience, therefore, to the extraordinary exigencies of their condition, the people of the city of San Francisco elected members to form a legislature, and clothed them with full powers to pass laws.

The communities of Sonoma and of Sacramento City followed the example.

Thus were three legislative bodies organized ; the two most distant being only one hundred and thirty miles apart.

Other movements of the kind were threatened, and doubtless would have been followed in other sections of the Territory, had they not been arrested by the formation of a State Government.

While the people of California were looking to Congress for a Territorial Government, it was quite evident that such an organization was daily becoming less suited to their condition, which was entirely different from that of any of the Territories out of which the new States of the Union had been formed.

Those Territories had been at first slowly and sparsely peopled by a few hunters and farmers, who penetrated the wilderness, or traversed the prairies in search of game or a new home ; and, when thus gradually their population warranted it, a government was provided for them. They, however, had no foreign commerce, nor anything beyond the ordinary pursuits of agriculture and the various branches of business which usually accompany it, to induce immigration within their borders. Several years were required to give them sufficient population and wealth to place them in a condition to require, or enable them to support, a State Government.

Not so with California. The discovery of the vast metallic and mineral wealth in her mountains had already attracted to her, in the space of twelve months, more than one hundred thousand people; an extensive commerce had sprung up with China, the ports of Mexico on the Pacific, Chili, and Australia.

Hundreds of vessels from the Atlantic ports of the Union, freighted with our manufactures and agricultural products, and filled with our fellow citizens, had arrived, or were on their passage round Cape Horn; so that in the month of June last there were more than three hundred sea-going vessels in the port of San Francisco.

California has a border on the Pacific of ten degrees of latitude, and several important harbors which have never been surveyed; nor is there a buoy, a beacon, a light-house, or a fortification, on the whole coast.

There are no docks for the repair of national or mercantile vessels nearer than New York, a distance of some twenty thousand miles round Cape Horn.

All these things, together with the proper regulations of the gold region, the quicksilver mines, the survey and disposition of the public lands, the adjustment of land titles, the establishment of a mint and of marine hospitals, required the immediate formation of a more perfect Civil Government than California then had, and the fostering care of Congress and the Executive.

California had, as it were by magic, become a State of great wealth and power. One short year had given her a commercial importance but little inferior to that of the most powerful of the old States. She had passed her minority at a single bound, and might justly be regarded as fully entitled to take her place as an equal among her sisters of the Union.

When, therefore, the reality became known to the people of that Territory that the government had done nothing to relieve them from the evils and embarrassments under which they were suffering, and seeing no probability of any change on the subject which divided Congress, they adopted, with most unexampled unanimity and promptitude, the only course which lay open to them—the immediate formation of a State Government.

They were induced to take this step not only for the reason that it promised the most speedy remedy for present difficulties, but because the great and rapidly growing interests of the Territory demanded it ; and all reflecting men saw, at a glance, that it ought not to be any longer, and could not under any circumstances, be much longer postponed.

They not only considered themselves best qualified, but that they had the right to decide, as far as they were concerned, the embarrassing question which was shaking the Union to its centre, and had thus far deprived them of a regularly organized civil government. They believed that, in forming a constitution they had a right to establish or prohibit slavery, and that in their action as a State, they would be sustained by the North and the South.

They were not unmindful of the fact, that while Northern statesmen had contended that Congress has power to prohibit slavery in the Territories they had always admitted that the States of the Union had the right to abolish or establish it at pleasure.

On the other hand, Southern statesmen had almost unanimously contended that Congress has not the constitutional power to *prohibit* slavery in the Territories, because they have not the power to *establish* it ; but that the people, in forming a government for themselves, have the right to do either. If Congress can rightfully do one, they can certainly do the other.

This is the doctrine put forth by Mr. Calhoun in his celebrated resolutions of 1847, introduced into the Senate of the United States, among which is the following :

" *Resolved*, That it is a fundamental principle in our political creed, that a people in forming a constitution have the unconditional right to form and adopt the government which they may think best calculated to secure their liberty, prosperity and happiness ; and, in conformity thereto, no other condition is imposed by the Federal Constitution on a State, in order to be admitted into this Union, except that its constitution shall be ' Republican ;' and that the imposition of any other by Congress would not only be in violation of the Constitution, but in direct conflict with the principle on which our political system rests."

President Polk, in his annual message, dated 5th December, 1848, uses the following language:

" The question is believed to be rather abstract than practical, whether slavery ever can or would exist in any portion of the acquired territory, even if it were left to the option of the slaveholding States themselves. From the nature of the climate and productions, in much the larger portion of it, it is certain it could never exist; and in the remainder the probabilities are that it would not.

" But, however this may be, the question, involving, as it does, a principle of equality of rights of the separate and several States, as equal copartners in the confederacy, should not be disregarded.

" In organizing governments over these Territories, no duty imposed on Congress by the Constitution requires that they should legislate on the subject of slavery, while their power to do so is not only seriously questioned, but denied, by many of the soundest expounders of that instrument.

" Whether Congress shall legislate or not, the people of the acquired Territories, when assembled in Convention to form State Constitutions, will possess the sole and exclusive power to determine for themselves whether slavery shall or shall not exist within their limits."

The people of California, therefore, acting in conformity with the views thus expressed, and what seemed to be the generally admitted opinion in the States, had every reason to suppose, and did suppose, that by forming a Constitution for themselves, and deciding this question in accordance with their own views and interests, they would be received with open arms by all parties.

In taking this step they proceeded with all the regularity which has ever characterized the American people in discharging the great and important duties of self-government.

As already stated, I arrived at San Francisco on the morning of the 4th of June.

The steamer in which I was a passenger did not stop at Monterey; I therefore did not see General Riley, nor had I any communication with him until about the middle of the month, when he came to San Francisco. A few days after my arrival his proclamation calling a Convention to form a State Constitution, *dated the third of June*, was received.

The people acted in compliance with what they believed to be the views of Congress, and conformably to the recommendations of the proclamation, and proceeded, on the day appointed, to elect members to a Convention for the purpose of forming a constitution, to be regularly submitted to the people for their ratification or rejection, and, if approved, to be presented to Congress, with a prayer for the admission of California, as a State, into the Union.

I desire here to make a brief and emphatic reply to the various unjust and most extraordinary accusations and insinuations which have been made respecting the movements of the people of California in forming their State Government.

I had no secret instructions, verbal or written, from the President, or any one else, what to say to the people of California on the subject of slavery; nor was it ever hinted or intimated to me that I was expected to attempt to influence their action in the slightest degree on that subject. That I never did, the people of California will bear me witness. In that Territory there was none of the machinery of party or of the press; and it is even more absurd to suppose that any *secret influences*, for or against slavery, could have been used there, than it would to believe that they could be successfully employed in Maryland or Georgia.

I therefore declare all assertions and insinuations, that I was secretly instructed to, or that I did in any way, attempt to influence the people of California to exclude slavery from their Territory, to be without foundation.

The election of delegates to the Convention proceeded regularly in pursuance of the proposed mode of holding it, and as far as I am informed, no questions were asked whether a candidate was a Whig or a Democrat, or whether he was from the North or the South. The only object seemed to be, to find competent men who were willing to make the sacrifice of time which a proper discharge of their duties would require.

As soon after my arrival at San Francisco as the arrangements of General Smith would permit, I proceeded with him to the interior of the country for the purpose of examining the gold region, and other interesting and important portions of it. I did not return until the 16th of August. The elections had taken place when I was in the mountains. I was taken ill on the 20th of that month, and was confined to my bed and room more than two months.

The Convention met on the 1st of September. So it will be seen that I was not present where any election was held, nor had I anything to do with selecting or bringing out candidates; and my illness is sufficient proof that I did not, and could not, had I been disposed, exercise any influence in the Convention, which was sitting one hundred and thirty miles from where I was.

Some intimations or assertions, as I am informed, have been thrown out that the South was not fairly represented in the Convention. I am told by two of the members of Congress elect from California, who were members of the Convention, that of the thirty-seven delegates designated in General Riley's proclamation, sixteen were from slaveholding, ten from the non-slaveholding States, and eleven who were citizens of California under the Mexican government, and that ten of those eleven came from districts below 36° 30'. So that there were in the Convention twenty-six of the thirty-seven members from the slaveholding States and from places south of the Missouri Compromise line.

It appears, on the journals of the Convention, that the clause in the constitution excluding slavery passed unanimously.

I now proceed to give the result of my inquiries, observations and reflections respecting the population, climate, soil, productions—the general character of grants of land from Mexico—the extent and condition of the public domain—the commercial resources and prospects—the mineral and metallic wealth of California.

POPULATION.

Humboldt, in his Essay on New Spain, states the population of Upper California, in 1802, to have consisted of—

Converted Indians..15,562
Other Classes........ 1,300
                                                                     ———
      Total..16,862

Alexander Forbes, in his history of Upper and Lower California, published in London
in 1839, states the number of converted Indians in the former to have been,

In 1831...18,683
  Of all other Classes, at... 4,342

      Total.. 23,025

He expresses the opinion that the number had not varied much up to
1835, and the probability is, there was very little increase in the white
population until the emigrants from the United States began to enter the
country in 1838.

They increased, from year to year, so that, in 1846, Col. Fremont had
little difficulty in calling to his standard some five hundred fighting men.

At the close of the war with Mexico it was supposed that there were,
including discharged volunteers, from ten to fifteen thousand Americans
and Californians, exclusive of converted Indians, in the Territory. The
immigration of American citizens in 1849, up to the 1st January last, was
estimated at eighty thousand—of foreigners, twenty thousand.

The population of California may therefore be safely set down at
115,000 at the commencement of the present year.

It is quite impossible to form anything like an accurate estimate of the
number of Indians in the Territory. Since the commencement of the
war, and especially since the discovery of gold in the mountains, their
numbers at the missions and in the valleys near the coast have very much
diminished. In fact the whole race seems to be rapidly disappearing.

The remains of a vast number of villages in all the valleys of the Sierra
Nevada, and among the foot-hills of that range of mountains, show that
at no distant day there must have been a numerous population where
there is not now an Indian to be seen. There are a few still retained in
the service of the old Californians, but these do not amount to more than
a few thousand in the whole Territory. It is said there are large numbers of them in the mountains and valleys about the head waters of the
San Joaquin, along the western base of the Sierra, and in the northern
part of the Territory, and that they are hostile. A number of Americans were killed by them during the last summer in attempting to pene-
trate high up the rivers in search of gold; they also drove one or two
parties from Trinity River. They have in several instances attacked

parties coming from or returning to Oregon, in the section of country which the lamented Captain Warner was examining when he was killed.

It is quite impossible to form any estimate of the number of these mountain Indians. Some suppose there are as many as 300,000 in the Territory, but I should not be inclined to believe that there can be one third of that number. It is quite evident that they are hostile, and that they ought to be chastised for the murders already committed.

The small bands with whom I met, scattered through the lower portions of the foot-hills of the Sierra, and the valleys between them and the coast, seemed to be almost of the lowest grade of human beings. They live chiefly on acorns, roots, insects, and the kernel of the pine burr—occasionally they catch fish and game. They use the bow and arrow, but are said to be too lazy and effeminate to make successful hunters. They do not appear to have the slightest inclination to cultivate the soil, nor do they even attempt it—as far as I could obtain information—except when they are induced to enter the service of the white inhabitants. They have never pretended to hold any interest in the soil, nor have they been treated by the Spanish or American immigrants as possessing any.

The Mexican government never treated with them for the purchase of land, or the relinquishment of any claim of it whatever. They are lazy, idle to the last degree, and, although they are said to be willing to give their services to any one who will provide them with blankets, beef and bread, it is with much difficulty they can be made to perform labor enough to reward their employers for these very limited means of comfort.

Formerly, at the missions, those who were brought up and instructed by the priests, made very good servants. Many of those now attached to families seem to be faithful and intelligent. But those who are at all in a wild and uncultivated state are most degraded objects of filth and idleness.

It is possible that government might, by collecting them together, teach them, in some degree, the arts and habits of civilization; but, if we may judge of the future from the past, they will disappear from the face of the earth as the settlements of the whites extend over the country. A very considerable military force will be necessary, however, to protect the emigrants in the northern and southern portions of the Territory

CLIMATE.

I now come to consider the climate. The climate of California is so remarkable in its periodical changes, and for the long continuance of the wet and dry seasons, dividing, as they do, the year into about two equal parts, which have a most peculiar influence on the labor applied to agriculture and the products of the soil, and, in fact, connect themselves so inseparably with all the interests of the country, that I deem it proper briefly to mention the causes which produce these changes, and which, it will be seen, as this report proceeds, must exercise a controlling influence on the commercial prosperity and resources of the country.

It is a well-established theory, that the currents of air under which the earth passes in its diurnal revolutions follow the line of the sun's greatest attraction. These currents of air are drawn toward this line from great distances on each side of it; and as the earth revolves from west to east, they blow from northeast and southeast, meeting, and of course causing a calm, on the line.

Thus, when the sun is directly, in common parlance, over the equator, in the month of March, these currents of air blow from some distance north of the tropic of Cancer, and south of the tropic of Capricorn, in an oblique direction toward this line of the sun's greatest attraction, and forming what are known as the northeast and southeast trade winds.

As the earth, in its path round the sun, gradually brings the *line* of attraction north, in summer these currents of air are carried *with* it; so that about the middle of May the current from the northeast has extended as far as the 38th or 39th degree of north latitude, and by the 20th of June, the period of the sun's greatest northern inclination, to the northern portions of California and the southern section of Oregon.

These northeast winds, in their progress across the continent, toward the Pacific Ocean, pass over the snow-capped ridges of the Rocky Mountains and the Sierra Nevada, and are of course deprived of all the moisture which can be extracted from them by the low temperature of those regions of eternal snow, and consequently no moisture can be precipitated from them, in the form of dew or rain, in a higher temperature than that to which they have been subjected. They therefore pass over the hills and plains of California, where the temperature is very high in summer, in a very dry state; and so far from being charged with moisture, they absorb, like a sponge, all that the atmosphere and surface of the earth can yield, until both become, apparently, perfectly dry.

This process commences, as I have said, when the line of the sun's greatest attraction comes north in summer, bringing with it these vast atmospheric movements, and on their approach produce the dry season in California, which, governed by these laws, continues until some time after the sun repasses the equator in September, when, about the middle of November, the climate being relieved from these northeast currents of air, the southwest winds set in from the ocean, charged with moisture—the rains commence and continue to fall not constantly, as some persons have represented, but with sufficient frequency to designate the period of their continuance, from about the middle of November until the middle of May, in the latitude of San Francisco, as the wet season.

It follows as a matter of course, that the *dry season* commences first, and continues longest in the southern portions of the Territory, and that the climate of the northern part is influenced in a much less degree, by the causes which I have mentioned, than any other section of the country. Consequently, we find that as low down as latitude 39°, rains are sufficiently frequent in summer to render irrigation quite unnecessary to the perfect maturity of any crop which is suited to the soil and climate.

There is an extensive ocean current of cold water, which comes from the northern regions of the Pacific, or, perhaps from the Arctic, and flows along the coast of California. It comes charged with, and emits in its progress, air, which appears in the form of fog when it comes in contact with a higher temperature on the American coast, as the Gulf stream of the Atlantic exhales vapor when it meets in any part of its progress, a lower temperature. This current has not been surveyed, and, therefore, its source, temperature, velocity, width and course have not been accurately ascertained.

It is believed by Lieutenant Maury, on what he considers sufficient evidence—and no higher authority can be cited—that the current comes from the coasts of China and Japan, flows northwardly to the peninsula of Kamtschatka, and, making a circuit to the eastward, strikes the American coast in about latitude 41° or 42°. It passes thence southwardly, and finally loses itself in the tropics.

Below latitude 39°, and west of the foot hills of the Sierra Nevada, the forests of California are limited to some scattering groves of oak in the valleys and along the borders of the streams, and of red wood on the ridges and in the gorges of the hills—sometimes extending into the plains. Some of the hills are covered with dwarf shrubs, which may be used as fuel. With these exceptions, the whole territory presents a surface without trees or shrubbery. It is covered, however, with various species of grass, and for many miles from the coast with wild oats, which, in the valleys, grow most luxuriantly. These grasses and oats mature and ripen early in the dry season, and soon cease to protect the soil from the scorching rays of the sun. As the summer advances, the moisture in the atmosphere and the earth, to a considerable depth, soon becomes exhausted ; and the radiation of heat, from the extensive naked plains and hill sides, is very great.

The cold, dry currents of air from the northeast, after passing the Rocky Mountains and the Sierra Nevada, descend to the Pacific, and absorb the moisture of the atmosphere, to a great distance from the land. The cold air from the mountains, and that which accompanies the great ocean current from the northwest, thus become united, and vast banks of fog are generated, which, when driven by the wind, has a penetrating, or *cutting* effect on the human skin, much more uncomfortable than would be felt in the humid atmosphere of the Atlantic, at a much lower temperature.

As the sun rises from day to day, week after week, and month after month, in unclouded brightness during the dry season, and pours down his unbroken rays on the dry, unprotected surface of the country, the heat becomes so much greater inland than it is on the ocean, that an under current of cold air, bringing the fog with it, rushes over the coast range of hills, and through their numerous passes, toward the interior.

Every day, as the heat, inland, attains a sufficient temperature, the cold, dry wind from the ocean commences to blow This is usually from

11 to 1 o'clock; and as the day advances the wind increases and continues to blow till late at night. When the vacuum is filled, or the equilibrium of the atmosphere restored, the wind ceases; a perfect calm prevails until about the same hour the following day, when the same process commences and progresses as before, and these phenomena are of daily occurrence, with few exceptions, throughout the dry season.

These cold winds and fogs render the climate at San Francisco, and all along the coast of California, except the extreme southern portion of it, probably more uncomfortable, to those not accustomed to it, in summer than in winter.

A few miles inland, where the heat of the sun modifies and softens the wind from the ocean, the climate is moderate and delightful. The heat in the middle of the day is not so great as to retard labor, or render exercise in the open air uncomfortable. The nights are cool and pleasant. This description of climate prevails in all the valleys along the coast range, and extends throughout the country, north and south, as far eastward as the valley of the Sacramento and San Joaquin. In this vast plain the sea breeze loses its influence, and the degree of heat in the middle of the day, during the summer months, is much greater than is known on the Atlantic coast in the same latitudes. It is dry, however, and probably not more oppressive. On the foot hills of the Sierra Nevada, and especially in the deep ravines of the streams, the thermometer frequently ranges from 110° to 115° in the shade, during three or four hours of the day, say from 11 to 3 o'clock. In the evening as the sun declines, the radiation of heat ceases. The cool dry atmosphere from the mountains spreads over the whole country, and renders the nights cool and invigorating.

I have been kindly furnished by Surgeon General Lawson, U. S. Army, with thermometrical observations, taken at the places in California, viz: At San Francisco, by Assistant Surgeon W. C. Parker, for six months embracing the last quarter of 1847, and the first quarter of 1848. The monthly mean temperature was as follows: October, 57°; November, 49°; December, 50°; January, 49°; February, 50°; March, 51°.

At Monterey, in latitude 36° 88' north, and longitude 121° west, on the coast, about one degree and a half south of San Francisco, by Assistant Surgeon W. S. King, for seven months, from May to November inclusive. The monthly mean temperature was : May, 56° ; June, 59° ; July, 62° ; August, 59° ; September, 58° ; October, 60° ; November, 56°.

At Los Angelos, latitude 34° 7', longitude west 118° 7', by Assistant Surgeon John S. Griffin, for ten months—from June, 1847, to March, 1848, inclusive. The monthly mean temperature was : June, 73° ; July, 74° ; August, 75° ; September, 75° ; October, 69° ; November, 59° ; December, 60°. This place is about forty miles from the coast.

At San Diego, latitude 32° 45', longitude west 117° 11', by Assistant Surgeon J. D. Summers, for the following three months of 1849, viz.: July, monthly mean temperature, 71° ; August, 75° ; September, 70°.

At Suttersville, on the Sacramento River, latitude 38° 32' north, longitude west 121° 34', by Assistant Surgeon R. Murray, for the following months of 1849 : July, monthly mean temperature 73° ; August, 70° ; September, 65° ; October, 65°.

These observations show a remarkably high temperature at San Francisco during the six months from October to March inclusive ; a variation of only eight degrees in the monthly mean, and a mean temperature for the six months of 51 degrees.

At Monterey we find the mean monthly temperature from May to November, inclusive, varying only six degrees, and the mean temperature of the seven months to have been 58°. If we take the three summer months, the mean heat was 60°. The mean of the three winter months was a little over 49° ; showing a mean difference, on that part of the coast, of only 11° between summer and winter.

The mean temperature of San Francisco, for the three winter months, was precisely the same as at Monterey—a little over 49°.

As these cities are only about one degree and a half distant from each other, and both situated near the ocean, the temperature at both, in summer, may very reasonably be supposed to be as nearly similar as the thermometer shows it to be in winter.

The mean temperature of July, August and September, at San Diego, only 3° 53' south of Monterey, was 72°. The mean temperature of the same months at Monterey was a little over 59°, showing a mean difference of 13°.

This would seem to indicate that the cold ocean current is thrown off from the southern part of the coast by Point Conception, and the islands south of it; and consequently its influence on the climate of San Diego is much less than at Monterey and San Francisco.

At Los Angelos, forty miles distant from the coast, the mean temperature of the three months is 74°; and of the three autumn months 67°; of the three winter months 57°.

At Suttersville, about one hundred and thirty miles from the ocean, and 4° north of Los Angelos, the mean temperature of August, September and October was 67°. The mean temperature of the same months at Monterey was 59°; showing a difference of 8° between the sea-coast and the interior, on nearly the same parallel of latitude. A much greater difference would undoubtedly appear if we had observation for the spring and summer months at Suttersville and the gold mines.

These variations in the climate of California account for the various and conflicting opinions and statements respecting it.

A stranger arriving at San Francisco in summer is annoyed by the cold winds and fogs, and pronounces the climate intolerable. A few months will modify if not banish his dislike, and he will not fail to appreciate the beneficial effects of a cool, bracing atmosphere. Those who approach California overland, through the passes of the mountains, find the heat of summer, in the middle of the day, greater than they have been accustomed to, and therefore many complain of it.

Those who take up their residence in the valleys which are situated between the great plain of the Sacramento and San Joaquin, and the coast range of hills, find the climate, especially in the dry season, as healthful and pleasant as it is possible for any climate to be which possesses sufficient heat to mature the cereal grains and edible roots of the temperate zone.

The division of the year into two distinct seasons—dry and wet—impresses those who have been accustomed to the variable climate of the Atlantic States unfavorably. The dry appearance of the country in summer and the difficulty of moving about in winter seem to impose serious difficulties in the way of agricultural prosperity, while the many and decided advantages resulting from the mildness of winter, and the bright, clear weather of summer, are not appreciated. These will appear when I come to speak of the productions of California. We ought not to be surprised at the dislike which the immigrants frequently express to the climate. It is so unlike that from which they come, that they cannot readily appreciate its advantages, or become reconciled to its extremes of dry and wet.

If a native of California were to go to New England in winter, and see the ground frozen and covered with snow, the streams with ice, and find himself in a temperature many degrees colder than he had ever felt before, he would probably be as much surprised that people could or would live in so inhospitable a region, as any immigrant ever has been at what he has seen or felt in California.

So much are our opinions influenced by early impressions, the vicissitudes of the seasons with which we are familiar, love of country, home and kindred, that we ought never to hazard a hasty opinion, when we come in contact with circumstances entirely different from those to which we have all our lives been accustomed.

SOIL.

The valleys which are situated parallel to the coast range, and those which extend eastwardly in all directions among the hills, toward the great plain of the Sacramento, are of unsurpassed fertility.

They have a deep, black, alluvial soil, which has the appearance of having been deposited when they were covered with water. The idea is strengthened by the fact that the rising grounds on the borders of these valleys, and many hills of moderate elevation have a soil precisely like that of the adjoining plains.

This soil is so porous, that it remains perfectly unbroken by gullies, notwithstanding the great quantity of water which falls in it annually during the wet season. The land in the northern part of the territory on the Trinity and other rivers, and on the borders of Clear Lake, as far as it has been examined, is said to be remarkably fertile.

The great valley of the Sacramento and San Joaquin has evidently been, at some remote period, the bed of a lake; and those rivers which drain it, present the appearance of having cut their channels through the alluvial deposit after it had been formed. In fact, it is not possible that they could have been instrumental in forming the plain through which they pass. Their head-waters come from the extreme ends of the valley, north and south ; and, were it not for the supply of water received from the streams which flow into them from the Sierra Nevada, their beds would be almost, if not quite, dry in the summer months. The soil is very rich, and, with a proper system of drainage and embankment, would, undoubtedly, be capable of producing any crop, except sugar cane, now cultivated in the Atlantic States of the Union.

There are many beautiful valleys and rich hill sides among the foot hills of the Sierra Nevada, which, when the profits of labor in mining shall be reduced, so as to cause its application to agriculture, will pro- bably support a large population. There is said to be a rich belt of well- timbered and watered country extending the whole length of the gold re- gion between it and the Sierra Nevada, some twenty miles in width. There is no information sufficiently accurate respecting the eastern slope of the great snowy range to enable us to form any opinion of its general character or soil. Some of its valleys have been visited by miners, who represent them as fully equal to any portion of the country to the west- ward of it.

The great valley of the Colorado, situated between the Sierra Madre and the Sierra Nevada, is but little known. It is inhabited by numerous tribes of savages, who manifest the most decided hostility toward the whites, and have hitherto prevented any explorations of their country, and do not permit emigrants to pass through it. Therefore parties from Santa Fe, on their way to California, are compelled to make a circuit of near a thousand miles northward to the Salt Lake, or about the same dis- tance southward by the route of the Gila. Although this valley is little known, there are indications that it is fertile and valuable.

The name of the river " Colorado" is descriptive of its waters ; they are as deeply colored as those of the Missouri or Red River, while those of the Gila, which we know flows through barren lands, are clear.

It would seem impossible for a large river to collect sediment enough in a sandy, barren soil to color its waters so deeply as to give it a name among those who first discovered and have since visited its shores. The probability, therefore, is, that this river flows through an alluvial valley of great fertility, which has never been explored. This conjecture is strengthened by the fact that the Indians who inhabit it are hostile, and oppose, as far as they can, all persons who attempt to enter or explore it. This has been their uniform course of conduct respecting all portions of the continent which have been fertile, abounding in game and the spontaneous productions of the earth.

As this valley is situated in the direct route from Santa Fe to California, its thorough exploration becomes a matter of very great importance, especially as it is highly probable that the elevated regions to the north of it, covered with snow during most of the year, will force the line of the great National Railway to the Pacific through some portion of it.

The soil I have described situated west of the Sierra Nevada, and embracing the plain of the Sacramento and San Joaquin, covers an area, as nearly as I can estimate, of between fifty and sixty thousand square miles, and would, under a proper system of cultivation, be capable of supporting a population equal to that of Ohio or New York at the present time.

PRODUCTS OF CALIFORNIA.

Previous to the treaty of peace with Mexico, and the discovery of gold, the exportable products of the country consisted almost exclusively of hides and tallow. The Californians were a pastoral people, and paid much more attention to the raising of horses and cattle than the cultivation of the soil.

Wheat, barley, maize, beans and edible roots, were cultivated in sufficient quantity for home consumption, but, as far as I am informed, not for exportation. At that time a full-grown ox, steer, or cow, was worth about two dollars. Beef cattle, delivered on the navigable waters of the bay of San Francisco, are now worth from $20 to $30 per head; horses, formerly worth from $5 to $10, are now valued at $60 to $150. The destruction of cattle for their hides and tallow has now entirely ceased, in consequence of the demand for beef. This demand will of course increase with the population; and it would seem that, in a very few years, there will be none to supply the market.

If we estimate the number of cattle, now in California, at 500,000 head, which is believed to be about the number—and the population at 120,000, for the year 1850—a low estimate—and suppose it to increase 100,000 per annum, there will be in the Territory or State, in 1854, 520,000 people.

If we adopt the estimate of those well acquainted with the demand, of half a beef, on an average, to each inhabitant, it appears there will be a consumption, in 1850, of 60,000 head; in 1851, of 110,000; in 1852, of 160,000; in 1853, of 210,000; in 1854, of 260,000. Making an aggregate of 800,000, which would absorb all the present stock, with is natural increase.

This is a very important matter, as connected with the amount of supply which that country will ultimately require from the Atlantic States of the Union. There is no other country on earth which has, or will ever possess, the means of supplying so great a demand.

It is now a well-established fact among the emigrants to California, that oxen possess greater powers of endurance than mules or horses ; that they will perform the distance with loaded wagons in less time, and come in at the end of the journey in better condition.

Cows are now driven in considerable numbers from Missouri, and the time cannot be far distant when cattle from the western States will be driven annually by tens of thousands to supply this new market.

If California increases in population as fast as the most moderate estimate would lead us to believe, it will not be five years before she will require more than 100,000 head of beef cattle per annum, from some quarter, to supply the wants of her people.

It must not be supposed that salt provisions may supply this vast demand. Those who have attempted to live on such food, during the dry season, have been attacked with scurvy and other cutaneous diseases of which many have died.

There is no climate in the world where fresh meat and vegetables are more essential to human health. In fact they are indispensable.

It must not be inferred that cattle driven across the plains and mountains, from the western States, will be fit for beef on their arrival in California. But one winter and spring on the luxuriant pastures of that country will put them in a condition which would render them acceptable in any Atlantic market.

These grazing grounds are extensive enough to support five times as many cattle as may be *annually* required; therefore, there will be no scarcity of food for them.

I am acquainted with a drover who left California in December last with the intention of bringing in ten thousand sheep from New Mexico. This shows that the flocks and herds east of the Rocky Mountains are looked to already as the source from which the markets on the Pacific are to be supplied.

The climate and soil of California are well suited to the growth of wheat, barley, rye and oats. The temperature along the coast is too cool for the successful culture of maize, as a field crop. The fact that oats, the species which is cultivated in the Atlantic States, are annually self-sowed and produced on all the plains and hills along the coast, and as far inland as the sea breeze has a marked influence on the climate, is sufficient proof that all the cereal grains may be successfully cultivated without the aid of *irrigation*.

It is quite true that *this auxiliary* was extensively employed at the missions, and undoubtedly increased the product of all crops to which it was applied, as it will in any country on earth if skilfully used. This does not prove, however, that it was *essentially necessary* to the production of an ample reward to the husbandman. The experience of all the old inhabitants is sufficient evidence of this. If their imperfect mode of culture secured satisfactory returns, it is reasonable to presume that a more perfect system would produce much greater results. There is abundant evidence to prove that, in the rich alluvial valleys, wheat and barley have produced from forty to sixty bushels from one bushel of seed, *without irrigation*.

Irish potatoes, turnips, onions, in fact all the edible roots known and cultivated in the Atlantic States, are produced in great perfection. In all the valleys east of the coast range of hills the climate is sufficiently warm to mature crops of Indian corn, rice, and probably tobacco.

The cultivation of the grape has attracted much attention at the missions, among the residents of towns, and the rural population, and been attended with much success, wherever it has been attempted. The dry

season secures the fruit from those diseases which are so common in the
Atlantic States, and it attains very great perfection.

The wine made from it is of excellent quality, very palatable, and can
be produced in any quantity. The grapes are delicious, and produced
with very little labor. When taken from the vines in bunches and suspended in a dry room, by the stems, they become partially dry, retain
their flavor, and remain several weeks, perhaps months, without decay.

Apples, pears and peaches are cultivated with facility, and there is
no reason to doubt that all the fruits of the Atlantic States can be produced in great plenty and perfection.

The grasses are very luxuriant and nutritious, affording excellent pasture. The oats, which spring up the whole length of the sea coast, and
from forty to sixty miles inland, render the cultivation of that crop entirely unnecessary, and yield a very great quantity of nutritious food
for horses, cattle, and sheep. The dry season matures, and I may say,
cures these grasses and oats, so that they remain in an excellent state
of preservation during the summer and autumn, and afford an ample supply of forage. While the whole surface of the country appears parched,
and vegetation destroyed, the numerous flocks and herds, which roam
over it, continue in excellent condition.

Although the mildness of the winter months and the fertility of the
soil secure to California very decided agricultural advantages, it is admitted that *irrigation* would be of very great importance, and necessarily
increase the products of the soil in quantity and variety, during the
greater part of the dry season. It should, therefore, be encouraged by
Government, in the survey and disposition of the public lands, as far as
practicable.

The farmer derives some very important benefits from the dry season.
His crops in harvest time are never injured by rain; he can with perfect confidence permit them to remain in his fields as long after they
have been gathered as his convenience may require; he has no fears that
they will be injured by wet or unfavorable weather. Hence it is that
many who have long been accustomed to that climate, prefer it to the
changeable weather east of the Rocky Mountains.

As already stated, the forests of California, south of latitude 39°, and west of the foot hills of the Sierra Nevada, are limited to detached, scattering groves of oak in the valleys, and of red-wood on the ridges and on the gorges of the hills.

It can be of no practical use to speculate on the causes which have denuded so large an extent of country, further than to ascertain whether the soil is or is not favorable to the growth of forest trees.

When the dry season sets in, the entire surface is covered with a luxuriant growth of grass and oats, which, as the summer advances, becomes perfectly dry. The remains of all dead trees and shrubs also become dry. These materials, therefore, are very combustible, and usually take fire in the latter part of summer and beginning of autumn, which commonly passes over the whole country, destroying in its course, the young shrubs and trees. In fact, it seems to be the same process which has destroyed or prevented the growth of forest trees on the prairies of the western States, and not any quality in the soil unfriendly to their growth.

The absence of timber and the continuance of the dry season are apt to be regarded by farmers, on first going into the country, as irremediable defects, and as presenting obstacles almost insurmountable to the successful progress of agriculture. A little experience will modify these opinions.

It is soon ascertained that the soil will produce abundantly without manure; that flocks and herds sustain themselves through the winter without being fed at the farmyard, and, consequently, no labor is necessary to provide forage for them; that ditches are easily dug, which present very good barriers for the protection of crops, until live fences can be planted and have time to grow. Forest trees may be planted with little labor, and in very few years attain a sufficient size for building and fencing purposes. Time may be usefully employed in sowing various grain and root crops during the wet or winter season. There is no weather cold enough to destroy root crops, and, therefore, it is not necessary to gather them. They can be used or sold from the field where they grow. The labor, therefore, required in most of the old States to fell the forests, clear the land of rubbish, and prepare it for seed, may here be applied to other objects.

All these things, together with the *perfect security of all crops, in harvest time from injury by wet weather*, are probably sufficient to meet any expense which may be incurred in irrigation, or caused, for a time, by a scanty supply of timber.

In the northern part of the Territory, above latitude 39°, and on the hills, which rise from the great plain of the Sacramento and San Joaquin, to the foot of the Sierra Nevada, the forests of timber are beautiful and extensive, and would, if brought into use, be sufficiently productive to supply the wants of the southern and western portions of the State.

I have spoken of the agricultural products and resources of the country, without reference to the remarkable state of things caused by the discovery of gold, which, it is probable will postpone for an indefinite time all efforts to improve the soil. As long as laborers can earn fifteen dollars or more per day, in collecting gold, they can very well afford to import their supplies from countries where the wages of labor are not more than from fifty cents to one dollar per day. It is not, therefore, to be supposed that the soil will be cultivated more than the production of vegetables, fruits, and other articles so perishable in their nature that they cannot be brought from a great distance, will require.

To secure this important market for the products and manufactures of the States east of the Rocky Mountains is undoubtedly an object of the greatest importance. It will be considered in its proper place.

PUBLIC DOMAIN.

The extent and value of the public lands, suitable for agricultural purposes in California, cannot be ascertained with any degree of accuracy until some very important preliminary questions shall have been settled.

It is not known whether the Jesuits who founded the mission, or their successors, the Franciscans, ever did, or do now hold any title from the Spanish crown to the lands which they occupied. Nor has any investigation been made to ascertain how far those titles, if they ever existed, have been invalidated by the acts of the priests, or the decrees of the Mexican government.

A superficial view of the matter would be very apt to lead to the supposition that the Jesuits, so celebrated for wisdom and cunning, would not fail to secure that which, at that time, would probably have been obtained by merely asking for it—a royal decree, granting to them all the lands they might require in that remote country for ecclesiastical purposes. There have been some intimations to that effect, but nothing is distinctly known. These missions embrace within their limits some of the most valuable lands in the Territory, and it is very important that it should be ascertained whether they belong to the government, or may justly be claimed by individuals.

Most of the land fit for cultivation south of latitude 39°, and west of the valley of the Sacramento and San Joaquin, is claimed under, what purport to be, grants from the Mexican government.

On most of these grants the minerals and metals are reserved to the government—conditions were coupled with many of them which have not been complied with. In others, the boundaries described embrace two or three times as much land as the grant conveys.

The Mexican law required all grants made by the Provisional Government, with few exceptions, to be confirmed by the Supreme Government. The great distance which separated them, and the unfrequent or difficult means of communication, made a compliance with the law so expensive and tardy, that it came to be almost disregarded.

There were other causes which led to this neglect.

Previous to the treaty with Mexico and the immigration of American citizens to that country, land was not regarded as of much value, except for grazing purposes. There was room enough for all. Therefore the claimants or proprietors did not molest each other, or inquire into the validity of titles.

These extensive grants are described by natural boundaries, such as mountains, bays and promontories, which, in many instances might allow of a variation of several miles in the establishment of a corner with chain and compass.

By the treaty of Guadalupe Hidalgo, the United States purchased all the rights and interests of Mexico to and in California. This purchase not only embraced all the lands which had not been granted by Mexico, but all the reserved minerals and metals, and also the revisionary rights which might accrue to Mexico from a want of compliance on the part of

10*

the grantees with the conditions of their grants, *or a want of perfection in the grants.*

It will be perceived that this is a subject of very great importance, not only to the people of California, but to the United States, and calls for prompt and efficient action on the part of the government. It is believed that the appointment of competent commissioners, fully empowered to investigate these titles, in a spirit of kindness toward the claimants, with power to confirm such titles as justice may seem to demand, or with instructions to report their proceedings and awards to Congress, for confirmation or rejection, will be the best and perhaps the only satisfactory mode of adjusting this complex and difficult question.

The lands in the northern part of the Territory, above the 39°, have not been explored or granted. They are supposed to embrace an area of about twenty millions of acres, a large portion of which is doubtless valuable for its timber and soil.

Comparatively few grants have been obtained in the great valley of the Sacramento and San Joaquin. This vast tract, therefore, containing, as is estimated, from twelve to fifteen millions of acres, belongs mostly to the government. South of this valley, and west of the Colorado, within the limits of California, as indicated in her constitution, there are said to be extensive tracts of valuable unappropriated land, and on investigation it will probably appear that there are many of them in detached bodies, which have not been granted.

do not speak of the gold region, embracing the entire foot hills of the Sierra Nevada, some five hundred miles long and sixty miles broad, in connexion with the public domain, which may be embraced in the general land system for sale and settlement, for reasons which will be hereafter assigned.

The survey of the public lands on a system suited to the interests of the country is a matter of very great importance. In the inhabited portions of the Territory the boundaries of Mexican grants, running as they do in all directions, will render the system of surveys by parallels of latitude and longitude quite impracticable.

In all parts of the country irrigation is desirable, and its benefits should be secured as far as possible by suitable surveys and legal regutions. Most of the valleys are watered by streams sufficiently large to be rendered very useful. It would, therefore, seem wise to lay off the land in conformity to the course of the hills and streams which bound and drain the valleys.

A system of drainage, which would also secure irrigation, is absolutely necessary to give value to the great plain of the Sacramento and San Joaquin. This valley is so extensive and level, that if the rivers passing through it were never to overflow their banks, the rain which falls in winter would render a greater portion of it unfit for cultivation. The foundation of such a system can only be established in the survey and sale of the land.

This can be done by laying out canals and drains at suitable distances, and in proper directions and leaving wide margins to the rivers, that they may have plenty of room to increase their channels when their waters shall be confined within them by embankments.

It would be well also to regulate the price of these lands so as to meet, in some degree, the expense of draining them.

This system would, when agriculture shall become a pursuit in California, make this valley one of the most beautiful and productive portions of the Union.

COMMERCIAL RESOURCES.

The commercial resources of California are, at present, founded entirely on her *metallic wealth*—her vast mineral treasures remaining undeveloped, and her fertile soil almost wholly neglected; and this must continue to be the case as long as labor, employed in collecting gold, shall be more profitable than in any other pursuit which can furnish the sinews of commerce.

The day is probably not distant, however, when her minerals, especially the quicksilver mines, will be extensively and profitably worked.

Gold is the product of the country, and is immediately available, in an uncoined state, for all the purposes of exchange. It is not there, as in other countries where the productions of the earth and of art are sent to markets—foreign or domestic—to be exchanged for the precious metals or other articles of value. There, gold not only supplies the medium of domestic trade, but of foreign commerce.

At first view, this state of things would seem to be unfavorable to all extensive intercourse with other parts of the world, because of the want of return freights of *home production* for the vast number of vessels which will arrive with supplies.

These vessels, however, making no calculations on return cargoes, will estimate the entire profits of the voyage on their outward freights, and become, on their arrival, willing carriers for a comparatively small consideration.

This tendency in the course of trade, it would seem, must make San Francisco a warehouse for the supply, to a certain extent, of all the ports of the Pacific, American, Asiatic, and the Islands.

Almost every article now exported by them finds a ready market in California, and the establishment of a mint will bring there also the silver bullion, amounting to more than ten millions per annum, from the west coast of Mexico, and, perhaps, ultimately from Chili and Peru, to be assayed and coined.

Vessels bound round Cape Horn, with cargoes for markets on the American coast of the Pacific, can, by taking advantage of the southeast trade winds, and "standing broad-off the Cape," make the voyage to San Francisco in as short a time as they can to Valparaiso or any port south of California. Vessels have sailed from our Atlantic ports to San Francisco in less than one hundred days, and they have been, in more than one instance, over one hundred and twenty days in going from Panama to San Francisco.

This astonishing difference, in time and distance, was caused by the course of the winds and the "gulf-stream" of the Pacific, mentioned in my remarks on the climate of California.

The vessels from our Atlantic ports took advantage of the winds by steering *from the Cape* as far into the Pacific as to be enabled to take a course west of the gulf-stream in sailing northward, thus availing themselves, first of the southeast, then of the northwest " trades," and avoiding opposing currents.

The vessels from Panama were kept back by calms, adverse winds, and currents. It will be perceived, therefore, that there can be no inducement for vessels bound round Cape Horn, with mixed or assorted cargoes, to stop at Valparaiso, Callao, Guayaquil, or any other port on the west coast, because the exports of all those places will seek a market at San Francisco ; and their supply of merchandize, as *return freight*, will be delivered at less expense than it can be by vessels direct from Atlantic ports, American or European. This tendency of trade to concentrate at San Francisco will be aided by the course of exchange.

Gold dust is worth but $17 per ounce in Chili. It is worth $18 at the United States Mint. If, therefore, a merchant of Valparaiso has ten thousand ounces in San Francisco, received in payment for lumber, barley, flour, or other produce, and desires an invoice of goods from the United States or Europe, he will gain $10,000 at the outset, by sending his gold to New York, besides saving something on the freight and insurance, and at least one month's interest.

The countries on the west coast of America have no exports which find a market in China, or other ports of Asia. San Francisco will therefore become not only the mart of these exports, but also of the products and manufactures of India required in exchange for them, which must be paid for, principally in gold coin or gold dust. Neither gold coin nor gold dust will answer as a remittance to China. Gold, in China, is not currency in any shape, nor is it received in payment of import duties, or taxes on land, or on the industry of the people.

The value of pure gold in China is not far from $14 the ounce. Hence, the importer of manufactures and products of India into San Francisco will remit the gold coin or dust direct to New York, for investment in sterling bills on London. These bills will be sent to London, and placed to the credit of the firm in China from whom the merchandise had been received, and who, on learning of the remittance having gone forward to their agents, will draw a *six months' sight bill* for the amount, which will sell in China at the rate of four shillings and *two* pence or *three* pence per dollar.

I have a statement before me from one of the most eminent merchants and bankers of New York, who was for many years engaged extensively in the India trade, which shows that the profit or gain on ten thousand ounces of gold thus remitted would be $34,434 44

And that the loss on the same quantity, sent direct to China,
would be 15,600 00
_____

Total difference in profit and loss in favor of the remittance
to New York, ... $50,034 44

It will thus be perceived, that nature has so arranged the winds and currents of the Pacific, and disposed of her vast treasures in the hills and mountains of California, as to give to the harbor of San Francisco the control of the commerce of that ocean, as far as it may be connected with the west coast of America.

Important as the commerce of the Pacific undoubtedly is, and will be, to California, it cannot now, nor will it ever compare in magnitude and value to the domestic trade between her and the older States of the Union.

Two years ago California did not probably contain more than 15,000 people. That portion of it which has since been so wonderfully peopled by American citizens, was, comparatively, without resources, and not supplied with the common comforts of shelter afforded by a forest country.

Notwithstanding the great distances emigrants have been compelled to travel to reach the Territory, more than 100,000 have overcome all difficulties and spread themselves over its hills and plains.

They have been supplied from distances as great as they themselves have passed, with not only the necessaries, but the comforts and many of the luxuries of life. Houses have been imported from China, Chili, and the Atlantic States of the Union. All the materials required in building cities and towns have been added to the wants of a people so numerous, destitute and remote from the sources of supply.

These wants will exist as long as emigration continues to flow into the country, and labor employed in collecting gold shall be more profitable than its application to agriculture, the mechanic arts, and the great variety of pursuits which are fostered and sustained in other civilized communities.

This may be shown, by mentioning the prices of a few articles. Last summer and autumn, lumber was sold in San Francisco at $300 to $400 per thousand feet. At Stockton and Sacramento City, at $500 to $600. At these prices, it could be made in the Territory, and many persons were engaged in the business. I perceive, by recent accounts, that the price had fallen at San Francisco to $75; at this price it *cannot* be made where labor is from $10 to $15 per day, and the difficulties attending its manufacture are much greater than in the Atlantic States. Lumber can be delivered in our large lumber markets for an *average* of the various qualities of $16, and freighted to San Francisco for $24, making $40 per thousand feet. This price would cause the manufacture of it in California to be abandoned. We may add $20 per thousand to meet any increase of price in the article itself, or in the freight, and the result would be the same.

It is probable that the demand, for several years to come, will not be less than twenty millions of feet per annum, which, at $40 per thousand, will be $8,000,000.

When California comes to have a population of 200,000, which she will have before the close of the present year, she will require near half a million of barrels of flour from some quarter, and no country can supply it as good and cheap as the old States of the Union. Including freight and insurance, this may be set down as an item of about $5,000,000. The article of clothing, allowing $20 to each person, would be $4,000,000.

There is no pretension to accuracy in these items, and they may be estimated too high, but it is quite as probable they are too low.

We have no data on which to found a calculation of what the value of the trade between the States east of the Rocky Mountains and California will be during the current year. I will venture the opinion, however, that it will not fall short of $25,000,000. It may go far beyond that sum. At present, I can perceive no cause which will retard or diminish emigration.

If the movement shall continue five years, our commerce with that Territory may reach $100,000,000 per annum. This is doubtless a startling sum, but it must be borne in mind that we have to build cities and towns, supply machinery for mining, coal for domestic purposes, and steam navigation, and all the multifarious articles used in providing the comforts and luxuries of life, for half a million of people, who will have transferred themselves to a country which is to produce, comparatively, nothing except minerals and the precious metals, and whose pursuits will enable them to purchase, at any cost, whatever may be necessary for their purposes.

It is difficult to imagine or calculate the effect which will be produced on all the industrial pursuits of the people of the old States of the Union, by this withdrawal from them of a half a million of producers, who, in their new homes and new pursuits, will *give existence* to a commerce almost equal in value to our foreign trade. Let no one, therefore, suppose he is not interested in the welfare of California. As well may he believe his interests would not be influenced by closing our ports and cutting off intercourse with all the world.

The distance round Cape Horn is so great that breadstuffs and many other articles of food deteriorate, and many others are so perishable in their nature that they would decay on the passage. This would be the case particularly with all kinds of vegetables and undried fruits. Until some more speedy mode of communication shall be established by which produce can be transferred, the farmers and planters of the old States will not realize the full value of this new market on the Pacific.

Many other important interests will be kept back, especially the consumption of coal. The American steamers now on the ocean, those on their way there and others shortly to be sent out will consume not far from one hundred thousand tons of coal per annum. The scarcity of wood in California will bring coal into general use as fuel as soon as it can be obtained at reasonable prices. Suppose there may be three years hence forty thousand houses, which shall consume five tons each per annum. This, with the steamers, would be a consumption of three hundred thousand tons. If delivered at $20 per ton it would compete successfully with the coal from Vancouver's Island and New Holland and amount to $6,000,000.

The construction of a railroad across the Isthmus of Panama would secure the market for these articles against all competition.

Some idea may be formed of the demand for them from the prices paid in San Francisco last autumn. Coal was sold at $60 to $100 per ton;

potatoes $16 per bushel; turnips and onions for 25 to 62½ cts. each; eggs from $10 to $12 per dozen.

The distance from Chagres to New York has recently been run in seven days. The same speed would carry a steamboat from Panama to San Francisco in ten days. Allow three days to convey freight across the Isthmus, on a railway, and both passengers and freight will be conveyed from New York to San Francisco in twenty days.

This celerity of movement would secure for American produce the entire market of California. Sailing vessels may be successfully employed between our Atlantic and Gulf ports and the terminus of the railway on this side of the Isthmus; and *propellers* from Panama to San Francisco. These latter vessels will be found peculiarly suited to that trade; they can use their steam through the calms of the Bay of Panama, and against head winds and currents going north, and their sails with favorable winds and currents coming south.

These modes of conveyance, in connexion with the railroad across the Isthmus, would be sufficiently expeditious and economical to turn the tide of commerce, between the Atlantic and Pacific States of the Union, into that channel. The tendency of our commerce on the Pacific to promote the employment of ocean steamers is of much importance as connected with the defence of our extensive line of coast from latitude 32° to 49°, the protection of the whale fishery, and other branches of trade on that ocean. The establishment of a line of heavy steamers to China would promote all these objects; increase our intercourse with the country, and probably be the means of opening communications with Japan. Money wisely employed in promoting these objects, it is believed, would add more to the power and prosperity of the country than its expenditure on any *general system* of fortification at the present prices of labor and materials. There is one point, however, of such vast importance that no time should be lost in taking the necessary steps to render it perfectly impregnable—that is the entrance to the harbor of San Francisco. On the strength of the works which may be erected to defend that passage will depend the safety of California in a time of war with a maritime power. Permit a hostile fleet to cast anchor in the harbor of San Francisco and the country would be virtually conquered.

The coast has not been surveyed, nor has its outline bean correctly ascertained. There are many rocks above and below the water-line, and small islands not mentioned or indicated on any chart, which render navigation near the land, especially at night, extremely dangerous.

An accurate survey of the coast, to commence at the most important points, the construction of light-houses, and the placing of buoys in proper positions, are objects of much importance, and, it is not doubted, will attract the early attention of government.

METALLIC AND MINERAL WEALTH.

The gold region of California is between four hundred and five hundred miles long, and from forty to fifty miles broad, following the line of the Sierra Nevada. Further discoveries may, and probably will, increase the area. It embraces within its limits those extensive ranges of hills which rise on the eastern border of the plain of the Sacramento and San Joaquin, and extending eastwardly from fifty to sixty miles, they attain an elevation of about four thousand feet, and terminate at the base of the main ridge of the Sierra Nevada. There are numerous streams which have their sources in the springs of the Sierra, and receive the water from its melting snows, and that which falls in rain during the wet season.

These streams form rivers, which have cut their channels through the ranges of foot hills westwardly to the plain, and disembogue into the Sacramento and San Joaquin. These rivers are from ten to fifteen, and probably some of them twenty miles apart.

The principal formation or substratum in these hills is talcose slate; the superstratum, sometimes penetrating to a great depth, is quartz. This, however, does not cover the entire face of the country, but extends in large bodies in various directions—is found in masses and small fragments on the surface, and seen along the ravines, and in the mountains overhanging the rivers, and in the hill sides in its orignal beds. It crops out in the valleys and on the tops of the hills, and forms a striking feature of the entire country over which it extends. From innumerable evidence and indications, it has come to be the universally admitted opinion among the miners and intelligent men who have examined this region, that the *gold, whether in detached particles and in pieces, or in veins, was created in combination with the quartz.* Gold is not found on the surface of the country, presenting the appearance of having been thrown up and scattered in all directions by volcanic action. It is only found in particular localities, and attended by peculiar circumstances and indications. It is found in the bars and shoals of the rivers, in ravines, and in what are called the dry diggings.

The rivers, in forming their channels, or breaking their way through the hills, have come in contact with the quartz containing the gold veins, and by constant attrition cut the gold into fine flakes and dust, and it is found among the sand and gravel of their beds at those places where the swiftness of the current reduces it, in the dry season, to the narrowest possible limits, and where a wide margin is, consequently, left on each side, over which the water rushes, during the wet season, with great force.

As the velocity of some streams is greater than others, so is the gold found in fine or coarse particles, apparently corresponding to the degree of attrition to which it has been exposed. The water from the hills and upper valleys, in finding its way to the rivers, has cut deep ravines, and, wherever it came in contact with the quartz, has dissolved or crumbled it in pieces.

In the dry season these channels are mostly without water, and gold is found in the beds and margins of many of them in large quantities, but in a much coarser state than in the rivers ; owing, undoubtedly, to the moderate flow and temporary continuance of the current, which has reduced it to smooth shapes, not unlike pebbles, but had not sufficient force to reduce it to flakes or dust.

The dry diggings are places where quartz containing gold has cropped out, and been disintegrated, crumbled to fragments, pebbles and dust, by the action of water and the atmosphere. The gold has been left as it was made, in all imaginable shapes; in pieces of all sizes, and from one grain to several pounds in weight. The evidences that it was created in combination with quartz are too numerous and striking to admit of doubt or cavil. *They are found in combination in large quantities.*

A very large proportion of the pieces of gold found in these situations have more or less quartz adhering to them. In many specimens they are so combined they cannot be separated without reducing the whole mass to powder and subjecting it to the action of quicksilver.

This gold, not having been exposed to the attrition of a strong current of water, retains, in a great degree, its original conformation.

These diggings, in some places, spread over valleys of considerable extent, which have the appearance of alluvion, formed by washings from the adjoining hills, of decomposed quartz and slate earth, and vegetable matter.

In addition to these facts it is beyond doubt true, that several vein-mines have been taken, showing the minute connection between the gold and the rock, and indicating a value hitherto unknown in gold-mining.

These veins do not present the appearance of places where gold may have been lodged by some violent eruption. It is combined with the quartz, in all imaginable forms and degrees of richness.

The rivers present very striking and, it would seem, conclusive evidence respecting the quantity of gold remaining undiscovered in the quartz veins. It is not probable that the gold in the dry diggings, and that in the rivers—the former in lumps, the latter in dust—was created by different processes. That which is found in the rivers has undoubtedly been cut or worn from the veins in the rock, with which their currents have come in contact. All of them appear to be equally rich. This is shown by the fact that a laboring man may collect nearly as much in one river as he can in another. They intersect and cut through the gold region, running from east to west, at irregular distances of fifteen to twenty, and perhaps some of them thirty miles apart.

Hence it appears that the gold veins are equally rich in all parts of that most remarkable section of country. Were it wanting, there are further proofs of this in the ravines and dry diggings, which uniformly confirm what nature so plainly shows in the rivers.

For the purpose of forming some opinion respecting the probable amount or value of treasure in the gold region, it will be proper to state the estimates which have been made of the quantity collected since its discovery

Gold was first discovered on the south fork of the American River, at a place called Sutter's Mill, now Culoma—late in May or early in June,

1848. Information which could be relied on announcing this discovery was not received in this city until late in the following autumn.

No immigration into the mines could, therefore, have taken place from the old States in that year. The number of miners was consequently, limited to the population of the Territory—some five hundred men from Oregon—Mexicans and other foreigners who happened to be in the country or came into it during the summer and autumn, and the Indians, who were employed by or sold their gold to the whites.

It is supposed there were not far from 5,000 men employed in collecting gold during that season. If we suppose they obtained an average of $1,000 each—which is regarded by well-informed persons as a low estimate—the aggregate amount will be $5,000,000.

Information of this discovery spread in all directions during the following winter; and, on the commencement of the dry season in 1849, people came into the territory from all quarters—from Chili, Peru, and other States on the Pacific coast of South America—from the west coast of Mexico—the Sandwich Islands, China and New Holland.

The emigration from the United States came in last, if we except those who crossed the Isthmus of Panama, and went up the coast in steamers, and a few who sailed early on the voyage round Cape Horn.

The American emigration did not come in by sea, in much force, until July and August, and that overland did not begin to arrive until the last of August and first of September. The Chilians and Mexican were early in the country. In the month of July it is supposed there were fifteen thousand foreigners in the mines. At a place called Sonorian Camp, it is believed there were at least ten thousand Mexicans. Hotels, restaurants, stores and shops of all descriptions, furnished whatever money could procure. Ice was brought from the Sierra, and ice-creams added to numerous other luxuries. An inclosure made of the trunks and branches of trees, and lined with cotton cloth, served as a sort of amphitheatre for bull-fights ; other amusements characteristic of the Mexicans were seen in all directions.

The foreigners resorted principally to the southern mines, which gave them a great superiority in numerical force over the Americans, and enabled them to take possession of some of the richest in that part of the country. In the early part of the season the Americans were mostly employed on the forks of the American and on Bear, Uba, and Feather rivers. As their numbers increased they spread themselves over the southern mines, and collisions were threatened between them and the foreigners. The latter, however, for some cause, either fear, or having satisfied their cupidity, or both, began to leave the mines late in August, and by the end of September many of them were out of the country.

It is not probable that during the first part of the season there were more than five or six thousand Americans in the mines. This would swell the whole number, including foreigners, to about twenty thousand the beginning of September. This period embraced about half of the season during which gold may be successfully collected in the rivers.

Very particular and extensive inquiries respecting the daily earnings and acquisitions of the miners lead to the opinion that they averaged an ounce per day. This is believed by many to be a low estimate ; but from the best information I was able to procure, I am of opinion that it approaches very near actual results. The half of the season, up to the 1st of September, would give sixty-five working days, and to each laborer, at $16 per ounce, $1,040. If, therefore, we assume $1,000 as the average collected by each laborer, we shall probably not go beyond the mark.

This would give an aggregate of $20,000,000 for the first half of the season—15,000,000 of which was probably collected by foreigners. During the last half of the season the number of foreigners was very much diminished, and, perhaps, did not exceed 5,000. At this time the American immigration had come in by land and sea, and the number of our fellow-citizens in the mines had, as was estimated, increased to between 40,000 and 50,000. They were most of them inexperienced in mining, and it is probable the results of their labors were not as great as has been estimated for the first part of the season and experienced miners, assuming that the average of half an ounce per day ought to be considered as reasonable, it would give an aggregate of about $20,000,000. If from this we deduct one-fourth on account of the early commencement of the wet season, we have an estimate of $15,000,000 ; at least five of which was collected by foreigners, who possessed many advantages from their experience in mining and knowledge of the country.

These estimates give, as the result of the operation in the mines for 1848 and 1849, the round sum of $40,000,000—one half of which was probably collected and carried out of the country by foreigners.

From the best information I could obtain, I am led to believe that at least $20,000,000 of the $40,000,000 were taken from the rivers, and that their richness has not been sensibly diminished, except in a few locations, which had early attracted large bodies of miners. This amount has principally been taken from the northern rivers, or those which empty into the Sacramento; the southern rivers, or those which flow into the San Joaquin, having been, comparatively, but little resorted to until near the close of the last season. These rivers are, however, believed, by those who have visited them, to be richer in the precious metal than those in the northern part of the gold region.

There is one river which, from *reported* recent discoveries, and not included in the description of those flowing into the great plain west of the Sierra Nevada, is as rich in gold as any of them. That is the *Trinity*, which rises north of the head waters of the Sacramento, and discharges into the Pacific not far from the fortieth degree of north latitude.

There are, as nearly as my recollection serves me, twelve principal rivers in which gold has been found; but most of the $20,000,000 in the above estimate was taken from six or seven of them, where it was first discovered and most accessible.

Adopting the hypothesis that the gold found in the beds of these streams has been cut or worn from the veins in the quartz through which they have forced their way, and considering the fact that they are *all rich*, and are said to be nearly equally productive, we may form some idea of the vast amount of treasure remaining undisturbed in the veins which run through the masses of rock in various directions over a space of forty or fifty miles wide, and near five hundred miles long.

If we may be allowed to form a conjecture respecting the richness of these veins from the quantity of lump or coarse gold found in the dry diggings, where it appears to occupy nearly the same superfices it did originally in the rock—its specific gravity being sufficient to resist ordi-

nary moving causes—we shall be led to an estimate almost beyond human calculation and belief. Yet, as far as I can perceive, there is no
plausible reason why the veins which remain in the quartz may not be
as valuable as those which have become separated from the decomposed
rock. This matter can only be satisfactorily decided by actual discoveries.

The gold region of California having attracted a large share of public
attention, it was to be expected that various suggestions and propositions
would be made with respect to the proper mode of disposing of it.

The difficulty in arranging a suitable plan has been the want of accurate information on which a well considered opinion might be formed.
Its distance from the seat of government, the conflicting statements and
reports respecting it, served only to bewilder and mystify the public
mind, and render a thorough examination of it necessary, to ascertain
whether its value is such as to render legislation necessary for its proper
protection and management.

If it appears, from the preceding part of this report, that it is sufficiently important to require laws suited to the condition and development of its wealth, we are necessarily brought to the consideration of the
proper rules and regulations to be adopted for that purpose.

The survey and sale of that section of country, under our present land
system, or any other mode which may be devised, would, undoubtedly,
cause very serious discontent among those who have gone, and all who
may desire to go there to collect gold, and a most unnecessary and un-
avoidable inequality in the distribution of wealth among the purchasers.

Sections and parts of sections of land, having no indications of gold on
the surface, but possessing untold treasures in the bowels of the earth,
might be sold for what would be a mere trifle in comparison of their real
value. Capitalists would overbid the daring, strong-armed day-laborer,
who had braved the storms of Cape Horn, or the privations of a journey
across the plains ; and, by the power and combination of resources, would
possess themselves of the most valuable mines which have been discovered, and employ skillful miners to examine the country with as much
secrecy as possible, for the purpose of making such discoveries as would

enable them in a great degree to monopolize the most valuable portions of the country.

It is much easier to imagine than describe the discontent, perhaps disorder, which would spring up among an hundred thousand freemen deprived the privilege of an equal enjoyment of, or participation in, what they have been in the habit of regarding as the common property of the people of the whole Union.

It is, perhaps, more than doubtful whether such laws could be enforced. The employment of troops for that purpose would not only be odious, but ineffectual; they would be more likely to set an example of insubordination, by desertion, than to compel obedience in others.

The people would unite with them in producing anarchy and confusion. No system, therefore, which is not in accordance with the interests of the people can be carried into successful operation. It is always fortunate when laws can be so framed as to harmonize those interests with the policy and duty of the government. It is believed that may be accomplished in this case.

While every American citizen in the mines is aware that he is on government property, and would consider any attempt to drive him away as an act of oppression, he at the same time feels that something is due from him for the privilege he enjoys, and he would willingly pay a reasonable sum to have those privileges defined, and to be protected in the enjoyment of them.

The gold in the rivers, the dry diggings and the ravines is accessible to any man who has the strength to use a pan or washer, a spade and pick-ax.

The employment of machinery may perhaps facilitate its collection, but it is not essential. Every man is master of his own movements. The case will be very different with the vein-mines, which yet remain in the rock. To work them successfully will require machinery, with horse or steam power, involving an expenditure of capital in proportion to the extent of the operations.

No prudent man will make such investments until his rights and privileges shall have been clearly defined by law. In the absence of all legal regulations, if a man were to discover a vein-mine and incur the expense of erecting machinery to work it, any other person, citizen or foreigner, might construct an establishment alongside of him, deprive him of his discovery, and destroy the value of his property. Hence it will be perceived that any law prescribing the privileges and duties of miners should be so framed as to secure the rights of all.

There is some fertile soil in the gold region—beautiful valleys and rich hill sides—which, under circumstances favorable to agriculture, would undoubtedly be valuable for that purpose; but at present, and as long as the collection of gold shall continue to reward labor so much more abundantly than the cultivation of the soil, the important matter to be considered is, the proper mode of disposing of the metallic wealth of the country.

The first step, in my opinion, should be to reserve the entire region where gold is found, from the operation of the pre-emption laws, and from sale, so that it may be now regarded as the *common treasure* of the American people, and hereafter as a rich inheritance to their posterity. Then provide for the appointment of a commissioner of the mines, and a sufficient number of assistant commissioners to carry the law into effect.

Let the office of the commissioner be established at some point convenient to the mines, say Sacramento Cicy, and the offices of his assistant on the principal rivers, and in the most productive districts. Provide that any and every American citizen, on application at the office of the commissioner, or any of his assistants, and by paying one ounce, or $16, or such sum as may be considered just and proper, shall be entitled to receive a license or permit to dig anywhere in the Territory for one year. Provide, also, that any one who shall *discover* or purchase of the discoverer, a vein-mine, shall be entitled to work it, to a certain extent, under proper regulations, on paying to the commissioner such per cent. on the proceeds of the mine as may be a suitable tax on the privileges granted. It will be necessary also to allow the miner to cut and use such timber and other building materials as his business requires; and, also, to allow those who work under permits the privilege of erecting cabins for shelter through the winter. Authorize the commissioner to lay out sites for the towns in convenient situations to the mines, and offer the lots for sale, reserving the metals and mineral, so that those who make mining a permanent pursuit may accumulate around them the comforts and enjoyments of civilized life. Let those who desire to cultivate gardens or farm-lots be accommodated. It will be necessary also to authorize the sale of timber and other materials, for building and other purposes. There may be other suggestions which do not now occur to me, but no doubt will, to those who may be charged with the preparation of any measure which may be brought forward on this subject.

I have suggested one ounce or $16 as the price of a permit or license to dig or collect gold for one year. This I regard as about the average value of one day's labor in the mines. This tax on 50,000 miners, the probable number next summer, will give a revenue of $800,000. On 100,000 miners—the probable number of 1851—it will give $1,600,000, beside the per centum on the vein-mines, and the sum received for town lots, timbers, &c., &., which would probably swell the amount to at least $2,000,000. Any variation in the tax imposed will, of course, increase or diminish this estimate.

A suitable amount of the money thus collected should be expended in constructing roads and bridges, to facilitate communication to and through the mining districts.

These facilities will so reduce the cost of living in the mines, that the miners will instead of lose by paying the tax. These are accommodations which the miners themselves will ever provide, because of the want of concert of action among them sufficient to accomplish such objects, but for which they will willingly pay any moderate contribution. A liberal per centum should be allowed out of this sum, as a school fund, and for the establishment of an university to educate the youth of California. Let it not be considered that this will be doing injustice to the older States of the Union. They will reap a harvest sufficiently rich in their intercourse with their younger sister on the Pacific to justify the most liberal course of policy toward her.

I have given $20,000,000 as the probable revenue for 1851, under the proposed system. This would discharge the interest on the amount stipulated in the treaty to be paid to Mexico for California and New Mexico, provide $300,000 per annum for a school fund, and the necessary improvements in mining districts, and create a sinking fund of half a million per annum, to pay the principal of the indemnity to Mexico.

An increase of the number of miners, or of the price of permits, would of course increase the revenue. If the vein-mines shall be found as extensive and productive as the best-informed persons suppose, the right to work them, properly secured by law, and the opportunity thus offered of using machinery to advantage, will justify the collection of a much larger per cent. on their gross product than it is proposed to require from those who labor with their own hands in the use of the simple means now employed in the collection of gold. The amount, therefore, collected from this source may ultimately be as large, perhaps larger, than that for permits.

If revenue is an object, there can be little doubt that, by the adoption of this system, the amount collected in a few years will be larger than the entire district would command in ready money, if offered for sale; and the interests and privileges of those employed in the mines will be secured from the grasping and monopolizing spirit of individual proprietors; California and the whole Union preserved from scenes of anarchy and confusion, if not bloodshed, which must result from a sale of the mining region to speculators, and an attempt to protect them in the enjoyment of their purchases.

The salaries of the commissioner and his assistants may easily be paid out of the amount received, in fixed sums, or in the form of a per centum.

I have proposed to exclude foreigners from the privilege of purchasing permits, and from working as discoverers or purchasers in the vein-mines. My reasons for recommending this policy are, that these mines belong to, and in my judgment should be preserved for, the use and benefit of the American people. I mean, of course, all citizens, native and adopted.

During the mining season of 1849, more than 15,000 foreigners, mostly Mexicans and Chilenos, came in *armed bands* into the mining district, bidding defiance to all opposition, and finally carrying out of the country some $20,000,000 worth of gold dust, which belonged *by purchase* to the people of the United States. If not excluded by law, they will return and recommence the work of plunder. They may, with as much right, gather the harvest in the valley of the Connecticut, the Ohio, or Mississippi. No other nation, having the power to protect it, would permit its treasure to be thus carried away. I would not allow them to purchase permits, or work vein-mines, because the contributions proposed to be required are so moderate that they will not cause the slightest inconvenience to the miners, and are not designed as an equivalent for these privileges. Foreigners, therefore, would willingly pay these small sums for permission to collect and carry away millions of dollars in value. The object is not only a suitable revenue, but to preserve for the use of our own fellow-citizens the wealth of that region.

This system of permits will make all who purchase them *police officers, to aid in excluding* from the mines all who are not entitled to, or who do not procure them. This will prevent deserters from the army or navy from being harbored and protected in the mines. Not being allowed to purchase permits, the assistant commissioners, aided by the miners, would soon detect and arrest them. Sailors belonging to the mercantile marine would be detected in a similar manner, and thus prevented from running away.

The commerce of the country would be protected from the disastrous consequences resulting from the abandonment of ships by their crews, which necessarily imposes a heavy tax on consumers, because merchants, as a measure of self-protection, must charge such losses on their cargoes, and consequently they fall on those who purchase. The army and navy would be saved from demoralization, and prepared for service in case of necessity.

Many of the emigrants to California, especially those from the western States, will remain and form a resident population; but there will be thousands and tens of thousands of young and middle-aged workingmen from all parts of the Union, who will resort to the mines for the purpose of obtaining the means to purchase a farm or establish themselves in some favorite pursuit, and as soon as they have secured a sufficient amount will return, and their places will be supplied by others who will go and do likewise.

This process has already commenced. Many who went out last spring have returned with an ample reward for their labors and privations.

The market in California for the products and manufactures of the other States of the Union will enhance prices, which, with the gold collected and brought home by laboring people, will diffuse a degree of wealth and comfort hitherto unknown among them.

The *quicksilver mines* of California are believed to be numerous, extensive, and very valuable. There is one near San José, which belongs to, or is claimed by, Mr. Forbes of Tepic, in Mexico. The cinnabar ore, which produces the quicksilver, lies near the surface, is easily procured, and believed to be remarkably productive.

Discoveries of other mines are reported, but no certain information respecting them has been made public. It is, undoubtedly, a fortunate circumstance that nature, in bestowing on California such vast metallic treasure, has provided, almost in its immediate neighborhood, inexhaustible stores of quicksilver, which is so essential in gold mining.

The policy of government with respect to these mines of cinnabar should, in my opinion, be quite different from that which I have felt it my duty to suggest for the management of the gold region.

As soon as the necessary explorations can be made, and proper information obtained, it will be well to offer these mines for sale, and commit their development to the hands of private enterprise.

It is believed that there are extensive beds of silver, iron, and copper ores, in the Territory; but there is no information sufficiently accurate respecting them, to justify any statement of their existence or value.

I have already alluded to the propriety of establishing a mint in California. This is important in many respects. At this time there is not coin to supply a currency. Much difficulty is experienced in procuring enough to pay the duties on foreign goods. The common circulating medium is, therefore, gold dust, which is sold at $15 50 to $16 per ounce. In the mines it is frequently sold much lower. The miners, the laboring men, are the sufferers from this state of things.

Those who purchase and ship gold to the Atlantic States make large profits; *but those who dig lose what others make.*

I have estimated that there will be $5,000,000 collected during the current year. At $16 per ounce, that sum will weigh 3,125,000 ounces.

Gold at the United States Mint is worth $18 per ounce, making a difference in value on that quantity, between San Francisco and New York of $6,250,000, which would be saved to the miners by the establishment of a mint.

I have also suggested its importance as a means of promoting and increasing our trade with the west coast of Mexico and South America.

It is not doubted that the construction of a railway across the Isthmus of Panama, and perhaps the establishment of other lines of communication between the two oceans, will give to the products and manufactures of the older States of the Union command of the market of California to the exclusion, in a great degree, of those of the west coast.

A mint will therefore become of the utmost importance, to give such marketable value to silver bullion as to enable the merchants of those countries to keep up and increase their intercourse with our principal ports on the Pacific.

The silver bullion shipped to Europe from the west coast of Mexico amounts to more than ten millions of dollars per annum. From the countries on the west coast of South America, probably an equal quantity. That from Mexico goes to pay for European importations into her ports on the Atlantic side.

A market at San Francisco for this bullion will be the means of substituting American and Chinese fabrics for those of European manufacture in all those countries. This will greatly increase the trade between China and California.

I have the honor to be, with great respect, your most obedient servant, [Signed]

T. BUTLER KING.

To Hon. JOHN M. CLAYTON, Secretary of State.